The Sociological Heritage of the Scottish Enlightenment

Edinburgh Studies in Scottish Philosophy

Series Editor: James A. Harris, University of St Andrews

Scottish philosophy through the ages

This series covers the full range of Scottish philosophy over five centuries – from the medieval period through the Reformation and Enlightenment periods, to the nineteenth and early twentieth centuries.

The series publishes innovative studies on major figures and themes. It also aims to stimulate new work in less intensively studied areas, by a new generation of philosophers and intellectual historians. The books combine historical sensitivity and philosophical substance which serve to cast new light on the rich intellectual inheritance of Scottish philosophy.

Editorial Advisory Board
Angela Coventry, University of Portland, Oregon
Fonna Forman, University of California, San Diego
Alison McIntyre, Wellesley College
Alexander Broadie, University of Glasgow
Remy Debes, University of Memphis
John Haldane, University of St Andrews and Baylor University, Texas

Books available
Thomas Reid and the Problem of Secondary Qualities, Christopher A. Shrock
Adam Smith and Rousseau: Ethics, Politics, Economics, edited by Maria Pia Paganelli, Dennis C. Rasmussen and Craig Smith
Imagination in Hume's Philosophy: The Canvas of the Mind, Timothy M. Costelloe
Essays on Hume, Smith and the Scottish Enlightenment, Christopher J. Berry
Hume's Sceptical Enlightenment, Ryu Susato
Adam Ferguson and the Idea of Civil Society: Moral Science in the Scottish Enlightenment, Craig Smith
Hume's Scepticism: Pyrrhonian and Academic, Peter S. Fosl
Adam Ferguson's Later Writings: New Letters and an Essay on the French Revolution, Ian Stewart and Max Skjönsberg
Thomas Reid and the Defence of Duty, James J. S. Foster
Scottish Philosophy after the Enlightenment, Gordon Graham
The Sociological Heritage of the Scottish Enlightenment, edited by Tamás Demeter

edinburghuniversitypress.com/series/essp

The Sociological Heritage of the Scottish Enlightenment

Edited by Tamás Demeter

EDINBURGH
University Press

Edinburgh University Press is one of the leading university presses in the UK. We publish academic books and journals in our selected subject areas across the humanities and social sciences, combining cutting-edge scholarship with high editorial and production values to produce academic works of lasting importance. For more information visit our website: edinburghuniversitypress.com

© editorial matter and organisation Tamás Demeter, 2024, 2026
© the chapters their several authors, 2024, 2026

Edinburgh University Press Ltd
13 Infirmary Street
Edinburgh EH1 1LT

First published in hardback by Edinburgh University Press 2024

Typeset in 11/13 Adobe Sabon by
IDSUK (DataConnection) Ltd, and
printed and bound by CPI Group (UK) Ltd,
Croydon, CR0 4YY

A CIP record for this book is available from the British Library

ISBN 978 1 3995 1233 6 (hardback)
ISBN 978 1 3995 1234 3 (paperback)
ISBN 978 1 3995 1235 0 (webready PDF)
ISBN 978 1 3995 1236 7 (epub)

The right of Tamás Demeter to be identified as editor of this work has been asserted in accordance with the Copyright, Designs and Patents Act 1988 and the Copyright and Related Rights Regulations 2003 (SI No. 2498).

Contents

List of Abbreviations vii
Series Editor's Introduction ix

1. The Sociological Heritage of the Scottish Enlightenment: An Introduction 1
   Tamás Demeter

Part I General Perspectives

2. Human Nature and Social Change: Historical Institutionalism in the Scottish Enlightenment 21
   Christopher J. Berry

3. Adventitious Sociology: Dispassion and Insight in the Scottish Enlightenment 46
   Kenneth Macdonald

Part II Sociological Ideas in the Scottish Enlightenment

4. Adam Ferguson as Founding Father of Sociology 85
   Craig Smith

5. 'Partly social, partly selfish': The Social Evolutionism of Henry Home, Lord Kames 103
   R. J. W. Mills

6. Pre-Weberian Charismatic Leadership and Aesthetics of Deference in the Scottish Enlightenment 134
   Spyridon Tegos

7. Sociology within the *Statistical Account of Scotland* 153
   Kenneth Macdonald

Part III The Sociological Afterlife of the Scottish Enlightenment

8. Hegel and the Notion of Retroactive Necessity in the Scottish Enlightenment — 199
   Dirk Schuck

9. Traces of Hume in Sociology — 219
   Angela M. Coventry

10. Hume and Durkheim: Common Views on Sociality — 244
    Catherine Dromelet

11. Westermarckian Evolutionary Perspective on Scottish Moral Sentimentalism — 269
    Otto Pipatti

12. In Praise of Adam Smith, or, The Workings of Commercial Society — 292
    John A. Hall

13. John Millar and Sociology: Disciplinary History and its Discontents — 330
    Nicholas B. Miller

14. 'Das Adam Smith Problem': A Sociological Reassessment — 355
    Aldo Mascareño and Leonidas Montes

15. The Foundational Document of the Sociology of Knowledge — 381
    Tamás Demeter

Notes on Contributors — 410
Index of Names — 414
Index of Subjects — 417

Abbreviations

BA	Henry Home, Lord Kames, *Essays upon Several Subjects concerning British Antiquities*
Corr.	*Correspondence of Adam Smith*
E	David Hume, *Essays Moral, Political, Literary*
ECS	Adam Ferguson, *An Essay on the History of Civil Society*
EHM	James Dunbar, *Essays on the History of Mankind in Rude and Cultivated Ages*
EHU	David Hume, *An Enquiry concerning Human Understanding*
EMPL	David Hume, *Essays: Moral, Political and Literary*
EPM	David Hume, *An Enquiry concerning the Principles of Morals*
EPMNR	Henry Home, Lord Kames, *Essays on the Principles of Morality and Natural Religion*
EPS	Adam Smith, *Essays on Philosophical Subjects*
HAm	William Robertson, *The History of America*
HLT	Henry Home, Lord Kames, *Historical Law-Tracts*
HV	David Millar, *An Historical View of the English Government*
Institutes	Adam Ferguson, *Institutes of Moral Philosophy*
Life	Dugald Stewart, *Account of the Life and Writings of Adam Smith*
LJA	Adam Smith, *Lectures on Jurisprudence 1762/3*
LJB	Adam Smith, *Lectures on Jurisprudence 1766*
LRBL	Adam Smith, *Lectures on Rhetoric and Belles Lettres*

NHR	David Hume, 'The Natural History of Religion'
OR	David Millar, *The Origins of the Distinction of Ranks*
OSA ('Old' Statistical Account)	*The Statistical Account of Scotland. Drawn up from the communications of the ministers of the different parishes by Sir John Sinclair, Bart*
Principles	Adam Ferguson, *Principles of Moral and Political Science*
SHM	Henry Home, Lord Kames, *Sketches on the History of Man*
T	David Hume, *A Treatise of Human Nature: Being an Attempt to Introduce the Experimental Method of Reasoning into Moral Subjects*
TMS	Adam Smith, *The Theory of Moral Sentiments*
WN	Adam Smith, *An Inquiry into the Nature and Causes of the Wealth of Nations*

Series Editor's Introduction

Philosophy has been taught and written in Scotland since the fifteenth century. The purpose of this series is to publish new scholarly work on any and every aspect of the history of Scottish philosophising, from John Mair to John Macmurray. Scotland's most celebrated philosophical achievements remain those produced by Hume, Smith, Reid, and their contemporaries in the eighteenth century. It is, however, no longer possible to believe that the Scottish Enlightenment had no indigenous roots. Nor is it possible to believe that there was no significant philosophy produced in Scotland once the Enlightenment was over.

There is no single set of intellectual concerns distinctive of and unique to philosophy as it has been taught and written in Scotland. Historical study of Scottish philosophy must be, to a significant extent, study of the changing nature of philosophy itself. It should be open to the idea that the preoccupations and methods of philosophers today may not be those of philosophers in the past. It should also concern itself with philosophical connections and intellectual affinities between Scotland, England, Ireland, and the rest of Europe, and, where appropriate, between Scotland and America.

James Harris

I

The Sociological Heritage of the Scottish Enlightenment: An Introduction

Tamás Demeter

The social sciences have been growing negligent of their own history. One can find a clear reflection of this tendency in university training: the historical content of degree programmes keeps diminishing at the expense of methodological training for various ways of data processing. Less and less engagement is required with the classics of these disciplines, and even less with their prehistory and emergence. The consequent vanishing of historical sensitivity is reflected in scholarly discourse: major generalist journals are less likely to publish papers focusing on historical topics that are considered only to be of antiquarian interest anyway. Thus, being squeezed out of the core fields of training, research and discourse in the social sciences, niche journals proliferate, but their reach outside specialist circles is rather limited. Disciplinary history is outsourced to intellectual historians and gradually their own history becomes as alien to the social sciences as the history of physics has become to physics.

This loss of historical interest and consciousness is not constrained to the history of the disciplines, but it is part of a broader culture of ahistoricity in the social sciences: they are barely sensitive to the lessons that history can provide. Economics and political science are increasingly interested in models whose connection to reality is frequently dubious. The inclination to learn from history has declined at the expense of an aspiration to understand idealised situations through mathematical modelling.[1] Sociology has developed in a different direction: it has retained more empirical content but at the expense of developing into an increasingly descriptive field of study whose survey methods of producing empirical data tend to lend support to less and less reliable conclusions and explanations.[2]

The loss of historical sensitivity has adverse consequences for theory construction and reduces the prospect of theories to provide insight into the processes taking place in contemporary society. The critique and interpretation of sociological theories are not merely historically relevant. Engagement with past sociological inquiry is a fertile source of inspiration for conceptual innovation: it provides an occasion for the revision of our received and unquestioningly deployed conceptualisations. With the decline of historical awareness these occasions become less numerous, and the alternative conceptual resources they could make available become impoverished. This has consequences for the prospects of empirical research as well: conceptual homogenisation deprives us from the ability to see phenomena from more than one point of view.

Despite its present peripheral status, conceptual innovation has been crucial in sociology. In comparison with the natural sciences, a distinctive feature of the social sciences is continuous conceptual innovation, and in consequence they have always been a very diverse field of inquiry. In historical retrospect, the history of social sciences does not lend much support for a properly Kuhnian paradigm-driven historiography. Talk about 'sociological paradigms' is of course abundant, and for didactic purposes such lax use of 'paradigm' is largely harmless. Yet it conceals the fact that the evolution of sociology is not congruent with that of the natural sciences. There have been no dominant conceptual schemes, values, methods and so on that could conquer the whole of sociological imagination at any given time and obliterate the memory and prospects of potential alternatives. There have always been resources for radically different ways of conceptualising social phenomena.

Different ways of conceptualisation reveal, or even create, different social realities – this is one lesson one can read from Ian Hacking's insightful explorations in the history of human sciences.[3] Another lesson one can derive from Hacking, and in different ways also from Peter Winch,[4] is that social phenomena, partly but crucially, are themselves of a conceptual nature, and the way this element is translated from the conceptual scheme of one sociological theory into that of another transforms the phenomenon itself. Society turns out to be a different place with different phenomena if it is conceptualised as a field of symbolic interactions or social conflicts or institutional structures, or some amalgam of these. Depending on one's conceptualisation, one's social reality will contain different phenomena and will require different strategies of engagement. This feature is reflected even within major approaches in fine-grained ways. If one takes 'class position' with Weber to arise from one's situation in the marketplace, rank, and party, or with Marx to arise from one's ownership of the means of production, or with Mannheim to reflect one's sphere of political activity, then one ends up with very different pictures of social stratification and the associated processes. And if one revises Marx's 'class' to reflect one's position in the process of redistribution, as did for example Konrád and Szelényi,[5] then one will have the resources to unmask self-proclaimed classless (communist) societies by the (Marxist) means of class analysis.

The Scottish Enlightenment is a rich source of conceptual innovations suitable for sociological deployment. Arguably, these concepts are not arranged into full-blown sociological theories or deployed with sociological awareness, and they frequently reflect what might be called, with Kenneth Macdonald, an 'adventitious sociology': a spontaneous and unreflective emergence of sociological insights.[6] However, this character of several sociological insights in the period can also be seen as a natural and unavoidable feature at the dawn of sociology, at its 'predisciplinary' phase, as we might call it with John Heilbron.[7] As Karl Mannheim aptly put it once, reality has not done us the favour of evolving in accordance with the disciplinary boundaries we find so natural today.[8] As new phenomena requiring new forms of inquiry emerged, they still had to be dealt with within the boundaries of existing disciplines. What might be called sociology in the Scottish Enlightenment cannot be clearly and distinctively detached from the neighbouring fields of history, moral philosophy, political economy and law.[9] It is hardly surprising to find that reflecting on the sociological features of reality started to emerge within less specialised disciplines and intertwined with other cognitive interests and insights.

Following Raymond Aron's suggestion, the emergence of sociology, as we have come to know it, presupposes two previous developments. The first is the emergence of social phenomena themselves in suitable complexity and a lack of transparency that makes them worthy objects of inquiry. When nothing lies hidden, when phenomena and reality coincide, then there is no need for science. Arguably, with the advent of *commercial society* in Scotland complexity would increase and transparency would decline significantly in comparison to preceding social formations, and this development required elaborate theorising for making social processes traceable. This form of socio-economic organisation is defined by an ever-increasing division of labour and specialisation that generate a field of socio-economic interaction where everyone must sell and buy the products of specialised labour – in an abstract marketplace.

It could be argued that conceptualising this form of socio-economic organisation as 'commercial society' reflects a different understanding and a more intense sociological sensitivity than the alternative label for the same organisation – 'capitalism' – and reflects different perceptions of social reality mediated by different concepts. Capitalism, especially in its Marx-inspired understanding, is primarily an economic concept that signifies a mode of production centred on capital investment, entrepreneurial organisation of economic activity, free market and ownership of the means of production. As capitalism forces its logic on to other, non-economic spheres of activity so it reveals its several, but derivative, sociological, legal and ideological consequences – while it retains the primacy of the economic. 'Commerce' in 'commercial society' is devoid of reductionistic overtones. It is an element in a system of mutual dependencies in 'that indissoluble chain of industry, knowledge and economy' that connects closely interacting fields of social life.[10] These interactions connect fields with different aims, logic and mechanisms. These 'moral causes' (for example, manners, customs, institutions) inculcate sometimes conflicting values, and their dialectics drives towards a transactional organisation of society that itself facilitates the widespread adoption of those values. Making transparent the intricate interaction of various causes driving social organisation dominates the Scots' sociological and economic imagination.

Aron's other prerequisite for the emergence of sociology is a suitable disciplinary environment for the study of this complexity, in which the fundamental metaphysical and methodological concepts are already in place and ready to be extended to social phenomena. This period of disciplinary evolution would arrive after Newton with the triumph of the experimental method of inquiry that advocated a search for lawlike regularities in nature, and experiment and observation as the only possible foundation of that inquiry. The ensuing attempt at the introduction of 'the experimental method of reasoning into moral subjects'[11] would soon become an established practice of producing knowledge and insights on human interactions. One distinguishing feature of the Scots' contribution arises from their interest in *causal mechanisms* and the *explanations* one can derive for them. Instead of constructing visions for ideal social arrangements, or arguments for the legitimacy and justification of some form of government, they were interested in how social phenomena arise, evolve and dissolve. This focus of interest facilitated the *naturalistic* flavour of Scottish social inquiry in both its providential and its agnostic forms.[12] Those adhering to some providential form of naturalism retained transcendent and religious concerns as a superadded framework for an interpretation of social phenomena. Thus they could maintain a common space of scholarly discourse focused on the phenomena themselves even with those of a more agnostic and irreligious orientation.

This interest in causal mechanisms is clearly reflected in the delineation of discernibly sociological problems in the processes of social organisation and institutionalisation:[13] family, social structure and stratification, gender issues, forms of social solidarity, ecclesiastical order and the social character of knowledge transmission were among the prominent foci of proto-sociological theory construction. Their discussion marked the emerging independence of social inquiry from more narrowly focused discourses of politics and political economy. In accordance with their descriptive and explanatory interest in mechanisms, the Scots' attitude to policy questions was frequently expressed in the form of conditionals – but this did not prevent them from evaluating and crticising government policies when it seemed necessary, as it did for Adam Smith in *The Wealth of Nations* (1776). Providing insights in 'if . . . then' conditionals might seem to many as indicating a lack of warmth in social causes. Alternatively, it can also be seen as reflecting a commitment to disinterested inquiry: as an exercise that, maybe unreflectively, pursues a proto-Weberian ideal of value-free inquiry – that is, an inquiry without commitments beyond theoretical choices concerning what and how to study.

Causal mechanisms are diachronic; organisation and institutionalisation are typically long-term processes – and Scottish social science traces them with a characteristic *historical sensitivity*. As opposed to survey and statistical methods or modelling, its recourse is typically history:[14] history provides a warehouse of data but it can be analysed to reveal patterns of action, and recurrent correlation of similar events can be analysed into triggering causes and constellations. Consequently, mathematical methods are practically non-existent: history is the great guide of social inquiry not mathematics. What little mathematics there is, is typically reflected in proportional thinking: as social phenomena are typically complex, the proportions of their constituents within a complexity is of significance.[15]

This volume contains case studies illustrating how sociological concepts and perspectives emerged in a less differentiated disciplinary environment and in the context of divergent scholarly and social motivations. This environment, as the essays collected here illustrate, provided a fertile soil for the emergence of sociological sensitivity and sociological concept building – without being the home of mature sociological theorising. Yet, as several chapters argue here, these concepts find echoes in subsequent sociological thought, testifying to the sociological significance of the Scottish heritage. This heritage is sometimes conscious, and in some cases it even provides an ideal to follow; in other cases the links are more blurred but, even there, conceptual congruences without direct historical connection illustrate clearly the significance of sociological sensitivity in the Scottish Enlightenment.

The essays of the volume are divided into three parts. The first contains two chapters that offer two different general perspectives on those aspects of Scottish Enlightenment thought that can be called sociological. For the Scots, as Christopher J. Berry points out, humans are social creatures by nature, and so the history of mankind is conterminous with the history of society: its manners, laws, property, norms and so on – in short, its institutions. The Scots are, accordingly, putting forward a history of society. In Dugald Stewart's terminology, this is a 'natural history', an enterprise which is underpinned by two pillars: the principles of human nature and circumstances. These differ because for Stewart and his fellow Scots the former implies constancy, the latter indicates variability. The 'principles' have to possess a basic fixity or constancy because without that premise it would not be feasible to write a history of mankind; there has to be a uniformity, or demonstrably sufficient invariance, in human nature. But unless the 'circumstances' varied, in time and place, there would be no subject for an aggregative history of society. While there is an element of ineliminable givenness (such as latitude and longitude) in these circumstances, what is decisive is the transformative and increasingly self-determining human response to them. The central argument of Berry's chapter is that these responses take on an 'institutional' form with the crucial codicil that these diverse 'forms' express themselves temporally, and he identifies these responses as coping mechanisms. The conjunction of the two principles means that the Scots write a history of institutions, but that enterprise is underwritten by a principled commitment to the constancy of human nature.

The chapter by Kenneth Macdonald defends and elaborates further his idea of a merely 'adventitious' sociology in the Scottish Enlightenment. This sociology displays a dispassionate approach to understanding social processes and is not deployed to underpin a moral vision. The essay continues Macdonald's argument that Adam Smith was not driven by his sociology of poverty to embrace a concern for the poor as underpinning his analyses.[16] Smith considers in a neutral and dispassionate way the thought that his approved taxes on luxuries are a driver of child poverty; his conclusion is unsentimental: 'it would not probably diminish much the useful population of the country'. In shifting the emphasis away from grand theory and moral vision, and towards adventitious sociology, the chapter also notes the difficulty of interpreting the translation and impact of 'grand theory' across time. Amartya Sen often invokes Smith as a precursor of Sen's own insights into capability deprivation. But Sen's account of Smith is based upon a misreading of Smith, and Macdonald suggests that adventitious sociology provides a less fraught ground of continuance. The chapter draws on illustrations from James Steuart, who is under-appreciated in the secondary literature, despite being an insightful proto-sociologist. Macdonald focuses on a hitherto unrecognised passage in which Steuart invents modern signalling theory, as currently deployed by economists and sociologists. This is noteworthy for the clarity with which Steuart lays out the underlying principles of such an explanation (though he deploys it only once). And the descriptor 'unrecognised' leads to a general puzzle for further inquiry: how are we to interpret such valid, but unregarded, precursors of modern sociology?

Part II contains chapters on sociological elements in central figures of the Scottish Enlightenment. Craig Smith focuses on Adam Ferguson who is widely considered the 'founding father' of the discipline: William Lehmann, Donald MacRae and Alan Swingewood have all made the case for Ferguson as a founding father. Ferguson certainly seems to stand at a pivotal point in the development of the sociological tradition. He represents a link between the methodological innovations of Montesquieu and the fascination with socialisation of Rousseau, on the one hand, and the grand system building of Hegel and Marx, on the other. In addition, Ferguson's discussion of the methodology of studying society in the early chapters of his *An Essay on the History of Civil Society* (1767) is perhaps the clearest statement of the Scottish Enlightenment's 'science of Man'. Smith examines the claims made on Ferguson's behalf for his position in the history of sociology from a new perspective: instead of examining Ferguson's purported contributions to sociological thinking in terms of their place in the development of sociology, Smith looks at their place within Ferguson's own writings and his wider system of thought. The chapter presents how important sociological ideas were to Ferguson, rather than assessing how important Ferguson's sociological ideas were to sociology: it explores how much of a sociologist Ferguson turns out to have been by looking at the place of sociological arguments in his overall thinking.

R. J. W. Mills presents the case of Henry Home, Lord Kames who experimented with the sort of social evolutionary history that we associate most with the Scottish Enlightenment, applying this style of thinking to a wide array of topics. He was particularly dedicated to one of the fundamental questions of the Enlightenment's 'science of human nature': whether man is fit for society. Having first explored this issue in his *Essays on the Principles of Morality and Natural Religion* (1751), Kames's final answer, found in *Sketches of the History of Man* (1774), was that we are 'partly social, partly selfish' but benefit most from being social. If what is important about the contribution of the Scottish Enlightenment to sociology is a sense that society is the product of various forces that can be empirically studied then Kames deserves a place at the table alongside Smith, Millar and Ferguson. Kames's case, in Mills's presentation, can also be read as an illustration of Berry's point: Kames sought to understand the underlying trajectory of the origin and development of specific institutions and behaviours, extracting from the diversity of historical evidence a system of providentially arranged developments. This took the form of an interplay between an unchanging human nature and the changing societal contexts in which humans existed. Key was the mode of subsistence, which led Kames to outline a stadial history of society. Within this, 'commercial society' does not end up as the perfection of but rather the corruption of society, in place of the desired balance between agriculture and commerce.

The chapter by Spyridon Tegos turns to Adam Smith to explore the aesthetic origins and the related emotional economy of social authority and charismatic leadership. In various works, Smith studies the rhetorical resources of inciting sentimental reactions towards greatness, the sources of wonder, admiration and surprise, and he sketches a 'natural history' that is a stadial explanation of the emergence of deference to authority. In *The Theory of Moral Sentiments* (1759) Smith examines the moderate aesthetic attachment to systems as a legitimate motivation of political action and introduces the notions of the spirit and love of system, and he concludes that authoritarianism and true statesmanship derive from an aesthetic attachment to systems. Moderation is rarely found among political reformers, obsessed by their allegedly well-drafted systems. The 'man of the system', this potential fanatic, according to Smith, often remains a factional leader but he can also transform himself into a man of public spirit, if he resists the enthusiasm for the unmediated implementation of allegedly perfect systems, so there must be a live feedback loop between theory and praxis. In Tegos's construal, Smith's true statesman, who inspires legitimate deference while relying on these resources, can be read fruitfully through a Weberian lens as a bearer of modern charismatic authority.

Part II closes with a second chapter by Kenneth Macdonald, which provides an analysis of John Sinclair's *Statistical Account of Scotland* (1791–9). The 'Old Statistical Account' (OSA) has, with its verbatim accounts from nine hundred or so ministers of the kirk, traditionally been mined as a source for the facts of life in eighteenth-century Scotland. This chapter, by contrast and uniquely, reads the OSA as providing an insight into how these ministers thought about the structure of their society – how, and whether, they thought sociologically. Of the several niceties this chapter offers, let me draw close attention to just one: the passages discussing curling because they create a pleasant organic connection between the visual appearance of the book's cover and its content. As it transpires, the ministers were perceptive about the social significance of curling, which transcended that of mere entertainment. They could see it as an instance of structured social competition and read it as an activity indicating collective mental health. They also indicate that curling was combined with local initiatives facilitating social cohesion through a contribution to poor relief efforts. Charles Martin Hardie's painting that we decided to use as cover image serves as a visual allegory of the present enterprise at various levels: it portrays a Scottish invention that reflects cooperation, competition, social structure and, in the background, an engagement with social issues combined with an aspiration for social improvement. In short, it reflects the sensitivities that have defined sociology from its earliest days.

Alongside Macdonald's other essay in this volume, this chapter contributes to an ongoing project: to place low-level insights, rather than grand theory, at the heart of the sociological legacy of Enlightenment Scotland. The aim of the chapter is not to provide a comprehensive overview of sociological insights one can excavate from the OSA but to ascertain whether these ministers could think sociologically, and the topics chosen (political unrest; religion; occupation and technology; the organisation of provision for the poor; the provision of inoculation against smallpox) aim to illustrate a reasonable range of sociological ways of thinking. Macdonald's answer on the evidence is that, on social matters, the ministers thought as rational economic sociologists. On the sociology of ideas, they are less sure-footed; but, by the end of the eighteenth century, this particular elite had absorbed a mode of thought about their social context that we might reasonably claim as 'sociological', objective and dispassionate.

The chapters collected in Part III explore the afterlife of the sociological heritage of Enlightenment Scotland. Dirk Schuck unearths the link from the Scottish Enlightenment through Hegel to modern Marxist social thought. In the introduction to the *Grundrisse* (1857–8), Marx famously claims that 'human anatomy contains a key to the anatomy of the ape'.[17] This apparent paradox has an epistemological meaning. Marx here invokes Hegel's notion of the history of society being constructed *post festum*: only from the standpoint of what has already happened are we able to see the evolvement of a natural and necessary development which would lead us to that stage. Schuck explores the connection between Hegel's insight and the theories of societal development in the Scottish Enlightenment. In this tradition, there is a great diversity of competing theories about the distinct (necessary) stages in the history of human society. Dismissing such historical speculations as inferior is itself based on precarious assumptions about the criteria that historical knowledge must meet. Hegel's analysis of the opposing forces to be found within human reason can help us see that, by denying ourselves such speculations, we fail to realise the full potential of our mind's capabilities.

Angela Coventry reviews Hume's widespread influence in the history of sociology. She argues that Hume's experimental science of human nature revealed the illusory pursuit of first causes in religion, the shortcomings of positing obscure forces in metaphysics and replaced the search for causes with the scientific study of descriptive generalisations or laws of nature. Auguste Comte continued Hume's project with the positive application of the scientific method to society. Ferdinand Tönnies considered Hume as one of the true inventors and expert practitioners of sociology, due especially to Hume's account of convention. Hume sees conventions as rules or systems of rules, like rules of language, justice or money, which are based on a sense of common or mutual interest that tends towards public utility. For Tönnies such conventions are the foundations of society. In *Community and Society* (1887), Tönnies treats conventions as necessarily serving a general utility to society but only on the condition that this utility is wanted and promoted by the members of society in the interests of their own utility. Hume's 1757 essay 'The Natural History of Religion' examines the historical and causal origins of religious belief. This procedure continued in sociological theories of the nineteenth and early twentieth centuries, especially in Comte and Émile Durkheim. Coventry also links Hume on the self to later sociological theories of the social self. Hume's account of the social origin of passions and sympathy allows that one can come to view and know oneself through the perspective of others. Similar ideas are dominant in G. H. Mead's account of the social construction of the self and in Lev Vygotsky's understanding of the effect of social relations on human mental development.

Catherine Dromelet elaborates on various aspects of a Hume–Durkheim connection. Steven Lukes and Warren Schmaus have already offered insights on the intellectual connections of Durkheim to the Scottish Enlightenment. Besides his engagement in the debate concerning causation and the categories of the understanding inspired by Hume, there is a further field where Durkheim seems to be indebted to the Scottish Enlightenment and to Hume in particular. As Dromelet argues, Durkheim's account of social organisation and the emergence of social order has striking affinities to those put forward by Scottish thinkers, particularly Hume. Against this background, Durkheim's social and moral theory can be read as a sociological appropriation of Hume's 'science of man', for example with respect to 'sympathy' as a social transmitter of emotions; to the role of social processes and structures in giving rise to moral sentiments; and to collective or public sentiments. The chapter reconstructs the way in which Humean ideas reached Durkheim. Then it turns to discussing the Humean understanding of central concepts that become operative in Durkheim's account of social organisation, morality and knowledge. Finally, Dromelet presents a Humean challenge to the idea of a Kantian influence on Durkheim's account of moral obligation and argues that Hume's psychosocial concepts of sympathy and custom anticipate some of the ideas in the Strong Programme of the Sociology of Knowledge.

Otto Pipatti's chapter retains the focus on sociology and morals while outlining an overview of the Scottish roots of Edward Westermarck's theory of morality. While largely forgotten today, Westermarck was a contemporary of the major classical sociologists and the first professor of sociology in Britain. The chapter begins with a brief look at Westermarck's life and career, and then it discusses Westermarck's conception of sociology and its relation to his study of morality. Throughout his writings, as it transpires in Pipatti's presentation, Westermarck stressed his debt to the Scottish moral sentimentalists, especially Hume and Smith. The rest of the chapter focuses on the Humean and Smithian elements of his thought, exploring how Westermarck read and understood their ideas and developed them further in his own theory of moral emotions. More specifically, it examines the emotional basis of moral judgements; the nature and characteristics of the moral emotions; the importance of sympathy, emotional contagion and aversion or disgust in how the moral emotions arise; the emergence and maintenance of moral norms; and objectification as a major element in moral judgements.

John Hall turns to Adam Smith and diagnoses his neglect in contemporary sociology, arguing in favour of reversing this situation – partly in opposition to Kenneth Macdonald's first chapter in the present volume, disputing Macdonald's claim concerning the lack of Smith's normative social concerns. As Hall argues, Smith had an initial impact on sociology. Members of the Progressive Movement working at the University of Chicago knew and wrote about his work, with Charles Cooley taking from Smith's *Theory of Moral Sentiments* his concept of the 'looking-glass self' and thereby founding the tradition of symbolic interactionism. However, these thinkers paid little attention to Smith's historical and comparative sociology. The main reason for remedying this situation is that sociology can be improved by taking Smith seriously. The chapter first introduces Smith's key insights on the way in which commercial sociability can ensure social cohesion, if policies are in place that prevent merchants from so capturing the state as to destroy the workings of this beneficent mechanism. Hall goes on to argue that Smith's concerns are still relevant when examining contemporary liberal capitalism, and he illustrates this with Thomas Philippon's recent analysis of the economy of the United States. Finally, Hall compares Smith to Marx, Weber and Durkheim, showing ways in which Smith fills gaps in their thought and in sociology's understanding of the modern world.

In recent decades, John Millar has become a canonical figure of the Scottish Enlightenment. This is partly due to Nicholas Miller's work, whose chapter here offers the first study of Millar's reception before the rise of modern scholarship on the Enlightenment in the mid-twentieth century. Intertwining theoretically and historically oriented approaches to disciplinary pasts, his chapter recasts John Millar's sociological reception and considers his enduring significance for sociological analysis. Millar first featured as part of nineteenth-century debates on gender relations in early history that crossed emerging disciplinary distinctions between sociology and anthropology. Around the turn of the twentieth century, sociologists and anthropologists identified him as an early discussant of the history of social inequality, sparking the interest of a range of German Marxists attempting to divine Marx's eighteenth-century influences. Werner Sombart weaponised this reception history in 1923 by arguing that Millar was the true progenitor of historical materialism, or what he renamed the 'technological-economic theory of history'. Hitherto, the ideological character of Sombart's celebration of Millar has not been noticed. The chapter reveals how Millar's legacy up to World War II was rarely nationalised as Scottish, having been mostly discussed outside Britain and in languages other than English. The chapter ends by suggesting that Millar's primary contributions to sociology lie in connection with history: stadial history as practice, rather than theory, contained the seeds of a historicist approach, with Millar's inquiry straddling fields we now associate with history and sociology.

Aldo Mascareño and Leonidas Montes direct our attention to the long-debated 'Adam Smith Problem', and a common misunderstanding of 'sympathy' and 'self-interest' arising from an all too narrow interpretation of the two concepts. They emphasise that Smith's concept of self-interest transcends that of mere selfishness and that *The Theory of Moral Sentiments*, besides developing the crucial concept of sympathy, offers a strong moral defence of self-interest. They are consonant with John Hall in suggesting that *The Wealth of Nations* (1776), in addition to its defence of self-interest, is rich in moral implications regarding the construction of a differentiated yet interdependent modern society. This idea of modern society allows a new sociological perspective: while self-interest emphasises autonomy and differentiation through division of labour, sympathy stresses the fact that there can be no interdependence without developing what modern sociology calls expectations of expectations – that is, without one's recognition of others' self-interest. A proper understanding of this framework connects sympathy with self-interest, as well as Smith's two main works. The chapter puts these concepts into dialogue with Niklas Luhmann's theory of social systems and argues along these lines that a proper comprehension of modern society requires a balancing act between self-interest (the foundation of autonomy and differentiation) and sympathy (the basis for social interdependence). Both Smith and Luhmann presuppose this interaction, so the Smithian connection foreshadows a Luhmannian understanding of the complexities of modern society.

Jerry Fodor famously labelled Hume's *Treatise of Human Nature* (1739–40) as 'the foundational document of cognitive science'.[18] Tamás Demeter's chapter argues that the significance of the *Treatise* is also foundational to the sociology of knowledge, especially as practised in its Strong Programme that originated in Edinburgh. This proposal is consonant with Catherine Dromelet's suggestion in her contribution to this volume. As this chapter points out, it is widely acknowledged that the strong naturalistic tendencies of Hume's epistemology anticipate the explanatory constructs of cognitive psychology, but it is much less frequently acknowledged that Hume's analyses of knowledge and cognition also extend to and invoke social causes. The chapter shows how central concepts and analyses of David Bloor's historical case studies can be conveniently translated into a Humean idiom. In this reconstruction, Hume's ideas on social 'ranks' and circles of 'sympathy' foreshadow Bloor's analyses of stratification in scholarly communities in terms of 'group' and 'grid' features (borrowed from Mary Douglas's anthropology). Similarly, Hume's idea of socially transmitted 'general rules' offers a possibility to translate Bloor's account of the influence of scientific socialisation on divergent ways of knowledge production. Affinities between Hume and Bloor should not be surprising as Bloor himself frequently cites Hume in support of his general perspective. In the chapter's presentation, however, these general affinities are substantiated by specific convergences between the different sociologically oriented conceptualisations of epistemic phenomena.

The present collection provides an overview of the sociological significance of Scottish Enlightenment thought, frequently in connection with the pre-history of the neighbouring disciplines of economics and political science. The volume does not aspire to be an exhaustive presentation of this significance and connections – that would be too much to hope for. Instead, it aims to transcend the sometimes all too rigid disciplinary boundaries and highlight the wide-ranging influence of Scottish Enlightenment philosophy. More generally, it aims to convince the reader that philosophy has an impact outside philosophy – in the present case, in the social sciences, and particularly in sociology.

Acknowledgements

The present volume has benefited from a workshop held in at Corvinus University of Budapest on 28–29 January 2021. The workshop has been supported by the MTA-BTK Lendület 'Morals and Science' Research Group and Corvinus University of Budapest. This project contributes to the research programme of MTA-BTK Lendület 'Value Polarizations in Science' Research Group.

Notes

1. For a recent, more detailed diagnosis on the consequences of ahistoricity in economics and economic policy see Adam Tooze, 'The Return of Depression Economics: Paul Krugman and the Twenty-First-Century Crisis of American Democracy' in Richard Bourke and Quentin Skinner (eds), *History in the Humanities and Social Sciences* (Cambridge: Cambridge University Press, 2022), pp. 354–78.
2. The present diagnosis is largely consonant with those offered in Iván Szelényi, 'The Triple Crisis of Sociology', *Contexts*, 20 April 2015. http://contexts.org/blog/the-triple-crisis-of-sociology
3. Particularly Ian Hacking, *Rewriting the Soul* (Princeton: Princeton University Press, 1995) and *Mad Travelers* (Charlottesville, VA: University of Virginia Press, 1998).

4. Peter Winch, *The Idea of a Social Science and Its Relation to Philosophy* (London: Routledge and Kegan Paul, 1958).
5. György Konrád and Iván Szelényi, *The Intellectuals on the Road to Class Power* (Brighton: Harvester, 1979).
6. For the idea see Kenneth Macdonald, 'Did British Sociology Begin with the Scottish Enlightenment?' in Plamena Panayotova (ed.), *The History of Sociology in Britain* (Cham: Palgrave Macmillan, 2019), pp. 37–70. For further elaboration see his 'Adventitious Sociology: Dispassion and Insight in the Scottish Enlightenment' in the present volume.
7. John Heilbron, *The Rise of Social Theory* (Minneapolis, MN: University of Minnesota Press, 1995).
8. Karl Mannheim, 'Die Gegenwartsaufgaben der Soziologie' in *Schriften zur Soziologie* (Wiesbaden: Springer VS, 2019), p. 81.
9. One should also note that political economy itself started to gain independence of moral philosophy only in this period. See Thomas Ahnert, 'The Philosophy Curriculum at Scottish Universities in the Eighteenth Century' in Aaron Garrett and James Harris (eds), *Scottish Philosophy in the Eighteenth Century, Volume II: Method, Metaphysics, Mind, Language* (Oxford: Oxford University Press, 2023), pp. 43–5.
10. David Hume uses this widely discussed phrase in 'Of Refinement in the Arts' in *Essays, Moral, Political, and Literary*, ed. E. F. Miller (Indianapolis, IN: Hackett, 1987), p. 271.
11. As the subtitle of Hume's *A Treatise of Human Nature, Being and Attempt to Introduce the Experimental Method of Reasoning into Moral Subjects*, originally published in two volumes in London, printed for John Noon, in 1739 and 1740.
12. On providential and agnostic naturalism in Scottish Enlightenment inquiry see Tamás Demeter, 'Philosophical Methods' in Aaron Garrett and James Harris (eds), *Scottish Philosophy in the Eighteenth Century, Volume II: Method, Metaphysics, Mind, Language* (Oxford: Oxford University Press, 2023), pp. 53–107, 71–3.
13. See for example Christopher Berry's chapter in the present volume, as well as his classic *Social Theory of the Scottish Enlightenment* (Edinburgh: Edinburgh University Press, 1997).
14. But Macdonald in Chapter 7 of the present volume introduces the *Old Statistical Account*, an early example of a sociological survey.
15. See for example Eric Schliesser, *Adam Smith: Systematic Philosopher and Public Thinker* (New York: Oxford University Press, 2023), pp. 325–9.

16. Macdonald first put forward this view in Kenneth Macdonald, 'Of Shame and Poverty; and on Misreading Sen and Adam Smith', *Adam Smith Review* 11 (2019), pp. 111–262. Available online: www.academia.edu/44011649
17. Karl Marx, *Grundrisse: Introduction to the Critique of Political Economy* (New York and London: Vintage Books, 1973), p. 105.
18. Jerry Fodor, *Hume Variations* (Oxford: Clarendon Press, 2003), p. 134.

Part I

General Perspectives

2

Human Nature and Social Change: Historical Institutionalism in the Scottish Enlightenment

Christopher J. Berry

The 'Scottish Enlightenment' is a short-hand term that generally characterises a set of ideas and arguments. In my own work I have focused more specifically on the ideas and arguments of those Scots who developed an analysis of society as having both synchronic and diachronic dimensions.[1] That is to say the components of society – laws, morals, customs and so on – more or less cohere or interlock in a particular era but these components gradually change to establish a new configuration. In this chapter I continue that focus by arguing that the Scots, with whom I am concerned,[2] are to be characterised as historical institutionalists. In developing my argument I examine the implicit relation between history and human nature.

The label 'historical institutionalist' is mine; it is not the Scots' own self-identification. However, the term 'institution' to refer to a component of 'society' is used by the Scots. Other examples will feature below, but to give two illustrative usages: Ferguson expansively refers to 'the institutions of men'[3] and Smith inter alia refers generally to 'human institutions' but also more particularly to coined money and mints as 'institutions'.[4]

I start by picking up a sentence in Dugald Stewart's *Life* of Smith. Prompted by Smith's *Considerations* on language, Stewart regards it as an 'interesting question' (that is, 'important' or 'significant') in the 'history of mankind' to discern by what 'gradual steps' the transition from the 'simple efforts of uncultivated nature' to a 'complicated' state has been made.[5] The phrase 'history of mankind' is one employed across the writings of the literati (as they self-identified). It is employed, among others, by Hume,[6] Smith,[7] Ferguson,[8] Stewart[9] and in the title of Dunbar's book.[10]

Millar's usage captures the theme of this chapter when he writes that he is illustrating the 'history of mankind ... by pointing out the more obvious and common improvements which gradually arise in the state of society and by showing the influence of these upon the manners, the laws and government of a people'.[11]

Since humans are social creatures then it means that the history of mankind is conterminous with the history of society – its manners, laws and government or 'institutions'. The universality of the former carries over into the latter. The Scots are putting forward a history of society. It is crucial to grasp the Scots' conception of the relation between these two 'histories'. Again that passage from Dugald Stewart gives a helpful clue. As he proceeds to outline, when direct evidence is missing then the natural, conjectural or theoretical historian (these are synonyms) can nonetheless consider in what manner humans 'are likely to have proceeded, from the principles of their nature, and the circumstances of their external situation'.[12]

Human nature and circumstances are thus the two pillars that support natural history. These differ because for Stewart and his fellow Scots the former implies constancy, the latter indicates variability. The 'principles' (first pillar) have to possess a basic fixity or constancy because without that premise it would not be feasible to write a history of mankind; there has to be a uniformity, or demonstrably sufficient invariance, in human nature (a point to which we shall return in Section 2). Unless the 'circumstances' (second pillar) varied, in time and place, there would be no subject for an aggregative history of society. While there is an element of ineliminable given-ness (such as latitude and longitude) in these circumstances, what is decisive is the transformative and increasingly self-determining human response to them. My contention is that these responses take on an 'institutional' form with the crucial codicil that these diverse 'forms' express themselves temporally. The conjunction of Stewart's two principles means that the Scots write a history of institutions but that enterprise is underwritten by a principled commitment to the constancy of human nature.

The institutions in question are uncontroversial. As well as Millar's 'manners, laws and government' they also incorporate other standard constituents, such as property, religion, kinship, ethical and social norms. In Section 1, I select, as sufficient for current purposes, religion and governance to illustrate in more detail the Scots' argument qua historical institutionalists. I then proceed, in Section 2, to examine the relation between institutional change and constant human nature.

1

Governance

Hume observes that American tribes live together 'without any establish'd government' and it is only in time of war that they 'pay submission' to 'their captain'.[13] Hume here is not forthcoming as to the basis of the captain's authority but in a late (posthumously published) essay he refers to those who possess superior personal qualities of 'valour, force, integrity or prudence' as commanding 'respect and confidence'.[14] The consensus among the Scots was that, from the available evidence suitably supported by concurrent testimony and comparison, the first mode of subordination was based on personal qualities. Millar states that in the 'rude period' of hunting and fishing there are no distinctions except those which arise from 'personal qualities either of mind or body',[15] qualities that Stuart finesses as 'force of body and vigour of mind'.[16] To those Smith, still referring to hunters, adds age as another specific factor.[17] This addition is echoed by Robertson who links 'age' and 'courage' as examples of 'personal qualities' that serve as the source of distinctions[18] and by Kames who refers to 'age' and 'experience'.[19]

For Smith those personal qualities 'naturally introduce subordination . . . antecedent to any civil institution'.[20] Antecedence supposes temporality. There is, of course, an intimate connection between government (Smith's 'civil institution') and subordination because it is assumed to be part of the meaning of 'government' that it is a hierarchical relationship of ruler over ruled.[21] While, as befits its unstable character, the answer to the question 'who rules?' among hunter-gatherers is initially transient and fluid, nonetheless there are sown some seeds of what will grow into institutional structures of governance. Picking up Stewart's 'second principle' of natural history, a salient circumstance of savage/rude/hunter-gatherer life is, as Hume had pointed out, warfare.

Millar hypothesises that someone adept at waging war will be conspicuous and that eminence will be enhanced by others becoming 'accustomed to follow his banner'.[22] The reference to 'custom' – a crucial component in the Scots' social theory that can be reasonably interpreted as a process of institutionalisation (see later) – was utilised by Hume for whom 'long continuance' of the state of war in the earliest societies results in the people being 'enured' to their submission to their leaders so that they come to accept their decisions to resolve peacetime disputes.[23] It is in this 'casual and imperfect' way, as an unintended consequence, that government commences;[24] it is a reaction not a deliberative positive act (like a contract).[25] Institutions or what Ferguson calls 'establishments' are, in his well-known phrase, the product of 'action' not 'design'.[26]

This same trajectory is traced by others. Millar follows Hume closely. The head of a rude society is originally the commander of forces who later turns his attention to settling internal disputes.[27] Both Kames[28] and Ferguson[29] illustrate this 'casual and imperfect' process by observing that government emerges gradually and is only restrained by rules after many 'errors in the capacities of magistrates and subjects' have been committed or until the people have suffered under 'vicious government'. One important reason for this priority of external to internal affairs is that initially internal disputes were expected to be settled privately – the principle of revenge was accepted. The ceding of the right of revenge by the 'multitude' to the chief to whom they have become enured is remarked upon by Stuart.[30] It is also stressed by Robertson who refers to it in several of his writings.[31] Compounding the power of custom, this represents the tentative beginning of a process of institutionalisation that Millar attributes to the 'progress of government'.[32]

The notion of 'progress' implies advance through time. Sociality is true of all humans but it is evident to experience that its institutional expression is, in Stewart's sense, 'circumstantial' and thus (increasingly) diverse. Nevertheless, by seeking a causal explanation for these expressions they can be revealed as non-random. Since the (Newtonian) criterion of successful natural science is the reduction of multiplicity to simplicity then the hallmark of successful social science is the reduction of the diversity of institutions to some intelligible pattern. There were two candidates on offer: space and time. The former was a species of physical causation (exemplified by climate); the latter was a central assumption of moral causation.

The Scots, following Hume (in his essay 'Of National Characters' [1748]), judged moral causes to have greater explanatory power than physical ones. In line with its root meaning in mores or customs, this mode of causation better captured not only the variety of institutional formation but also that this variety changed over time. To pick up my earlier comment, it establishes that 'institutions' reflect temporally the diversity of human responses to environmental circumstances. Institutions, we can say, are coping mechanisms. Humans as they cope with (to use Stewart's phrase) their external situation come in time to live in an environment of their own creation; their 'circumstances' themselves have increasingly become human or 'moral'. The record of this progressively effective coping process is an account of 'improvement'; it is the stuff of history and the key to the Scots as historical institutionalists.

This is not to deny physical causes any role. Millar states that, when searching for the causes of the 'amazing diversity' of circumstances, 'we must undoubtedly resort, first of all, to the differences of situation'. These differences include 'the fertility or barrenness of the soil' and 'the nature of its productions' but the significant consequence is that these physical circumstances generate a response: they affect the 'species of labour requisite for procuring subsistence'.[33] Kames similarly argues that in cold climes, the hardness of the ground makes cultivation of corn difficult so that in response only hunting or herding are practised, while in the 'torrid zone' the inhabitants subsist only on vegetable food.[34] Ferguson judges that 'the torrid zone everywhere round the globe ... has furnished few materials for history' and stands in a stark and crucial contrast to the 'temperate zone'.[35] That zone is the scene of the 'principal honours of the species' because it is there that mankind has developed or progressed. In our terms, this means that in that zone the coping responses are cumulative and autopoietic.

In a key quotation for my argument, Robertson expresses this when he comments on the relative sway of moral and physical causes; climate produces greater effects on 'rude nations' than in 'societies more improved' because 'civilized men' can through their 'ingenuity and inventions ... supply the defects and guard against the inconveniences of any climate'.[36] As they develop, humans are able increasingly to dominate nature ('supply the defects') because they are not determined rigidly by their environment ('hard determinism'). They have, rather, 'ingenuity', the capacity to learn from experience and 'invent' improvements, somewhat in the manner of 'a boy' employed to operate a fire-engine who, purely for his own benefit, hit upon a more efficient mechanism.[37] Those inventions that enhance 'coping' are retained through habit and custom (a process of institutionalisation or 'soft determinism'[38]) and so improvement upon improvement – the process of 'civilisation' – becomes possible, albeit neither certain nor immune to regression. Dunbar, who explicitly follows Robertson and who of all the Scots gives the most careful analysis of 'climate',[39] argues that 'the series of events, once begun, is governed more perhaps by moral than physical causes'.⁴⁰ This is because the impact of the latter varies with 'the general state of human improvement'⁴¹ so that they are of 'the least relative moment in the most flourishing stage of arts and sciences'.⁴² Humans have the increasing capacity to control their environment; the extent of that control is an index of development.⁴³ But how that control is exercised manifests and solidifies itself in their institutions so that, as Dunbar puts it, the extent of any improvement correlates 'in a high degree with the progress of civil arts'.⁴⁴

With his phrase 'civil arts' Dunbar intimates the link with governance as one of those institutions that can be assessed historically and thus implicitly serve as an index of improvement.⁴⁵ This is a gradual process but within it different phases or stages can be identified. This stadial approach takes on a distinctively institutional form in the Scots. Although the outlines are commonly shared, the definitive accounts are provided by Smith and Millar, in their lectures at Glasgow University. In their jurisprudence classes, they articulated for their students how property, and thus the need for juridical and governmental regulations, evolved. For their pedagogic purposes they divided this evolution into four stages.⁴⁶ In Smith's lectures of 1762/3 he unequivocally refers to 'four distinct states which mankind pass thro' – hunter, shepherd, agriculture and commerce.⁴⁷ (In the 1766 version they are called hunting, pasturage, farming and commerce.)⁴⁸ In Millar's (unpublished) lectures on government, they are explicitly said to be 'stages in the acquisition of property'.⁴⁹

In the initial hunter stage where property is indistinguishable from possession (a point emphasised by Kames but also by Smith who perhaps follows him),⁵⁰ its transient character means there is little to regulate and governance based on the personal qualities and age is sufficient. There is a rough-and-ready equality that correlates with 'universal poverty'.⁵¹ However, the second stage sees a marked change with property now taking the form of the unequal 'ownership' of herds. But this inequality marks a more permanent differentiation and with that 'some degree ... of civil government' is introduced.⁵² On Smith's account, this introduction is a self-interested move by the owners of the herd (the rich). They require 'government' to preserve 'that order of things which can alone secure them in the possession of their own advantages'. Smith had originally made this argument in his *Lectures* where property in the age of shepherds is said bluntly to make government 'absolutely necessary' and to be so because otherwise the poor would attack the rich.[53] The governance of a Tartar khan is 'despotical'.[54] Hence rule and what passes for 'law' in the second stage is inherently capricious – it depends on the khan's whim and in consequence will lack generality or inclusivity.

Exactly the same can be said of governance in the third stage. The establishment of property in land does not produce any shift in the basis of subordination. Just as the chief in pastoral times is the one with the largest herd (and thus most retainers) so the leader in agricultural societies is the one with the most land (and thus most retainers).[55] The same crucial relationship of dependency applies in both ages. Upholding this relationship is not merely the 'brute' fact of material dependency but also a consolidative, complementary set of legitimating beliefs about that rule which are institutionally embodied in manners or 'habits of thinking'.[56] Millar, in the context of the pastoral stage, provides a particularly clear example of this chain of reasoning: 'thus the son, who inherits the estate of his father, is enabled to maintain an equal rank . . . which is daily augmented by the power of habit and becomes more considerable as it passes from one generation to another'.[57]

Habits can thus be understood as coping mechanisms that form institutions. That is to say, habits, as repeated effective responses to circumstances, establish an institutional environment or order; the effectiveness of which increases as the order becomes more established. As I have argued elsewhere,[58] institutions established in this way are correspondingly 'sticky'; the 'uniform continuance of custom', in Smith's phrase, is powerful.[59] One significant consequence of this stickiness is that the Scots as exponents of historical institutionalism see social change as necessarily gradual and typically inadvertent.[60]

The *locus classicus* of this is Smith's account of the implosion of the feudal mode of governance resting on customary dependency. It is a crucial and definitive characteristic of a commercial society that this dependency is absent. Owing to the pervasiveness of exchange – including decisively land[61] – then property is 'subjected to a constant rotation' and this 'prevents it from conferring upon the owner the habitual respect and consideration derived from a long continued intercourse between the poor and the rich'.[62] In other words, the institutional framework of governance shifts.

At the heart of this shift is the overturning of the institutions of feudalism whereby the 'great proprietors', as Smith calls them, were 'judges in peace' as well as 'leaders in war'.⁶³ The eventual separation of these roles into distinct institutions heralds the fourth commercial stage. This happened 'by chance' as the offspring of social growth and attendant multiplication of business. Smith judges this to constitute 'the great advantage' of 'modern times ... and the foundation of that greater Security which we now enjoy'.⁶⁴ Prior to this separation, the power/authority of the feudal lords was exercised without any effective external control. Hence they were, for example, able to levy, as they saw fit, taxes on travellers through their lands and any traders who remained within their demesnes were in a 'servile' condition.⁶⁵ But the corollary of this was that these proprietors had no authority or clout beyond their boundaries. One consequence of this localisation or segmentation of power was that there could be no consistency of decision between localities nor any 'external' guarantee of consistency within a 'jurisdiction'. Steuart made the point eloquently when he contrasted the circumstance where the 'laws' are liable to change 'through favour or prejudice to particular persons or particular classes' to one where people are 'governed by general laws', which are 'established so as not to be changed but in regular and uniform way'.⁶⁶

This regularity is institutionalised as the rule of law, whereby, in Hume's characterisation, the administration of government 'must act by general laws that are previously known to all the members' and when that obtains the government is free.⁶⁷ This connection between liberty and the absence of capricious will by those in power was commonly made and, of course, was not the prerogative of the Scots.⁶⁸ Among the Scots, in addition to Steuart and Hume, the same link is made, for example, by Hutcheson,⁶⁹ by Wallace,⁷⁰ by Kames⁷¹ and by Ferguson⁷² as well as Smith.⁷³

This shift from personal rule to the impersonal rule of law not only exemplifies the diachronic dimension to institutions but illustrates their synchronicity. Hence the abstractness and impersonality of law in the fourth stage mirrors the abstractness and impersonality of commerce ('the market') in that both repose on beliefs and expectations. When rule is not capricious but predictable then, provided the rules are kept, individuals can reasonably expect that they will be free to pursue their own interests (the very definition of 'natural liberty' according to Smith).⁷⁴ In a commercial society everyone is to 'some extent a merchant',⁷⁵ that is to say they are involved in a complex series of impersonal interdependent relations in pointed contrast to the personal dependency of relations in earlier stages. A manufacturer spends time *now* producing a particular product in the expectation that anonymous others will *later* want it, and that belief about their desire is itself premised on the belief that others are *now* producing different products. Hume captures this network of beliefs in his comment that

> the poorest artificer, who labours alone, *expects* at least the protection of the magistrate, to ensure him the enjoyment of the fruits of his labour. He also *expects* that when he carries his goods to market and offers them at a reasonable price, he shall find purchasers and shall be able, by the money he acquires, to engage others to supply him with those commodities which are requisite for his subsistence.[76]

Indicative of the complexity of a modern commercial society, Hume continues that last quotation by remarking that 'in proportion as men extend their dealings and render their intercourse with others more complicated, they always comprehend in their schemes of life a greater variety of voluntary actions which they *expect*, from the proper motives, to co-operate with their own'. This complexity stands in stark contrast to the simplicity and uniformity of early societal structures. Millar remarks that

> however such people [rude and barbarous] may happen to be distinguished by singular institutions and whimsical customs, they discover a wonderful uniformity in the general outline of their character and manners; an uniformity no less remarkable in different nations the most remote from each other.[77]

Similarity of circumstances or conditions is a general cause that produces as an effect similarity of manners which, as Millar's quotation testifies, incorporate institutions.[78] Hence the 'wonderful uniformity' of the manners of rude people is the product of similar circumstances and the similarity of the response to them.[79] But against the backcloth of a natural history of mankind, as Stewart had characterised it, there is a move from simple to complicated;[80] as exemplified by the institutional shift from immediate governance by particular individuals to mediated governance via the general or abstract rule of law.

To reinforce that picture, I choose the natural history of religion as a second example of the Scots as historical institutionalists. Stewart himself identified Hume's essay 'The Natural History of Religion' as a work that exemplified 'theoretical' history.[81]

Religion

The development of governance from the institutions of personal rule and despotic and capricious overlordship to those that embody the predictable authority and impersonality of law follows, as befits the complementary syn- and diachronic dimensions of sociality, a similar course in the institutions that embody religious belief and practice. When it comes to 'savages', the 'circumstances' (Stewart's second principle) are characterised in similar terms across the Scots as a whole but the explanatory role played by human nature (the first principle) exhibited some divergence. Some argued that belief in religion is a primary principle in human nature,[82] some that is a secondary principle but still rooted in universal principles of human nature (most explicitly by Hume, who roots it in the passions of hope and fear, and implicitly by Smith and Dunbar) while others were non-committal (Ferguson). Those differences aside, I will in Section 2 argue that for institutionalists they are not decisive because there is a shared conviction that human nature functions as a constant principle and also a shared agreement on the historical trajectory. In outline, it is the development from the institutions of polytheistic belief and practice to monotheistic belief and practice.

Though Hume[83] and Kames[84] disagree about the source of religion, both state that polytheism is the earliest expression of religious belief. Hume identifies a universal or natural propensity in mankind to ascribe malice or good-will to everything that 'hurts or pleases us' hence the polytheistic personification of trees, mountains and streams.[85] For Dunbar 'in ages of ignorance and simplicity, mankind are so prone to credulity and admiration' that these 'propensities' lead them to the 'acknowledgement and adoration of invisible powers'.[86] These 'powers' will vary according to the particular circumstances, so, as Ferguson observes, maritime nations will conceive of a deity as 'monarch of the seas' while for those based on land the deity is 'the ruler of the seasons'.[87] In either case the inhabitants cope with the uncertainties and tribulations of their environment (circumstances) by creating religious institutions, such as ceremonies that (say) require sacrifices to appease the gods to obtain safe sea-passage. What that quotation from Ferguson also illustrates is the shared imagery of governance, itself symptomatic of institutional synchronicity.[88] Savages cope with the ever-present exigencies of warfare by institutions of governance in order to increase efficacy and order just as they cope with natural or environmental uncertainty and calamity by seeking order and solace through their religion (a form of 'collective psychotherapy' as it has been nicely termed[89]).

Hume is careful to point out – and this is a central part of my overall argument – that the human propensity to personify will operate 'if not corrected by experience and reflection'.[90] This is why Hume more precisely defines polytheism as the 'uninstructed' religion of primitive mankind.[91] That savages are ignorant is a point made again and again by Hume and not only by him.[92] What marks out, and lies at the root of, the ignorance of savages is their not knowing what truly constitutes cause and effect. This assertion is clear in Hume[93] and Kames,[94] and for Robertson the savages' inability to comprehend the causes of occurrences produces the fanciful belief that there is 'something mysterious and wonderful in their origin'.[95]

This ignorance is attributable to their circumstances and this attribution now enables religious speculation and practice to fit into the broader schema of institutional development, from 'ignorance to knowledge' or from 'rude to civilized manners'.[96] For Hume 'primitive Man' is a necessitous creature, pressed by 'numerous wants and passions'.[97] Trying to meet pressing needs with limited resources means a lack of leisure and that shortcoming means no time to stand back from immediate exigency to reflect and acquire instruction. For Millar, 'science and literature' are the 'natural fruit of leisure'.[98] 'Free' time is required to enable humans to begin the process of tracing the causal links that for the 'ignorant multitude' remain unknown.[99] Given that ignorance marks out the early ages in the history of mankind then the growth of 'science', the uncovering of the causal processes at work, like the increasing predominance of moral causes, is an index of improvement or 'civilisation'. Those revelations track institutional development.

Robertson remarks that those who labour for subsistence have no leisure or capacity for refined speculation.[100] (For reasons to be explored in Section 2, this deficiency is not limited to Amerinds.) What is crucial is the *opportunity* to reflect. The link between the creation of that opportunity and social development is a feature of Smith's *History of Astronomy* (a component of his posthumous *Essays*). In a familiar fashion, 'savages', he conjectures, live in a pre-philosophical age where subsistence is precarious and life is short. They are preoccupied with immediate questions of survival and have neither the time nor the inclination to look into the causes of things. When confronted by startling irregularities in their experience, their response is to invoke some 'invisible designing power'.[101] In a Humean (ultimately Lucretian) fashion (and Hume is a big influence on *Astronomy*), this invocation is based on their own emotions such as fear or love and for Smith, too, this is the source of polytheism. (He makes much the same point in the *Moral Sentiments*.)[102]

However, with the gradual establishment of institutions that support order and security there comes, Smith continues, for those with sufficient leisure ('liberal fortune'), the opportunity to pay closer attention to the world around them and practise philosophy or science (the terms are interchangeable) and begin the process of tracing causal links.[103] (As straightforwardly formulated in his brief essay *Ancient Physics*, 'as ignorance begot superstition, science gave birth to the first theism'.)[104] This process is underpinned by institutional development. In Stewart's terms, this development is from simplicity to complexity or differentiation; as here by a social division between those who possess a fortune and those who don't. Kames's more elaborate stadial theory generates the same associations as it plots how 'men improve in natural knowledge' becoming thereby 'skilful in tracing causes from effects' until they arrive at 'true religion'.[105]

To generalise: religious belief moves from polytheism (particular and concrete) to monotheism (general and abstract). These beliefs are embedded in social institutions of religious practice/worship (Hume explicitly refers to monasteries as 'religious institutions'[106]). There is a gradual shift from idolatry, auguries and sacrifices to intellectual appreciation of Design and in tandem there is a move to increasingly established rule-governed institutions away from those initially represented by charismatic 'conjurors and wizards'.[107] The increasing institutionalisation from shaman to a priestly caste and a priesthood reflects the general process of social differentiation; religious institutions take a variety of forms – an established national church, an international church, an array of sects – all having their own internal rules and offices.

To conclude this section and to act as a harbinger, I want to pick up the Smithian observation that the development of scientific knowledge is the concomitant of social differentiation. One institutional expression of that differentiation is the relative exposure to education. The significance of this can be best appreciated within the context of the relation between history and human nature, the theme of Section 2.

2

As exemplified in governance and religion, the Scots have charted a course of institutional development. That course is the history of mankind-in-society. Humans have transformed their situation, turning as Smith rhapsodised 'primitive forests into agreeable and fertile plains', establishing 'cities and commonwealths' and inventing and improving 'all the sciences and arts that make human life noble and glorious'.[108] But, in line with Stewart's characterisation, this transformation is of 'circumstances' not of 'human nature'. Notwithstanding that those circumstances are historical, increasingly 'moral' and the product of human action, they do not go 'all the way down' to be constitutive; as Hume avers, the 'universal principles' of human nature remain 'constant'.[109]

There are a number of factors that support this 'non-contextual'[110] interpretation of the meaning of historical institutionalism in the Scots. The first is methodological or philosophical. In order for there to be an enterprise that pretends to be a history of mankind there needs to be a constitutive subject matter. History and social science generally would be impossible if every age and every society was in some deeply significant sense *sui generis*; it would literally be incomprehensible if the Algonquin (say) were so distinctive in their behaviours and institutions that these bore no relation to the Apache let alone to Gauls or Glaswegians. This is, of course, at one level platitudinous, a mere illustration of Terence's aphorism *homo sum* . . . but, given the Scots' commitment to social science and causal analysis, it takes on a more telling form. The whole thrust of Newton's methodological programme of explanatory parsimony would be rendered nugatory if different sets of social institutions across space and time were conceptually opaque. Of course, societies differ but it is only because the Scots accept that fact that there is a reason to seek an explanation for those differences.[111] Diversity necessarily presupposes uniformity, since the ability to identify differences presupposes some basic commonality because without that it is impossible to judge whether others do have beliefs or conceptual frameworks different from one's own.[112]

On a less methodological and more substantive footing, institutions, as coping mechanisms, are adaptations to constants in human nature. To co-opt Hume's example of housing,[113] humans need shelter whether this be a cave or a palace. That need is rooted in the universal requirement to avoid or ameliorate cold, heat, drought, flood and so on. And that requirement itself is a consequence of the uniform human aversion to pain. The difference between a cave and a palace represents the temporal variety of human institutions, exemplified here in governance and religion. Smith concludes *The Theory of Moral Sentiments* with the apposite statement that 'natural sentiments of justice' attain an 'accuracy and precision' in 'civilized nations' that is missing where the people remain 'rude' and barbarous. Here again we have the paradigmatic contrast between rude irregularity and the cultivated 'regular system of justice', together with the assumption that 'justice' is not some local peculiarity but a ubiquitous ('natural') aspect of generic human social co-existence.[114]

There is an underlying value judgement here. As we saw when discussing religion, the correlate of ignorance is superstition; Hume even propounds the dictum that 'from the grossness of its superstitions we may infer the ignorance of the age'.[115] The 'chief characteristic', Hume declares elsewhere, that distinguishes civilisation from barbarism is the 'indissoluble chain' of industry, humanity and knowledge.[116] Humans are more industrious, humane and knowledgeable because of social change; they become 'less oppressed with their own wants' as they gradually improve their circumstances through the development of institutions of commerce, governance, law, learning, 'culture' and so on.[117]

This is indeed an 'improvement'; knowledge is better than ignorance, just as industry is better than sloth and humanity than cruelty.[118] From this it follows that the Scots' commitment to historical institutionalism is not value-neutral; some ways of living are superior to others. The institutions of commercial society, such as the rule of law and extensive markets, which result in better food, clothing and habitation as well as more freedom than anything experienced by an absolute 'African king',[119] have on those grounds in the eyes of the Scots proved to be the most effective coping mechanisms that have yet been developed. The propensity to 'truck, barter and exchange' has expressed itself more effectively, and to the overall social benefit of 'universal opulence', in the manufacture even of a 'coarse and rough woollen coat', which implicates anonymously thousands in its production, rather than in two-way direct exchange of a bow for some venison.[120]

To understand institutions as historically evolved coping mechanisms has two key implications. First, though commercial society is better than what went before, it is not perfect (as all the Scots to varying degrees accepted).[121] As historians especially sensitive to the contingencies of accident and not necessarily benign unintended consequences, they are no subscribers to a Hegelian *Weltgeist* (there is no *List der Vernunft* at work) or even to a Condorcetian commitment to '*la perfectibilité de l'homme*', to an ever-consolidating progress of reason. The antisocial aspects of human nature such as selfishness, avidity, pride or misalignment of priorities (preferring the contiguous to the remote, as Hume put it – hence the need for governance) are not always going to be corralled or successfully channelled by the institutional framework.

The second implication speaks directly to Stewart's characterisation of natural history. The circumstantially contrived institutional responses to what Hume calls the 'unnatural necessity' of the human condition does not (certainly in contrast to Hegel) produce any change in human nature.[122] It follows from this that the savage 'character', with its ignorance and superstition, does not belong exclusively to some far-away (in either time or space) society but is also characteristic of a considerable portion of eighteenth-century British society (generically labelled the vulgar). The vulgar of today are akin to the savage in the past in that both are relatively uninstructed; the explanation is the same, it cross-cuts spatio-temporal location. Hence Kames's remark that, even in an 'enlightened age', 'superstition' is not eradicated but 'is confined among the vulgar'.[123] Despite his disagreement with Kames, Hume, in broadly similar terms, declares that 'the vulgar in nations which have embraced the doctrine of theism *still* build it upon irrational and superstitious principles'.[124] This is a consequence of the 'propensity of mankind toward the marvellous', which – and this is the central point – though it may 'receive a check from sense and learning can never be thoroughly extirpated from human nature'.[125] To similar if opposite effect, the fundamental principles of morality are not relative because, no matter how deep rooted a social institution, these principles are based on the 'strongest and most vigorous passions of human nature', which, as with infanticide, though they may be 'warpt', they 'cannot be entirely perverted'.[126] For Smith, 'an instructed and intelligent people are *always* more decent and orderly than an ignorant and stupid one'. Hence the need to provide publicly subsidised education to offset the ignorance of the inferior ranks in commercial societies in order prudentially to reduce 'delusions of enthusiasm and superstition' which in 'ignorant nations' occasion the 'most violent disorders'.[127] The decisive variable is institutional: the availability, and distribution, of resources to provide instruction and accretion of social capital.

It is true that instruction and experience enable individuals increasingly to think 'abstractly'. For example, knowing that lightning is a natural regularity that is causally explicable as an electrical discharge supersedes an explanation of it as the irregular work of the 'invisible hand of Jupiter' as an expression of his displeasure.[128] But this difference is circumstantial; it does not imply any inherent limitation on either the savage's or, in a commercial society, a porter's 'mental capacity'.[129] Smith accounts for the different 'characters' of a porter and a philosopher institutionally, by 'education' as well as 'habit, custom', as a consequence of the division of labour rather than an expression of any original or natural difference.[130]

The porter/philosopher example illustrates intra-societal, while the temporal priority of polytheism to monotheism or personal to impersonal rule illustrates inter-societal differences. But, as we have argued, the inter/intra-societal differences cross-cut, as Millar illustrates when he argues that it would be 'as vain' to look for liberty and independent spirit in 'uncultivated parts of the world' as in an 'English waggoner' or 'persons of low rank in the highlands of Scotland'.[131]

In summary, it is a key insight of the Scottish Enlightenment that, thanks to their social scientific account of social or moral causation, differences in behaviour and values are largely a product of institutions. Though varied across time and space these institutions are not random; as recurrent coping mechanisms or responses to the requirements of social life that are rooted in the constant and uniform principles of human nature they are open to scientific explanation. For the Scots the best way to dispel any idea of randomness was to chart these responsive institutions historically. The differences in governing institutions from rule by the 'strong man' to rule by law were explicable by the evolving circumstances to which they were, more or less, adequate and cumulative responses. The content of religious belief and practice is similarly circumstantially responsive. These circumstances, and thus these responses, are not fixed and thus, in principle and with all due allowance for stickiness, open to improvement. This potential for amelioration, and sensitivity to its gradual character, is underwritten by the Scots' preoccupation with the history of mankind-in-society. As here articulated, it was their scientific conviction that this 'history' is (as here reconstructed) properly grasped as a history of the institutions that comprise a 'society'.[132]

Notes

1. Christopher J. Berry, *Social Theory of the Scottish Enlightenment* (Edinburgh: Edinburgh University Press, 1997); Christopher J. Berry, *The Idea of Commercial Society in the Scottish Enlightenment* (Edinburgh: Edinburgh University Press, 2013). I have also summarised what I diffidently called the 'Berry line' at the end of Chapter 1 in Christopher J. Berry, *Essays on Hume, Smith and the Scottish Enlightenment* (Edinburgh: Edinburgh University Press, 2018).
2. At the conclusion to the opening chapter of my *Social Theory* I identified eight key exponents – Hume, Smith, Millar, Kames, Ferguson, Robertson, Dunbar plus Gilbert Stuart though he was based in England. Without excluding others, some of whom I cite, this octet continues to play a central role in this chapter.
3. Adam Ferguson, *An Essay on the History of Civil Society* [1767], D. Forbes (ed.) (Edinburgh: Edinburgh University Press, 1966), p. 279 (hereafter ECS).
4. Adam Smith *An Inquiry into the Nature and Causes of the Wealth of Nations* [1776] (Indianapolis, IN: Liberty Press, 1981), III.1.3/377; I.iv.7/40 (hereafter WN). For the role of institutions in Smith see Nathan Rosenberg, 'Some Institutional Aspects of the *Wealth of Nations*', *Journal of Political Economy* 68 (1960), pp. 557–70; Hyun-Ho Song, 'Adam Smith as an Early Pioneer of Institutional Individualism', *History of Political Economy* 27 (1995), pp. 25–48, though the former focuses on their constraining role in a commercial society and despite the latter's discussion of 'the logic of the evolution of institutions' (p. 44) Smith's historical account is not developed. The best account that treats the role and place of institutions temporally in Smith is Eric Schliesser, *Adam Smith: Systematic Philosopher and Public Thinker* (Oxford: Oxford University Press, 2017). My discussion is self-evidently less confined.
5. Dugald Stewart, *Account of the Life and Writings of Adam Smith* (hereafter *Life*) included in Adam Smith, *Essays on Philosophical Subjects* (Indianapolis, IN: Liberty Press, 1982), p. 292 (hereafter EPS).

6. David Hume *An Enquiry concerning Human Understanding* [1748], T. Beauchamp (ed.) (Oxford: Oxford University Press, 1999), p. 103 (hereafter EHU).
7. For example, WN_IV.vii.c.80/626.
8. ECS p. 3.
9. *Life* p. 293.
10. James Dunbar, *Essays on the History of Mankind in Rude and Cultivated Ages*, 2nd ed. (London: 1781) (hereafter EHM).
11. John Millar, *The Origin of the Distinction of Ranks*, 3rd ed. [1779] in W. Lehmann (ed.), *John Millar of Glasgow* (Cambridge: Cambridge University Press, 1960), p. 180 (hereafter OR).
12. *Life* p. 293.
13. David Hume, *A Treatise of Human Nature* [1739/40], D. and M. Norton (eds) (Oxford: Oxford University Press, 2002), 3.2.8.2, followed by page reference to *A Treatise of Human Nature*, revised edition, L. Selby-Bigge and P. Nidditch (eds) (Oxford: Clarendon Press, 1978), p. 540 (hereafter T).
14. David Hume, 'Of the Origin of Government' in *Essays: Moral, Political and Literary*, E. Miller (ed.) (Indianapolis, IN: Liberty Press, 1985), p. 39 (hereafter EMPL).
15. OR p. 247, cf. p. 204.
16. Gilbert Stuart, *A View of Society in Europe in Its Progress from Rudeness to Refinement*, 2nd ed. [1792] (Bristol: Thoemmes Reprint, 1995), p. 37.
17. WN V.i.b.6/711. See also Adam Smith, *Lectures on Jurisprudence 1762/3*, R. Meek, D. Raphael and P. Stein (eds) (Indianapolis, IN: Liberty Press, 1982), v.129/321 (hereafter LJA).
18. William Robertson, *The History of America* [1777] in *Works*, in one volume, D. Stewart (ed.) (London: William Ball, 1840), pp. 827–8 (hereafter HAm).
19. Kames (Henry Home, Lord), *Sketches on the History of Man*, 2 vols (Dublin, 1774), I, p. 414 (hereafter SHM).
20. WN V.i.b.4/710. Cf. ECS p. 63, also Adam Ferguson, *Principles of Moral and Political Science* [1792], 2 vols (Hildesheim: G. Olms, 1995), I, p. 260 (hereafter Principles).
21. See John Millar, *An Historical View of the English Government* [1797/1803], M. Salber Phillips and D. Smith (eds), in one volume (Indianapolis, IN: Liberty Press, 2006), p. 799 (hereafter HV).
22. OR p. 247, cf. p. 254.
23. EMPL p. 40.
24. EMPL p. 39.

25. The rejection of 'contractarianism' (with the possible exceptions of Hutcheson and Reid) was the standard argument in the Scots (see Berry, *Social Theory*, ch. 2).
26. ECS p. 122. While the sociological legacy of the Scots' alertness to 'unintended consequences' is well known (see Craig Smith, *Adam Smith's Political Philosophy* (London: Routledge, 2006) for a nuanced survey), what is less appreciated is that their account of institutionalisation is a forerunner of Institutional Economics as manifest, for example, in Thorstein Veblen when he argues 'institutions are . . . a cumulative sequence of habituation and the ways and means of it are the habitual response of human nature to exigencies that vary' ('The Limitations of Marginal Utility', *Journal of Political Economy* 17 (1909), pp. 235–45, p. 239). See text below for similar expressions in the Scots.
27. OR pp. 254–5, cf. HV p. 123.
28. SHM I, p. 414. See also Kames, *Historical Law-Tracts*, 2nd ed. (Edinburgh, 1779), pp. 39, 306 (hereafter HLT).
29. ECS p. 63, cf. ECS p. 100.
30. Stuart, *View of Society*, p. 37, cf. Stuart, *Historical Dissertation concerning the Antiquity of the English Constitution* (Edinburgh, 1768), p. 90.
31. See HAm p. 828, cf. Robertson, *View of Progress in Europe* [1769] in *Works*, p. 322, *The History of Scotland* (1759) in *Works*, p. 97.
32. I IV p. 107.
33. OR p. 175.
34. SHM I, p. 58.
35. ECS pp. 110, 108.
36. HAm p. 850.
37. WN I.i.8/20.
38. For example, Berry, *Social Theory*, pp. 82–5.
39. Cf. Berry, *Essays*, ch. 4 [1974]; Clarence Glacken, *Traces on the Rhodian Shore* (Berkeley, CA: University of California Press, 1967), pp. 596–601.
40. EHM p. 239.
41. EHM p. 297.
42. EHM p. 317.
43. Engels's depiction of the human mastery over nature (fully to be realised in the communist future) is only one later exemplification of this view; see emphatically *Herr Eugen Dühring's Umwälzung der Philosophie* (Stuttgart: Dietz, 1894), p. 264.
44. EHM p. 360.

45. Government is Hume's most frequently cited example of a moral cause in his essay on National Characters in EMPL.
46. Despite much commentary, explicit reference to four stages is relatively rare. For a detailed account of its limited employment see Berry, *Commercial Society*, ch. 2.
47. LJA 14–16.
48. Adam Smith, *Lectures on Jurisprudence 1766*, R. Meek, D. Raphael and P. Stein (eds) (Indianapolis, IN: Liberty Press, 1982), 150/460 (hereafter LJB).
49. Millar's list is Hunters and Fishers or mere Savages; Shepherds, Husbandmen; Commercial People. This is from the 1787 version but it is repeated identically in the two other surviving versions (1789, 1790), GUL MS Gen 289–91. But this is not isolated and Millar repeats the classification in his lectures on the Institutes of Justinian in 1789 version (GUL MS Gen 812) while the fourfold classification is, if anything, clearer in the 1793 version (GUL Hamilton MS117).
50. See Kames, *Essays upon Several Subjects concerning British Antiquities* (Edinburgh, 1747), p. 127n. Cf. Kames, *Elucidations respecting the Common and Statute Law of Scotland* (Edinburgh, 1777), p. 228; Smith LJA i.41/18, also LJB 150/460.
51. WN V.i.b.7/712.
52. WN V.i.b.12/715.
53. LJA iv.26/208.
54. WN V.i.b.7/713.
55. Cf. WN III.iv.6/414.
56. Ferguson, *Principles* I, p. 215. This argument had been captured by Hume in his judgement that all government, even the 'most despotic', is founded on 'opinion', which is how the few are able to govern the many (EMPL p. 32).
57. OR p. 250.
58. In Berry, *Essays*, ch. 5 [2000].
59. Adam Smith, *The Theory of Moral Sentiments* [1759/1790], D. Raphael and A. MacFie (eds) (Indianapolis, IN: Liberty Press, 1982), v.2.15/210 (hereafter TMS).
60. See Smith, especially WN III, iv.10/418. Cf. Stefano Fiori, 'Adam Smith on Method: Newtonianism, History and the "Invisible Hand"', *Journal of the History of Economic Thought* 4 (2012), pp. 411–35 who in an argument akin to mine declares 'institutions are human devices that can exhibit a kind of autonomous life owing to the limited capacity for both rationality and prevision' (p. 428). Fiori also stresses the inertial character of institutions.

61. See HLT 104; John Dalrymple, *Essay toward a General History of Feudal Property in Great Britain* (London, 1757), p. 94.
62. Cf. Millar OR, p. 291: 'This fluctuation of property, so observable in all commercial countries, and which no prohibitions are capable of preventing, must necessarily weaken the authority of those who are placed in the higher ranks of life. Persons who have lately attained to riches, have no opportunity of establishing that train of dependence which is maintained by those who have remained for ages at the head of a great estate. The hereditary influence is thus, in a great measure, destroyed; and the consideration derived from wealth is often limited to what the possessor can acquire during his own life.'
63. WN III.iv.7/415.
64. Adam Smith, *Lectures on Rhetoric and Belles Lettres*, J. Bryce (ed.) (Indianapolis, IN: Liberty Press, 1983), p. 176. Cf. WN III.iv.4/412.
65. WN III.iii.3/397–8.
66. James Steuart, *Principles of Political Oeconomy* [1767] in *Works*, 6 vols (London: Cadell & Davies, 1805), I, p. 314.
67 Hume, EMPL p. 41.
68. See for example John Locke, *Two Treatises of Government* [1689], P. Laslett (ed.) (New York: Mentor Books, 1965), §142, p. 409. Nor was it exclusively British. From Boisguillbert onwards, French authors, in their own context, made the same point.
69. Francis Hutcheson, *A Short Introduction to Moral Philosophy* [1757], L. Turco (ed.) (Indianapolis, IN: Liberty Press, 2007), p. 258.
70. Robert Wallace, *Characteristics of the Present Political State of Great Britain* [1758] (New York: Kelly Reprint, 1961), p. 215.
71. Kames, *Essays upon Several Subjects in Law* (Edinburgh, 1732), p. 20; Kames, *Principles of Equity*, corrected 2nd ed. (Edinburgh, 1760), p. 268.
72. Principles II, p. 477.
73. TMS VI.11.1.13/223.
74. WN IV.vii.c.44/606.
75. WN I.iv.1/37.
76. EHU p. 154; my emphasis.
77. HV p. 382.
78. Cf. Robertson, HAm p. 806; Millar, HV p. 28.
79. In his *View of Progress* [1769], Robertson notes that Tacitus' account of the 'barbarous Europeans' is corroborated by the accounts of Lafitau and Charlevoix on the 'various tribes and nations of savages in North America'. The points of similarity that he identifies are institutional – subsistence by hunting and fishing, the limited power of 'magistrates',

minimal 'criminal jurisdiction' (*Works*, p. 371). Ferguson (ECS p. 87) similarly compares Charlevoix and Tacitus on gift giving.

80. As a generalisation this becomes a common trope in nineteenth-century 'sociology', as exemplified inter alia in Tönnies' shift from *Gemeinschaft* to *Gesellschaft* or Spencer's trajectory from homo- to heterogeneity. Spencer also emphasises 'institutions' but, unlike Comte, shows little interest in the Scots' writings. For brief comment on the Scots' legacy see Berry, *Social Theory*, ch. 8 and in the specific British context see K. Macdonald, 'Did British Sociology Begin with the Scottish Enlightenment?' in P. Panayatova (ed.), *The History of Sociology in Britain* (Cham: Palgrave, 2019), pp. 37–69.

81. *Life* p. 293.

82. SHM II, p. 383; John Gregory, *A Comparative View of the State and Faculties of Man* [1765] in *Works of the late John Gregory* (Edinburgh, 1788), vol. II, p. 241; George Turnbull, *The Principles of Moral Philosophy* [1740] (Indianapolis, IN: Liberty Press, 2005), I, pp. 231ff.

83. David Hume, *The Natural History of Religion* [1757] in *A Dissertation on the Passions and The Natural History of Religion*, T. Beauchamp (ed.) (Oxford: Oxford University Press, 2007), p. 37 (hereafter NHR).

84. SHM II, p. 389.

85. Hume makes frequent recourse to the notion of 'propensity'. This gives him some conceptual 'wriggle-room', as manifest in his comment that the 'universal propensity to believe in invisible intellectual power if not an original instinct being at least an attendant of human nature' (NHR 86). For other examples in that work see pp. 49, 55, 59, 77, as well as in the *Treatise* (T 1.3.14.25/167). Smith of course gives the most famous instance when he says that to truck, barter and exchange is a 'propensity' in human nature, but he also speculated it might itself be derivative of speech (WN I.ii.1/25; cf. LJA vi.56/352, LJB 221/493). Dunbar (see text) also employs the term as do Kames (SHM I, p. 49) and Ferguson, who like Smith treats it as a synonym of 'disposition', although he differentiates it from 'inclination' (*Principles* I, p. 209), but see Schliesser (*Adam Smith*, p. 27) who glosses Smith's 'propensity' as a 'stable inclination'.

86. EHM p. 205.

87. Principles I, p. 169.

88. Millar makes the synchronicity evident: 'The admiration of a military leader in rude countries, has frequently proceeded so far as to produce a belief of his being sprung from a heavenly original and to render him the object of that adoration which is due the Supreme Being' (OR p. 256).

89. Spyridon Tegos 'Civility and Civil Religion before and after the French Revolution: Religious and Secular Rituals in Hume and Tocqueville', *Genealogy* 4 (2020), pp. 1–14, p. 3.
90. NHR p. 40.
91. Cf. Berry, *Essays*, ch. 6 [2000].
92. NHR p. 41, EMPL p. 61, EMPL p. 271.
93. NHR p. 41.
94. SHM II, p. 389.
95. HAm p. 843.
96. OR p. 176.
97. NHR p. 35.
98. HV p. 507, OR p. 176.
99. Cf. EPS p. 50.
100. HAm p. 840.
101. EPS p. 49.
102. III.5.4/164. For one of the few accounts that explore the natural history of religion in TMS see Colin Heydt, 'The Problem of Natural Religion in Smith's Moral Thought', *Journal of the History of Ideas* 73 (2017), pp. 73–94.
103. EPS p. 50.
104. EPS p. 114.
105. SHM II, pp. 402, 404.
106. David Hume, *The History of England*, 3 vols (London: George Routledge, 1894), II, p. 159.
107. HAm p. 843.
108. TMS IV.i.10/183.
109. EHU p. 150, cf. p. 153.
110. I coined this term initially in Christopher J. Berry, *Hume, Hegel and Human Nature* (The Hague: Martinus Nijhoff, 1982), exploited it generally in Christopher J. Berry, *Human Nature* (London: Macmillan, 1986) and returned to it in the more specific context of Hume reprinted in Berry, *Essays*, ch. 12 [2007] which comments on a range of interpretations (especially those contrary to my own) of that passage in Hume's *First Enquiry* (EHU p. 150).
111. For Stewart (*Life* p. 293) natural history is opposed to that 'indolent philosophy, which refers to a miracle whatever . . . it is unable to explain'. Cf. Millar OR p. 175, Hume EMPL p. 111.
112. See, inter alia, Donald Davidson, 'On the Very Idea of a Conceptual Scheme' in his *Inquiries into Truth and Interpretation* (Oxford: Clarendon Press, 1984), pp. 183–98; Bernard Williams, *Truth and Truthfulness* (Princeton: Princeton University Press, 2004), ch. 3.

113. Cf. Hume, *An Enquiry concerning the Principles of Morals* [1751], T. Beauchamp (ed.) (Oxford: Oxford University Press, 1998), p. 97.
114. TMS VII.iv.36/341. Hence Smith's pronouncement that without justice society would 'crumble into atoms' (TMS II.ii.3.4/86) – an argument trailed by both Hume (T 3.2.2.22/p. 497) and Kames (*Essays on the Principles of Morality and Natural Religion* (Edinburgh, 1751), p. 61), who is commended by Smith for differentiating the strictness of the obligation to justice in contrast to other social virtues (TMS II.ii.1.5/80).
115. Hume, *History* III, p. 113. As Hume was well aware, there is, of course, nothing new in this association; he cites, for example in his essay 'Of Suicide', Cicero's *De Divinatione* in this regard (EMPL p. 579).
116. EMPL p. 271.
117. OR p. 176.
118. Cf. EMPL p. 328.
119. WN I.i.11/24.
120. WN I.i.10–11/22.
121. Even the most committed to the merits of commerce identified downsides such as Hume (with worries about credit (EMPL pp. 349–65)), Smith (with concerns about ill-effects of the division of labour in book 5 of WN V.i.f.61/788) and Millar (with remarks on the negative consequences for the dignity of women (OR p. 225)). Others like – among many others – Ferguson in the *Essay* or Kames in his *Sketches* are more pointed in their critiques, though not on the same grounds.
122. Cf. Berry, *Essays*, ch. 9 [1982]; Christopher J. Berry, *The Idea of Luxury: A Conceptual and Historical Investigation* (Cambridge: Cambridge University Press, 1994), ch. 8.
123. SHM II, p. 417. Kames makes frequent use of the metaphor of 'ripening' – what the seed requires is the right environment. He uses the metaphor in the context of the 'sense of the Deity' (SHM II, p. 404), marriage (SHM I, p. 328) and norms (*Principles of Equity*, I, p. 8).
124. NHR p. 53; my emphasis.
125. EHU p. 176. Though the context is the debunking of miracles, Hume makes it clear that the propensity's remit is wider; 'extraordinary' travellers' tales generate the universally 'agreeable emotion' of 'surprize and wonder' and thereby give a tendentious credence to the tales (cf. EHU p. 175). There is similarly a 'propensity' to return back to idolatry (NHR p. 59). It follows that because of its roots in human nature Hume, unlike some of the

French *philosophes*, cannot think religious belief will disappear; see Donald T. Siebert, *The Moral Animus of David Hume* (Newark, DE: University of Delaware Press, 1990), p. 64. That Hume was not hostile to 'religion as such' and accepted that historically it had played a civilising role, see Timothy M. Costelloe, '"In Every Civilized community": Hume on Belief and the Demise of Religion', *International Journal of the Philosophy of Religion* 55 (2004), pp. 171–85, pp. 183, 181, but for the view that Hume endorsed the 'revolutionary aspiration of making God obsolete' see Scott Yenor, 'Revealed Religion and the Politics of Humanity in Hume's Philosophy of Common Life', *Polity* 38 (2006), pp. 395–415, p. 405.
125. EHU p. 176.
126. TMS V.2.1/200, cf. VII.iv.36/341.
127. WN V.i.f.61/788; my emphasis.
128. EPS p. 50.
129. Cf. Frank E. Manuel, *The Eighteenth Century Confronts the Gods* (Cambridge, MA: Harvard University Press, 1967), p. 179, cf. p. 183, who judges that for Hume 'the vulgar and the primitive mind were the same'.
130. Smith, WN 1.iii.4/28–9. Cf. LJB 220/493. Jennifer Pitts, *A Turn to Empire* (Princeton: Princeton University Press, 2005), p. 37 argues that Smith does 'not attribute societal development to enhanced mental capacities', although she does see other Scots (Millar and Robertson) as 'at times' making that connection. However, she overstates her case. I want to claim that my notion of institutions as coping mechanisms captures the mutual reciprocity between human 'ingenuity' and circumstances (cf. Robertson in text above).
131. OR p. 295.
132. I am grateful to Craig Smith for his comments on an earlier draft. Versions of this paper were delivered as lectures at Fudan University, Shanghai and at Boston College. I thank professors Li Hongtu and Ouyang Xiaoli at the former, and Ryan Hanley at the latter, for their kind invitations.

3

Adventitious Sociology: Dispassion and Insight in the Scottish Enlightenment

Kenneth Macdonald

Introduction

The most sociologically innovative contribution of the Scottish Enlightenment is to be found in its adventitious sociology – the in-passing reflective speculation on the actual social processes observed by the writers; that speculation but contingently connected to their central analytic theses. Such adventitious sociology is more pertinent for the history of sociology than the larger, apparently social, theories of these writers. In this chapter I want to explore this thought further, stressing that such adventitious sociology is not only insightful but also remarkably value free.

But first some further discussion on the place of grand theory in the transmission of ideas. I have, in an earlier paper,[1] challenged some of the specific claimed influences, by way of grand theory, on sociology. My argument was that some eighteenth-century sociological theses were misascribed, whilst others 'ported' to our present less straightforwardly than claimed. But a further aspect deserves consideration: these grand theories (such as stadial theories or conjectural history) were, perhaps surprisingly, not deployed by these writers in understanding *their* present context. That may be a contrarian view: Brewer, as part of his argument for the importance of 'conjectural history', wrote:

> sociological discourse finds its origin partly in a *special type of history* [*conjectural history*] and . . . it began to be deployed by Ferguson in eighteenth-century Scotland *because* it enabled analytical discussion of *social change in Scotland*.[2]

'Conjectural history' fits ill as a description of Ferguson's empirical, grounded approach:

Who would, from *mere conjecture*, suppose that the naked savage would be a coxcomb and a gamester? ... Yet these particulars are a part in the description which is delivered by those who have had *opportunities of seeing* mankind in their rudest condition.[3]

But additionally – and most pertinent for my present argument – Ferguson gives little evidence of applying his overarching schema, however we describe them, to 'social change in Scotland'. Indeed, he gives little evidence of engaging (explanatorily) with any of the detail of eighteenth-century Scottish life as he develops his framework. Search, and we may find a couple of instances; for example, an aside on genteel ladies' difficulties in entertaining gentlemen on wet afternoons,[4] or this on the way in which evaluative terms reflect actors' interests: 'in the cant [*occupational*] language of merchants, a *good* man means a person that is solvent, and full able, as well as willing, to fulfil his engagements'.[5] But such instances are passing rare and *uncharacteristic* of Ferguson's style. My previously cited instances of Ferguson's adventitious sociology were all methodological (such as his insight that historical fiction is revealing more of the time *in which*, than the time *of which*, it was written).[6] In this, Ferguson is not unique. These theorists – however empirical their narrative of the *genesis* of the eighteenth century – are precisely *not* offering a sociology of their own actualised present. Millar, for example, on 'distinction of ranks', provides impressively anthropological discussion of the evolving historical condition of women (and deserves credit for foregrounding this issue).[7] The naive modern reader might anticipate an upcoming chapter, carrying an informed *insider's* account of contemporary gender relationships, on life as lived in Millar's present. But just as Millar reaches his eighteenth-century present, he reverts to generalisations, his discussion moving variously between affluent ancient Rome and modern Europe, explicitly eschewing what we might think to be sociology:

> It is *not* intended . . . in this discourse, to consider those variations, in the state of women, which arise from the *civil or religious government* of a people, or from such other causes as are *peculiar to the inhabitants of different countries*.[8]

What sort of possible discussion do I find missing? Take an example. Families, for agricultural labourers in eighteenth-century Scotland, formed an economic unit; the cash payments generated by women's 'manufacture' (knitting, spinning) forming an important resource, sometimes more reliable than male agricultural employment. One respondent to the *Statistical Account* frets about the resulting destabilisation of this model when machines reduce the price of spinning:

> *Single women* may ... find employment in some other branches of manufacture; but it does not appear in what other way *married women*, who must sit always at home with their children, can contribute anything to the support of their families.[9]

The issues may have been more visible by the end of the century but were present when Millar wrote: it would have been sociologically fruitful to read his contemporaneous detailed reading of the interplay here between the economic and the social structure of the family. And the 'blindness' extends even to their recent historical past. Hume, in his encyclopedic *History of England*, attaches appendices on 'manners' and 'learning', but the comments are largely superficial, with impercipient disparagement – as this on the *Faerie Queene*: 'allegory ... too seldom ... ingenious'.[10]

The other reason to hesitate over large theories is the difficulty in identifying connections between such high-level theories. Whilst the evidence is that Keynes had no direct awareness of Steuart, there may still remain some 'history of ideas' point in articulating how Steuart's perspective-on-economics-taken-as-a-whole has some synchrony with Keynes's perspective-on-economics-taken-as-a-whole.[11] But *explicit* connections may raise problems. For example, here is Sen making an attribution he often invokes (though the bracketed phrase appears nowhere in Smith): 'Adam Smith ... felt impelled to define "necessaries" in terms of their effects on the freedom to live nonimpoverished lives (such as "the ability to appear in public without shame"). Thus, the view of poverty as capability deprivation ... has a far-reaching analytical history';[12] or, later, with Rothschild: 'A capability based approach of poverty and deprivation can draw substantially on Smith's pioneering analysis';[13] and Nussbaum sees a similar link for her related, but distinct, analyses: 'I shall argue, Smith's work paves the way for my "Capabilities Approach"'.[14] All three authors elsewhere write insightfully on Smith, but these particular claims, I have argued, are based on a misreading of Smith on shame and poverty.[15] Less erudite modern writers are unlikely to read Smith in detail before citing his influence. Does it matter? The concept of 'capabilities' is, in its varying instantiations, complex and powerful. It can stand, as it were, on its own feet. A derivation from *Smith* or from *misread-Smith* or *not-from-Smith-at-all* may not matter?

Do the issues become simpler if we consider transmission not to us but to writers closer to the eighteenth century? We know that Hegel read Steuart with attention, and a case can be made for some influence.[16] Marx, sitting in the British Library, also studied Steuart.[17] Consider a small, but in its way not uninformative, result of Marx's scholarship – here prefaced by a well-known (because insightful and portable) passage from the introduction to the *Grundrisse*:

> The solitary and isolated hunter or fisherman, who serves Adam Smith and Ricardo as a starting point, is one of the unimaginative fantasies of 18th century romances *à la* Robinson Crusoe ... They saw this individual not as a historical result, but as the starting-point of history; not as something *evolving* in the course of history, but posited by nature ... This delusion has been characteristic of every new epoch hitherto.[18]

Less well-known, because less cited, is Marx's *conclusion* to that passage: 'Steuart ... avoided this naive view'.[19] Does Marx's careful attending-to-Steuart matter, if that attending-to is itself subsequently disattended-to? And there is a further issue: is Marx's analysis of Steuart's exceptionalism correct? I read Berry's interpretation of Steuart's concept of the public good – 'For Steuart, there truly is a contextually dependent common interest ... [this] underlies Steuart's argument that a Smithian reliance on mutual self interested interactions is an insufficient mechanism to realise the public good'[20] – as supporting the thought that Steuart's non-naivety does not inhere in his differing 'seeing' of the *individual* but in his particular conceptualisation of common interest. (And, a final twist, Marx's own explanation for that avoidance of naivety – he suggests that Steuart 'as an aristocrat, tended rather to regard things from a historical standpoint'[21] – is at best eccentric.)

This twisted little tale (of an influence, subsequently not registered and perhaps anyway initially misperceived) is obviously only one little tale, not in itself a knock-down argument against conventional history of ideas. My concern though is that it is precisely the kind of difficulty we start to experience once we attempt to trace the detail of *any* intellectual lineage.

We know that the 'reading' of authors changes over time. The shifting interpretation of Smith is a truth universally acknowledged. It follows that a reader, call the reader 'X', sitting between our time and Smith's, will (from our perspective) often 'misread' Smith. If X is influenced by that reading, that influence may (from our perspective) be based on a 'misreading'. Are we (given *our* assumptions) then justified in taking that misreading as evidence of the intellectual influence of *Smith's ideas*? Of course, we can give a careful account of how X's 'misreading' – being a function of its time and place and context – influenced X's thought. And that would indeed be a sort of history. We would be documenting how the *fact-of-Smith* affected subsequent intellectual argument. So Smith, as 'misperceived' in X's time, gives rise to certain thoughts in X; without the *fact-of-Smith* this, we might argue, would not have happened. Whether that narrative is to count as tracing the impact of Smith's *ideas* is more debatable. And we face identical problems if we then move to discuss how later thinkers (Y, Z) were in turn 'influenced by X's thoughts'; and we by them.

This whole puzzle is embedded within a larger issue. The shifting interpretation of Smith is indeed a truth universally acknowledged; but that observation entails the thought that *our* readings of Smith fall within this flux. It would be folly to imagine that – through some comic cosmic chance – *we* happen to be living at the unique time point when accounts-of-Smith match the ideas-of-Smith. That our account of Smith is finally correct is perhaps a delusion we require in order to interpret (for example, I find myself insisting that my account, below, of a non-evaluative Smith – based strictly on Smith's-words-on-the-page – is intrinsically more robust than interpretations which parachute-in fashionable, but undocumented, emphases). Nevertheless, as Steuart, displaying his sociological acuity, remarks: 'Every writer values himself upon his impartiality; because he is not sensible [*aware*] of his fetters'.[22]

The instances of adventitious sociology – being more anchored in the *puzzle* explained – may be less susceptible to these concerns. For example, Smith considering how rental differences between Edinburgh and London are driven by norms of home ownership ('A dwelling-house in England means everything that is contained under the same roof. In France, Scotland, and many other parts of Europe, it frequently means no more than a single storey');[23] or considering how the family situation of French financiers leads them to happily purchase government annuities;[24] or Kames explaining why in Holland female and male children inherit equally;[25] or Hume anticipating Kuhn on the importance of scientific revolution;[26] or Millar explaining why it was, historically, in the financial self-interest of the church 'that people of inferior condition should be rendered capable of acquiring property'.[27] Or Steuart, as we shall see, inventing social mobility cross-tabulations well before they are ever used. Or Steuart, again as we shall see, weighing the differing social display patterns of financiers and landowners, or thinking through how taxpayers might be nudged to disregard vehicle tax. The *analysis* strategies are not, for the writer, integral to any general analytic argument (though the derived *conclusions* may be). But one could see how, for example, Smith's account of the social position of financiers might form the kernel of a sociological paper.[28]

These bits of in-passing eighteenth-century sociology may be more portable, and better straws-in-the-wind for the incipient development of sociology, than apparently grander social theories. But they come with their own second-order interpretative issues. If I show (as I hope to, below) that Steuart invented signalling theory – unnoticed, and in passing – the import of that may be perplexing. To this I return.

But I wish here to take a short pause for an 'aside to camera' (soliloquy would be too grand a model). As with the cinematographic device, this will not advance the plot (argument) in any way, but it may assist an understanding (or undermining) of that plot. My day job is as an empirical quantitative sociologist with an interest in statistical techniques.[29] The sociology seminars I habitually attend are determinedly anchored in the quantitative analysis of data. This instantiation of sociology is contestable (particularly within the UK) but it is an active, and European, intellectual thread. From this perspective, as I read these eighteenth-century writers, moments of academic sibship come *not* as they are articulating their grand theories (which are not my grand theories, or even the grand theories of my more discursive contemporaries) but when they are puzzling over the *detail* of the social world they inhabit. It is at those moments that their voices fall closest to, are echoic of, the voices I would hear in a graduate sociology seminar. Whence my concern both to document these instances and to try and understand how they come about – they matter if we are to articulate the ways in which the past speaks to the present. This also undergirds my concerns in Chapter 7 in this volume, exploring how the university-educated of the Scottish late eighteenth century thought about their *social* world.[30] Now to return to more conventional academic mode.

Thinking Dispassionately about the Social

My overarching chapter title notwithstanding, any attempt to cover, in acceptable detail, all the writers of the Scottish Enlightenment would consume more words than available. So the remainder of this chapter centres on the relation to adventitious sociology of just two writers: Adam Smith and James Steuart (with perhaps the hope that, having witnessed the argument around two, we may be left with some insight as to how it might apply to others). Though they write with differing emphases they are, in a way that the proponents of high theory were not, concerned to explicate the circumambient world they inhabit. Smith is included because he is inescapable (when Sinclair's parish ministers, at the end of the century, invoke writers on socio-economic issues, it is uniquely Smith they reference) but also – importantly – because one popular reading of his sociological involvement would, if validated, present a challenge to the overall theme of this present volume. Steuart is included because he is a quirky and undervalued thinker, capable of insightful sociological moves (despite writing, much of the time, convolutedly,[31] about money-supply). Though it appears the two had met,[32] their relation was fraught. Steuart, whose *Inquiry* preceded Smith's, was studiously ignored by Smith ('Without once mentioning [Steuart's book], I flatter myself, that every false principle in it, will meet with a clear and distinct confutation in mine').[33]

I devote a later section of this chapter to contrasting Steuart's inquiry (into the principles of political economy) with Smith's inquiry (into the nature and causes of wealth) and use a further section to assess Steuart's sociological understanding, ending with the issues sparked by his, earlier mentioned, invention of signalling theory. But I want to begin with consideration of Smith and in particular the common claim that he is not-dispassionate on behalf of the poor.

Smith, of course, is the better-known writer, and many of his empirical social insights have become familiar through academic repetition. *An Inquiry into the Nature and Causes of the Wealth of*

Nations (hereafter WN) is rich in documentation of social inequality – of wages, education, mortality, political access – and it is tempting to read such 'sociological' insights as not adventitious but as central to, intrinsic to, Smith's project. Once that move is made it becomes a small step to see such descriptions – since they would *for us* demand remedial action on the things described – as showing that Smith wrote recognising the need for remediation. This, for example, is Nussbaum reflecting on the social facts within WN, facts that 'WN appears to regard as highly important, *urgently in need of correction*'.³⁴

This style of reading Smith has become established orthodoxy. As careful a scholar as Schliesser chooses, though the move may not be required by his central thesis, to endorse the approach: 'I elaborate on the line of argument that has been developed during the last three decades that has explained and *emphasised* Smith's attempts to *further the interests* of the working poor'.³⁵ Acceptance of these arguments is not confined within Smith studies; here, for example, is a view from a major political science journal:

> There is now broad agreement among Smith scholars that he *regarded poverty as deeply problematic and sought ways to combat it,* a consensus that includes those who approach his thought from the contemporary right, such as Himmelfarb, as well as the contemporary left, such as Fleischacker.³⁶

This view of a 'passionate' Smith has certain attractions (it may serve as a counterweight against simple-minded *laissez-faire* interpretations) and allows a neat insertion of Smith into a long sociological tradition (as in the Sen claims assessed above, or Ringen's assertion that the 'relative understanding of the problem [of poverty] is firmly rooted in the writings of Adam Smith'³⁷). But I regard these 'consensus' readings as profoundly mistaken.

Judgement on that 'consensus' has particular import for the present volume. One of the central overarching themes of our individual contributions, as I understand them, is the thought that the *detached* theoretical interest, and the descriptive-explanatory stance, adopted by several Scottish moral philosophers in their proto-sociological moments was a distinctive feature of their thought, distinguishing them from their foreign counterparts. It would follow, as a defensible claim, that many of the epistemic values that later would be associated with sociological inquiry (that is, value-free, objective, explanatory inquiry into the structures and processes of society) did emerge first in this Scottish tradition. If the interpretation of a 'passionate' Smith were to stand scrutiny, that overarching theme would lose a central – vital? – support.

In my extended contribution to the 2019 *Adam Smith Review*[38] I examined in detail and *in context* (that *in context* being the consequential analytic move) each of the Smith passages (such as the 'but equity, besides' passage) invoked, and re-invoked, by proponents of the consensus view. In each case, I argued, if we attend to the words-on-the-page, to what Smith actually wrote, we see no evidence for a writer who *regarded poverty as deeply problematic and sought ways to combat it*. What we find in the text is not a concerned twenty-first-century interventionist agenda central to Smith's argument but instead adventitious, and dispassionate, sociological insights that never get in the way of Smith's expressed concern with the nature and causes of the wealth of nations.

For the more determined proponents of the consensus view, the absence of Smith's words-on-the-page is apparently no deterrent. Once the assumption is made (that Smith intends a moral gloss) it becomes easy to import, onto even Smith's sparsest rendition of factual inference, the desired gloss. This, for example, is Fleischacker, describing:

> the 'indirect ethics' I have attributed to Smith . . . Smith accomplishes ethical ends *without actually mentioning ethical terms*, writes so that ethical concerns come, as if *naturally, to the surface* without having to be dragged there by preachy pronouncements.[39]

Smith himself disparaged such 'double doctrine' textual readings.[40] But Fleischacker puts his analysis strategy with admirable forthrightness; other writers present interpretations following, but not acknowledging, this model. It has at least two ineluctable flaws. Firstly, what is seen as rising *naturally* to the surface is observer-dependent (manifestly our twenty-first-century *natural* is not Smith's); if we are to invoke *our* ethics we need *evidence* that Smith would share *our* reading. Consider, for example, the assurance that Smith 'makes a number of proposals *which he believes will make it easier for the poor to rise socially*: the abolition of apprenticeship requirements and the laws of settlement, and the reform of a number of tax policies'.[41] Whatever the mobility outcomes of these proposals might be, the *text* provides no evidence for the claimed Smith *belief* and *intention*. For example, one of Fleischacker's references is to an extended discussion of land-tax, in which Smith demonstrates how 'a practice which is hurtful to the *whole community* might perhaps be sufficiently discouraged'⁴² and further proposes 'a system of administration . . . as might contribute a good deal to the *general* improvement . . . of the *country*'.⁴³ That is what Smith writes, and his *professed* incentive is amply sufficient to motivate his prose; there is *nothing* in the cited text supporting the assertion that he *believes* this *will make it easier for the poor to rise socially*. Such imported ascriptions require evidence.

The second flaw – which I take to be a catastrophic flaw – is that the 'indirect ethics' attribution, once invoked, is not *defeasible*. How, if we make this assumption, can we expect ever to show, of a particular empirical or analytical passage, that Smith was *not* aiming to accomplish ethical ends? Potential for falsification (as Popper noted) is a reasonable request to make of any theory wishing to be taken seriously.

Why, absent the extreme Fleischacker move, the temptation to import normative assumptions?

Firstly, it comes from the thought that to document inequality, to 'see' inequality, must entail an aversion to inequality, a realisation of its iniquity. Nussbaum writes percipiently on Smith's ethics in *The Theory of Moral Sentiments* (hereafter TMS) but pivots on this misreading:

> In an ironic reversal of [*the old 'Adam Smith Problem'*], it is WN, a work commonly reputed as callous, that understands *with keen sympathy* the depth to which human abilities stand in need of material goods and institutional arrangements. But the (allegedly) softer and more humane *TMS* retains a deep attachment to some problematic Stoic doctrines.⁴⁴

The ascription of subjective perception ('understands with *keen sympathy*') is going beyond the words-on-the page; we have no direct evidence for that ascribed feeling (even the 'human abilities' phrasing is a Nussbaum addition to Smith's discussions). We are dealing with an eighteenth-century thinker; we are not entitled to merely *assume* that he felt as we might feel about the sociological analyses he presents.

Secondly, Smith's argumentative arcs are frequently long. Individual observations, phrases, must be read in context to appreciate their valence for Smith, their role in *his* argument. It is too easy for a modern reader, in haste, to lift the decontextualised phrase.

Reverting for a moment to Smith's discussion of shame and linen-shirts, that discussion is located within a sequence reflecting on 'taxes upon consumable commodities', within *that* evaluating the response of the '*creditable* day labourer'[45] to *falling* into shirtless poverty. It does not speak directly to the state of mind – the 'shame'? – of the shirtless poor (as Smith elsewhere notes: 'all men, sooner or later, accommodate themselves to whatever becomes their permanent situation').[46] Few discussions of Smith on shame and poverty attend to that context.

Each invocation of a 'concerned' Smith tends to be supported by reference to other (supposedly grounded) invocations – *so yet another example of the Smith we know to be concerned* – but this, on the part of the consensus, is logically no better than bootstrap levitation. Of course, *if we grant* the premise, any *particular* unevidenced reading may seem plausible; the difficulty is that the premise rests solely on the sum of such unevidenced grantings. To counter such moves, each attempted ascription must be individually unpicked. That is what I attempted – at length – in the *Adam Smith Review* piece, and will not replicate now.

But another route to re-establishing a dispassionate Smith – separating him from *our* moral intuitions – is to look at the conclusions to which Smith accepts his analyses lead. These conclusions are implausible if viewed as attempts, by one with keen sympathy, to advance the interests of the working poor. They become unsurprising (if occasionally unlovely) when viewed as part of a project to enhance the *wealth of nations*.

Consider education. Smith is in favour of universal education (even if here, uncharacteristically, vague on implementation detail).[47] But listen to Smith's depiction of the *utility* of educating the poor:

> An instructed and intelligent people . . . are always more decent and *orderly* . . . more disposed to *respect* [*their lawful*] *superiors* . . . less apt to be misled into . . . *unnecessary opposition* to the measures of government. In free countries, where the safety of government depends very much upon the favourable judgment which the people may form of its conduct, it must surely be of the highest importance that they should not be disposed to *judge rashly or capriciously* concerning it.[48]

Education, as he presents it, prevents disorder, avoids 'unnecessary opposition' to the measures of government and enables a 'favourable', non-capricious view of the government's conduct, thus ensuring the 'safety of government'. Perhaps useful for the wealth of a nation? But this does not sound like advocacy for empowerment of the poor. Himmelfarb's gloss on this passage reads: 'the laborer . . . by dint of his education . . . was to be a *free and full participant in society*'.[49] If Smith were indeed thinking the thoughts that Himmelfarb ascribes to him, it would become a puzzle why he penned the restricted passage that he did. Rothschild, on the same passage, waxes even more lyrical: 'This is the Enlightenment idyll, of *universal public discussion* among thoughtful, reflecting, self-respecting individuals.'[50] Again the puzzle. If that is the idyll in Smith's mind, why did he merely write, approvingly, of a people 'disposed to *respect* [*their lawful*] *superiors*'?

Or take the famous 'but equity, besides' passage (which I have contextualised and examined more fully elsewhere):[51] 'It is but equity, besides, that they who feed, clothe, and lodge the whole body of the people, *should have such a share* of the *produce of their own labour* as to be themselves *tolerably* well fed, clothed, and lodged.'[52] The restraint, the limitation, of Smith's implied support for the poor is apparent if we contrast this with an appeal, five years earlier,[53] from (the much maligned) Arthur Young:

> If the *real* distresses of the poor are in question . . . if they are not clothed in a warm and decent manner – well lodged – and nourished plentifully with wholesome food . . . in the name of God force the purses of the rich . . . raise the price of labour – increase your [poor] rates – do whatever the necessity of the case requires[54] [original emphasis]

Young aims for 'plentiful, wholesome' food, 'warm' clothing, for 'well lodged' workers. Smith, the claimed innovative advocate for the poor, wishes only for them to be '*tolerably* well fed, clothed, and lodged'. Rothschild's continuing gloss – 'Smith argued for *high wages* . . . on grounds of equity'[55] – further misrepresents that argument; there is nothing in the text about '*high* wages' (Smith begins the section by referring to the modest gains, which he has just documented, in living standards over the last century, and it is this modest gain he is analysing). Fleischacker, not uncharacteristically, reads Smith as addressing a further offstage audience (not apparent in the text):

> *To those* who wanted to restrain the poor from buying *luxury goods*, *Smith says* that it is 'but equity' for the lower ranks of society to have a fair share of the food, clothes, and housing they themselves provide.[56]

Again the puzzle: if that is indeed Smith's intention, why no mention of luxury goods? Why offer the poor only a *share of the produce* of their own labour? (It is far from clear that the produce of an agricultural labourer, however apportioned, would yield much in the way of luxury goods, given eighteenth-century pricing; and Smith leaves undefined how we might specify a 'share'.) And remember that Smith *himself* was one of those prepared to 'restrain the poor from buying luxury goods': 'Taxes upon the luxuries of the poor ... I am so far from disapproving, that I look upon them as the best of sumptuary laws'.[57]

Consider further these taxes on 'luxuries'. Earlier, rival Steuart had proposed taxes on 'necessaries', which would be met by a rising price of labour:

> The best of all taxes are moderate excises; the most productive excises are those imposed on the *necessaries* of life. They raise the price of living universally and proportionably, and therefore enable every industrious man to raise the price of his labour in proportion to the tax he pays.[58]

Smith (part of his 'without once mentioning' debate with Steuart) opposes taxes on necessaries, precisely *because* they feed through into the price of labour:

> As the wages of labour are everywhere regulated partly by the demand for it, and partly by the average price of the necessary articles of subsistence ... a tax upon the necessaries of life operates exactly in the same manner as a direct tax upon the wages of labour ... *The middling and superior ranks of people, if they understand their own interest, ought always to oppose all taxes upon the necessaries of life*, as well as all direct taxes upon the wages of labour. *The final payment* of both the one and the other *falls altogether upon themselves*.[59]

Note that whilst Steuart's analysis focused on consequences for the 'industrious man', Smith's considers the impacts for the 'middling and superior ranks of people'. Smith even develops his argument to a position where he is willing to contemplate a luxury tax (upon 'fermented liquors') which falls *principally* on the poor:

> Though the expence [*i.e. expenditure*] of those inferior ranks of people ... taking them individually, is very small, yet the whole mass

> of it, taking them collectively, amounts always to by much the largest portion of the whole [expenditure] of the society . . . The taxes upon [expenditure], therefore, which fall chiefly upon that of the superior ranks of people . . . are likely to be much less productive than either those which fall indifferently upon the [expenditure] of all ranks, or even those which *fall chiefly upon* that of the *inferior ranks* . . . The excise upon the materials and manufacture of home-made [*i.e. non-foreign*] fermented and spirituous liquors is accordingly, of all the different taxes upon [expenditure], *by far the most productive*; and this branch of the excise falls very much, perhaps principally, upon the [*expenditure*] *of the common people* . . .[60]

This is the voice of an empirical, dispassionate writer, considering what constitutes a productive tax; he is prepared to countenance a productive (and, for Smith, here properly imposed, on 'luxuries' not 'necessaries') tax which 'falls . . . perhaps principally, upon the [*expenditure*] *of the common people*'.[61]

Smith pushes this even further. He clearly delineates, follows through, the impact, on the *disorderly* poor, of taxes upon these luxury goods. He sees – but is apparently unbothered by – a clear consequential link to extreme childhood poverty (his analysis can stand as piece of adventitious sociology, or perhaps adventitious social policy):

> Upon the sober and industrious poor, taxes upon [luxuries] act as *sumptuary laws* . . . *Their* ability to bring up families, in consequence of this forced frugality . . . is frequently, perhaps, increased by the tax . . . All the poor, indeed, are not sober and industrious, and the dissolute and disorderly might continue to indulge themselves . . . *without regarding the distress which this indulgence might bring upon their families* . . . [*they*] however, seldom rear up numerous families, their children generally perishing from neglect . . . Though the advanced price of the luxuries of the poor, therefore, might increase somewhat the distress of such disorderly families, *it would not probably diminish much the useful population of the country*[62]

That conclusion makes sense (albeit cold-hearted sense – dispassion much in evidence) if we see – only if we see – Smith as centrally interested in the *wealth* of nations.

It is in the light of such examples that I wish to dissociate from the observed 'broad agreement among Smith scholars that he *regarded poverty as deeply problematic and sought ways to combat it*'. The invocation of a supposedly evaluative Smith is extrinsic to Smith's texts (and, incidentally, extrinsic to what little we know of Smith's life).[63]

Two Disjoined *Inquiries*, Considered

Since both Steuart and Smith write about economics, and the history of their differential reception is primarily the history of early economics, it is unsurprising that most comparative commentary focuses on their economic doctrines. I, however, wish, given my present remit – considering impacts on sociology and social policy – to reflect more generally on their wider intellectual strategies. Steuart throughout is more interventionist in social arrangement than Smith;[64] his subtitle is 'an essay on the science of domestic policy in free nations' and, as he observes, 'A government must be continually in *action*, and one principal object of its attention must be the consequences and effects of *new* institutions'.[65] He ponders how to *deploy* taxes, in a way Smith does not, for social goals: 'the intention of taxes, as I understand them, is only to advance the public good (by throwing a part of the wealth of the rich into the hands of the industrious poor)'.[66] But his analyses are, I would argue, still dispassionate. He is (as identified in the Berry comment, cited above) concerned with the common good and with some abstract idea of good governance. His concern, like Smith's, is not with the poor as such. And his main sociological insights, are, as we shall see, still adventitious – innovations he makes in passing, without always encapsulating their import.

Treatment of population (its growth and the constraints upon it) can serve as a useful expository wedge to reveal the difference between our two writers. Here is Smith discussing remuneration levels:

> there is however a certain rate *below which it seems impossible to reduce* . . . the ordinary wages even of the lowest species of labour. A man['s] . . . wages must at least be sufficient to maintain him . . . [and] somewhat more; otherwise it would be impossible for him to *bring up a family*, and the race of such workmen *could not last beyond the first generation* . . . *this* rate [is] evidently the *lowest which is consistent with common humanity*[67]

As you might anticipate from my discussion so far, that 'common humanity' phrase is a standing temptation to those wishing to read

Smith as compassionate, caring; it may be worth exploring this further before spelling out the *population* implications, as Smith presents them.

'Common humanity' invites reading as a gesture to a moral basis for some sort of desired minimal wage. For example, Rothschild observes: 'His principles of commerce are *always* circumscribed by other laws, of justice and equity ... Wages ... *are also "regulated" by "common humanity"*'.[68] And even Nussbaum's nuanced rendition invites us to see the constraint benignly.

> He shows sympathy with wage regulations that favor workmen: all workmen should be guaranteed that 'lowest rate that is consistent with common humanity', which means enough to maintain a household with a wife and enough children to guarantee that two survive to adulthood.[69]

Some readers go further: 'Could it be that "common humanity" refers to a certain moral responsibility that reflects a principle of natural justice ...?'[70] Are these readings justified? For Smith, 'humanity' does not encapsulate a principle of justice, natural or otherwise; he is explicit that, in *contrast* to the requirements of justice, the rules 'which ascertain the actions required by ... humanity ... are ... vague and *indeterminate*'.[71] Read in context,[72] it is clear that the phrase 'common humanity' is here doing little *ethical* work – it is functioning more as a depiction of 'the *minimal* human condition'.

Quite how minimal is apparent in Smith's following discussion of a 'long stationary' country (China) where the 'lowest class of labourers, *therefore*, notwithstanding their scanty subsistence, must some way or another make shift to continue their race':[73]

> the competition of the labourers ... [reduces] them to this *lowest* rate which is consistent with *common humanity* ... The poverty of the lower ranks of people in China far surpasses that of the most beggarly nations in Europe.[74]

It is clear from Smith's description of such a labourer's sustenance that he is envisaging barest subsistence, not what any warm fellow feeling might advocate:

> If by digging the ground a whole day he can get what will purchase a small quantity of rice in the evening, he is contented. The condition of artificers [*craftsmen*] is, if possible, still worse ... they are continually running about the streets ... begging employment.[75]

Further, it is pertinent that Smith takes this minimum 'common humanity' level as *irrelevant* to the experience of impoverished labourers in eighteenth-century Scotland: 'There are many plain symptoms that the wages of labour are *nowhere* in this country regulated [*i.e. determined*[76]] by this *lowest rate which is consistent with common humanity.*'[77] This is not (in any accepted sense) a minimum wage discussion. So I read Smith's argument as about minimum *subsistence* levels, not, *pace* Rothschild, as about wages regulated by what later generations might call 'common humanity'.

The level Smith is invoking, subsistence level, is potentially a brake upon population, keeping it within its sustainable limits:

> in civilized society it is only among the inferior ranks of people that the scantiness of subsistence can set limits to the further multiplication of the human species; and it can do so in *no other way than by destroying a great part of the children which their fruitful marriages produce* . . . It is in this manner that the demand for men, like that for any other commodity, *necessarily* regulates the production of men; quickens it when it goes on too slowly, and stops it when it advances too fast.[78]

This is presented, by Smith, neutrally, factually, without negative comment. We are at liberty to agree or disagree with Smith's demography; that is a separate discussion. But here is no deployed 'keen sympathy' for the poor. Smith's analysis is, however, of a piece with Smith's indifference (noted above) to the child poverty implications of his taxation policy ('it would not probably diminish much the useful population'). Again, Smith is aware of class differentials in infant mortality (and the further peculiar disadvantages of the impoverished: 'In foundling hospitals, and among the children brought up by parish charities, the mortality is still greater than among those of the common people').[79] But, however tempting it may be to assume that Smith therefore sees this requiring remediation, there is, as I have elsewhere argued at length, *nothing* in WN to sustain an interventionist reading of his differential mortality insights.[80]

Steuart, by contrast, is more disposed to consider government involvement and is concerned to assess population in terms of its social *utility*:

> The *use* of inhabitants is to be mutually serviceable one to another . . . and to the society in general. Consequently, every state should, *in good policy*, first apply itself to make the inhabitants they have

> answer *that* purpose, before they carry their views towards augmenting their numbers. I think it is absurd to wish for new inhabitants, without first knowing how to employ the old . . . I shall then begin by supposing that inhabitants require rather to be *well employed* than increased in numbers.[81]
>
> If it . . . happens, that an additional number produced do no more than feed themselves, then I perceive no advantage gained to the society by their production.[82]

Underlying this is Steuart's interventionist approach to social policy, with a wider remit for the emergent discipline of political economy:

> I have explained the term [political economy], by pointing out the *object* of the art; which is, to provide *food, other necessaries, and employment to every one* of the society. (This is a very simple and a very general method of defining a most complicated operation.) To provide a proper employment for all the members of a society, is the same as to *model* and *conduct* every branch of their concerns.[83]

This motivation is manifestly absent from WN. So Steuart naturally starts to explore the planning implications – on youth unemployment, and claims to full employment:

> A statesman should make it his endeavour to employ as many of every class as possible, and when employment fails in the common run of affairs, to *contrive new outlets for young people* of every denomination.[84]
>
> Whenever . . . anyone is found . . . who is willing to work for his bread, but who can find no employment, there is a *breach of the contract, and an abuse*.[85]

Within this framework, Steuart's account of population and its constraints reads very differently from Smith's:

> Let me . . . consider the generation of man in a political [*i.e. social policy*] light, and it will present itself under two forms. The one is a *real multiplication*; the other only as *procreation*.
>
> Children produced from parents who are able to *maintain* them, and bring them up to a way of getting bread for themselves, do really multiply and serve the state. Those born of parents whose subsistence is *precarious* . . . have a precarious existence . . . Many such will perish for want of food, but many more for want of ease . . .

> When marriage is contracted without the requisites for multiplication, it produces a procreation, attended with the above-mentioned inconveniences; and as by far the greater part of inhabitants are in the lower classes, it becomes the *duty of a statesman to provide against such evils*, if he intends, usefully, to increase the number of his people.[86]

For Steuart, 'statesman' serves as a placeholder for a government attending to the true interests of the state,[87] so that last clause references 'the duty of a government to provide against such evils'.

This sense of a government's duty to intervene – even if merely from the motive of population increase – is explicitly linked to actions, which (unlike Smith's descriptive analyses of subsistence as a population limiter hitting the poorest) would bring benefit to the poor. But also note – and here Smith and Steuart are alike – that Steuart's analysis is dispassionate, *not* driven by appeals to our *concerns* for the poor but by concern for health of the polity.

The discussion flowing from this leads Steuart into interesting paths. The first forms a piece of adventitious sociology – perhaps more accurately, adventitious sociological method. The second is a novel, even eccentric, proposal for quite extreme intervention. In contrast to Smith, whose most adventurous flight of fancy – 'a new Utopia' as he calls it – requires merely an extension of the geographic scope of taxation,[88] Steuart is minded to consider how our underlying social structures might be *other* than they are (a stirring of the nascent discipline of social policy). But first the more mundane, though for the eighteenth century quite innovative, sociological methodology.

Steuart, thinking of population in a 'political light', in relation to the arrangement of the *polis*, and wishing to ensure adequate workforce, comments:

> Every plan proposed for *this* purpose, which does not proceed upon an exact recapitulation [*enumeration*] of the inhabitants of a country, parish by parish, will prove nothing more than an expedient for walking in the dark ... I would recommend ... to have one [list] [*i.e. a cross-tabulation*] made out, classing all the inhabitants, *not only by the trades they exercise, but by those of their fathers*.[89]

Sinclair – who cites this passage as one of his two 'enlightenment thinker' invocations in defence of his OSA project – misreports

Steuart as here listing a prerequisite for *any* plan 'for benefiting a nation'.⁹⁰ The desired tabulations are, for Steuart, tied to one particular project (workforce planning); though, once entertained, they admittedly have more general import. By the twentieth century, father/son transition tables were to become a standard sociological analytic tool, to assess the comparative 'openness' of modern industrial societies and to document patterns of absolute and relative mobility. But Steuart's thought had to wait some time for its instantiation; it was over a century after he wrote that the first such published table appeared – in Karl Pearson's 1904 analysis of 'contingency of occupations of fathers and sons', using a table supplied by Emily Perrin.⁹¹

Steuart's focus is occupational planning, not 'social mobility' in the parlance of twentieth-century sociology. But what is of interest is that his mode of thought, his way of thinking about society, leads him to advocate a specific form of data collection and presentation that was later to become important. Adventitious sociological methodology – innovative, not fully deployed by the writer.

Smith talks of population fluctuation in terms of very broad social classes (perhaps because he sees occupational barriers as potentially highly permeable – 'The arts of weaving plain linen and plain silk, for example, are almost entirely the same. That of weaving plain woolen is somewhat different; but the difference is so insignificant, that either a linen or a silk weaver might become a tolerable [woollen] workman in very few days';⁹² or again, on watchmaking: 'to explain to any young man . . . how to construct the machines, cannot well require more than the lessons of a few weeks'⁹³). Steuart in contrast is interested in the reproduction of quite narrow occupational groups:

> When I come to the lower classes, I examine for example that of shoemakers, where I find a certain number [*of shoemakers*] produced. This number I first compare with the number of shoemakers actually existing, and then with the number of marriages subsisting among them (for I suppose recapitulations [*enumerations*⁹⁴] of every kind) from which I discover the fertility of marriage, and the success of multiplication in that part . . . I have said, that I imagine it an advantage that every class should support [*produce*] at least its own numbers; and when it does more, I should wish (where it possible) that the higher classes might be recruited from the lower, rather than the lower

from the higher; the one seems a mark of prosperity [*prospering*⁹⁵], the other of decay: but I must confess that the first is by far the most difficult to be obtained.⁹⁶

There are three noteworthy points in that quotation. Firstly, Steuart (for all his willingness to think afresh) is clearly assuming that by occupational default the sons of shoemakers become shoemakers. Secondly, more interestingly, Steuart, as he thinks through the detailed application of his scheme, realises that his initial data-collection proposal (father/son occupation data) does not, by itself, supply the information that would be required to answer his policy questions (whence that addition of occupationally specific marriage rates and derived fertility rates). Thirdly, and most strikingly, by the end of the paragraph Steuart has started to 'read' his data in terms of social mobility (a pattern of upward social mobility is, he infers, a sign that a country is prospering, whilst downward mobility marks a society in decay). And he is alert to the policy difficulty of realising his preferred mobility pattern. Adventitious sociology indeed: he does not take the next step of saying that the collection of similar data from other European countries would enable comparative, quantitative discussion of relative prospering. But he has – however imperfectly – assembled the pieces that would enable such a step.

Armed with the notional data, and the principle that 'the higher classes might be recruited from the lower, rather than the lower from the higher', Steuart however does proceed to devise policy to maintain occupational numbers over time (he believes that people would be more disposed to marriage – so, under the constraints of eighteenth-century norms, more prolific – were they not faced with the financial burden of children):

> According ... to circumstances [*i.e. where needed*], and in consistence with these principles, I would encourage marriage by taking the children off the hands of their parents. Where marriage succeeds the worst ... a great encouragement should be given to it: perhaps the whole [*of the children*] should be taken care of [*by the state*] ... My view [*is*] ... having such a number of children *yearly taken care* of as shall answer the multiplication proposed [*the numbers in each occupation*], and that these be proportionally raised from each class, and from each part of the country, and produced from *marriages protected by the state*, distinguished from the others.⁹⁷

Adventitious Sociology 67

The proposal is hedged with caveats and the detail a mite unclear; but, in outline, bold. It meshes with a suggestion, later in his *Inquiry*, of a labour-pool for national service:

> For the *augmentation* of this class [*the military*], I would receive all male children who should be given or exposed by their parents. These should be bred [*trained*] to every sort of labour for which the state has occasion, and the numbers might be carried to 20% above that which might be judged necessary in time of the hottest war. Out of this class only, the standing [*military*] forces might be recruited: those who remained might be employed in every public service; such as working in arsenals, docks, highways, public buildings, etc. *By taking care of the children of this whole class, the numbers would rise to whatever height might be judged necessary* . . . This is a good scheme . . . the execution is gradual; therefore no sudden revolution is implied.[98]

Perhaps no sudden revolution but certainly a revolution. And, however we decide to rate Steuart's proposals for occupational planning (with its comingled willingness to think unconventionally about some social arrangements whilst holding fast to conventional views of social position), the impetus to the by-product – that empirical table '*classing all the inhabitants, not only by the trades they exercise, but by those of their fathers*' – is worth cherishing.

I have been stressing Steuart's, as against Smith's, willingness to consider radical social restructuring in pursuit of the 'science of domestic policy'. But perhaps underlying this for Steuart is a sharper sense of the social weight of action than is to be found in Smith. Consider their differentiated treatments of what Smith calls 'unproductive' labour. As has often been remarked, Smith's model would not look kindly upon a service-based economy. Here is Smith:

> The labour of some of the most respectable orders in the society is, like that of menial [*domestic*] servants, unproductive of any value, and does not fix or realize itself in any permanent subject, or vendible commodity, which *endures* after that labour is past . . . [*for*] churchmen, lawyers, physicians . . . like the declamation of the actor, the harangue of the orator, or the tune of the musician, the work of all of them *perishes* in the very instant of its production.[99]

We can see what is driving Smith – concern to anchor that 'vendible commodity' – and the distinction does have import in Smith's economic framework. But in forcing the distinction he commits himself to a socially implausible claim: that the work of churchmen, lawyers, physicians 'perishes in the very instant of its production'. Steuart – perhaps arriving at the same allocation of *things* – reaches for a differing *description*: 'incorporeal'. And that description permits a more acceptable analysis:

> The first species of the *things incorporeal*, which may be purchased with money, is personal service; such is the attendance of a menial servant, the *advice* of a physician, of a lawyer, the assistance of skilful people *in order to acquire knowledge*, the service of those employed *in the administration of public affairs* ... There is a kind of resemblance between the species here enumerated, and what we called the useful value in *consumable commodities*. In the one and the other [*i.e. in both*], there is an equivalent given for a man's time usefully employed ... whereas here [*things incorporeal*], for want of a permanent and transferable substance, the personal services though producing *advantages which are sufficiently felt*, cannot however be *transferred* for the adequate price they cost.[100]

Both Steuart and Smith are concerned to stress the non-transferability of 'incorporeal', non-'vendible' production. Smith, in his eagerness to distinguish, ends by misdescribing – 'the work of all of them *perishes* in the very instant of its production'. In contrast, Steuart – noting 'the assistance of skilful people *in order to acquire knowledge*' – better captures our (surely justified) sense that such labour can generate lasting effects.

Steuart's Sociology

The dominant motive for my chapter is to assert the role of adventitious dispassionate sociology, within the Scottish Enlightenment's contribution to the genesis of a present discipline that itself – at least in some of its manifestations – might have some claim on dispassion and insight. But within that broad theme I have a minor aim: the rehabilitation of James Steuart as an Enlightenment thinker of substance, at least when viewed from the perspective of the non-economic social sciences. I have already, I hope, indicated why his preparedness (and ability) to think 'outside of the box' is refreshing and how on some topics he is demonstrably more socially nuanced than Smith, and I have touched on one of his surprising methodological suggestions. I wish to spend a further few paragraphs indicating why, beyond these examples, I find Steuart of interest.

He has a clear understanding of relativism and change, not given to seeing the Enlightenment as the highest point of human progress (perhaps this is what underlies the Marx approval, noted earlier):

> All simplicity of manners is only relative. Our fathers looked upon the manners of their ancestors as simple, these again admired the simplicity of the patriarchs; and perhaps the time may come, when the manners of the 18th century may be called the noble simplicity of the ancients[101]

and his pragmatic theory of knowledge is appealing: 'when I say I *believe* any proposition, I mean no more than that I reason and act upon the hypothesis of its being true'.[102] Thinking about the world around him, he appears sociologically attentive. He has an awareness of the tensions of socially intersecting roles:

> If there were but one man upon earth, his duty would contain no other precepts than those dictated by self-love. If he comes to be a father, a husband, a friend, his self-love falls immediately under limitations . . . If he comes to be a judge, a magistrate, he must frequently forget that he is a friend, or a father.[103]

When 'doing economics', as when designing taxation, he is alert to the social costs of implementation, thinking of ways to nudge people into acceptance. For example, in place of a retrospectively collected tax on carriages, he proposes a point-of-manufacture tax upon carriage-wheels:

> The price [of wheels] would immediately rise; but this rise would soon become familiar to the man who has the carriage; and he would then be no more hurt by this additional expense, than if it had proceeded from some new and expensive fashion of wheels . . . very soon nobody would enquire how it came about, nor once complain of the tax.[104]

Again, like Smith, he provides small, insightful, adventitious sketches of micro-social processes; this, for example, on the 'display' of financiers (with the additional observation that their social role is still unformed):

> They are not exposed to the many hidden expenses incident to [*i.e. falling on*] land-proprietors. They are a class in the state but lately known; the capital of their wealth is hid; and opinions concerning

their figure and rank are as yet unformed. Whereas [*in contrast*] the family of a landed proprietor is known; his expense *may surpass* that of his predecessors without much observation [*comment*]; but if it should *fall below* it, he commonly sinks in the estimation of his neighbours ... An heir to a landed estate, is bred up from his infancy with the notion of living like his father: the son of a monied man has commonly very different sentiments; and even when any of this class takes a turn to expense [*expenditure*], the lustre of it is all displayed round their own bodies; that is, in their own house, and in their own families: no country seats, hounds, horses, servants in every quarter, family interest to keep up ... .[105] [emphases original]

Steuart, again somewhat like Smith, has a fascination with the unintended consequences of particular institutions, as in this analysis of the side-effects of aggrandisement (and an ensuing exposition of the economics of tourism):

When I see a rich and magnificent monastery of begging friars adorned with profusion of sculpture, ... incrustations of marble, beautiful pavements ... Here then is an effect of charity, which I have heard condemned by many ... 'What prostitution of riches!' say they: 'how usefully might all this money have been employed, in establishing manufactures, building a navy, and many other good purposes?' Whereas I am so entirely taken up with the *effects* arising from the execution of the work, that I seldom give myself time to reflect upon its intention. The building of this monastery has fed the industrious poor, has encouraged the liberal arts, has improved the taste of the inhabitants, has opened the door to the curiosity of strangers ... The miraculous tongue of St Anthony of Padua, has brought more clear money into that city than the industry of a thousand weavers could have done.[106]

In a subtle and ingenious paper on unintended consequences in the Scottish Enlightenment,[107] Craig Smith emphasises the role that such consequences played in their thought. But his paper focuses down to their depiction of unintended *order*[108] and ends by being more sympathetic to grand theory than I would choose. What I here wish to stress is the importance, to these writers (as in this Steuart example), of *seeking* unintended consequences as a heuristic method for their social science – they value 'reason and understanding, by which we are capable of discerning the *remote consequences* of all our actions, and of *foreseeing* the advantage or detriment which is likely to result from them'.[109] Stuart identifies the unintended consequences of monastery construction, and the profitable tourism fallout from reliquary veneration. Locating such unintended consequences is a prime move in constructing their dispassionate, social explanations (though *'unanticipated consequences'* might be a more apt descriptor than 'unintended', since theirs is not, at base, an intentionalist morality).

And Steuart, like the other writers of the Scottish Enlightenment, generates insightful pieces of adventitious sociology. He, for example, like Smith, is aware of class-related mortality – though his plurality of detrimental causes is again more nuanced than Smith's:

> If it be true, as I think it is, from what I have seen and observed, that numbers, especially of children, among the lower classes, perish from the effects of indigence; either directly by want of food, or by *diseases constructed gradually* from the want of convenient ease; and that others perish from want of [medical] care . . .[110]

But, and unlike Smith, Steuart takes this as an impetus to leverage the practised collection of demographic *data* away from its then-prevailing geographic focus (data by *city*) to a *social* focus (data by *class*):

> All this [*variation in mortality*] I agree may be true; but I should be glad to see in what proportion it *is* so, and to be certain of the fact. I want to know the diseases of the rich and of the poor; I want to have as particular *details of the births and deaths of every class*, as I can have of those of the cities of Paris London or Breslaw.[111] I want to know *from what parents* those multitudes of poor . . . sprung; and most of all to have such *accounts from different countries*, where different manners prevail. For no just conclusion can be drawn from the comparison of facts, without *examining circumstances*.[112]

Here again Steuart – almost in passing – in pursuit of his central concerns, makes a sociological suggestion – the collection of *class*-specific demographic data, in contrast to the common practice of his contemporaries – that has implications beyond his concerns. There are obvious parallels with his 'invention' of social mobility tables (and notice here his reasoned desire for cross-national comparative data, as a device for 'examining circumstances'). But I want to end with an even more striking instance.

An Unsettling Instance of Adventitious Sociology

My final example of Steuart's adventitious sociology is, I think, intriguing in its own right, but more intriguing for the interpretative expositional problem it entails.

It comes from his 1769 report on the 'interest' of the County of Lanark (to which the 1805 reprint added this subtitle: 'which (in several respects) may be applied to that of Great Britain in general').[113] The substantive issue, underlying my example, is itself slight. It was a commonplace eighteenth-century observation that young women, servant girls, spent money on decorations and dress. Sinclair's parish ministers, some thirty years afterwards, consistently note that whereas the wealthy devote their extra resources to housing and furniture, the poor favour dress:

> among those of both sexes who are unembarrassed with the cares and expense of a family, the advanced wages of labour have had an obvious tendency to cherish the *idle vanity of dress* [114]
>
> The young woman . . . now *sinks all the money she makes in dress and ornament* . . .[115]

Steuart also notes this behaviour and wishes to explain it. Vanity (particularly female vanity) might have been thought a tempting explanation for a gentleman such as Sir James (as it was to be for these turn-of-the-century clergy). But this is what Steuart actually writes:

> The women [of Lanark] also form a considerable class [*group*], and may subsist with great ease by spinning. Their lowest gains amount from twenty pence to two shillings per week. With this they are clothed and nourished, and many of them, while young and unmarried, we see decently *ornamented with little superfluities of dress*; which they hold out [*i.e display*], I suppose, as a *fund at their disposal* for the maintenance of children, in case any young fellow should wish to take them for a wife. *Were it not, therefore, for the use of ribands, and such little ornaments now in fashion, a country lad could form no judgement of the industry and frugality of the young women of*

the parish. I call the buying such superfluities as ribands, the greatest proof of frugality; because every unnecessary expense must be cut off before they can purchase an ornament, which, from the wedding day, the husband expunges out of the list of his wife's expenses; as she had formally expunged all other superfluities, in order to acquire what now she finds to be superfluous. Thus all that possibly can be spared, is[116] provided for the subsistence of the children during their infancy.[117]

His analysis is that *by spending money on superfluities* the women 'hold out', or *manifest*, their earning capacity (and their habits of thrift, since such purchases required the habit of saving). These signals, being visible, provide information to the observer (these country lads) – information which is deemed relevant to mate choice. The modern signalling theorist would recognise this analytic move. It explains the information – and the point of the information – carried by the active purchasing of ribbons and explains why *this* action (because of its information-carrying utility). Steuart emphasises the *frugality* information contained in this superficially *extravagant* purchase ('because every unnecessary expense must be cut off before they can purchase an ornament'). That '*must be cut off before they can purchase*' phrase also underlines his perception – again necessary for signalling theory – that the signal cannot readily be faked. Steuart's next move, with its unthinking assumption of male authority, may remind us that we are still in the eighteenth century (these superfluities 'from the wedding day, *the husband expunges* out of the list of his wife's expenses'); but notice also the assumption that women are active participants in the economic unit of the family[118] and share in the perception of the need to redirect resources (the superfluities 'now *she finds* to be superfluous') to the subsistence of the children during their (preearning) infancy.

This is classic signalling theory. The justification of an activity, the understanding of an activity, is to be found not in the concrete product (ribbons) but in the utility to the individual of providing signalling information (mate choice); that signal providing not-easy-to-fake information.

This I think is a nice example for a number of reasons. I am not laying an imposed expectation upon Steuart – his prose is not tortured to read it as I have just read it. The insights are Steuart's, and *expressed by him* – 'I call buying such superfluities the greatest proof of frugality' – so do not fall foul of Quentin Skinner's scathing aspersions on the 'mythology of doctrines': 'The danger of converting some scattered or quite incidental remarks by a classic theorist into his "doctrine" on one of the mandatory themes [the topics currently regarded as constitutive of the subject]'.[119] Steuart's remarks are – in and of themselves – expressive of the fact that Steuart here perceives the value of ribbons as signals, not things. His analysis is a neat, possibly veridical, application of signalling theory (signalling theory might variously be claimed by both sociologists and economists; I am happy to interpret it as 'sociological economics'). But Steuart does not observe 'I have found a new way of thinking about, of conceptualising, apparently economic phenomena'. Nor does he, as far as I can see, elsewhere make use of this analytic strategy. Though it would not be displeasing to encounter an early signalling theorist who cited Steuart as a precursor, I am sceptical of finding any such. Further, as far as I am aware, this Steuart move goes unremarked in the academic commentary on Steuart's thought.

So what are we to make of this, which is a genuine, but underdeveloped, insight, not integral to the general intellectual narrative of the writer?[120] Is noting it equivalent to merely picking up a peculiar pebble from the beach, remarking on its fascinating structure (almost a *lusus naturae*, as it were) but with no inferences to be drawn?

An alternative account is that it forms some evidence that the way of thought of a particular group or era is such that it predisposes to demonstrable insights of this kind – these Scottish eighteenth-century writers embodied a way of thinking about the world which encouraged insights of this nature. This then becomes an interesting fact about the context – it is after all by providing frameworks within which thoughts of this kind occur that social science will advance. Of course, to articulate the *manifest* themes in Steuart's economic and social thought remains important in understanding broad sweeps of intellectual history. But in another sense Steuart's grand theories are irrelevant (in the sense that no economist or social scientist today would pick up Steuart's framework as he wrote it and try to run with it as an explanatory tool or device).

What matters about these eighteenth-century Scots is not the grand theories that they left us but the cast of mind to which they predisposed us. Which is why I see this adventitious sociology as important.

Notes

For constructive and challenging comment on an earlier draft I am grateful to Richard Breen and John Goldthorpe, and to all the participants (but particularly Tamás Demeter) at the workshop on the present volume, in Budapest (actually and virtually), January 2022. I also acknowledge helpful comment from an Edinburgh University Press reviewer.

1. Kenneth Macdonald, 'Did British Sociology Begin with the Scottish Enlightenment?' in Plamena Panayotova (ed.), *The History of Sociology in Britain: New Research and Revaluation* (Cham: Palgrave Macmillan, 2019), pp. 37–69. Available online: https://link.springer.com/content/pdf/10.1007%2F978-3-030-19929-6_2.pdf. That chapter spent time, as the present does not, on evaluating traditional narratives as to influence.
2. John Brewer, 'Conjectural History, Sociology and Social Change in Eighteenth-Century Scotland' in D. McCrone et al. (eds), *The Making of Scotland* (Edinburgh: Edinburgh University Press, 1989), p. 14. Throughout I silently add italics for expositional clarity; where these are in the original, it is so noted.
3. Adam Ferguson, *An Essay on the History of Civil Society* (Edinburgh: Kincaid & Bell, 1767), p. 115 (henceforth ECS).
4. 'The men of this country, says one lady, should learn to sew and to knit, it would hinder their time from being a burden ... to other people ... I tremble at the prospect of bad weather; for then the gentlemen come mopping to us for entertainment; and the sight of a husband in distress, is but a melancholy spectacle' (ibid. p. 64).
5. Adam Ferguson, *Principles of Moral and Political Science* (Edinburgh: Creech, 1792), i, p. 302; he makes the same point more formally in his *Institutes of Moral Philosophy* (Edinburgh: Kincaid et al., 1773), p. 167.
6. Ferguson, ECS p. 115.
7. John Millar, *The Origin of the Distinction of Ranks* (London: Murray, 1779), p. 57 (henceforth OR).
8. OR p. 108
9. *The Statistical Account of Scotland. Drawn up from the communications of the ministers of the different parishes by Sir John Sinclair, Bart* (Edinburgh: Creech, 1791–9), v, p. 63 (henceforth OSA).
10. David Hume, *The History of England* (London: Cadell, 1778), iv, Appendix 3.68; I would read Spenser's allegory as more 'ingenious' – see Kenneth Macdonald, 'Allegorical Landscape in the *Faerie Queen* (Books I to III)', *Durham University Journal* 32 (1971), pp. 121–4.

11. Paul Chamley, 'Sir James Steuart inspirateur de la théorie générale de Lord Keynes?', *Revue d'économie politique* 72 (1962), pp. 303–13; for careful evaluation, see Ragip Ege, 'The New Interpretation of Steuart by Paul Chamley' in Ramon Tortajada (ed.), *The Economics of James Steuart* (London: Routledge, 1999), pp. 84–101.
12. Amartya Sen, *Social Exclusion: Concept, Application, and Scrutiny* (Manila: Asian Development Bank, 2000), p. 4.
13. Emma Rothschild and Amartya Sen, 'Adam Smith's Economics' in K. Haakonssen (ed.), *Cambridge Companion to Adam Smith* (Cambridge: Cambridge University Press, 2005), pp. 319–65, at p. 360.
14. Martha Nussbaum, *The Cosmopolitan Tradition* (Cambridge, MA: Harvard University Press, 2019), p. 144.
15. Kenneth Macdonald, 'Of Shame and Poverty; and on Misreading Sen and Adam Smith', *Adam Smith Review* 11 (2019), pp. 111–262, at pp. 119–32. Available online: www.academia.edu/44011649
16. Dominique Caboret, 'The Market Economy and Social Classes in James Steuart and G. W. F. Hegel' in Tortajada, *Economics of James Steuart*, pp. 57–75.
17. See Angela Coventry, 'Traces of Hume in Sociology', in this volume.
18. Karl Marx, *Economic Works 1857–61* (New York: International Publishers, 1987), p. 17.
19. Ibid. p. 17.
20. Christopher Berry, 'James Steuart on the Public Good' in J. M. Menudo (ed.), *The Economic Thought of Sir James Steuart* (London: Routledge, 2020), pp. 3–13, at p. 12.
21. This is the elided portion of the 'Steuart . . .' sentence quoted above.
22. James Steuart, *An Inquiry into the Principles of Political Oeconomy* (London: Millar & Cadel, 1767), i, p. xii.
23. Adam Smith, *An Inquiry into the Nature and Causes of the Wealth of Nations*, R. H. Campbell et al. (eds) (Oxford: Oxford University Press, [1776] 1976) (henceforth WN), I.x.b.52.
24. WN 5.3.35–6.
25. Henry Home, Lord Kames, *Sketches of the History of Man* (Edinburgh: Creech, 1774), i, p. 205.
26. David Hume, *Essays, Moral and Political* (Edinburgh: Kincaid, 1742), ii, p. 73.
27. Millar, OR p. 274.
28. Macdonald, 'Did British Sociology Begin with the Scottish Enlightenment?', p. 53.
29. By way of evidence for my quantitative enthusiasms over the years, I list some Macdonald papers (two with co-authors): 'The marginal adjustment of mobility tables, revisited', osf.io/preprints/socarxiv/

z4u2d, (2023); 'Family Investments in Children: What the Interactions and the Data Do not Say', *European Sociological Review* 27 (2011), pp. 281–6; 'Russia and Youth Crime: A Comparative Study of Attitudes and Their Implications', *British Journal of Criminology* 47 (2007), pp. 2–22; 'Sex Differences in Political Knowledge in Britain', *Political Studies* 51 (2003), pp. 67–83; 'Return to Indianapolis: A Note on the Logic of Model Construction', *American Journal of Sociology* 89 (1983), pp. 683–7.

30. Kenneth Macdonald, 'Sociology within the *Statistical Account of Scotland*', in this volume.
31. Steuart's exposition is convoluted, but excusably so: eighteenth-century coinage carried both a 'face' value and 'intrinsic' value (of that gold and silver); the exchange value of all, and so their relation to each other, fluctuated over time and over trading nation (and as coins wore with age).
32. As evidence for Smith and Steuart meeting: 'Adam Smith has been heard to observe, that he understood Sir James's system better from his *conversation*, than his volumes', p. 378 in *Anecdotes of the life of Sir James Steuart* in *The Works, Political, Metaphysical and Chronological of the Late Sir James Steuart* (London: Cadell and Davies, 1805), vi, pp. 361–91.
33. *Correspondence of Adam Smith*, ed. E. C. Mossner and I. S. Ross (New York: Oxford University Press, second edition, 1987) (henceforth *Corr.*), letter 132.
34. Nussbaum, *Cosmopolitan Tradition*, p. 150.
35. Eric Schliesser, *Adam Smith: Systematic Philosopher and Public Thinker* (Oxford: Oxford University Press, 2017), p. 194.
36. Dennis Rasmussen, 'Adam Smith on What Is Wrong with Economic Inequality', *American Political Science Review* 110 (2016), pp. 342–52, at p. 343.
37. Stein Ringen, 'Direct and Indirect Measures of Poverty', *Journal of Social Policy* 17 (1988), pp. 351–65, at p. 353.
38. Macdonald, 'Misreading Sen and Adam Smith'.
39. Samuel Fleischacker, *On Adam Smith's Wealth of Nations: A Philosophical Companion* (Princeton: Princeton University Press, 2004), p. 208.
40. Adam Smith, *Essays on Philosophical Subjects*, ed. W. P. D. Wightman and J. C. Bryce (Oxford: Oxford University Press, 1983), p. 112.
41. Samuel Fleischacker, 'Adam Smith on Equality' in Christopher Berry et al. (eds), *The Oxford Handbook of Adam Smith* (Oxford: Oxford University Press, 2013), pp. 485–99, at p. 494.
42. WN V.ii.c.14.

43. WN V.ii.c.16.
44. Nussbaum, *Cosmopolitan Tradition*, p. 144.
45. WN V.ii.k.3.
46. Adam Smith, *The Theory of Moral Sentiments*, ed. D. D. Raphael and A. L. Macfie (Oxford: Oxford University Press, [1759] 1976), III.3.30–33 (hereafter TMS).
47. Macdonald, 'Misreading Sen and Adam Smith', pp. 142–4.
48. WN V.i.f.61.
49. Gertrude Himmelfarb, *The Idea of Poverty: England in the Early Industrial Age* (London: Faber, 1984), p. 60.
50. Emma Rothschild, 'The Debate on Economic and Social Security in the Late Eighteenth Century: Lessons of a Road Not Taken', *Development and Change* 27 (1996), pp. 331–51, at p. 337.
51. Macdonald, 'Misreading Sen and Adam Smith', pp. 170f.
52. WN I.viii.36.
53. Attribution of 'earlier' matters, because the consensus view chooses to see Smith as a first-mover: '*More than anyone else before him*, Smith urged an attitude of respect for the poor, a view of them as having equal dignity with every other human being' (Fleischacker, *On Adam Smith*, p. 205). Minimally, the Arthur Young quote shows this to be not true.
54. Arthur Young, *The Farmer's Tour through the East of England* (London, 1771), iv, p. 352.
55. Emma Rothschild, 'Adam Smith and Conservative Economics', *Economic History Review* 45 (1992), pp. 74–96, at p. 84.
56. Samuel Fleischacker, 'Adam Smith and the Left' in Ryan Hanley (ed.), *Adam Smith: His Life, Thought, and Legacy* (Princeton: Princeton University Press, 2016), pp. 478–93, at p. 485.
57. Corr. 299.
58. James Steuart, *The Principles of Money Applied to the Present State of the Coin of Bengal*, 2nd ed. (London, 1772), p. 85. [*Works*, v, p. 93].
59. WN V.ii.k.1–5, 9.
60. WN V.ii.k.43–4.
61. Fleischacker reads Smith on taxation differently. ('He even suggests, in a couple of places, that the government *arrange* its taxes so that "the indolence and vanity of the rich" can contribute to the well-being of the poor', *On Adam Smith*, p. 494.) I directly address such misinterpretations in 'Misreading Sen and Adam Smith', pp. 180f.
62. WN V.ii.k.7.
63. See Macdonald, 'Misreading Sen and Adam Smith', pp. 190–3.

64. Consider: an article entitled 'Adam Smith's expressed social policy recommendations' (as distinct from stances he might be *intuited* to have supported) would be short.
65. Steuart, *Inquiry*, i, p. 7.
66. Ibid. p. 388.
67. WN I.viii.14–16.
68. Rothschild, 'Adam Smith and Conservative Economics', p. 85.
69. Nussbaum, *Cosmopolitan Tradition*, p. 156.
70. Amos Witztum and Jeffrey T. Young, 'The Neglected Agent: Justice, Power, and Distribution in Adam Smith', *History of Political Economy* 38 (2006), pp. 437–71, at p. 441.
71. TMS III.6.9; as an aside of interest – of corrective interest because Smith is often thought crass in his relation to women – note that he holds, pejoratively, this 'humanity' responsible for the *irregularity* whereby 'the *attempt* to ravish is not punished as a rape' though the '*real* demerit . . . is undoubtedly the same in both cases' (TMS II.iii.2.4).
72. Macdonald, 'Misreading Sen and Smith', pp. 163f.
73. WN I.viii.25.
74. WN I.viii.24.
75. Ibid. p. 24.
76. Though Smith sometimes deploys 'regulated' in the more familiar modern sense of legal regulation, he also uses it, as here, to point to simple causal determination: for example, 'the quantity of industry annually employed is necessarily *regulated* by the annual demand' (WN I.x.b.46), 'custom everywhere *regulates* fashion' (WN I.ix.20).
77. WN I.viii.28.
78. WN I.viii.39–40.
79. WN I.viii.38.
80. Macdonald, 'Misreading Sen and Adam Smith', pp. 207f.
81. Steuart, *Inquiry*, I, p. 60.
82. Ibid. p. 82.
83. Ibid. p. 15.
84. Ibid. p. 65.
85. Ibid. p. 83.
86. Ibid. p. 72.
87. Steuart first introduces the term 'statesman' as 'a *general term* to signify the head, according to the form of government' (*Inquiry*, I, p. 2). While he habitually writes as if this 'head' were an (abstract) *individual*, the 1805 edition replaces 'head' by 'legislature and supreme power' (*Works*, i, p. 2). Conceptually, the best modern translation of Steuart's 'statesman' must be simply 'government'.

88. WN V.ii.68.
89. Steuart, *Inquiry*, i, pp. 72–3.
90. Sir John Sinclair, *Analysis of the Statistical Account of Scotland* (Edinburgh: Tait, 1831), i, pp. 60.
91. See John Goldthorpe, 'Sociology and Statistics in Britain: The Strange History of Social Mobility Research and Its Latter-Day Consequences' in Panayotova (ed.), *The History of Sociology in Britain*, pp. 339–87, at p. 346.
92. WN I.x.c.42.
93. WN I.x.c.16.
94. As in the use of 'recapitulation' in the previous Steuart quotation.
95. 'Prosperity' means something like 'growth, prospering' (as distinct from wealth) – here (as in WN) its antithesis is 'decay', 'decline' (not poverty, per se).
96. Steuart, *Inquiry*, i. p. 73.
97. Ibid. pp. 73–4.
98. Ibid. p. 450.
99. WN III.ii.2.
100. Steuart, *Inquiry*, i, p. 369.
101. Ibid. p. 456.
102. Steuart, *Works*, vi, p. 34.
103. Steuart, *Inquiry*, i, p. xiii.
104. Ibid. ii, p. 52.
105. Ibid. ii, p. 478.
106. Ibid. i, p. 468.
107. Craig Smith, 'The Scottish Enlightenment, Unintended Consequences and the Science of Man', *The Journal of Scottish Philosophy* 7 (2009), pp. 9–28.
108. Ibid. p. 10.
109. TMS IV.2.6.
110. Steuart, *Inquiry*, i, p. 76.
111. For the significance and context of that Breslau reference, see John Goldthorpe, *Pioneers of Sociological Science* (Cambridge: Cambridge University Press, 2021), pp. 20–3.
112. Steuart, *Inquiry*, i, p. 76.
113. Steuart, *Works*, v, p. 279.
114. OSA x, p. 51.
115. OSA ii, p, 390.
116. The 1805 reprint (*Works*, v, p. 294) has '*will then be*' rather than '*is*'.
117. James Steuart, *Considerations on the Interest of the County of Lanark* (Glasgow: Duncan, 1769), p. 16.

118. A correct perception: the OSA, for example, throughout reports women's earnings (and economic management) as central to the survival of poor families – often more stable than male earnings.
119. Quentin Skinner, 'Meaning and Understanding in the History of Ideas', *History and Theory* 8 (1969), pp. 3–53, at p. 7.
120. For a more sceptical discussion of similar issues in Aristotle and Smith, see Macdonald, 'Misreading Sen and Adam Smith', pp. 112–14.

Part II

Sociological Ideas in the Scottish Enlightenment

4

Adam Ferguson as Founding Father of Sociology

Craig Smith

Introduction

In histories of sociology it is commonplace to find Adam Ferguson cited as a founding father of the discipline. Often lauded as the 'first real sociologist', Ferguson is singled out from among the thinkers of the Scottish Enlightenment as being especially influential on the development of the modern discipline of sociology.[1] This tendency is mirrored in the literature that focuses on the study of Ferguson himself, with both of the pioneering monographs on Ferguson focusing on his thinking about society from a sociological perspective.[2] From this perspective Ferguson represents a link in a story that tells of the pre-history of sociology. He represents a link between the methodological innovations of Montesquieu and the fascination with socialisation of Rousseau on the one hand, and the grand system building of Hegel and Marx on the other.[3]

This view of Ferguson and his place in the history of sociology has been subject to some sceptical interrogation. Duncan Forbes observed that much more would need to be added to Ferguson's ideas before they became sociology,[4] while Kenneth Macdonald has pointed out that having elements of what would become the sociological method and sociological concepts is not the same thing as trying to do sociology.[5] This, it seems, is obvious in the sense that both the term sociology and its classical formulation post-date Adam Ferguson's lifetime. And yet the founding fathers of disciplines rarely reveal the science as fully formed and replete with all of its intellectual tools, so saying that he is not quite doing sociology yet hardly precludes considering him as an ancestor in other senses. Moreover, there is good evidence that Adam Ferguson was widely read and admired by other transitional thinkers to whom sociology traces its early steps. Both Hegel and Marx refer to

Ferguson, and refer to him on matters that are invoked to place both him and them in the sociological tradition.⁶ Both Forbes's and Macdonald's approaches implicitly cede the point that Ferguson and the thinkers of the Scottish Enlightenment were assembling some of the building blocks of what would come to be sociology. Perhaps, then, John Brewer's 'proto-sociology' is a nicer expression. That said, however, looking at Ferguson as a proto-sociologist is still viewing things through a sociological lens.⁷

One key element that is often thought to distance Ferguson's work from sociology proper is the absence of an idea of a value-free mode of social enquiry, one that is self-consciously scientific, determined to remain objective and yet aware that the agent and his preconceptions are themselves formed by social experience. These ideas are most clearly articulated by the classical sociologists of the nineteenth and twentieth centuries and, though they have been questioned by a critical tradition sceptical of the possibility of freeing analysis from normative commitments, they remain an important part of the discipline's self-identity.

In this chapter I want to approach things from another perspective. My aim is to understand what Ferguson thought about and did with those elements of his thought that have been used to claim him as a progenitor of sociology. I look at their place within his own writings and his wider system of thought. My aim, in so doing, is to look at how important these proto-sociological ideas were to Ferguson, rather than to assess how important Ferguson's proto-sociological ideas were to sociology. Put another way, my aim is to explore just how much of a sociologist Ferguson turns out to have been by looking at the place of sociological arguments in his overall thinking. In doing so I hope to demonstrate that Ferguson is an important precursor of sociology in another, overlooked, sense: that his work is committed to the idea of separating the objective study of society from normative and political imperatives to social action.

The chapter proceeds by outlining the elements of Ferguson's thinking that have been held to anticipate sociology. I then examine the function of these within Ferguson's argument with particular attention to his overall methodology, before finally exploring the link between Ferguson's sociological arguments and his conception of his own intellectual enterprise. In doing so I will suggest that Ferguson's proto-sociological ideas play a vital role in his moral science – his attempt at an objective scientific study of humanity that would in turn support his normative moral philosophy – and that, in so trying to separate the objective study of society from the value-driven assessment of those societies, he is representative of a tension that remains between sociology and philosophy to this day.

Ferguson's Sociological Ideas

Ferguson's reputation as a proto-sociologist is usually traced to some combination of the following ideas:

> His rejection of great legislator myths and state of nature arguments in favour of social explanations.[8]
> His belief that humans were social animals and unintelligible outside a social context.[9]
> His adoption of the method of conjectural or theoretical history common to the Scottish Enlightenment as a means of comparative analysis to explore social humans.[10]
> The identification of the phenomena of unintended consequences and the recognition that the social was the product of the interaction of individuals rather than an expression of deliberately designed human artifice.[11]
> Strictures on the importance of empirical data and the danger of ethnocentric bias in data gathering and analysis.[12]
> The idea that the myths of a society serve as a source of data about the society's belief structures.[13]
> The development of a stadial theory and of an early form of functional analysis.[14]
> The anticipation of conflict sociology in his stress on the centrality of external conflict to social cohesion.[15]
> The identification of civil society as a new form of social formation.[16]
> The exploration of the division of labour and some negative effects that it had on individuals that prefigure ideas of anomie and alienation.[17]

As befits an assertion of founding father status, many of these refer to key methodological commitments or concepts that have become central to the discipline. On the side of methodology we have: empiricism, social theory, the ubiquity of the social, socialisation, ethnocentrism, unintended consequences, conflict sociology, functionalism, stadial theory and myth as evidence. On that of key concepts: civil society, the division of labour and alienation. It is worth pausing briefly to illustrate each of these and demonstrate that they are indeed explicit concerns in Ferguson's thinking rather than the product of reading back with hindsight.

Ferguson's commitment to science is ubiquitous. We need look no further than the choice of the name *Principles of Moral and Political Science* (1792) as the title of his final work, and the division of the subject matter in that book (descriptive science in volume one and normative philosophy in volume two) indicates Ferguson's agenda and commitments to the self-consciously empirical and scientific exploration of society. In this he is well within the mainstream of the Scottish conjectural historians. But, as I have argued elsewhere, this phrase is singularly inappropriate in describing Ferguson's method, as the whole thrust of his social theory is a rejection of the conjectures of Rousseau and a demand that inquiry be based on generalisations from empirical evidence.[18] Annette Meyer has noted that Ferguson's empiricism is combined with a near total disinterest in metaphysics.[19] While religious and providential arguments do appear in Ferguson's work they generally do not impinge on the descriptive generalisations. There is a good reason for this. Ferguson is committed to placing his normative prescriptions on as solid a basis as possible. The problem with earlier attempts to understand society was that they mingled their normative preferences with their attempts at description. In the early chapters of *An Essay on the History of Civil Society* Ferguson rejects legislator and contract theories on the basis that they are not supported by the empirical evidence and instead represent fanciful abstractions grounded in the author's favoured normative commitments.[20] Mixing the descriptive and the normative modes of enquiry is a key failing that Ferguson sees in his predecessors and contemporaries.

In the same passages Ferguson is clear that the social is the proper subject matter of inquiry. Whole societies and not isolated individuals are the locus of profitable inquiry. This is a corollary of the fact that there is a 'Principle of Society in human nature',[21] one which is so obvious an observation as not to be worth arguing over. Social life is a result of a universal 'disposition to society'[22] and the human character is formed in society. Habituation, custom and socialisation loom large in the analysis of social relationships. As he puts it: 'Men form themselves into society and the Society reacts upon its members to an Effect that contributes more than any other circumstance to the Form which its members Assume and the Rank that they bear . . .'[23] This natural sociability, combined with the propensity for habit formation in group interaction, produces 'a general conformity of thought'[24] where the 'authority of prevailing opinions makes at least one bond of society'.[25] Different societies develop different practices and beliefs as a result of this process of a universal human nature engaging in its social dimension in response to differing circumstances. If 'We have not any sufficient reason to believe that men, of remote ages and nations, differ from one another otherwise than by habits acquired in a different manner of living . . .',[26] then we have a baseline for a comparative social science.

As a result, Ferguson believes that 'all actions of men are equally the result of their nature'[27] and all conditions in which humanity is found are equally states of nature. Those who condemn a form of behaviour as being 'unnatural' are guilty of regarding the 'general and prevailing sense or practice of mankind'[28] at one time or place as an eternal standard. While Ferguson does believe that moral science can identify universal elements of human experience, it must not do so in a thoughtless and superficial fashion. Avoiding such ethnocentric assumptions is a key concern in Ferguson's collection of evidence through the comparison of the practices of diverse societies.

From here it is but a short step to the observation that social phenomena cannot be understood as the result of deliberative activity. Ferguson's awareness of the centrality of unintended consequences to genuine social explanation is perhaps best captured by the oft-quoted observation that 'nations stumble upon establishments, which are indeed the result of human action, but not the execution of any human design'.[29] This leads Ferguson to explore a series of functionalist explanations. He even makes explicit use of the concepts of 'function'[30] and 'superstructure'[31] to describe what he is doing.[32] Moreover, the preoccupation with unintended consequences and the use of functionalist ideas to account for them come together in those passages where Ferguson is held to prefigure conflict sociology. When Ferguson observes that 'Without the rivalship of nations, and the practice of war, civil society itself could scarcely have found an object, or a form. Mankind might have traded without any formal convention, but they cannot be safe without a national concert',[33] he is tracing the functional origin of the modern state to an unintended consequence of conflict between groups. This is something he later develops into a theory of the origin of national identity and culture. In so doing Ferguson makes the case that the myths and stories shared by a people, though false, provide a fruitful source of information on their belief systems.[34]

Ferguson also makes use of a stadial theory, but his use of the theory departs from the mainstream four stage theory deployed by Adam Smith, John Millar and others. Ferguson's 'highly idiosyncratic'[35] version of stadialism operates with three stages rather than four. And unlike his compatriots he does not distinguish the stages based on economics, or what Marx would later call the mode of production.[36] For Ferguson societies are distinguished between savage, barbarian and civilised on the basis of the political and legal institutions that have developed. This stress on the political elements of civilisation cuts against the Marxist-inspired reading of Ferguson as aligned with a supposed proto-materialist theory that emerges from stadialism, but it does not sever the economic from the political because Ferguson believed that the legal and political institutions create the space for economic activity. If there is a base/superstructure in Ferguson, it is the social phenomena of politics and the law that are base and economics that is superstructural.

It is here that we come to Ferguson's analysis of civil society. It is clear that Ferguson does not deploy this term in precisely the same way as modern thinkers do: to indicate an arena of social action that lies between the family and the state. Yet for all that, as Christopher Berry has argued, Ferguson clearly did identify such a 'space' in his thinking and understood that it was important to understand such a 'space' if we were to understand the operation of the modern societies that he called civil societies.[37] In so doing a favourite theme of Ferguson's analysis is the impact of the division of labour and the danger that arises from the separation of particular roles that are necessary for social cohesion. The fear that we might 'break the bands of society'[38] lies behind the debates about Ferguson's debt to classical republicanism and claims of his influence on the development of later ideas of alienation as central to the experience of modern societies. In his discussion of this, particularly prominent in the *Essay*, Ferguson dwells on the dangerous nature of the separation of the roles of statesman and warrior, seeing it as a form of corruption and, in military terms, a disaster for national defence and politics.[39]

Now, recall that my interest here is not in the similarity of these ideas to their later appearance in the sociological tradition, nor is it in claims that Ferguson is uniquely responsible for the genesis of these ideas. Instead my focus is on the role these methodological and conceptual notions play within Ferguson's own thinking. The brief summary above serves to show that these ideas are indeed present in Ferguson's discussion of the methodology of social inquiry and that they generate concepts that are of particular concern to him as sources of moral corruption in modern civil society. All of this, I would like to suggest, can better be understood within the context of Ferguson's self-conception of his system of ideas than it can through the lens of his place in the development of sociology.

Moral Science and Moral Philosophy

Elsewhere I have attempted to outline the coherence of Ferguson's system of ideas by identifying how key elements of it fit together as an intellectual project.[40] In doing so I make use of the distinction around which Ferguson structures his final published work, the *Principles of Moral and Political Science*. To make the distinction clear I use the term 'moral science' to apply to empirical elements of Ferguson's project, the identification of the different elements which are, in fact, related to human moral experience and the study of how they do in fact interact through the study of self, society and history. What I call 'moral philosophy' is the normative application of this to arguments about how human beings ought to act. Moral science informs moral philosophy because it provides us with reliable systematic knowledge of what human beings are and how they interact in society. Finally, what I call 'moral education' is the application of moral science and moral philosophy in a practical pedagogy which prepares the student and reader for practical moral decision-making in a modern society.

Ferguson saw himself as developing a scientific approach to the study of moral subjects. His conception of science is broadly conventional, a blend of Bacon and Newton similar to that of others in the Scottish Enlightenment.[41] But in Ferguson's case there is also another important influence: Aristotle. Ferguson's debt to Aristotle is not mediated by the scholastic adaptation of the ancient thinker. Instead Ferguson returns to the source and is inspired by Aristotle's own project. What I mean by this is that he sees that the basis of a successful understanding of what humans should do must be based on an accurate understanding of what they are and of the societies that they live in. Moral philosophy needs a solid foundation and that foundation must be based on solid evidence. As he puts it, 'notorious facts are foundation enough, upon which we may safely erect the fabric of moral science, so far as it is of any importance to mankind'.[42]

Ferguson's aim in the first volume of the *Principles* is to produce an empirically based account of human nature and human society. This was to be a matter of facts. As Ferguson would have it:

> the facts are presented not as discoveries, but as the data, from which to infer the judgements and conclusions of the second part, relating to the foundations of choice, or what man ought to wish for himself, for his country, and for mankind.[43]

And, lest we think that this is a position that Ferguson comes to later in life, we can consult the description of his project in *The Institutes of Moral Philosophy* (1769). Here he states that:

> Before we can ascertain rules of morality fitted to any particular nature, the fact relating to that nature should be known. Before we can ascertain rules of morality for mankind, the history of man's nature, his dispositions, his specific enjoyments and sufferrings, his condition and future prospects, should be known.[44]

The project remains the same throughout his career.

To be absolutely clear: it is central to Ferguson's methodology that empirically based moral science should precede and inform normative moral philosophy. The two are distinct modes of inquiry linked in a common enterprise. The clarity with which Adam Ferguson links together the two sides of his argument has led many to see his approach as one where the empirical and normative are indistinguishable. An example of this is where David Allan describes Ferguson as 'in no sense the purveyor of a descriptive science of society' and a 'shameless partisan for the cause of virtue'.[45] I think that Allan was wrong about this, and that Ferguson is both a moralist and a descriptive moral scientist, but more importantly that he was conscious of these two as distinct yet interdependent activities. The evidence for this comes in the repeated attempts to separate the descriptive 'science' from the prescriptive 'philosophy'. Ferguson, as Lisa Hill observes, operates with a 'procedure that is simultaneously empirical and normative',[46] but crucially he is clear that these are separate, though interdependent, aspects of his method. As Hill notes, Ferguson rarely lets his moral commitments 'interfere with the empirical evidence'.[47] There is a very simple reason behind this for Ferguson: insufficient attention to the distinct nature of these two modes of inquiry has retarded progress in both.

This can work in more than one way. In the case of his fellow Scottish thinkers Adam Smith and David Hume he thinks that they have correctly identified the distinction between a descriptive theory of human moral experience and a prescriptive moral philosophy.[48] The problem is that they have mistaken the former activity as the limit of their ambition and, in refusing to put the conclusions of their moral science to work in the service of a prescriptive account of morality, have left their systems half-finished.[49]

What humans do blame is different from what they ought to blame and 'The subject of morality has been greatly perplexed by the blending of these two questions together.'[50] Ferguson's point is that moral science can provide us with a history of moral opinions and with an account of human nature which will serve as the basis for a moral philosophy of what humans should do. The facts of what is done do not prevent us from choosing what is better. In Ferguson's view this is one place where ancient philosophy has the advantage over modern philosophy. While modern philosophy has correctly adopted the scientific technique as a secure means of inquiry, it has gone astray in jettisoning some of the old ideas such as that of a *summum bonum* and a systematic normative framework of morality that flows from it. The problem was not with these per se but rather with inattention to the separate tasks of the descriptive study of humans and then the identification of values appropriate to them.

For Ferguson the fact that we are social leads to the universal development of benevolence as a moral value. This gives him a bridge between the findings of his moral science and the prescriptive code of morality that he develops in the second volume of the *Principles*. Here he works through what he sees as the normative implications of the first volume. Man is 'formed for society, and is excellent in the degree in which he possesses the qualifications of an associate and a friend'.[51] Trite as this observation may seem it can serve Ferguson as the basis of his response to the major problems that he sees in civil society. What I have called Ferguson's moral philosophy then takes the form of an identification of the principles that ought to guide our moral decision-making. As he would have it:

> But there being some circumstances common in the situation and disposition of all mankind; such as, their being united in society, and concerned in what relates to their fellow creatures; men universally admire qualities which fit the individual to promote the good of mankind; as, wisdom, justice, courage, and temperance.[52]

Or again:

> The distinction of right and wrong is coeval with human nature: It is perceived without instruction, in acts of fidelity and beneficence, or of perfidy and malice. These are the topics of praise and blame, in every nation and in every age. That, indeed, which in one instance is considered a benefit, in another instance is considered as harm or detriment.[53]

For Ferguson the fact that we are social leads to the universal development of benevolence as a moral value. As he stressed in the opening chapters of the *Essay*, a human who lived in one of the imaginary states of nature or who had grown to maturity in isolation could tell us nothing about human behaviour. It is an empirical fact that humans are social; they are found in society everywhere and as a result they all come to display benevolence. Similarly, when humans come to cooperate in groups there are certain functions that arise from the very nature of communal life.

The 'Principle of Society in human nature'[54] and the 'fact' of human sociability mean that humans are social before they are rational. Man, according to Ferguson, 'is born in society, and, while unconscious of benefit or wrong, is anxiously preserved in his state'.[55] The development of society cannot be an act of calculated self-interest as some have supposed because humans were social before they were rational enough to form such a concept.[56] The move to the discussion of normative moral principles that might rest on this becomes possible because of this universality. Again, this is a position consistent across his writings but it receives its clearest statement in the *Principles*:

> Society, in which alone the distinction of right and wrong is exemplified, may be considered as the garden of God, in which the tree of knowledge of good and evil is planted; and in which men are destined to distinguish, and to chuse, among its fruits.[57]

Society is the 'atmosphere' or 'vital air' in which morality is 'kindled'.[58] But we need some additional steps in the argument to move from the fact that humanity is social to particular claims about the moral value of particular actions. This is because all human actions, good, evil or indifferent, exist in a social setting. Moral philosophy must identify from among these which social actions tend to the good of society. Evil is antisocial, but even evil acts take place in a social setting. So Ferguson believes that we can use benevolence to understand why it is that we should prefer actions that preserve society to those that threaten social cohesion. Crucially this is not because such actions are in our individual interest; instead it is because they embody a sense of the good derived from our sociability. Ferguson is then able to deploy proto-sociological arguments to discuss the development of the 'sense of a public'[59] within a society and from there to examine a number of social forces that may contribute to 'weaken the bands of society'[60] and break the acquired sense of 'mutual dependence'[61] that holds nations together.

Proto-Sociological Concerns in Moral Science

Having deployed moral science to provide a descriptive account of human behaviour in civil society, Ferguson is able to identify the potential danger of the separation of the human character created by the division of labour. This separation creates two major problems for Ferguson. The first of these is a problem of social cohesion. This is the empirical observation that a society where the distinction of statesman and warrior is allowed to take hold and where military service and skill become professionalised has a structural flaw that threatens the dissolution of the society. Part V and Part VI of the *Essay* represent an attempt to theorise such a decline and fall inspired largely by the experience of the Roman Republic. Ferguson's point is that nations rise and fall and the reasons for this can be identified by empirical study. The second is the problem of what to do about this.

Shifting to a normative mode, Ferguson then begins to identify prescriptive goals. Given that human beings are naturally social and that the ultimate good for humans is a social good (benevolence), then the structural problems faced by civil societies need a solution. If moral philosophy tells us that a civil society is a good society, one that allows us to pursue our normative ideals, then the potential dissolution of such a society is a pressing matter of moral concern. This observation then informs Ferguson's policy prescriptions. His support for a militia as a complement to the standing army, his educational programme that seeks to instil a sense of duty in those who will manage the state and his opposition to demagogues, to democracy and to radical politics are all driven by his identification of them as dangers to the stability of society.[62] Moral science has informed both the content of his normative moral philosophy through the identification of a *summum bonum* of benevolence and the particular problems that he saw as pressing for his own society, chiefly those that threaten the dissolution of the social bonds.

The usefulness of thinking about Ferguson in the context of his own ideas about moral science as a basis for moral philosophy is that it provides an important caveat against those who would read Ferguson as a nostalgic figure steeped in the civic republican tradition. Ferguson did indeed draw on republican or civic humanist ideas, but in doing so he was not backward-looking, nostalgic or a 'rear-guard'.[63] His thinking exists at a pivotal point where the 'limits'[64] of the civic tradition have been reached. As David Allan notes, Ferguson did not want to go back to the ancient republics because he saw that circumstances had changed and that society now meant civil society.[65] He is a student of civil society precisely because he saw that this form of society was new and needed to be studied if we were to create a secure basis for moral philosophy in these new types of society.

Conclusion

I began by asserting that my concern is not with Ferguson's place in the genesis of sociological ideas. Instead it is with the place of these ideas in Ferguson's thinking. In looking for the place of these ideas in Ferguson's thinking we discover that they are deeply embedded in his sense of his own project. His awareness that a descriptive theory of human life in society was a necessary prerequisite for a successful moral philosophy that could inform human attempts to address the problems generated by modern civil societies is central to his approach. My suggestion has been that the proto-sociological elements of Ferguson's methodology – his empiricism, conjectural history, focus on the social and socialisation, awareness of unintended consequences and ethnocentrism, and use of functionalist explanation, stadial theory, conflict sociology and myth as evidence – are part of a conscious attempt to create what he called a moral science. In developing this methodology Ferguson was quite aware that his own society was a new type of social formation and his development of the concept of civil society was an attempt to explore this, just as those passages which have been read since Karl Marx as anticipations of the idea of alienation and problems created by the division of labour point to the moral and political challenges of this new type of society. Moreover, the second part of Ferguson's project, his prescriptive moral philosophy, forms a part of the solution to these problems. His moral philosophy serves as a basis for a moral education that allows the leaders of civil society to guard against the problems that Ferguson has identified and inculcates in them a sense of service and duty that embodies the *summum bonum* of benevolence.

For Adam Ferguson a discussion of human values must be based on evidence drawn from a value-free observation of the nature of its subject, the human in society. It is perhaps fitting that a figure seen as a precursor of the 'value-free' discipline of sociology saw that such objectivity was necessary to the successful conduct of moral philosophy. In our academy the two are divided by jealously guarded disciplinary and methodological boundaries. Perhaps the lesson of looking into Ferguson as proto-sociologist is that it would be better for both sociology and moral philosophy if these boundaries were not so rigidly policed.

Notes

1. Donald G. MacRae, 'Adam Ferguson' in T. Raison (ed.), *The Founding Fathers of Social Science* (Harmondsworth: Penguin, 1969), pp. 17–26, p. 17. See Alan Swingewood, 'Origins of Sociology: The Case of the Scottish Enlightenment', *British Journal of Sociology* 21 (1970), pp. 164–80; Gladys Bryson, *Man and Society: The Scottish Inquiry of the Eighteenth Century* (Princeton: Princeton University Press, 1945); and Tom Bottomore and Robert Nisbet, *A History of Sociological Analysis* (London: Heinemann, 1978).
2. W. C. Lehman, *Adam Ferguson and the Beginnings of Modern Sociology* (New York: Columbia University Press, 1930); David Kettler, *Adam Ferguson: His Social and Political Thought* (New Brunswick, NJ: Transaction Press, 2005), 2nd ed.
3. On Ferguson and Montesquieu see Sheila Mason, 'Ferguson and Montesquieu: Tacit Reproaches?', *British Journal for Eighteenth*

Century Studies 11 (1988), pp. 193–203; Alexander Broadie, *Agreeable Connexions: Scottish Enlightenment Links with France* (Edinburgh: John Donald, 2012); and Donald Winch, *Adam Smith's Politics: An Essay in Historiographic Revision* (Cambridge: Cambridge University Press, 1978).

4. Duncan Forbes, 'Introduction' in Adam Ferguson, *An Essay on the History of Civil Society 1776*, ed. D. Forbes (Edinburgh: Edinburgh University Press, 1967), pp. xii–xli and Duncan Forbes, 'Natural Law and the Scottish Enlightenment' in R. H. Campbell and A. Skinner (eds), *The Origins and Nature of the Scottish Enlightenment* (Edinburgh: John Donald, 1982), pp. 186–204.
5. Kenneth Macdonald, 'Did British Sociology Begin with the Scottish Enlightenment?' in Plamena Panayotova (ed.), *The History of Sociology in Britain* (Cham: Palgrave Macmillan, 2019), pp. 37–69.
6. Craig Smith, *Adam Ferguson and the Idea of Civil Society: Moral Science in the Scottish Enlightenment* (Edinburgh: Edinburgh University Press, 2019), pp. 150–1.
7. John D. Brewer, 'Putting Adam Ferguson in His Place', *The British Journal of Sociology* 58 (2007), pp. 105–22, p. 106 also refers to Ferguson giving things a 'sociological twist', cited by John D. Brewer, 'Adam Ferguson and the Theme of Exploitation', *The British Journal of Sociology* 37 (1986), pp. 461–78, p. 473. See also John D. Brewer, 'Conjectural History, Sociology and Social Change in Eighteenth Century Scotland: Adam Ferguson and the Division of Labour' in D. McCrone, S. Kendrick and P. Straw (eds), *The Making of Scotland: Nations, Culture and Social Change* (Edinburgh: Edinburgh University Press, 1989), pp. 13–30.
8. Fania Oz-Salzberger, 'Introduction' in Adam Ferguson, *An Essay on the History of Civil Society*, ed. F. Oz-Salzberger (Cambridge: Cambridge University Press, 1994).
9. Christopher J. Berry, *Social Theory of the Scottish Enlightenment* (Edinburgh: Edinburgh University Press, 1997).
10. H. M. Höpfl, 'From Savage to Scotsman: Conjectural History in the Scottish Enlightenment', *Journal of British Studies* 17 (1978), pp. 19–40.
11. Ronald Hamowy, *The Scottish Enlightenment and the Theory of Spontaneous Order* (Carbondale, IL: Southern Illinois University Press, 1987); F. A. Hayek, 'The Results of Human Action not Human Design' in *Studies in Philosophy, Politics, and Economics* (London: Routledge and Kegan Paul, 1967), pp. 96–105; and Eugene Heath, 'Ferguson and the Unintended Emergence of Social

Order' in Eugene Heath and Vincenzo Merolle (eds), *Adam Ferguson: Philosophy, Politics and Society* (London: Pickering & Chatto, 2009), pp. 155–68.
12. Craig Smith, 'Adam Ferguson and Ethnocentrism in the Science of Man', *History of the Human Sciences* 26 (2013), pp. 52–67.
13. Kettler, *Adam Ferguson*.
14. Broadie, *Agreeable Connexions*; Lehman; *Adam Ferguson*; and Lisa Hill, *The Passionate Society: The Social, Political and Moral Thought of Adam Ferguson* (Dordrecht: Springer, 2006).
15. Lisa Hill, 'Eighteenth-Century Anticipations of the Sociology of Conflict: The Case of Adam Ferguson', *Journal of the History of Ideas* 62 (2001), pp. 281–99.
16. See Jean Cohen and Andrew Arato, *Civil Society and Political Theory* (Cambridge, MA: MIT Press, 1992); Ernest Gellner, *Conditions of Liberty: Civil Society and Its Rivals* (Harmondsworth: Penguin, 1994); Edward Shils, *The Virtue of Civility: Selected Essays on Liberalism, Tradition, and Civil Society*, ed. Steven Grosby (Indianapolis, IN: Liberty Fund, 1997); John Varty, 'Civic or Commercial? Adam Ferguson's Concept of Civil Society' in R. Fine and S. Rai (eds), *Civil Society: Democratic Perspectives* (London: Frank Cass, 1997), pp. 29–48; J. Ehrenberg, *Civil Society: The Critical History of an Idea* (New York: New York University Press, 1999), pp. 91–6; Richard Boyd, 'Reappraising the Scottish Moralists and Civil Society', *Polity* 23 (2000), pp. 101–25; Fania Oz-Salzberger, 'Civil Society in the Scottish Enlightenment' in K. Kaviraj and S. Khilnani (eds), *Civil Society: History and Possibilities* (Cambridge: Cambridge University Press, 2001), pp. 58–83; Christopher J. Berry, 'The Scottish Enlightenment and the Idea of Civil Society' in A. Martinos (ed.), *Sociadade Civil: Entre Miragen e Oportunidade* (Coimbria: Faculdade de Lettres, 2003), pp. 99–115; Brett Bowden, 'The Idea of Civilisation: Its Origins and Socio-Political Character', *Critical Review of International Social and Political Theory* 7 (2004), pp. 25–50.
17. See Ronald Meek, 'The Scottish Contribution to Marxist Sociology' in R. L. Meek (ed.), *Economics and Ideology and Other Essays* (London: Chapman and Hall, 1967), pp. 34–50; Ronald Hamowy, 'Adam Smith, Adam Ferguson, and the Division of Labour', *Economica* 35 (1968), pp. 249–59; Hiroshi Mizuta, 'Two Adams in the Scottish Enlightenment: Adam Smith and Adam Ferguson on Progress', *Studies in Voltaire* 191 (1981), pp. 182–99; Andrew Skinner, 'A Scottish Contribution to Marxist Sociology?' in I. Bradley and M. C. Howard (eds), *Classical and Marxian Sociology* (London:

Macmillan, 1982), pp. 95–121; Ted Benton, 'Adam Ferguson and the Enterprise Culture' in P. Hulme and L. Jordanova (eds), *The Enlightenment and Its Shadows* (London: Routledge, 1990), pp. 101–20; Lisa Hill, 'Adam Smith, Adam Ferguson and Karl Marx on the Division of Labour', *Journal of Classical Sociology* 7 (2007), pp. 339–66. More recently Ferguson and his fellow conjectural historians have been given a place in the development of ideas that would become the concept of race. See Silvia Sebastiani, 'National Character and Race: A Scottish Enlightenment Debate' in T. Ahnert and S. Manning (eds), *Character, Self, and Sociability in the Scottish Enlightenment* (London: Palgrave Macmillan, 2011), pp. 187–205 and Silvia Sebastiani, *The Scottish Enlightenment: Race, Gender, and the Limits of Progress* (London: Palgrave Macmillan, 2013). As Ferguson is a minor player in that discussion, I leave it aside for the purposes of this chapter.
18. Smith, *Adam Ferguson*, pp. 55, 77.
19. Annette Meyer, 'Ferguson's "Appropriate Stile" in Combining History and Science: The History of Historiography Revisited' in Eugene Heath and Vincenzo Merolle (eds), *Adam Ferguson: History, Progress and Human Nature* (London: Pickering & Chatto, 2008), pp. 131–45, pp. 140, 145.
20. Adam Ferguson, *An Essay on the History of Civil Society*, ed. Fania Oz-Salzberger (Cambridge: Cambridge University Press, [1767] 1995), pp. 7–16 (henceforth ECS).
21. Adam Ferguson, *Principles of Moral and Political Science*, 2 vols (New York: AMS Press, [1792] 1973), 1, p. 26 (henceforth Principles).
22. Principles 1, p. 48.
23. Adam Ferguson, *The Manuscripts of Adam Ferguson*, ed. Vincenzo Merolle (London: Pickering & Chatto, 2006), p. 83.
24. Principles 1, p. 135.
25. Principles 1, p. 218.
26. Principles 1, p. 221.
27. ECS p. 15.
28. Principles 1, p. 15.
29. ECS p. 119.
30. ECS p. 49, 83; Principles 1, p. 12; Adam Ferguson, *The History of the Progress and Termination of the Roman Republic*, University of Michigan: Historical Reprint Series (New York: J. C. Derby, 1856), p. 29.
31. Principles 1, p. vii; ECS p. 159.
32. Lisa Hill (*Passionate Society*, p. 102) is among those who see Ferguson's 'Providentialist functionalism' as an important indication of the

centrality of religion to his thinking. Crucially, though, the providential interpretation of history seldom trespasses on the descriptive account of the evolution of the practices under discussion.

33. ECS p. 28.
34. ECS pp. 77, 111–12.
35. Ronald L. Meek, *Social Science and the Ignoble Savage* (Cambridge: Cambridge University Press, 1976), p. 154.
36. For a discussion of how Ferguson's stadial theory differs from that of his peers see David Allan, *Adam Ferguson* (Aberdeen: AHRC Centre for Scottish and Irish Studies, 2006), p. 81 and Duncan Forbes ('Introduction', p. xxv) who point out that property and economic concerns have a less central role in Ferguson's account than Smith's, a point denied by Ronald Meek (*Social Science*, p. 150). Meek, rightly in my view, points out that, like Montesquieu and Hutcheson, Ferguson does not 'privilege' property and subsistence (*Social Science*, pp. 34–5) and provides a more sociologically sophisticated stadial theory than is appreciated by those who read Marxian determinism into him.
37. Berry, 'The Scottish Enlightenment and the Idea of Civil Society'.
38. ECS p. 207.
39. ECS p. 218.
40. Smith, *Adam Ferguson*.
41. Ferguson explicitly cites Bacon as an inspiration (Principles 1, p. 2), and cites Newton's principles of reasoning and empiricism with approval (Principles 2, pp. 16, 118).
42. Principles 1, p. 155. As he puts it elsewhere: 'I am ambitious to show that there is a science of manners or of Ethics, no less than of Jurisprudence or of Politics, and for this purpose would willingly point out a method, by which to derive the offices or duties of a virtuous life from principles at once so comprehensive and unquestionably evident, as to enable every person to fill up the detail for himself' (Principles 2, pp. 321–2).
43. Principles 1, p. 10.
44. Adam Ferguson, *Institutes of Moral Philosophy* (London: Routledge/Thoemmes Press, [1769] 1994), pp. 9–10 (henceforth Institutes).
45. Allan, *Adam Ferguson*, p. 21. Richard Sher takes a less extreme view and argues that Ferguson 'bound together his science of society and his ideology more tightly than did Hume – so tightly, in fact, that they frequently appear indistinguishable' (Richard B. Sher, *Church and University in the Scottish Enlightenment: The Moderate Literati of*

Edinburgh (Edinburgh: Edinburgh University Press, 1985), p. 196). While this seems closer to the truth of Ferguson's intentions, it suffers from the pejorative implications of the term ideology which suggest that Ferguson's political commitments shape his argument.
46. Hill, *Passionate Society*, p. 57.
47. Ibid. p. 7.
48. Smith, *Adam Ferguson*, pp. 25–7.
49. For discussions of Ferguson as moral philosopher see Gordon Graham, 'Adam Ferguson as a Moral Philosopher', *Philosophy* 88 (2013), pp. 511–25; Eugene Heath, 'Ferguson's Moral Philosophy' in Vincenzo Merolle (ed.), *The Manuscripts of Adam Ferguson* (London: Pickering & Chatto, 2006), pp. xlvii–lxxvi.
50. Institutes p. 109. See also Principles 1, p. 161.
51. Principles 2, p. 41.
52. Institutes p. 39.
53. Principles 1, p. 300.
54. Principles 1, p. 26.
55. Principles 1, p. 30.
56. ECS p. 23.
57. Principles 1, p. 268.
58. Principles 1, pp. 268–9.
59. ECS p. 211.
60. ECS p. 182.
61. ECS p. 182.
62. Adam Ferguson, *Reflections Previous to the Establishment of a Militia* (London: R. & J. Dodsley, 1756).
63. Sher, *Church and University*, p. 398; Richard B. Sher, 'Adam Ferguson, Adam Smith and the Problem of National Defence', *Journal of Modern History* 61 (1989), pp. 240–68, pp. 244, 263–4.
64. John Robertson, 'The Scottish Enlightenment at the Limits of the Civic Tradition' in I. Hont and M. Ignatieff (eds), *Wealth and Virtue: The Shaping of Political Economy in the Scottish Enlightenment* (Cambridge: Cambridge University Press, 1983), pp. 137–78.
65. Allan, *Adam Ferguson*, p. 118. See Anna Plassart, *The Scottish Enlightenment and the French Revolution* (Cambridge: Cambridge University Press, 2015), pp. 145–51, who reads Ferguson as part of the republican tradition, but as free of nostalgia.

5

'Partly social, partly selfish': The Social Evolutionism of Henry Home, Lord Kames

R. J. W. Mills

Henry Home, Lord Kames (1696–1782) was one of the most prominent Scottish social theorists and, through his patronage and example, led the way for his contemporaries.[1] He experimented with the sort of social evolutionary history that we associate most with the Scottish Enlightenment, applying this style of thinking to a wide array of topics. He was particularly dedicated to one of the fundamental questions of the Enlightenment's 'science of human nature': whether man is fit for society. Having first explored this issue in his *Essays on the Principles of Morality and Natural Religion* (1751), Kames's final answer, found in *Sketches of the History of Man* (1774), was that we are 'partly social, partly selfish' but benefit most from being social.[2] In exploring how he got to this point, we get a sense of Kames's perspective that social context determines how human nature works. Despite this, Kames does not usually appear with any prominence in accounts of the history of sociology, even ones that view the social theorists of the Scottish Enlightenment as pioneering figures in that discipline's formation.[3] He does appear with greater prominence, by contrast, in accounts of the history of anthropology.[4] E. E. Evans-Pritchard went as far as to claim that 'we have all the ingredients of anthropological theory in the nineteenth century and even at the present day' in works such as those of the Scottish jurist.[5] I want to make the case here that Kames warrants inclusion alongside Adam Smith, Adam Ferguson and John Millar as proto-sociologists, and will do so for similar reasons as those cited for describing Kames as a proto-anthropologist. After all, musing on Kames's contribution, Evans-Pritchard elsewhere opined that 'all the Scottish moral philosophers wrote the same books'.[6]

Kames was interested in man as a 'social being' and with charting the 'progress of men in society'.[7] He contributed to that move, necessary for the emergence of sociology, away from an understanding of a fixed human nature that existed prior to and was unaffected by participation in society. Kames believed that there were universal principles of human nature, but how they developed was influenced by the social conditions of the individual. The leading thinkers of the Scottish Enlightenment are often seen, alongside Montesquieu and sometimes Rousseau, as encouraging a new perception of human behaviour as a product of society.[8] Due to this, the Scots and Montesquieu dealt with the issue of social diversity in a way earlier social contract theorists of politics, such as Hobbes and Locke, could not. A historical argument can be made here that Kames, through his patronage, support and conversation as much as his publications, encouraged the thinkers of the Scottish Enlightenment to historicise their thought about man and society. This chapter, though, will only briefly survey Kames's historical role as a father-figure to the Scottish Enlightenment's social theory, before directing the bulk of our attention to his writings.

If the great achievement of Scottish Enlightenment social theory was to historicise the study of human nature and society then Kames was at the forefront of this development.[9] As such, he has been treated unfairly by his exclusion from histories of sociology. The most general methodological principles we can extract from his writing are (1) that the various institutions and behaviours of specific societies can be understood in terms of a trajectory of societal progress from savagery to civilisation, with his later writings viewing this as a stadial progression of societies based on changes in the mode of subsistence; (2) that those institutions and behaviours developed in an interconnected fashion, and should not be viewed separately; (3) that when substantiating claims about societal change we should draw evidence from societies across geography and time; and (4) that humans possess a common nature made up of inherent principles of behaviour, but how these principles develop differ according to the societal circumstances in which the individual finds themselves. All of these place Kames firmly at the centre of the proto-sociological thinking attributed to the Scottish Enlightenment and not, per Ronald Meek long ago, on its 'fringes'.[10] Indeed, one possible reason for Kames's frequent exclusion from the Scottish proto-sociological mainstream is that the pioneering discussions of the Scottish Enlightenment's relationship to sociology, which set the agenda of subsequent discussions, all viewed Kames primarily as a legal theorist of limited relevance to social theory.[11] This was, I suggest, an oversight.

Kames as a Significant Figure for Scottish Enlightenment 'Sociology'?

Kames was a principal local stimulus behind the emergence of the Scottish school of social theory. Especially after he was appointed to the bench in 1752 (and acquired the title of Lord Kames), he was a patron of many of the leading thinkers of the Scottish Enlightenment. His biographer Alexander Fraser Tytler claimed that, especially after 1752 but also before, Kames utilised his many 'opportunities of promoting every species of improvement'.[12] Kames's 'example and encouragement' were 'beneficial in exciting a literary spirit' amongst the professionals of mid-eighteenth-century Edinburgh.[13] It was likely just as much with regard to Kames's acts as a patron as his philosophical writings that Adam Smith reputedly opined that 'we must every one of us acknowledge Kames for our master'.[14]

Similarly, Kames had a key role in the early dissemination of the stadial history of social institutions. The periodisation of societal development based on mode of subsistence is present in embryonic form in the Appendix to Kames's *Essays upon Several Subjects concerning British Antiquities* (1747). Something similar was present in Kames's *Principles*, where he charted the importance of man's 'hoarding appetite', as much as 'reason and reflection', in driving forward changes in subsistence.[15] But the brief discussion in the *Principles* was shorn of any societal elements and just outlined man's shift from hunting due to the precarity of subsistence, first by the 'contrivance' of domesticating animals and then by cultivating land.[16] Similarly, the account in *British Antiquities* focused on a shift from foraging to agriculture, rather than the three-stages approach – hunting, shepherding, farming – subsequently adopted. The explicit periodisation of stages of society is only fully fleshed out in Tract III of the *Historical Law-Tracts* (1758), where Kames charts the progress of conceptions of property.[17]

Kames's discussion of the distinct stages of society was not the first published by an eighteenth-century Scot, as Sir John Dalrymple had done this the previous year in his *Essay towards a General History of Feudal Property in Great Britain* (1757).[18] But Dalrymple acknowledged that he wrote his *Essay* with access to Kames's legal papers, presumably including the *Historical Law-Tracts* which Kames had composed several years before its publication.[19] Complicating matters is the likelihood that Adam Smith developed his own stadial theory when he was giving his lectures in Edinburgh (c. 1750–1), which Kames probably attended and patronised.[20] Noticeably, Kames's 1751 *Principles*, a work about man as a 'social being', did not discuss societal change in stadial terms and only in the 1758 second edition did he incorporate such language.[21] It has also been conjectured that Smith had Kames in mind in 1755 when he criticised others for borrowing from his lectures without crediting him.[22] What we can say, however, is that Kames published several historically minded treatments of human behaviours and institutions that embodied the new enlightened Scottish approach, especially in the *Historical Law-Tracts* and *Sketches*.

Kames was at the forefront of the Scottish Enlightenment's grappling with how to develop new methodologies for studying human nature and society in historical context. Björn Eriksson has argued the Scots' self-awareness they were going through an epistemological rupture about how human nature should be studied reflects that they were beginning to undertake a new form of study. Kames is as important a figure here as Smith, Millar or Ferguson. This is not least the case for his famous passage in the *Historical Law-Tracts* where he outlined how he dealt with charting the course of historical change and contemplated the role of writing histories based on 'conjectural facts'.[23] Kames's mechanistic definition of man, for example, as a complex machine consisting of many 'different springs of action' which was influenced in its workings by exogenous factors rendered human nature, to borrow Andreas Rahmatian's phrase, as 'similar to a research object in Newtonian physics'.[24] The various progressive histories that Kames undertook, especially in the *Sketches*, indicate a thinker concerned with how to proceed with synthesising the wealth of information he has in the pursuit of the subtopics of the 'history of mankind' and trying to understand how these factors influenced

Kames's Understanding of 'Society'

While he did not outline a detailed explanation at any one point, Kames reiterated his understanding of what society was in all his writings from the *Principles* onwards. 'Society' refers to groups of two or more individuals consistently living with or near each other and collaborating for their 'mutual assistance'.[25] The 'true spirit of society' consisted in enjoying 'mutual benefits, and in making the industry of individuals profitable to others as well as to themselves'.[26] The 'great advantage of society' is that the 'cooperation of many' allows us to develop 'arts, manufactures and commerce', leading to lives of plenty, security and the means by which we can develop fully as humans.[27] The best context for individual flourishing is the 'well regulated society' in which man is capable of 'high improvements'.[28] To endure, society must 'provide against mutual injuries' and there must be 'mutual trust and reliance upon engagements' and 'favours received should be thankfully repaid'.[29] As we will see below, the conditions for true society only emerged following the establishment of agriculture.

Kames maintained that the character of social interaction was heavily influenced by the society's mode of subsistence. This position first appeared in embryonic form in the Appendix to Kames's *British Antiquities* (1747), but with many elements that changed by the publication of *Historical Law-Tracts*. The first mode of subsistence was not hunting or fishing but foraging. When 'acorns were the food of man' and his wants were 'easily supplied', there was 'neither use nor appetite for society'.[30] Feeding off fruits and nuts, humans 'originally' lived in 'scattered habitations, with little intercourse, except among the members of the same family'.[31] The first social groupings were 'originally formed by accidental circumstances' and governments, likewise, emerged either as an 'effect of choice [or] some measure of accident'.[32] Man left the foraging life following the beginning of the 'culture of corn', which in turn led to 'more extensive intercourse', 'mutual assistance' and eventually to humans herding 'together in towns and villages'.[33] Social proximity led to increased 'opposition of interests', the need to appeal to judges in the form of 'men of weight and probity' within the society, from there fixed judges and then on to established governments.[34]

Kames's account of the relationship between extent of society and mode of subsistence was different a decade later. In *Historical Law-Tracts*, he now saw primeval humans as hunters not foragers. But, like foragers, hunters were 'averse to society', living in 'scattered habitations with little intercourse' beyond their own families.[35] Kames now saw the next stage of society being the 'shepherd life', which led to the 'conjunction of families for mutual defence', though they were bound together only by a 'local connection'.[36] The social tie between shepherds is 'slight indeed' as it involves only arrangements for responding to an occasional event, such as an immediate threat from other tribes.[37] In both the hunter-fisher and shepherd stage of life, the 'bonds of society' are 'too lax' for the benefits to be truly felt.[38] Indeed, Kames can be read here as claiming that neither the hunter nor shepherd life is actually a social one.

Society only really comes into proper existence with the establishment of agriculture and only makes a 'capital figure' when both 'husbandry and commerce flourish'.[39] Key here are the establishment of a reliable form of subsistence, fixity of dwellings and food production and the emergence of both labour undertaken in pursuit of a common goal and the division of labour. The growth of specific jobs in such a division places individuals into an 'intimate society of mutual support' and 'compacts them within a narrow space'.[40] The demands of agricultural production place the individual into an 'intimate union among a multitude of individuals', leading to the discovery of 'social duties' and the beginning of the process by which the social passions come to influence us as much as our dissocial ones.[41] By bringing 'men together for mutual assistance', agriculture encourages the establishment of the sophisticated notions of property beyond mere possession, leading to the 'performance of promises and covenants'.[42] The overlapping factors of increased social interaction, cooperation and mutual duties, the growing importance of property lead, after a time, to ascertaining and enforcement of laws to maintain social cooperation and thus to government. Society predated politics.

The preceding suggests Kames warrants being placed alongside Smith, Ferguson and Millar as 'genuine precursors who defined both a method of inquiry and a concept of society as a distinct object of study'.[43] We find in Kames the sort of 'conception of a social system of organic sociality [and] routinized acts' held to be characteristic of early sociology.[44] But before we get ahead of ourselves, we should note that in his progressive histories of society Kames is interested in human nature first and foremost, rather than society. The overriding intention in the *Principles* and *Sketches*, for example, is to answer the question of whether man is a social creature and, if so, to what extent and why. The unit of analysis, ultimately, is human nature as it exists in and out of society, with Kames interested primarily in how specific aspects of human nature developed with the context of certain forms of societal interaction. The object he always has view in these two books is not 'society' but 'man' – hence Book II of the *Sketches* is named 'The Progress of Man in Society'. Thus while Kames has a keen sense of what society is, what types of society there are, the criteria we should use to taxonomise those societies and the plotting of societal development, he is fundamentally interested in how different societies affect our pursuit of the worldly perfection of our providentially framed nature as human beings.

Man as a Social Animal

Kames was concerned not with Georg Simmel's question of 'how is society possible?' but with the prior question of whether man was 'qualified for society' in the first place.[45] In this, he was contributing to one of the European Enlightenment's major intellectual endeavours: ascertaining whether humanity was naturally sociable or whether it needed some form of enforced socialisation and punitive control for society to endure. Beneath Kames's aphoristic claim that 'man, by his nature, is fitted for society, and society is fitted for man by its manifold conveniences' lay a complicated perspective on human sociality.[46] Humans were characterised by what Kant would later term 'unsocial sociability': humans were clearly social creatures but had natures consisting of both social and dissocial passions that needed to be managed in certain ways to ensure the continuation and flourishing of society and its members.[47]

Kames argued that the inherent tendencies of our common human nature, with our innate moral sense at the helm, are both the cause and 'cement' of society.[48] Much of the *Principles* and the *Sketches* should be read as Kames explicating those aspects of human nature that made us social beings and made societies endure. His accounting of the social qualities of human nature, developed especially in the *Principles*, is an explicitly a priori argument: without these innate principles, society would never come into existence and would never endure. We possess, for example, a shared moral sense. This makes society possible: should we not all participate in this shared sense of right and wrong, morals would be as unique as individual faces, and conflict would be the inevitable result. The most important judgement within the moral sense keeping society together is our sense of justice.[49] It is also only in society that we can be truly happy, as many aspects of our natures can only be practised and satisfied in interaction with others. We are 'fitted by our nature for society' because of the 'natural affections' of 'pity, benevolence, friendship, love, dislike of solitude and desire of company'.[50] Kames, likewise, holds that we have a sense of property, which tells us what objects are 'ours' and what objects are 'theirs'. This 'sense of property owes not its existence to society'; rather it is society that 'owes its existence to the sense of property'.[51] Kames does not believe we have a fully formed set of beliefs about possessions, but rather holds that our inherent sense of property informs and develops as a consequence of life in society. Other inherent tendencies of human nature central to the form of society include, for example, our 'principles of veracity and fidelity'.[52] We tend to tell the truth and we tend to keep our promises, and we need to do both for society to endure.

Yet Kames's discussion of society in the *Sketches* sees this understanding of human nature placed into historical context. The *Principles* were written to 'illustrate the nature of man, as a social being', yet contained very little of the historicised treatment of human nature found subsequently in the *Sketches*.[53] The position was very different in Book II of the *Sketches*, where Kames was concerned with explaining how the findings of his studies in the 'natural history of man' should inform the issue of whether humans are sociable creatures. The gradual but never final victory of the social passions over the dissocial was to be understood in contexts of increasing socialisation in situations of growing plenty and the division of labour. Humans became fit for society through socialisation itself, over time and influenced by historical processes of long duration, especially changes to the means of subsistence.

The problem Kames faced in the *Sketches*, having spent twenty years scouring travel literature and ancient histories for examples of human behaviour and institutions, was that the anthropological testimony of mankind was one of frequent societal breakdown, persecution, violence and oppression. The 'chief articles in the history of every state' demonstrate that societies are plagued by 'envy, malice, revenge, treachery, deceit, avarice, ambition, &c &c' and are regularly destroyed by faction.[54] Similarly, 'all histories are full of the cruelty and desolation occasioned by differences in religious tenets'.[55] Surveying this accumulated material, Kames described himself as 'utterly at a loss' at reconciling the joys and horrors of man's life in society.[56] The answer he developed following taking a 'second view of the natural history of man' was twofold.[57] We have to first accept that human nature is a 'compound of principles and passions, some social, some dissocial'.[58] And then we must realise that God has set the social scene as the location where we are to face down challenges in ways that allow us to undertake virtuous actions befitting our nature as humans.

Similar to Ferguson, whose *Essay on the History of Civil Society* (1767) he admired, Kames believed that conflict is not only inherent in society but it is the very basis of human flourishing.[59] Any society in which the dissocial passions had been extirpated would be dull, unchallenging and ultimately would render the individual weak and oversensitive. Conflict and discord are necessary, lest we become morally and physically flabby: 'agitation is requisite to the mind, as well as the body'; it is the 'element of man, and the life of society'.[60] The challenges we face by the dissocial passions both of ourselves and of others give us an opportunity as individuals to be tested, learn and show character, and thus live virtuous and meaningful lives. To be engaged in activity of both sorts is for man to be 'in his element, and in high spirits'.[61] We learn to inure ourselves from distress and misfortune; the practice hardens us; we become brave. Without agitation, challenge or conflict, we sink 'into languor and despondence' – we would descend into nothing more than 'an oyster or a sensitive plant'.[62] A 'uniform life of peace, tranquillity and security' would render life 'tasteless'.[63]

Kames here was arguing against two themes in the debate over humanity's purported sociability. The first was the desirability of an earlier golden age untainted by the social horrors that Kames had enumerated. Regardless of whether it ever existed, the supposedly perfect society of the golden age would provide no motivation for exercise of either body or mind. In such a scenario, humans would become soft simpletons; underdeveloped versions of themselves unable to attain the potential of a fully exercised human nature. Evil both of the natural and moral kind thus 'contributes more to the enjoyment of life, as well as to the improvement of our faculties and passions, than an uniform state, without variety, and without hopes and fears'.[64] Conversely, Kames sought to distinguish his claim from Bernard Mandeville's argument that our private vices (say, vanity satisfied via conspicuous consumption) resulted in public benefits (thus stimulus of the economy and thence prosperity). It is not vicious action itself that leads to benign social outcomes. It is the existence of vice that provides us with an opportunity to be virtuous, and it is the virtuous action that leads to the beneficial social outcome, not the original evil. The evils we face are for our ultimate good: we can 'rest on the faith, that whatever is, is the best'.[65]

Kames's position that agitation in society is necessary to enable us to reach our full potential as humans butts up against the materialistic, mechanistic and (at least in the *Principles*) deterministic elements of his conception of human nature. In the *Principles*, Kames argued that God had placed within human nature a 'deceitful feeling' that we possessed free will and were subject to a long chain of causes and effects put into motion by the supreme being.[66] A quote from the *Principles* captures this conception:

> Man is a complex machine, composed of various principles of motion, which may be conceived as so many springs or weights, counteracting or balancing one another. When these are accurately adjusted, the movement of life is beautiful, because regular and uniform. But if some springs or weights be withdrawn, those which remain, acting now without opposition for their antagonists, will disorder the balance, and derange the whole machine.[67]

What was developed in the *Sketches* more fully was the argument that the determining factors on which principles of action move the human machine is the character of social interaction and the mode of subsistence. We can borrow here Christopher Berry's notion of the 'stickiness' of human behaviours and institutions, with Kames depicting established social practices as 'riveting men to their location situation'.[68] The existence of a set of inherent principles of action that function under the influence of social context means that societies are characterised by social conformity of shared inner conviction and behaviour.[69]

While humans share a 'common nature', the principles of action only 'ripen' to full functionality in societies characterised by secure subsistence, consistent sociality and political stability – constitutive of what Kames often terms a 'well-ordered state'.[70] Life in the earlier stages of society is characterised by insecurity of subsistence and threat of harm from within one's own tribe, other tribes, natural events like storms and from wild animals. Such a social context means that certain principles of action, especially fear, dominate over other principles of action – we are less than fully human if our social surroundings are unsafe. The growth of security and stability leads to a concurrent growth in the fully-roundedness of our humanity. In such situations, we benefit from a process of constant, consistent interaction with others, in which our repeated experience of specific kinds of predictable, reliable and safe social engagement leads to the internal balancing of our innate principles of action and the realisation of our full humanity. The previously domineering passion of fear 'lessens gradually as our circle of acquaintance enlarges' and as we develop 'consciousness of security in the social state'.[71]

In the *Principles*, Kames mainly framed the 'progress of society' as a shift from the savage state to that of civil society which resulted from incremental improvement over the long term. Following his immersion in historical research in the years after publication of the *Principles*, Kames now viewed the development of society in stadial terms. In the savage stage, 'man is almost all body, with a very small proportion of mind', whereas in the 'maturity of civil society, he is complete both in mind and body'.[72] Outside of society, man is a 'timid animal' due to his inherent weakness as an individual.[73] In the hunter-state, man becomes bolder, crueller and more violent, influenced by the practice of slaughtering animals for food. The second stage of society, shepherding, is a 'calm and sedentary life' that softens the 'harsh manners of hunters'.[74] Agriculture, the beginning of civilisation, cultivates benevolence because it requires the 'union of many hands in one operation'.[75] In doing so, he identified the specific moments along the 'refinement [of] our nature' and the growing 'prevalence of the social affections in the progress of society'.[76]

We become sociable in contexts where sociability is possible. Unlike some of his German Enlightenment counterparts, there is no way of reading Kames as a moral relativist. Kames believed in a suprasocial, immutable standard of right and wrong, which scholars have usually identified as being framed by a Stoic understanding of the natural order of things. Man has a fixed nature given to him by God, which only develops fully in situations of stable social existence in which the individual interacts constantly with other humans. There are universal and true standards for human behaviour, and these are rendered clear to us by the functioning of our common human nature. The diversity of social contexts in which humans act greatly influences the precise character of how their innate senses manifest themselves, and occasionally Kames writes in providentialist terms of how well-suited specific behaviours are to specific levels of social development. While he clearly viewed moderately sized agricultural and commercial societies with limited luxury consumption as the ideal form for human flourishing, he also held that the 'spring and principles of man are adjusted with admirable wisdom to his external circumstances',[77] which is to say that the workings of the inner nature of the hunter-fisher have been providentially framed to suit that situation, even if that situation is not the best form of human life. Kames believed we could, and he did, chart a trajectory of progress towards more perfect forms of human behaviour and sociality. Different societies can be judged according to whether they align with our common human nature or whether they pervert that nature. Indeed, the *Sketches* sees Kames trying to inform his readers about what needs to change in developed societies to stop them from degenerating: to understand the progress of society is to be able to change it.

This can be illuminated by examining how Kames thought about commerce and 'commercial society'. What is important here is not bartering between individuals, which is as old as humanity itself, but the employment of individuals in commerce.[78] For Kames, the emergence of significant commerce does not entail a different mode of subsistence, for most societies at least.[79] This is clear from a passage which is often read as Kames arguing for a four stages theory of society:

> In the temperate climates of the old world, there is great uniformity in the gradual progress of men from the savage state to the highest civilization; beginning with hunting and fishing, advancing to flocks and herds, and then to agriculture and commerce.[80]

The enumeration of stages here is in a series of couples (hunting *and* fishing, flocks *and* herds, and agriculture *and* commerce). He uses the same coupling of 'agriculture and commerce' when arguing for the necessity of salutary laws.[81] More importantly, as mentioned above, society reaches its perfection when 'husbandry and commerce' flourish together. However, significant commerce (that is, more than bartering) is not quite coeval with agriculture, however, as the former first requires the creation of surplus by the latter. Kames views industry, manufactures and commerce as emerging in conditions of abundance established by successful agriculture.[82] The development of this trifecta is unlike previous transformations of society, as the latter involved entirely new modes of subsistence, for example from hunting to shepherding.

The analysis of the role of commerce in Book II of the *Sketches* often takes the form of finding the right balance between agriculture and commerce within a society. To function best, Kames believed, societies need to rely on homegrown agriculture, in terms both of being self-reliant and of preventing the moral, physical and military weakness that results from opulence and luxury, but also require some commerce to enable improvement of arts and manufactures.[83] Kames spends much of Book II warning his readers about the perils of Britain becoming too much of a 'manufacturing and commercial country' at the expense of agriculture, and the dangers of its transformation into a 'manufacturing and commercial people', a development which threatens moral breakdown and military weakness.[84]

Much stands out for us here. Firstly, given that the Scots are regularly and fairly criticised for not explaining the shift from one stage of life to another, Kames is very clear about the processes involved in the emergence of commerce out of agriculture – be these, for example, the emergence of the division of labour, the establishment of more complex notions of property or the importance of food surpluses. Secondly, Kames's critique of commerce is clearly framed in the language of early modern republicanism and it is plausible that the traditional character of his assessment of 'commercial states' sets him apart from subsequent sociological treatments.[85]

Thirdly, and more boldly, I would argue that far from being the perfection of social development, Kames believed that 'commercial states' were corrupt societies unmoored from agriculture that soon degenerated and were conquered by more morally and militarily vigorous neighbours.[86] Two examples here are the Venetian Republic and Carthage, both 'commercial states' in which the people were 'all employed in arts, manufactures, and navigation'.[87] And both found that the wealth created by their commerce 'extinguished patriotism', rendered their male population 'effeminate' and their politics 'unjust, violent, and tyrannical', and raised the prospect of ultimate financial ruin having bankrupted their neighbours.[88] The perfect form of society is one in which there is both mature agriculture and significant commerce, with the two in balance. Primarily commercial societies are ones in which things have gone awry. While we can identify in the *Sketches* an implicit four stages model of society in the sense that commercial societies emerged after agricultural ones, the former are not an improvement on the latter but a degenerative development.

Government and Patriotism

A key innovative feature of enlightened Scottish social theory was that it explored not political society but civil society. If this is one marker of the emergence of sociological thought, Kames epitomised it.[89] Admittedly, he did not consistently invoke the terminology of 'civil society' like Adam Ferguson, to be deployed in distinction from 'political society'. Kames does use the term with that meaning on occasion, but he often also uses it to refer to a highly developed, refined society.[90] It remains true that Kames has the social unit rather than the political unit in view, and that the former exists separate from and yet is foundational to politics. This leads Kames to develop insights on how the nature of a society informs its political character.

As part of this, Kames shared with Ferguson, Smith and Millar the perspective that government did not appear as the result of an intended act of contract or agreement between peoples *per* seventeenth-century social contract theory but as something growing alongside the development of subsistence, property and the changing quality of social interaction. In *Historical Law-Tracts*, Kames averred that it is a 'universal maxim' that 'the advances of government towards perfection are strictly proportioned to the advances of the society towards intimacy of union'.[91] In the *Sketches*, however, the great expansion of political authority and the extent and enforcement of law occurs at a very specific moment in the progress of society where the dissocial passions threaten societal collapse. Kames identifies this process as evidence that 'providence extracts order out of confusion'.[92]

Once society reaches the agricultural stage of development, strong government becomes necessary for its continuation. In the hunting state, instead of government there is authority 'exercised by heads of families'.[93] In the shepherd state, similarly, society elders come together to resolve disputes but there are no courts or supra-familial umpires. Things change with agriculture. Partly this is an issue of demography: 'government is essential to a society of any extent' and agriculture allows for greater food production and thus increased population size.[94] But it is primarily to do with the need to quell the 'passions inflamed by opulence' that agriculture, and the subsequent progress in the arts, manufactures and commerce, bring about.[95] Men begin to trample over their innate sense of justice and honour in pursuit of the gratification of newly aroused selfish desires. These further agitate the dissocial passions, leading to a multiplication of the 'causes of discord' which 'threaten a total dissolution of society'.[96] Societal breakdown is precluded only by the 'unwearied, though silent, operation of the social appetite'.[97]

It is at this moment that societies submit themselves to greater political authority. This process is driven by the workings of the social appetites and moral sense, rather than by the imposition of authority by the already powerful onto the weak or by the lawgiver-figure found in Machiavelli's *Prince* or Rousseau's *Social Contract*. In times of intense societal discord men, by 'dire experience', realise that 'they must either renounce society or qualify themselves for it'.[98] The lesson learnt from 'infinite struggles' is that men prefer to be in society with others than in continual conflict with them.[99] The 'universal conqueror' of rebellious man is neither reason nor the power of the strongest but human nature itself, in the form of our innate appetite for society.[100] Emerging out of the horrors of human interaction wracked by the dissocial passions, we become 'solicitous about the good-will of others; and here to justice and good manners'.[101] Having come close to losing all the benefits of society, men are now 'better qualified ... than formerly' to live socially.[102]

While our innate social affection drove this realisation, it was demonstrably not sufficient alone to ward off the dissocial passions resulting from the economic transformation brought about by the establishment of agriculture. Instead, the principal means that emerged for escaping the threat of such collapse was the formation of strong and stable government enforcing property laws backed up by the threat of punishment. Government enforced 'perpetual restraint' of behaviour that 'deadens even the most fervid passions'.[103] In conditions where doing wrong will get you punished by a force greater than a rival individual, men 'acquire a habit of repressing their turbulent passions'.[104] Through constant enforcement, men become 'by degrees regular and orderly' in their social intercourse and are 'easily restrained from doing wrong'.[105] The 'authority of good government' and the 'restraint of law' encourage the return of stability and predictability over social interaction, leading to the resurgence of the 'kindly affections' and our 'appetite for society', calming the temper and sweetening our manners.[106] The establishment of government came at a moment of general exhaustion amongst society's members recoiling from constant discord, which is to say there is still an element of a social compact about Kames's account of the formation of government, even if it is placed in a broader historical context and lacks the specific moment of all individuals coming together.

Strong, reliable government according to known, fixed rules meant that the severity of punishment could decline. Punishment for transgressions is necessarily mild in early societies because there is barely any sense of joint government over tribal families. Punishments increase in rigour in line with government's authority over a people that is 'not yet well disciplined' and battling over the spoils of agricultural opulence.[107] Recalcitrant men are broken into sociability and eventually 'become regular and orderly under a steady administration'.[108] From this position punishment can become milder. As Kames summarises, 'thus government, after passing through all the intermediate degrees from extreme mildness to extreme severity, returns at last to its original temper of mildness and humanity'.[109] There is a symbiotic socialisation element here too: the newfound mildness of society teaches all individuals, including sovereigns and magistrates, to 'moderate their turbulent passions' such that 'mild and courtly behaviour' take over in newly polished, sociable agricultural and commercial societies.[110]

The fact that major steps in the progress of society are ultimately predicated upon the features of universal human nature is also evident in Kames's discussion of the appropriate extent for a well-ordered society. The most appropriate size of society is one large enough that we are not near our enemies, but not so large that we lose our ties with our fellow countrymen. Hunter societies were small and the proximity of individuals to others engendered 'discord and resentment without end'.[111] The establishment of agriculture, and with it arts, manufactures and commerce, allows for population increases. People are removed 'farther from their enemies', and this moderate distance 'renders them more gentle'.[112] This includes urban living, where we can be anonymous in the crowd and choose our social interactions. Ironically, then, the lack of unavoidable interaction with other fellow human beings beyond our own families allows the individual to 'relish the comforts of social life'.[113]

Attachment to our country and our fellow countrymen is the height of the social affections. A patriotic people is always 'pure and correct'.[114] Our awareness of our membership of a group or society, and our attachment to that society, however, develop in line with the stage of social development. While members in a tribe of hunters are part of a group united by a common language and a shared goal in capturing prey, they have 'no notion of a *patria*; and scarce any notion of society'.[115] The notion of society – mutual assistance, shared goals – they do have is that inspired by specific expeditions against enemies of their tribe or in the hunting of wild beasts. Shepherds have a clearer sense of common interest, Kames holds, but not quite a sense of a *patria*, given their nomadic existence. With the establishment of agriculture, fixed dwellings and property and, soon after, regular government, we find a sense of patriotism emerging.

Things go awry, however, if societies expand beyond the possibilities of maintaining broad social connections. Life in large states can weaken our social links because we are no longer in direct contact with members of our group. The weaker our social ties, the less our social affections direct our actions and the more selfish we become. We still, however, seek the society of groups. Thus, within larger societies, we split up into 'orders, associations, fraternities, and divisions' where we are better able to maintain 'social connections'.[116] Humans are not natural cosmopolitans. We retain a competitiveness and hostility towards nearby societies, which Kames sees as beneficial, when within limits, to social cohesion and common defence.[117] Our social appetites do not and cannot extend to the whole of humanity. We are designed for and are satisfied by social participation within 'moderate bounds'.[118] If we are placed into social scenarios in which we are held to be members of some tremendously large body (say, as Europeans rather than Britons) then our social affections weaken for lack of tangible objects and the dissocial passions can rise once again.[119]

Kames has a similar judgement about the strength of the 'bonds of society', by which he meant the demands that the society can legitimately place on the individual.[120] The 'perfection of human society' involves establishing a 'just degree of union' between preserving individual 'freedom and independency' and maintaining societal 'peace and good order'.[121] While they need to be of a certain strength for individuals to feel the benefit of social interaction, these bonds may 'also be overstretched'.[122] Societies in which the fruits of the individual's industry are dedicated to the common interest are 'unnatural and uncomfortable'.[123] Personal liberty is destroyed if our labour is directed by the state and the fruits of that labour are confiscated, and the individual is placed into a situation of dependence upon the whole society. Human nature, likewise, would be stunted: man's propensity for appropriation, for example, would be curtailed by communal property. The benefits of this propensity, through its effects on industry and subsequently prosperity, include the most dignified natural affections of generosity, benevolence, charity, gratitude and compassion. We cannot give or receive any of these if all is directed from above. Communal ownership would leave the 'noble principles' of human nature 'destitute of objects and exercise'.[124] Without being exercised, man becomes a 'very grovelling creature . . . scarce elevated above' the rest of the animals.[125] Hayek and Friedman would approve.

Cautionary Notes on an Enlightened Heuristic

Older scholarship was concerned with the links between Scottish Enlightenment social theory and Marxist historical materialism. Kames's contribution certainly contains a strong line in social determinism, especially in the *Principles*, but it collapsed under the pressure of historical evidence in his *Sketches*. In the latter work, Kames sought to identify the broad patterns, alignments and concurrences of institutions, morals and manners. Yet he repeatedly identified certain societies which did not exhibit the characteristics he would have expected given their place in his reading of the progress of society. Similarly, Kames often discussed specific social phenomena as progressing along trajectories that bore little direct relationship to socio-economic development. The clearest example of this is his discussion of the six (then seven) stages of the development of theology. Dominant theological positions transition from one form to another for purely internal reasons – for example, polytheism changes to henotheism – and without any reference to exogenous factors.

We could view this as a feature of Kames's approach to the 'history of man'. The individual sketches of specific social institutions and behaviours regularly buckle under the weight of contradictory historical examples, such that any simple theory of societal progress fails. A good illustration is how Kames's expectation about the influence of climate upon social development does not match up with his reading of human history. Through encouraging the easy transition to agriculture and the establishing security of subsistence, the temperate climates of the civilisations of antiquity contributed to the 'gradual progress of men from the savage state to the highest civilization'.[126] The similarly temperate areas of the Americas, however, do not experience the same development. Instead, there is no consistency to how societies on the American continents developed. Some societies were stuck as hunters, others became farmers having never been shepherds and the Mexican and Peruvian nations were an inexplicable mix of civilisation and savagery. As Rahmatian notes, 'Kames does not offer a solution to these contradictions'.[127]

Likewise, we should not read Kames as a stadial theorist of society who narrowly saw his own time of developed agriculture, manufactures and commerce as both the endpoint and the height of social development. He is open to the charge of taking those characteristics of his own society that he values highly as evidence of correct human nature and then reading back into history a trajectory of development leading up to his present. From here, we can find in Kames's social evolutionism many of the strands that develop into the 'evolutionist, generalising, ethnocentric, stereotyping, racializing, exoticising, anthropological theories of the nineteenth century and beyond'.[128] There is certainly some truth in this, borne out by the inspiration many nineteenth-century anthropologists took from Kames.

Yet Kames is less complacent about his own time that such a reading suggests. He exhibits a Tacitean belief in the unstoppable rise and fall of societies. The seeds of degeneration grow within the bowels of refinement because the latter situation is 'too agreeable to be lasting'.[129] Complacency and refinement lead to degeneration: 'morality declines in proportion as a nation polishes', a maxim that does not suggest a congratulatory belief in European moral superiority, though it might of cultural superiority.[130] Opulence and luxury are 'diseases' that tear apart societies.[131] The development of manufactures produces wealth, and wealth produces luxury, and consumption of luxury leads to the dramatic decrease in the social affections.[132] Look at an 'opulent city' engaged in 'extensive commerce' and you will see, claims Kames, that 'selfishness becomes the ruling passion: friendship is no more, and even blood-relation is little regarded'.[133] This is not a cyclical theory of history in the sense that morally corrupt commercial society degenerates back into limited agricultural society (or, equally, back to hunting). While it is not a cyclical theory of modes of subsistence, there are cyclical elements of moral progress and decay. We have gone full circle in that, 'in the progress of manners, men end as they began', as selfish creatures in the 'most polished state of society' as they were in the 'first and most rude state'.[134] In a 'state of degeneracy [characterised] by luxury and voluptuousness', 'civilized' man is worse off than 'savage' man as the former has 'neither mind nor body', while the latter only lacks 'mind'.[135]

We might be wrong, then, in viewing Kames as reflective of any purported complacency and self-regard of (Scottish) Enlightenment social theory. The emergence of commerce-led society did not mark the end of history: Kames's analysis identified a cycle of moral progress and decay. As George W. Stocking argued, Kames was able to identify both positive elements to earlier cultures and negative ones about the present.[136] More important, however, is Kames's sense that by understanding the world, we could change it. He was primarily concerned with the difficulties being experienced by mid-eighteenth-century civil societies in western Europe as they came under the control of extensive commerce, growing prosperity and luxury consumption, and the social affections were being weakened. What Kames offered in the *Sketches* was information that might aid a 'second progress', a second go at societal development, in which the lessons he drew from observing the moral corruption occasioned by too much commerce could help societies escape the cycle of refinement and degeneration.[137]

Another charge against Kames is that his much-vaunted empiricism and innovative progressive histories were mere window-dressing that supported his already established speculative theories of human nature. Rahmatian's charge is that Kames (and all the enlightened Scottish social theorists) utilised a 'dogmatic approach from *a priori* principles' to set up an account of human nature and then 'calculatingly' chose historical evidence to support their pre-established views.[138] Kames deployed facts to aid him 'construct an argument in favour of certain Enlightenment ideas' and thus composed social theories that were not 'really evidenced-based' though he presented them as though they were.[139] There is something to the charge, but it misses the mark. We can find littered throughout Kames's writing passages where he describes a new methodology and indicates a concern with how to approach thinking about human nature and society anew. It is in the *Historical Law-Tracts*, where Kames famously discusses the possibility of 'tracing the history of law through dark ages', that we get one of the Scottish Enlightenment's principal accounts of 'conjectural history'.[140] Where the historical record is lacking, we can turn to 'hints from poets and historians, by collateral facts, and by cautious conjectures drawn from the nature of government, of the people, and of the times'.[141] Indeed, it seems highly plausible this is the source of Dugald Stewart's unfortunately influential account of 'conjectural history'.[142] Piece together these 'conjectural facts' – an interesting phrase – alongside the few recorded facts we do have, and Kames believed we can join them all 'in one regular chain'.[143] The goal of such a conjectural history is an account of the 'progress' of a specific human institution or behaviour that is applicable to 'all nations, in the capital circumstances at least'.[144] This requires a form of what we might be tempted to call comparative sociology, in which we draw together the 'facts and circumstances' of a specific phenomenon in all different countries and, by aligning them, extract a sense of the 'natural' progress of things.[145]

Let me note two things here. One is that the extent of conjecture depends on the extent of archival material and the historical record: it is a method used to help us understand 'dark ages', not *all ages*. As such, the 'conjectural' element of any history peters out the further along the history we go. This suggests that 'conjectural history' as an all-encompassing term describing the sort of studies Kames undertook would be incorrect. This feeds into my earlier claim that Kames did not draw a firm distinction between an age of agriculture and an age of commerce: the ample historical record of this level of social development was too nuanced for such a blunt division. The second is that, especially in the *Sketches*, Kames is distinctly humble about the demands of empiricism and the limitations of speculation. He admits his lack of confidence about what 'degree of conviction' his probabilistic reasoning about the natural progress of various human behaviours and institutions warrants.[146] Kames describes his *Sketches*, a work of often copious historical example, as the 'substance of various speculations'.[147] Similarly, Kames said he abandoned many more conjectural theories in the face of contradictory empirical evidence.

Kames's own perception of what he was doing was that it was more securely rooted in empirical reality of human nature. He was critical of those who developed systems of moral philosophy based on only one aspect of human nature – a move Kames attributed to their desire to surprise the world with some novel thought. The axioms that formed the a priori elements stemmed from prior observation of human nature. He was also critical of those rationalist natural theologians, with Samuel Clarke being the prime example, who held that the means by which we reached our moral and religious knowledge was sophisticated ratiocination. Repeatedly, and in common with the other Scots, Kames argued against the utility of speculation and hypotheses in framing accounts of human nature and civil society. In the *Principles*, for example, he held that hypotheses were mere 'castles in the air' if there was 'no data either to verify or refute' the claims.[148] Both groups of thinkers were criticised for development philosophies that bore very little relation to how humans actually think, feel and act in society. In the face of philosophies of human nature that he believed purely speculative, Kames held his own account to be girded by factual observations in the natural history of man.

It is possible that Kames, regardless of his professions of being grounded in fact and writing in opposition to the purely speculative, did himself succumb to the same faults. It is possible to read the *Principles* as a speculative theory of human nature and social change that is then fleshed out by the facts of ancient history and travel writing in the *Sketches*.[149] To an extent this is a sound interpretation, though the intellectual historian in me wants to suggest it is anachronistic to accuse a mid-eighteenth-century social theorist of failing to meet the standards of a subsequent professional discipline. Moreover, what we find in Kames's works following his 'historical turn' after 1751 is a willingness to set aside theoretical simplicity and draw out the nuances and complexities of human nature and the progress of institutions and behaviours. This turn to history in itself is indicative of a thinker modifying their views in the face of evidence. The account of the development of monotheism in the *Principles*, for example, posited a simple progression of belief as we move from savagery to civility. By contrast, in the *Sketches*, Kames set out a six (subsequently seven) stage theory of theological development. The modification of this position resulted from his immersion in historical research.

Similarly, in the *Sketches*, Kames had developed an account of the 'dissocial passions'. This took the place of his account in the *Principles* of the opposition of selfishness and sociality.[150] In the latter case, Kames was able to argue that in fact social action regularly aligns with self-interest and that society does not ultimately involve a conflict between the two. But in the *Sketches*, the dissocial passions are precisely those in opposition to and which threaten society if they are allowed to dominate human action. And the reason for this change is that Kames studied the 'history of mankind' and saw that potentially catastrophic conflict is endemic to all societies due to a powerful strain of unsociality in our common nature. This shift in Kames's thought is reflective of the fact that, from the early 1750s onwards, he was (a) modifying his earlier published positions in the face of that evidence but also (b) on occasion, including discussion of evidence that contradicted his speculative theories. Kames had set himself a Herculean task: to comprehend all human history and narrow it down into a series of digestible sketches. No wonder he failed.

And to what purpose? The study of the 'history of mankind' was undertaken in the pursuit of the final causes of human life as framed by a supreme being. The fact that Kames undertook many of his investigations for reasons of natural theology places him at several steps remove from contemporary sociology. In this, I must differ from Rahmatian's view that Kames was as irreligious as David Hume but 'only more circumspect'.[151] Kames was clearly not an orthodox Christian and his study of human nature resulted in contemporary accusations that he abandoned many of the tenets of orthodox Presbyterianism. But he was some form of enlightened deist who believed in the existence of a supreme being whose will for humankind could be learnt from the study of human nature, and that whatever conforms to our nature conforms to God's will for us. We might also reject Mary Poovey's claim that Kames's providentialism was characteristic of wider enlightened Scottish social theory.[152] His reliance upon final causes and the natural theological purpose of his studies of man in society are qualitatively more serious, substantial and clear-cut than that found in Smith, Ferguson and Millar.

Conclusion

Alan Swingewood's judgement that 'what is significant about the contribution of the Scottish Enlightenment to sociology is the clear awareness that society constituted a process, the product of specific economic, social and historical forces that could be identified and analysed through the methods of empirical science' is equally true of Kames as it is of Smith, Millar and Ferguson.[153] For Kames, the principles of human nature were universal, but they were gradually revealed or gradually matured into full use as states developed. The causes of specific social institutions or social behaviours had to be placed into a wider context of several factors. Society results from our common nature and not from convention. One of the achievements of enlightened Scottish social theory was the separation of society and government, and the study of the former as something other than a factor of the latter. What Kames sought to understand was the underlying trajectory of the origin and development of specific institutions and behaviours, extracting from the diversity of historical evidence a system of providentially arranged developments. This took the form of an interplay between an unchanging human nature and the changing societal contexts in which humans existed. Key was the mode of subsistence, which led Kames to outline a stadial history of society. Within this, 'commercial society' does not end up as the perfection of but rather the corruption of society, in the place of the desired balance between agriculture and commerce.

Notes

I would like to thank Tamás Demeter for originally inviting me to contribute to this collection and for his comments on this chapter. It has also been immeasurably improved by commentary from Chris Berry, Craig Smith and Niall O'Flaherty, though I imagine they will disagree with some about 'commercial society'.

1. For overviews see Arthur Edward MacGuinness, *Henry Home, Lord Kames* (New York: Twayne Publishers, 1970); William C. Lehmann, *Henry Home, Lord Kames, and the Scottish Enlightenment: A Study in National Character and in the History of Ideas* (The Hague: Martinus Nijhoff, 1971); Ian Simpson Ross, *Lord Kames and the Scotland of His Day* (Oxford: Clarendon Press, 1972). In terms

of analysing Kames's thought, these have now been superseded by Andreas Rahmatian, *Lord Kames: Legal and Social Theorist* (Edinburgh: Edinburgh University Press, 2015).

2. Henry Home, Lord Kames, *Sketches of the History of Man*, ed. James Harris, 3 vols (Indianapolis, IN: Liberty Fund, [4th edition, 1788] 2007), III, p. 721 (henceforth SHM). On the *Principles* see Ari Helo, 'The Historicity of Morality: Necessity and Necessary Agents in the Ethics of Lord Kames', *History of European Ideas* 27:3 (2001), pp. 239–55; R. J. W. Mills, 'Lord Kames's Analysis of the Natural Origins of Religion: The *Essays on the Principles of Morality and Natural Religion* (1751)', *Historical Research* 89:246 (2016), pp. 751–75.

3. Alan Swingewood, 'Origins of Sociology: The Case of the Scottish Enlightenment', *The British Journal of Sociology* 21 (1970), pp. 164–80; Björn Eriksson, 'The First Formulation of Sociology: A Discursive Innovation of the 18th Century', *European Journal of Sociology / Archives Européennes de Sociologie / Europäisches Archiv Für Soziologie* 34 (1993), pp. 251–76; John Brewer, 'The Scottish Enlightenment and Scottish Social Thought c.1725–1915' in J. Holmwood and J. Scott (eds), *The Palgrave Handbook of Sociology in Britain* (Basingstoke: Palgrave Macmillan, 2014), pp. 3–29; and Piet Strydom, *Discourse and Knowledge: The Making of Enlightenment Sociology* (Liverpool: Liverpool University Press, 2000). More critically, see also Kenneth Macdonald, 'Did British Sociology Begin with the Scottish Enlightenment?' in Plamena Panayotova (ed.), *The History of Sociology in Britain* (Cham: Palgrave Macmillan, 2019), pp. 37–69.

4. George W. Stocking, 'Scotland as the Model of Mankind: Lord Kames' Philosophical View of Civilization' in T. H. H. Thoresen (ed.), *Toward a Science of Man: Essays in the History of Anthropology* (The Hague: Mouton, 1975), pp. 65–89; Alan Barnard, 'Through Radcliffe-Brown's Spectacles: Reflections on the History of Anthropology', *History of the Human Sciences* 5 (1992), pp. 1–20.

5. Edward Evans-Pritchard, *Social Anthropology* (London: Cohen & West, 1951), p. 25.

6. Edward Evans-Pritchard, *A History of Anthropological Thought* (London: Faber & Faber, 1981), pp. 14–15.

7. Henry Home, Lord Kames, *Essays on the Principles of Morality and Natural Religion*, ed. Mary Catherine Moran (Indianapolis, IN: Liberty Fund, [third edition, 1778] 2005), p. 3 (henceforth EPMNR); Kames, SHM II, p. 337.

8. Alan Swingewood, *A Short History of Sociological Thought* (Basingstoke: Macmillan, 1991), p. 9.
9. Ronald L. Meek, 'The Scottish Contribution to Marxist Sociology' in *Economics and Ideology and Other Essays* (London, 1967), pp. 34–50 at p. 37; Daniel Carey, *Locke, Shaftesbury, and Hutcheson: Contesting Diversity in the Enlightenment and Beyond* (Cambridge: Cambridge University Press, 2006), pp. 11, 196–7.
10. Meek, 'Scottish Contribution to Marxist Sociology', p. 36.
11. For example, Roy Pascal, 'Property and Society: The Scottish Historical School of the Eighteenth Century', *The Modern Quarterly* 1 (1938), pp. 167–79; Meek, 'Scottish Contribution to Marxist Sociology'; Andrew S. Skinner, 'A Scottish Contribution to Marxist Sociology?' in J. Bradley and M. Howard (eds), *Classical and Marxian Political Economy* (London: Palgrave Macmillan, 1982), pp. 79–114.
12. Alexander Fraser Tytler, Lord Woodhouselees, *Memoirs of the Life and Writings of the Honourable Henry Home of Kames*, 2 vols (Edinburgh, 1807), I, p. 159. On Kames's attempts at improving Scottish agriculture see Charles B. Bow, 'The "Final Causes" of Scottish Nationalism: Lord Kames on the Political Economy of Enlightened Husbandry, 1745–82', *Historical Research* 91 (2018), pp. 296–313.
13. Tytler, *Memoirs of Kames*, p. 160.
14. Tytler, *Memoirs of Kames*, p. 160.
15. EPMNR pp. 47–8.
16. EPMNR p. 47.
17. Henry Home, *Essays upon Several Subjects concerning British Antiquities* (Edinburgh, 1747), especially the footnote on pp. 127–8 and 192–9 (henceforth BA); Henry Home, Lord Kames, *Historical Law-Tracts* (Edinburgh, 1758), Tract III (henceforth HLT).
18. Sir John Dalrymple, *Essay towards a General History of Feudal Property in Great Britain* (London, 1757), pp. 86–8.
19. Dalrymple, *Feudal Property*, p. iii; Ross, *Kames*, p. 204.
20. Ronald L. Meek, *Social Science and the Ignoble Savage* (Cambridge: Cambridge University Press, 1976), ch. 4.
21. See Moran's commentary in EPMNR pp. 241–2.
22. But see Ronald L. Meek, 'Smith, Turgot and the "Four Stages" Theory' in *Smith, Marx, & After* (New York: Springer, 1977), pp. 18–32.
23. Cf. Eriksson, 'First Formulation of Sociology', p. 267.
24. Rahmatian, *Lord Kames*, p. 56.
25. EPMNR p. 36.

26. HLT p. 78. See also SHM III, p. 724 where he opines that 'one great purpose of society, is to furnish opportunities of mutual aid and support'. Reciprocity is key to Kames's understanding of society, as indicated by his arguments that (a) polygamous marriages lack 'proper society' and (b) 'sweet is the society of a pair fitted for each other' in monogamous marriages. See SHM I, p. 267.
27. SHM III, p. 719.
28. HLT p. 78.
29. HLT p. 78.
30. BA p. 194.
31. BA p. 194.
32. BA p. 194.
33. BA pp. 194–5.
34. BA p. 195.
35. BA p. 194; HLT p. 78.
36. HLT p. 78.
37. HLT p. 78.
38. HLT p. 125.
39. SHM I, p. 179.
40. HLT p. 78.
41. HLT p. 78.
42. Henry Home, Lord Kames, *Principles of Equity* (London, 1767), p. 15; SHM III, p. 719.
43. Swingewood, *A Short History of Sociological Thought*, p. 7. Cf. Goran Therborn, *Science, Class and Society: On the Formation of Sociology and Historical Materialism* (London: NLB, 1977), p. 162.
44. Eriksson, 'First Formulation of Sociology', p. 265.
45. SHM II, p. 357; Georg Simmel. 'How Is Society Possible?', *American Journal of Sociology* 16 (1910–11), pp. 372–91.
46. HLT p. 124.
47. Immanuel Kant, 'Universal History from a Cosmopolitan Viewpoint (1784)' in *Political Writings*, ed. Donna M. Brinton and Janet M. Goodwin (Cambridge: Cambridge University Press, 1991), p. 44. Thesis 4.
48. EPMNR p. 19.
49. Kames is known for his criticism of his friend Hume's claim that justice was an artificial virtue that arose from conventions which were themselves the results of long-running social interaction.
50. EPMNR p. 54. As Kames puts it in the *Sketches* (II, p. 358), 'the whole train of social affections' demonstrates our 'fitness for society and our happiness in it'.

51. EPMNR p. 49.
52. EPMNR p. 52.
53. EPMNR p. 3. By contrast, the *Principles* contained a greater sense of the societal influence on the formation of religious belief than it did on the formation of morals.
54. SHM II, p. 359.
55. SHM II, p. 361.
56. SHM II, p. 351.
57. SHM II, p. 361.
58. SHM II, p. 361.
59. See Craig Smith, *Adam Ferguson and the Idea of Civil Society: Moral Science in the Scottish Enlightenment* (Edinburgh: Edinburgh University Press, 2018), esp. p. 126.
60. SHM II, p. 364; III, p. 903.
61. SHM II, p. 364.
62. SHM II, p. 364.
63. SHM II, p. 365.
64. SHM II, p. 370.
65. SHM II, p. 370.
66. EPMNR p. 252. On Kames's position on free will see James Harris, *Of Liberty and Necessity: The Free Will Debate in Eighteenth-Century British Philosophy* (Oxford: Oxford University Press, 2005), pp. 88–107.
67. EPMNR p. 63.
68. SHM II, p. 361; Christopher J. Berry, 'Sociality and Socialisation' in *Essays on Hume, Smith and the Scottish Enlightenment* (Edinburgh: Edinburgh University Press, 2018), pp. 75–88 at p. 79.
69. Rahmatian, *Lord Kames*, p. 60.
70. For example, EPMNR p. 46.
71. EPMNR p. 43.
72. SHM I, p. 333.
73. SHM I, p. 176.
74. SHM I, p. 176.
75. SHM I, p. 177.
76. Henry Home, Lord Kames, *Elements of Criticism*, ed. Peter Jones, 2 vols (Indianapolis, IN: Liberty Fund, [6th edition, 1785] 2005), p. 82.
77. HLT p. 127.
78. SHM I, p. 74. This quote is from a Sketch entitled 'Of the Origin and Progress of Commerce' which, despite its title, is actually about 'how far industry and commerce are affected by the quantity of circulating coin'. See I, p. 80.

79. We might note in passing that, given that the Scots are criticised for not explaining the shift from one form of society to another, it is noticeable that Kames is quite clear about how commerce emerges from established agriculture.
80. SHM II, p. 565.
81. SHM I, p. 57.
82. For example, SHM III, p. 719.
83. For example, SHM III, p. 498.
84. For example, SHM II, pp. 501, 494.
85. See Christopher J. Berry, *The Idea of Luxury: A Conceptual and Historical Investigation* (Cambridge: Cambridge University Press, 1994), ch. 6.
86. See also James Harris's assessment in his 'Introduction', in SHM I, pp. ix–xx, which positions Kames as ambivalent and undecided on the issue of 'whether the corrupting effects of commerce are outweighed by the possibilities it opens up of refinement and improvement' (p. xvii).
87. SHM II, p. 495. See also II, p. 423.
88. SHM II, p. 408, II, p. 385 and I, pp. 85–6. See also I, p. 332. Kames draws the historical lesson for Britain from the Italian commercial city-states, for example at I, p. 209.
89. Therborn, *Science, Class and Society*, p. 159; Strydom, *Discourse and Knowledge*, p. 184.
90. For example, SHM III, p. 761.
91. HLT p. 79.
92. SHM II, p. 362.
93. HLT p. 78.
94. SHM II, p. 383.
95. SHM II, p. 372.
96. SHM II, p. 362.
97. SHM II, p. 362. We might note in passing this same process is repeated as the focus of societies shifts from agriculture to commerce, though now in conditions where government already exists.
98. SHM II, p. 362.
99. SHM II, p. 362.
100. SHM II, p. 362.
101. SHM II, p. 362.
102. SHM II, p. 363.
103. SHM I, p 178.
104. SHM II, p. 372.
105. SHM II, p. 372.

106. SHM I, p. 178; HLT p. 89.
107. SHM II, p. 373.
108. SHM II, p. 373.
109. SHM II, p. 374.
110. SHM II, p. 388.
111. SHM I, p. 178.
112. SHM I, p. 178.
113. SHM II, p. 178.
114. SHM II, p. 417.
115. SHM II, p. 416.
116. SHM II, p. 349.
117. See also Iain McDaniel, 'Unsocial Sociability in the Scottish Enlightenment: Ferguson and Kames on War, Sociability and the Foundations of Patriotism', *History of European Ideas* 41 (2015), 662–82.
118. SHM II, p. 350.
119. I say Britons here rather than Scots, as Kames defended eighteenth-century Britain as a highly successful society, though one under threat from its own opulence. The sceptical reader might think this was convenient for Kames.
120. HLT p. 125.
121. HLT pp. 124–5.
122. HLT p. 125.
123. HLT p. 125.
124. HLT p. 126.
125. HLT p. 126.
126. SHM II, p. 565.
127. Rahmatian, *Lord Kames*, p. 152.
128. Rahmatian, *Lord Kames*, p. 116.
129. SHM I, p. 204.
130. SHM III, p. 771.
131. For example, Kames SHM III, p. 761.
132. Berry, *The Idea of Luxury*; Christopher J. Berry, *The Idea of Commercial Society in the Scottish Enlightenment* (Edinburgh: Edinburgh University Press, 2013).
133. SHM I, p. 179.
134. SHM I, p. 179.
135. SHM I, p. 333.
136. Stocking, 'Kames' Philosophical View'.
137. SHM II, p. 429.
138. Rahmatian, *Lord Kames*, p. 196.
139. Rahmatian, *Lord Kames*, p. 203.

140. HLT p. 36.
141. HLT p. 36.
142. See Christopher Berry's chapter in this collection.
143. HLT p. 37.
144. HLT p. 36.
145. HLT p. 37.
146. SHM I, p. 3.
147. SHM I, p. 3.
148. EPMNR pp. 55, 171.
149. Rahmatian, *Lord Kames*, 157.
150. For example, SHM I, p. 200.
151. Rahmatian, *Lord Kames*, p. 51.
152. Mary Poovey, *A History of the Modern Fact: Problems of Knowledge in the Sciences of Wealth and Society* (Chicago: University of Chicago Press, 1998), pp. 227–8.
153. Swingewood, *Short History*, p. 21.

6

Pre-Weberian Charismatic Leadership and Aesthetics of Deference in the Scottish Enlightenment

Spyridon Tegos

Introduction

Adam Smith offers several hints pointing to a liberal 'history and theory' of prestige in modernity – anticipating Max Weber and other sociologists and jurists from the nineteenth century onwards. In this context, personal (or 'personified') authority attracts attention despite its vestigial status while titled aristocracy is receding in modernity. In *Economy and Society*, Max Weber famously distinguishes between three ideal-typical genres of authority: traditional, rational-legal and charismatic. The latter amounts to a personal form of heroic or prophetic grace, not necessarily parochial or doomed to eclipse in modernity. In his successive accounts of charisma,[1] Weber moves to a more critical assessment regarding its revolutionary potential and especially the threat that represents for personal freedom. In this chapter I tackle the Smithian conception of charismatic leadership and its potential echoing of Weberian categories that often go unnoticed. In this context I shift the attention to the aesthetical background of political deference simultaneously in works such as Edmund Burke's *Philosophical Enquiry into the Origin of Our Ideas of the Sublime and Beautiful* but also in early Smithian works such as the *Lectures on Rhetoric and Belles Lettres* and the *History of Astronomy* and *History of Ancient Physics*, rarely debated and considered in this specific context. First, I explore Burke's analysis of the connection between political subordination and the feeling of sublime. In this sense, wonder and admiration are linked to the sentiments of astonishment, reverence, respect and deference; then a second association is established between the above-mentioned sentiments and the feeling of delight in front of grandeur and magnificence.

Secondly, I turn to Adam Smith's *Lectures on Rhetoric and Belles Lettres*, which contains fairly understudied sources of rhetorical categories regarding sentimental reactions towards greatness. In his precocious epistemological essays on the *History of Astronomy* and *History of Ancient Physics*, Adam Smith also examines the intellectual sentiments of wonder, admiration and surprise. On several occasions he sketches a 'natural history' that is a stadial explanation of the emergence of deference to authority. The 'invisible hand of Jupiter' marks the ignorance, timidity and raw fear of the primitive mind as well as the gratitude that he feels towards the social or divine powerful hand that delivers him from his precarious conditions of living. The transition to pagan Greek – that is, mainly Athens and Minor Asia – civilised context that offers relative security and leisure also gives way to an aesthetic admiration of less anthropomorphic accounts of deity.

In the next section I turn to *The Theory of Moral Sentiments* where Smith examines the moderate aesthetical attachment to systems as a legitimate motivation of political action and introduces the notions of the spirit and love of system. According to Smith, authoritarianism and true statesmanship derive from the same aesthetical attachment to systems. Moderation, a key element in Adam Smith's science of politics, is rarely found among political reformers, obsessed by their allegedly well-drafted systems. Ultimately, I turn to the 'man of the system': this potential fanatic, according to Smith, who often remains a factional leader. Nonetheless he can also transform himself into a man of public spirit if he resists the enthusiasm for the unmediated implementation of allegedly perfect systems; this view of politics deems necessary an active feedback loop between theory and praxis. In this chapter I argue that Smith's true statesman who inspires legitimate deference can be read fruitfully through a Weberian lens as a bearer of modern charismatic authority.

The Irish Legacy: Edmund Burke – Political Deference Aestheticised

In the *Philosophical Enquiry into the Origin of Our Ideas of the Sublime and Beautiful*, Edmund Burke develops the psychological foundations of human imagination towards beautiful and terrifying objects in the natural world and human society. The *Enquiry* contains a theory of passions leading to a full-fledged anthropology relevant to politics. In this context, a theory of subordination and political deference intertwined with the sublime spectacle of political power looms large.

In this account, the passions belonging to self-preservation turn on pain and danger, and are considered as inspiring terror: 'A mode of terror, or of pain, is always the cause of the sublime.'[2] Whenever the prospective pain or danger is sensed without the agent being overwhelmed by a situation of real threat, the emotion of terror confers what Burke terms 'delight', a bittersweet sentiment that operates in security, when a remote danger is perceived as a release from uneasiness and therefore as a diminution of pain: 'Whatever excites this delight, I call sublime.'[3] In the *Enquiry* II, Burke delivers a cursory account of the sublime-driven sentiments and passions and their respective functions. The passage deserves to be quoted at length:

> The passion caused by the great and sublime in nature, when those causes operate most powerfully, is astonishment; the astonishment is that state of the soul, in which all its motions are suspended, with some degree of horror. In this case the mind is so entirely filled with its object, that it cannot entertain any other, nor by consequence reason on that object which employs it. Hence arises the great power of the sublime, that far from being produced by them, it anticipates our reasonings and hurries us on by an irresistible force. Astonishment, as I have said, is the effect of the sublime in its highest degree; the inferior effects are admiration, reverence and respect.[4]

It is evident that any rationalisation *ex post* misses the instinctive nature of the process. Burke dwells at some length on the linkage between astonishment and admiration on the one hand and terror on the other.[5] As he shrewdly notes, Greek and Roman languages bear witness to this association, deeply rooted in classical culture. Its implication, though, seems to pass unnoticed, according to Burke. In this chapter I focus on the connection between aesthetics of sublime and deference.

Admiration, reverence and respect address status alongside natural phenomena or works of art. The spectacle of social and political power yields deference[6] and initiates a peculiar perception of aestheticised politics. The distinction between amiable and awful virtues offers a prominent entry to this connection between the conception of sublime and deference. Burke elaborates on the

Humean distinction[7] between amiable and awful characters such as Caesar and Cato respectively; the sublimity of Cato's character has 'much to admire, much to reverence, and perhaps something to fear; we respect him but we respect him at a distance'.[8] Echoing Roman *auctoritas*, Burke's analysis brings to the fore the distance and estrangement involved in the father-inspired reverence and respect.[9] In this sense, Burke notices that real or metaphoric obscurity is a necessary condition 'to make any thing very terrible'. This applies to despotic governments and theocratic regimes par excellence: 'Those despotic governments, which are founded on the passions of men, and principally upon the passion of fear, keep their chief as much as may form the public eye. The policy has been the same in many cases of religion.'[10]

In the section on power, quite tellingly, Burke dissects power in shifting the attention to the animal world and the holy books. His main line of argumentation consists in separating the useful and beneficial to us that can be wielded at will and therefore subjected to us, and the magnificent and grandiose power that greatly surpasses our forces and leads to the 'grand and commanding conception' of the sublime.[11] It has to be noted that deference in front of the sublime spectacle of political power, the 'union of sacred and reverential awe' inspired by 'dread majesty', extends well beyond theocratic regimes: 'Thus we are affected by strength which is natural power. The power that arises from institution in kings and commanders, has the same connection with terror. Sovereigns are frequently addressed with the title of *dread majesty* . . .' (italics added).[12]

In this new section added in the 1759 edition, dedicated to power and its impact, as well as in the *Reflections on the Revolution in France*, Burke clearly states that modern, civilised governments are based more on respect and reverence, therefore on the sublime of power, than on unmixed fear and terror. Hence a certain aesthetical attachment to supreme authority is firmly embedded in modern deference, based on sublime delight, and should be understood as separate from despotic obsequiousness.[13] As we shall see below, Adam Smith further elaborates on this Burkean insight regarding modern forms of political deference, in between traditional and charismatic forms of authority in the Weberian taxonomy. The Burkean background of different aspects of Smith's thought has been rightly highlighted[14] without paying particular attention to the early Smithian works, though. However, one can find in the early works remarkable analysis of wonder and admiration regarding greatness and status that runs parallel to and enriches Burke's reflections. To this we now turn.

Adam Smith: Wonder and Admiration of Greatness from the *Lectures on Rhetoric and Belles Lettres* to the *History of Astronomy*

Surprisingly, Smith scholars rarely turn to the *Lectures on Rhetoric and Belles Lettres* (hereafter LRBL) for relevant reflections on admiration. Yet Smith's lectures on rhetoric and criticism include a great deal of intriguing material regarding wonder and admiration. 'Mythological history' regards gods and 'the most amazing part of their conduct'. In Smith's evolutionary account of human culture, poets were the first historians and they mobilise the 'language of wonder' in order to treat their subject par excellence, which is the marvellous, 'for in that stile amazement and surprise naturally break forth'.[15] As a result, 'In all countries we found poetry has been the first Species of writing, as the marvellous is that which first draw the attention of unimproved men.'[16] In the following lecture Smith further delineates his account of forms of writing in Europe. Poetry as mythological history of heroes and centaurs is routinely associated with the marvellous, 'as that which was most likely to please a rude and ignorant people. Wonder is the passion which in such people will be more excited.'[17] Therefore tragedy succeeds to the 'fabulous accounts of heroes' and novels succeed to the 'wild and extravagant Romances which were the first performances of our ancestors in Europe'.[18]

Heroes and high-status individuals also become objects of admiration. Smith defines the object of admiration in the LRBL: 'there are two Sorts of Objects that excite our admiration viz when an object is Grand, when it is beautiful'.[19] While examining the modes of 'describing or expressing internal invisible objects', Smith sets out to anatomise the internal and external factors that determine the sentiment of admiration: 'A mind not ruffled by any violent passions, but calm and tolerably serene; filled with some degree of joy not so great as to withdraw the attention, is that state of mind in which one is disposed to admiration.'[20] The country life seems to be an appropriate example of such a state of mind, triggering 'rapturous' expressions from poets. Smith offers a detailed account of bodily and mental reactions stemming from an 'easily pleased temper' in front of a beautiful object:

> he is fixt in the place he was in, his arms fall loose by his sides, or if the emotion is very violent are laid across his breast, he leans forward and stretches out his neck, with his eyes fixt on the object and little opened. The affection he feels is mixt with some degree of desire and hope towards the object and this inclines to draw nearer towards it.[21]

On the contrary, when the object is grand, he is 'fixt to his place, but does not, as in the first case desire to approach the object, he rather inclines to draw back'. The admiration triggered is strongly reminiscent of the Burkean sublime. In the LRBL, Smith's analysis mainly regards the worship of anthropomorphic deities or heroic figures. Smith states that this is 'what we properly call admiration. It does not partake of hope or desire but rather of reverential awe and respect, that gives one a fear of displeasing.' Reverential awe and respect also occur in front of great individuals, heroes, warriors and eminent social superiors such as royalty, a crucial connection between aesthetics and social and political sentiments in *The Theory of Moral Sentiments*.[22]

If one bears these conceptual insights in mind, the interpretation of the *History of Astronomy* gains in scope and depth.[23] In Section III, Smith shifts his narrative from a psychologically oriented philosophy of science to sociology of religion.[24] Everything turns on the specific status of 'superstitious wonder and admiration' within the transition from primitive, 'rude' religion[25] to account for natural phenomena to a systematic approach to things in a civilised context.

During the first stages of history, human subsistence is profoundly precarious and curiosity attains a *minimal* form of expression. The wonder and surprise due to phenomena that do not directly threaten human existence are not taken to be causes of trouble for the tranquillity of imagination. Therefore, apart from the emergency of day-to-day survival, the only fears and anxieties that count are the ones deriving from terrifying natural phenomena, compelling humans to search for the 'hidden chains that bind together the seemingly disjoined appearances of nature'.[26]

In Section III, 'Of the Origin of Philosophy', Smith accounts for the origins of polytheism. I suggest that the core of Smith's narrative is built around a single idea: the 'rudest forms' of religious superstition stand beyond the level of 'surprise and wonder', beyond 'anxious curiosity'. In the first stages of the savage condition, men experience a great deal of weakness and a permanent insecurity that cause the 'cowardice and pusillanimity' underpinning the primitive state of mind.[27]

In this context, the sentiment of amazement looms large. It is directed to 'awful or terrible' irregularities of nature: 'Comets, eclipses, thunder, lightning, and other meteors, by their greatness naturally overawe him, and he views them with *a reverence that approaches to fear*' (emphasis added);[28] we have to bear in mind that the ultimate end of natural philosophy is 'the repose and tranquillity of the imagination'.[29] Further irregular natural phenomena are not exclusively 'awful and terrible'; they lose their irregularity insofar as they can be classified. Therefore the origin of polytheism can be established, pinpointed in the 'vulgar superstition which ascribes all the irregular events of nature to the favour or displeasure of intelligent, though invisible beings, to gods, daemons, witches, genii, fairies'.[30]

Smith invokes the sociological factors of law, security and order, thereby calling forth his 'four-stage' scheme of the progress of society. The lack of security and order hinders the development of 'curiosity about the seemingly disjoined appearances of nature, which are dealt with by invoking the favour or displeasure of gods',[31] hence the conclusion that 'civilisation replaces fear with wonder'.[32] In short, fear and superstitious 'terrors of religion' obstructed the development of more rational and less timorous modes of explanation.

Admiration of a 'Systematic' Universe

In order to restore the mind's tranquillity disturbed by emotional shocks due to unaccountable phenomena, human imagination[33] naturally invents analogies[34] with things already seen and known.[35] The reverential admiration of the savage for beautiful or beneficial 'irregularities of nature' leads to a sentiment of gratitude towards the 'invisible hand of Jupiter'. In civilised societies, men have more occasions to confirm their strength and security over nature and therefore are less prone to conjure up invisible beings to explain the 'seemingly disjoined phenomena'.[36] In this case, the emergence of a leisure class marks a novel disposition – 'those of liberal fortunes are less disposed to employ, for this connecting chain, those invisible beings whom the fear and ignorance of their forefathers had engendered'.[37] Greek colonies of Asia Minor are praised for having attained a degree of security and stability due to their social development: they have overcome extreme poverty and, as a result, they have achieved a certain 'distinction of ranks' and 'regular subordination' which is the opposite of despotism assimilated to anarchy destructive of security[38] and favourable to superstition.

Being less prone to pusillanimity and terror, they respond to any break of this regularity – that is, to any form of wonder – by setting up explanatory systems accounting for natural phenomena as a whole.[39] This systematic attitude puts an end to piecemeal, invisible hand–type explanations, leading to an approach that renders the 'whole course of the universe consistent and of a piece'.[40] In this setting, the sentiment of admiration springs out of the beauty and greatness of the intellectual achievement consisting in the reconstruction of an imaginative order. Thus Adam Smith explores the alternative path to primitive servile deference based on fear and ignorance and sketches a natural history of demystification of power that amounts to moderate political deference. The deflationary tone of this approach drives him away from the Burkean background that remains an indispensable reference regarding the link between aesthetics and deference to authority. The crucial component is the particular twist that Smith gives to the notions of spirit and love of system that his British predecessors lack, as Smith himself states.

Adam Smith: Aesthetic Attachment to Systems in the *Theory of Moral Sentiments*

The language of moral sentiments often envelops an aesthetic vocabulary,[41] famously in the cases of Shaftesbury and Hutcheson but also regarding less-known figures of the Scottish Enlightenment. In this context, Smith's concept of admiration emerges in various instances in TMS regarding moral virtues considered as unusual and rare compared with the standard capacities of human nature. In Smith's theory of moral sentiments, the respectable virtues are explicitly more admired than the amiable ones. Heroic virtues such as magnanimity go beyond propriety, consensus and decorum and are directed towards a grandiose, magnificent phenomenon that captivates human imagination. In Smith's terms, the 'great leader of science and taste' triggers surprise and wonder but also commands our admiration, providing the ground for applause of intellectual virtues.[42] This excellence goes beyond the ordinary appeals to our admiration insofar as the beauty of the moral character requires our respect. Indeed, we approve the behaviour of the magnanimous and 'from our experience of the common weakness of human nature, we are surprised, and wonder how he should be able to act so as to deserve approbation. Approbation, mixed and animated by wonder and surprise, constitutes the sentiment which is properly called admiration, of which, applause is the natural expression'.[43] Regarding the style of expression, the 'respectable virtues are those which are most suited to a commendatory discourse where we should excite the admiration and wonder of the audience'.[44] Amiable virtues such as humanity are often associated with contemptible vices such as cowardice and want of resolution. In this context, Smith conflates admiration and wonder, evoking 'the language of admiration and wonder' most suitable to respectable virtues, consisting in 'amplicatives and superlatives' which 'are the terms we commonly make use of to express our admiration and respect'.[45] It remains an open question whether Smith introduces an 'aesthetic morality'[46] in the sense of an appeal to aesthetic norms[47] or whether this language is merely rhetorical; yet it becomes clear that admiration of moral beauty and sublimity echoes aspects of the abovementioned intellectual admiration.

Yet Smith's analysis cuts deeper and sheds light on an original layer of the problem. He dwells at length on this permanent trait of human nature, the obsessive accumulation of (unused but disposable) means that converge to an end:

> the exact adjustment of the means for attaining any conveniency or pleasure, should frequently be more regarded than that very conveniency or pleasure, in the attainment of which their whole merit would seem to consist, has not, so far as I know, been yet taken notice of by any body.[48]

In TMS IV.i, Smith accounts for the 'beauty which the appearance of utility bestows upon all the productions of art and the extensive influence of this species of beauty'. Smith claims right from the start that the 'fitness of any system or machine to produce the end for which it was intended, bestows a certain propriety and beauty upon the whole, and renders the very thought and contemplation of it agreeable'.[49] Against a background framed by an implicit criticism of Hume's conception of utility, Smith moves on to a sharp distinction between the consideration of the fittingness of means as useful to an end and the end itself.[50] Smith does not reduce the beautiful and harmonious to the useful but he distinguishes between the 'the beauty of an object in its suitedness to be useful as opposed to its actual usefulness'.[51]

Adam Smith: The Man of System and the (pre-Weberian) Charismatic Leader

The love of system is a peculiar Smithian concept. By contrast the spirit of the system strikes one as a shared preoccupation for many proponents of the French and Scottish Enlightenments. Condillac's famous *Treatise of Systems* (1749) introduces a minute taxonomy of scientifically and philosophically ungrounded 'abstract' systems, within which the spirit of system predominates. Throughout the text, Condillac makes a crucial distinction between abstraction soundly understood and metaphysical abstraction.[52] In his treatise, the spirit of system impedes focus on the 'faits bien constatés' (the facts rightly noticed)[53] and disrupts the development of the scientific experimental method. A similar controversy goes on in the domain of economics: embracing naturalism and empiricism blended with forms of teleology, the group known as the Physiocrats that Smith met while in France bears witness to this anti-system-building stance, battling from the mid-eighteenth century onwards against the construction of mathematical and mechanical model-systems and in favour of sensibility for 'nature's ways'; yet some of its members or followers, especially Turgot, are also accused of being victims of the spirit of system in their political decisions.[54]

In his well-known 'Letter to the Authors of the *Edinburgh Review*', Smith speaks very highly of the French Encyclopedia project of D'Alembert and Diderot, praising the 'peculiar talent of the French nation, to arrange every subject in that natural and simple order, which carries the attention, without any effort, along with it'.[55] The antithesis between a metaphysical spirit of system and an empirically driven and scientifically updated systematic spirit pervades the *Preliminary Discourse to the Encyclopedia* (1751). In his famous apology of the systematic spirit, D'Alembert defends the reduction of many orders of principles to the strictly necessary in order to account for natural phenomena in the simplest and most efficacious way. It this context, the spirit of system predominates in Aristotelian, Christian and modern Cartesian metaphysics and impedes science from making relevant observations and collecting the right data; it also immunises science from reality checks and feedbacks, giving undue weight to the metaphysical guarantee of truth, namely God. A system without pretension to envelope totality is a system that does not need unconditional principles.[56]

Smith shares D'Alembert's 'Baconianism' in the sense that knowledge and science should enhance human practice and foster improvement; as a result he is suspicious of system builders. Smith's praise and vehement critique of the physiocratic system in *Wealth of Nations* IV are amply discussed and beyond the scope of this chapter. Rather, Smith's critique of the man of system, undoubtedly inspired by those controversies but going well beyond them, is directly related to the love of system. The man of system, 'very wise in his own conceit', admires excessively his 'ideal plan of government' and does not respect the intermediary groups and corporation, 'the great orders and society', that check and balance sovereign power. Driven by an excessive, self-indulgent spirit of system, he wants to

> arrange the different members of a great society with as much ease as the hand arrange the different pieces upon a chess-board ... in the great chess-board of human society, every single piece has a principle of motion of its own, altogether different from that which the legislature might chuse to impress upon it.[57]

Therefore he is blinded by his own sublime vision of economics and politics. Fascination of beautiful systems gives way to delusions of grandeur:

> The man of system ... is often enamoured with the supposed beauty of his own ideal plan of government, that he cannot suffer the smallest deviation from any part of it. He goes on to establish it completely ... without any regard either to the great interests, or to the strong prejudices which may oppose it.[58]

Therefore frenetic implementation of reforms advances insensible to local mores and customs and irresponsive to frustrated, well-embedded social aspirations.

Yet Smith's account is more sophisticated and cuts deeper. The aesthetic appeal of systems is considered as a modern phenomenon and marks progress over traditional and charismatic authority, in the Weberian sense, as we shall see below. The spirit of system can be a legitimate ground of authority under specific conditions. In the context of the aesthetic appeal of the spirit of system within appropriate bounds, close but different to the Burkean sublime of power, the figure of the true statesman gains relevance. Smith thinks that a form of moderate charismatic leadership is possible although rare: 'This spirit of system commonly takes the direction of that more gentle public spirit; always animates it, and often inflames it even to the madness of fanaticism.'[59] Therefore, provided a check that generates a moderate spirit of system, this proves that modern statesmanship is not chimerical: 'Some general, and even systematical, idea of the perfection of policy and law, may no doubt be necessary for directing the views of the statesman.'[60]

In order to better grasp the advance of modern charismatic leadership in the Smithian sense, based on a leader's capacity to elevate himself above the factional, arrogant leader obsessed by a love of system to a true statesman, we can profitably juxtapose the two excerpts from TMS. The first regards the natural deference towards royalty that evokes servile submission and debasement; Smith's narrative can hardly avoid cynicism but is stunningly lucid and informative on the nature of sentimental loyalty to royalty. To some extent, Smith deconstructs the Burkean sublime of royal supreme power that has nothing to do with charisma:

> and their conduct [of the rulers] must, either justly or unjustly, have excited the highest degree of all those passions, before the bulk of the people can be brought to oppose them with violence, or to desire to see them either punished or deposed. *Even when the people have been brought this length, they are apt to relent every moment, and easily relapse into their habitual state of deference to those whom they have been accustomed to look upon as their natural superiors.* They cannot stand the mortification of their monarch. *Compassion soon takes the place of resentment, they forget all past provocations, their old principles of loyalty revive, and they run to re-establish the ruined authority of their old masters, with the same violence with which they had opposed it.* The death of Charles I brought about the Restoration of royal family ... [italics added].[61]

At this juncture, Weber's classical analysis of charisma in *Economy and Society* can provide valuable insights.[62] Weber's multilayered analysis goes beyond the scope of this chapter. Rather, I shift the attention to Weber's account of the routinisation of charisma within which traditional and charismatic authority merge as sources of legitimacy. Earlier in the text Weber made clear that charismatic authority is often but not always revolutionary as it emerges in extraordinary situations, amidst anxiety and enthusiasm in front of an unprecedented conjuncture. Yet it always inverts hierarchies and overthrow customs, law and traditions. The 'bearer of charisma enjoys loyalty and authority by virtue of a mission believed to embodied in him' while 'patriarchal power serves the demands of everyday life and persists in its function'.[63] The routinisation of charisma, as Weber calls the institutionalisation of charismatic rule after the founder's death, enables charisma and tradition, otherwise antagonistic, to merge.[64] Beyond rational regulations, both charisma and tradition rest on 'the belief in the sanctity of an individual's authority, which is unquestionably valid for the ruled . . .'; 'both rest on a sense of loyalty and obligation that always has a religious aura'.[65] In this sociological mode of thought, instead of upsetting everything traditional as in *statu nascendi*, charisma becomes a force of legitimation. Charisma is perceived as a sacred source of authority very much in the sense encountered previously in Burke's analysis of power. This mode of legitimation of authority draws heavily on religion and the mystification involved in the alleged religious aura of authority. Unlike Burke, the Weberian sociological interpretation better captures a layer in Smith's thought regarding the demystification and the emphasis on the modus operandi of charisma.

This proto-sociological way of thinking in Smith enhances a different take on moderate leadership. The principled, context-sensitive and moderate charismatic leader triggers a different type of feelings.[66] In this case, Smith evokes the modern charismatic leader and the influence that he exercises on his followers combined with persuasion and rhetorical skills, far from titled aristocracy's ritualised behaviour:

> The leader of the successful party, however, if he has authority enough to prevail upon his own friends to act with proper temper and moderation (which he frequently has not), may sometimes render to his country a service much more essential and important than the greatest victories and the most extensive conquests. He may re-establish and improve the constitution, and from the very doubtful and ambiguous character of the leader of a party, he may assume the greatest and noblest of all characters, that of the reformer and legislator of a

great state; and, by the wisdom of his institutions, secure the internal tranquillity and happiness of his fellow citizens for many succeeding generations.[67]

Going beyond Weberian categories, Smith's modern charismatic leader is not exceptional in the sense of having a heroic or extraordinary mission and he does not revolutionise structures, institutions and practices of everyday life. He stands out in his exceptional perception of moderation and self-restraint. Can this form of authority generate the necessary prestige for a sustainable structure of power? Be this as it may, Smith's insight regarding the aesthetic appeal of systems compared with personified authority as sources of legitimacy remains a profound analytical tool.

Conclusion

In the *Lectures on Jurisprudence*,[68] Adam Smith draws on the legacy of Roman *auctoritas* and seeks to determine the conditions of a transition from paternalistic deference to the impersonal authority of the laws. Yet he is aware that the 'impersonality' of law and institutions may be insufficient to bind. Despite systematic efforts to mitigate its impact on rationally stirred politics, reverence to authority remains a source of legitimacy in modern politics invoking an emotional foundation that ultimately remains supra-rational.

The man of system instantiates the congenital vice of philosophers and other intellectuals: the obsession with the beauty of allegedly perfect social or political systems that, once implemented, will supposedly complete the proposed moral, social or political reform or revolution. Although some idea or system is acknowledged as necessary for any theory to get off the ground, Smith is eminently sceptical about leaders totally obsessed by their projects of change irrespective of context. The real charisma is found in resistance to the excessive appeal of systems. Smith acknowledges that aesthetical attachment to systems potentially marks progress compared with traditional deference to charismatic authority because it depersonalises charisma, provided that some form of deference to authority is necessary for any sustainable regime. The main advantage of Smith's true statesmanship is unsurpassable coolness as an antidote to the self-delusion that has so often seized leaders' minds throughout human history.

Notes

1. E. Thomas Dow, Jnr, 'An Analysis of Weber's Work on Charisma', *The British Journal of Sociology* 29 (1978), pp. 92–3.
2. Edmund Burke, *A Philosophical Enquiry into the Origin of Our Ideas of the Sublime and Beautiful*, ed. Paul Guyer (Oxford: Oxford University Press, [1757] 2015), IV.viii, p. 109.
3. *Enquiry*, IV.v, p. 107, I.xviii, p. 43: 'The passions which belong to self-preservation, turn on pain and danger; they are firmly painful when their cause immediately affect us; they are delightful when we have an idea of pain and danger, without being actually in such circumstances; this delight I have not called pleasure, because it turns to pain, and because it is different enough from any idea of positive pleasure. Whatever excites this delight, I call sublime. The passions belonging to self-preservation are the strongest of all passions.'
4. Burke, *A Philosophical Enquiry*, II.ii, p. 48.
5. Ibid.: 'Θάμβος is in Greek either fear or wonder; εινός is terrible or respectable; αιδέω to reverence or to fear; *Vereor* in latin, is what αιδέω is in greek. The Romans used the verb *stupeo*, a term which strongly marks the state of an astonished mind, to express the effect either of simple fear or of astonishment'.
6. See the seminal study by Catherine Marshall, *Political Deference in a Democratic Age* (Cham: Palgrave, 2021), ch. 2, 'The Constitution of Political Deference', pp. 17–46.
7. Burke, *A Philosophical Enquiry*, III.x, p. 89. 'The authority of the father, so useful to our well-being, and so justly venerable upon all accounts, hinders us from having that entire love for him that we have for our mothers, where the parental authority is almost melted down into the mother's fondness and indulgence.' For useful context, Richard Bourke, *Empire and Revolution: The Political Life of Edmund Burke* (Princeton: Princeton University Press, 2015), pp. 143–4.
8. Burke, *A Philosophical Enquiry*, III.x, p. 89.
9. Burke, *A Philosophical Enquiry*, III.x, p. 89.
10. Burke, *A Philosophical Enquiry*, pp. 48–9.
11. Burke, *A Philosophical Enquiry*, p. 54.
12. Burke, *A Philosophical Enquiry*, p. 55.
13. Bourke, *Empire and Revolution*, p. 149: 'However, it followed from Burke's analysis that a depleted level of power, especially under conditions of reduced ill will on the part of whoever is in authority, diminished the intensity of the terror it could provoke, so that the

symbols of power displayed before the public in a civilised regime could foster subjection based on reverence rather than unadulterated dread. Submission could be elicited on the basis of sublime delight without needing to evoke excessive fear. This insight would prove important to Burke's understanding of political psychology. It appeared to show that awe and veneration can sustain authority in politics in the absence of unmitigated servility. It also implied that admiration flourishes in a context of deference where power commands respect without the threat of immediate danger. This implication argued against natural histories of government that traced the origins of subjection solely to gratitude for protection from fear. As Burke saw it, not only did the fear of authority continue to exact obedience but, further, the feeling of submission could be agreeable to the mind as terror relaxed into the sentiment of respect.'

14. Inter alia, the seminal studies of Donald Winch, *Riches and Poverty: An Intellectual History of Political Economy in Britain, 1750–1834* (Cambridge: Cambridge University Press, 1996), and 'The Burke-Smith Problem and Late Eighteenth-Century Political and Economic Thought', *The Historical Journal* 28 (1985), pp. 231–47.

15. LRBL XIX, ii.44, p. 104 in Adam Smith, *The Glasgow Edition of the Works and Correspondence of Adam Smith* (Oxford: Oxford University Press, 1976–1983). The following abbreviations are used for Adam Smith's works: TMS *Theory of Moral Sentiments* in vol. I; WN *An Inquiry into the Nature and Causes of the Wealth of Nations* in vol. II; EPS *Essays on Philosophical Subjects* in vol. III (*The History of Astronomy, History of Ancient Physics, Of the Nature of Imitation that takes place in what are called Imitative Arts*); LRBL *Lectures on Rhetoric and Belles Lettres* in vol. IV; LJA, LJB *Lectures on Jurisprudence* (A, B) in vol. V.

16. LRBL XIX, ii.45, p. 104.

17. LRBL XX, ii.61, p. 111.

18. LRBL XX, ii.62, p. 111.

19. LRBL IX, i.117, p. 48.

20. LRBL XIII, i.163, p. 68.

21. LRBL XIII, i.164, p. 68.

22. For context on the connections between admiration and propriety see Stephen J. McKenna, *Adam Smith: The Rhetoric of Propriety* (Albany, NY: SUNY Press, 2006), especially pp. 94–8.

23. For a synthesis and useful context, Craig Smith, 'The Essays on Philosophical Subjects' in Ryan Hanley (ed.), *Adam Smith: His Life, Thought and Legacy* (Princeton: Princeton University Press, 2016) pp. 87–104.

24. Christopher Berry, 'Smith and Science' in Knud Haakonssen (ed.), *The Cambridge Companion to Adam Smith* (Cambridge: Cambridge University Press, 2006) p. 119, following S. Moscovici, contends that the 'section changes tack by developing a sociological rather than a psychological argument'.
25. Christopher J. Berry, 'Rude Religion: The Psychology of Polytheism in the Scottish Enlightenment' in Paul Wood (ed.), *The Scottish Enlightenment: Essays in Reinterpretation* (Rochester, NY: University of Rochester Press, 2000), pp. 315–44: 'Polytheism is necessarily the religion of the savage because that is the finding of the science of man' (p. 327). In line with a broad acceptance of Lockean psychology, the Scottish school of 'natural history of mankind' stipulates that the development from childhood to adulthood and from infancy to maturity 'is "natural" in the sense that is predictable and normal (rather than inevitable). This is natural progression and it is this that "natural history" traces. What it traces generically is the "natural progress" from (in Millar's version) "ignorance to knowledge and from rude to civilized manners", or from "the rude" to the "cultivated" (Dunbar's subtitle of *Essays on the History of Mankind*), or again, as Stewart and Robertson put it, from the "simple" to the "complicated". The natural history of religion is a specific version of this generic tale.'
26. EPS *History of Astronomy*, III.1.
27 EPS *History of Astronomy*, II.5–12.
28. EPS *History of Astronomy*, III.1.
29. EPS *History of Astronomy*, II.12, IV.13.
30. EPS *History of Astronomy*, III.2; *History of Ancient Physics*, II.11.
31. Berry, 'Smith and Science', p. 119.
32. Christopher Longuet-Higgins, 'The History of Astronomy: A Twentieth-Century View' in P. Jones and A. S. Skinner (eds), *Adam Smith Reviewed* (Edinburgh: Edinburgh University Press, 1992), p. 83.
33. Anthony Skinner, 'Early Writings: Science and the Role of Imagination' in *A System of Social Science, Papers Relating to Adam Smith* (Oxford: Clarendon Press, 1996).
34. On the excesses of the use of analogy see EPS *History of Astronomy*, II.12 and IV.50 where Smith discusses Kepler's uses and misuses of the principle of analogy. See also Eric Schliesser, 'Wonder in the Face of Scientific Revolutions: Adam Smith on Newton's Proof of Copernicanism', *British Journal for the History of Philosophy* 13 (2005), pp. 697–732, and his *Adam Smith: Systematic Philosopher and Public Thinker* (Oxford: Oxford University Press, 2017).

35. EPS *History of Astronomy*, II.12, IV.56–7.
36. EPS *History of Astronomy*, III.50
37. EPS *History of Astronomy*, III.53
38. EPS *History of Astronomy*, III.50
39. EPS *History of Astronomy*, IV.50: 'While the great objects of nature thus pass in review before them, many things occur in an order to which they have not been accustomed. Their imagination, which accompanies with ease and delight the regular progress of nature, is stopped and embarrassed by those seeming incoherences; they excite their wonder, and seem to require some chain of intermediate events, which, by connecting them with something that has gone before, may thus render the whole course of the universe consistent and of a piece.'
40. On the background of Newtonian natural theology in Britain, see John Gascoigne, 'From Bentley to the Victorians: The Rise and Fall of British Newtonian Natural Theology', *Science in Context* 2 (1988), pp. 219–56.
41. For a balanced account of the links between aesthetics and morality in Smith, see Karen Valihora, *Austen's Oughts: Judgment after Locke and Shaftesbury* (Newark, DE: University of Delaware Press, 2010).
42. TMS I.i.4.3, p. 20.
43. TMS I.ii.2.1, p. 31.
44. LRBL XXII, ii, p. 104.
45. LRBL XXII, ii, p. 104.
46. Robert Fudge, 'Sympathy, Beauty, and Sentiment: Adam Smith's Aesthetic Morality', *The Journal of Scottish Philosophy* 7 (2009), pp. 133–46.
47. Emily Brady, 'Adam Smith's Sympathetic Imagination and the Aesthetic Appreciation of Environment', *Journal of Scottish Philosophy* 9 (2011), p. 97.
48. TMS IV.1.4, p. 180. See Robert Mitchell, 'Beautiful and Orderly Systems: Adam Smith on the Aesthetics of Political Improvement' in Eric Schliesser and Leonidas Montes (eds), *New Voices on Adam Smith* (London: Routledge, 2006).
49. TMS IV.i.1, p. 178.
50. TMS IV.i.1, p. 179.
51. Samuel Fleischacker, *On Adam Smith's* Wealth of Nations: *A Philosophical Companion* (Princeton: Princeton University Press, 2004), p. 116.
52. Étienne Bonnot de Condillac, *Traité des systèmes* (Whitefish, MT: Kessinger Publishing, [1769] 2009).

53. Condillac, *Traité des systèmes*, p. 24.
54. Jennifer Riskin, 'The "Spirit of System" and the Fortunes of Physiocracy', *History of Political Economy* 35 (2003), Annual Supplement, pp. 49, 54–69.
55. EPS p. 245.
56. Arnault Scornicki, 'Comme une envie de système. De Hegel à l'Encyclopédie', *Labyrinthe* 34 (2010), pp. 54–6.
57. TMS VI.ii.2.17, p. 234.
58. TMS VI.ii.2.17, pp. 233–4.
59. TMS VI.ii.15, p. 232.
60. TMS VI.ii.18, p. 263. See the commentary of Eric Schliesser, 'Adam Smith on Political Leadership' in R. J. W. Mills and Craig Smith (eds), *The Scottish Enlightenment. Human Nature, Social Theory and Moral Philosophy: Essays in Honour of Christopher J. Berry* (Edinburgh: Edinburgh University Press, 2021), pp. 141–3.
61. TMS I.iii.2.3, p. 53. See also Spyridon Tegos, 'Deference to Authority in Adam Smith', *The Adam Smith Review* 12 (2020), pp. 117–33.
62. Max Weber, *Economy and Society: An Outline of Interpretative Sociology*, ed. Guenther Roth and Claus Wittich (Berkeley, CA: University of California Press, [1922] 2013).
63. Weber, *Economy and Society*, p. 1117.
64. Weber, *Economy and Society*, p. 1124.
65. Weber, *Economy and Society*, p. 1124.
66. Paul Sagar, *The Opinion of Mankind, Sociability and the Theory of the State from Hobbes to Rousseau* (Princeton: Princeton University Press, 2018), pp. 227–8, claims that Smith, in this context, anticipates Weber's balancing between the 'ethic of principled conviction' and the 'ethic of responsibility'. Instead, I focus on the aspects of pre-modern as opposed to modern charismatic authority involved in Smith's analysis.
67. TMS VI.ii.13–14, pp. 231–2.
68. LJA p. 129. See also p. 321: 'Several things tend to give one an authority over others. 1st, superiority of age and wisdom which is generally its concomitant. 2dly, superior strength of body; and these two it is which give the old an authority and respect with the young. 3d, superior fortune also gives a certain authority, caeteris paribus; and 4thly, the effect is the same of superior antiquity when everything else is alike'.

7

Sociology within the *Statistical Account of Scotland*

Kenneth Macdonald

Introduction

We are concerned, in this volume, to assess whether, and in what mode, the intellectual framework of the Scottish Enlightenment enabled sociological thought. One indicator might be the 'sociological' awareness, broadly defined, of educated Scots by the end of the eighteenth century. A possible target group would be the near one thousand respondents whose more-or-less verbatim reports, collected by Sir John Sinclair, form the twenty-one volumes of the *Statistical Account of Scotland; drawn up from the communications of the ministers of the different parishes* (1791–9).[1] Consideration of their *mode* of thought (*not* its content) on some potentially sociological topics constitutes the subject of this chapter.[2]

Sinclair's ministers are an apt choice, for a number of reasons. They are engaged, under his direction, in reportage on the state of the country:

> the idea I annex to the term ['statistical'], is an enquiry into the state of a country, for the purpose of ascertaining the *quantum of happiness* enjoyed by its inhabitants, and the means of its future improvement.[3]

Their accounts are available, with an exceptionally high response rate. Though trained to theology, the ministers are not isolated from the general intellectual climate: 'Without doubt, in the course of their professional education, most of the clergy receive a tincture of the liberal arts',[4] but that professional education would, if anything, give a bias *against* naturalistic interpretation of social phenomena (so they form a good test-case). Considered as a historical descriptive source, the OSA, given the imbalance between parish and population, yields disproportionate space to rural Scotland (cities are underdescribed – Edinburgh particularly, served by a woefully inadequate[5] account from Creech, Sinclair's publisher). But for my purposes – centring on *how* this group thinks – that is not a problem, and the stilling of those Edinburgh elite voices is no bad thing; again, that bias leverages the import of any sociological thinking found. That the group is solely male is to be regretted, but eighteenth-century universities were male territory; the bias remains unfortunate but, again, perhaps leverages the import.

This chapter, given my focus, does not deploy, or assess, the OSA as a historical account of late eighteenth-century Scotland. A useful conspectus of some of the ethnographic material is found in Steven;[6] unfortunately, with some honourable exceptions,[7] even today there is a shortage of sustained *quantitative* analysis of the data garnered.

There are, however, three sociologically pertinent themes which I also ignore. The *first* is the impact of the *fact* of the OSA on the subsequent development of social arithmetic census-taking mensuration. This was Sinclair's active intent:

> it is to be hoped, that the example of Scotland . . . will soon be *imitated* by other nations. For that purpose, a specimen of the work is been *translated into French*, and transmitted to *every person of power*, political influence, or literary merit on the continent of Europe.[8]

He correctly perceived some successes ('The . . . *Board of Agriculture* . . . would never have taken place had it not been for this enquiry').[9] More contestable is his claim to be pathfinder for the British Census of 1801 ('The *practicability* of obtaining an accurate statement of the population of a country having been *proved* [*by OSA*] . . . Abbott . . . was *thence led*, in 1800, to being forward a plan for a general census of Great Britain');[10] the more conventional narrative sees that proposed head-count as a response to an English problem[11] of grain shortage. Untangling this would be a potentially fruitful line of enquiry, but it requires a historian's skills, not mine, and would move the narrative focus outwith the eighteenth century. The *second* road not taken is an assessment of Sir John Sinclair's *own* contribution to sociological thought. Sinclair is characteristically regarded as a 'doer' (as above), not a thinker; a revaluation may be due. Besides bringing about the OSA, he provided its intellectual framework and justification – as in his repeated refrain: 'the science of statistics is in politics, what anatomy is in medicine, laying the best foundation of all useful improvements'.[12] His *Analysis* of the OSA, thirty years later, attempts theoretical organisation of its garnered empirical matter:

> A populous nation, to a common observer, seems to be a *mass of confusion* and disorder ... In order to *explain* this ... interesting subject, it is necessary to consider a political [*i.e. organised*] society as divided into *twenty-seven* [*occupational*] *classes*, arranged under three ... heads ...[13]

The attempt to see order through defining occupational classes is a sociological move. Of course his resulting, structured, socio-economic classification has flaws, but he presents it, rightly, as a step forward from Adam Smith's categorisations (explicitly criticising Smith's failure to recognise intellectual labour as 'productive');[14] this could be seen as part of a long lineage of sociological analysis. But that is not, here, my focus.

The *third* area of possible, but unexplored, interest is the intellectual genesis of Sinclair's project: how anchored within the concerns of the thinkers of the Scottish Enlightenment? Sinclair was a student at the University of Edinburgh when 'moral philosophy was taught by Ferguson',[15] but his biography does not report him as attending these classes. He moved to Glasgow,[16] 'chiefly that he might attend the lectures of John Millar, Professor of Civil Law';[17] but there is every indication that Sinclair regarded Millar *not* as a social theorist, merely as an 'eminent jurist ... His attendance on the lectures of Professor Millar was preparatory to admission into the Faculty of Advocates'.[18] Sinclair himself, in his short history of Scottish exceptionalism, does not include either Ferguson or Millar amongst Scottish luminaries in the 'metaphysical, moral, and political sciences'.[19] The two Enlightenment thinkers whom Sinclair does cite, in his justification for the *Statistical Account*, are Dugald Stewart and James Steuart. Dugald Stewart appears in support of the claim that 'it is impossible to establish solid general principles, without the previous study of particulars'.[20] The reference Sinclair gives is to a very long chapter in Stewart's *Elements*: that chapter does indeed contain the sentence cited[21] but within an articulated theoretical framework with other emphases ('In order to lay a *solid foundation* for the science of politics, the *first step* ought to be, to ascertain that form of society which is perfectly *agreeable* to *nature and to justice*; and what are the *principles of legislation* necessary for maintaining it').[22] This, though not antithetical to Sinclair's project, in no wise prefigures, or appears to entail or require, the *Statistical Account*. My reading is that Stewart's 'particulars' are more analytic than Sinclair's incorporation would have them; where Stewart talks of something closer in design to the OSA ('a *general survey of the complicated structure* of society')[23] he sees it only as a device to check 'sanguine and inconsiderate projects of reformation'. To James Steuart is ascribed the assertion that without a detailed parish-by-parish enumeration, all plans for 'benefiting a nation' are only a 'vain and deceitful expedient for walking in the dark'.[24] Steuart is indeed in favour of mensuration, but his discussion[25] was of occupational population planning – the widening of this to *all* plans benefiting a nation (and that 'vain and deceitful') are Sinclair's embellishments. Perhaps (echoing the *second* topic above) here are grounds to discuss Sinclair's own intellectual contribution: his insistence on *systematic* inquiry into the state of a country? Whereas Hume looks kindly on Adam Smith's writing being 'so much illustrated by *curious* facts',[26] Sinclair is prepared to berate Smith for lack of 'accurate information' and structured facts: 'without a knowledge of those facts which statistical enquiries bring to light, no theory of political economy, however imposing in its *appearance*, can ... be safely reduced [*i.e. applied*] to practice'.[27] But a full account of OSA derivation has also to handle Sinclair's professed indebtedness to Continental precursors, as well as the arguments which led to support from the General Assembly of the Church of Scotland.[28] Again, resolution is beyond my present remit.

Some general observations on the response of the ministers within the *Statistical Account* may be helpful as context. Expectedly, perhaps particularly so given the framing, the writers are all anchored in the *particularity* of their parishes, alert to climate and varying soil ('most seasons, the ground is *bomb-proof* in the middle of March, and mere *puddle* for some time thereafter');[29] they display a keen farming interest in land surface and underlying strata (one garners the lifetime observations of the local well-digger).[30] They are aware of the importance of fuel – contrast Adam Smith whom Jonsson characterises as 'blind to the new importance of mineral energy'[31] – and report in detail on peat and coal supplies (and on the coal tax: 'impolitic, partial and oppressive').[32] Their energy sources are either geographically constrained (water) or laborious to move (coal, peat) or expensive to maintain (horses), and the materials of eighteenth-century agriculture remain rebarbatively physical. Rural ministers encourage (and carefully document) enclosures and improvement, but stone is needed for these enclosures – '[here], stones, for stone walls of any kind, are extremely scarce'[33] – and fertiliser is bulky, heavy: 'The quantity of dung bestowed on an acre is usually between 30 and 40 double [*two-horse*] carts'.[34] Unsurprisingly they are concerned over the state of the roads. Further, given the time and cost overheads of transportation, parishes are often presented as circumscribed units – 'The parish can well *supply itself* with provisions'.[35] *Production*, particularly in rural parishes, is salient, even for poets: '*Mr Robert Burns*, a gentleman well known by his poetical productions, who rents a farm in this parish, *is of opinion that the west country cows give a larger quantity of milk.*'[36]

The ministers' suggestions for melioration of condition are reform of salt duties (which, hindering food preservation, damaged production and export); reform of coal duties (which diverted time to peat-lifting and hindered fertiliser manufacture from limestone); provision of better roads, harbours and canals (often accompanied by carefully detailed information on possibilities); school improvement; spread of proven agricultural practice; introduction of *appropriate* manufactures. The detail they see as a strength of OSA – 'Our historians . . . chiefly employ themselves in . . . giving inaccurate accounts of . . . wars, and political contests, overlooking unfortunately, the more important details of *industry*, *trade*, and *population*'[37] – and they are enthused by Sinclair's project: with 'the *locality* and minuteness of the circumstances which it contains'.[38] This detail they see as both practically relevant and significant for social theory: 'enabling us to form a proper estimate of privileges peculiar [*unique*] to our own times . . . more safe and candid to compare our political condition with that of our fathers, than with . . . visionary theories of perfection'.[39]

Two aspects may strike the modern reader as surprising. Ministers, as we might expect, enumerate their parishioners in terms of 'examinable persons'; the opening exchange of that examination, the *Shorter Catechism*, is stark and memorable:

Q: What is the chief end of man?
A: Man's chief end [*purpose*] is to glorify God and to enjoy him forever

We might anticipate this would inform their answers on 'amelioration'. Not so. One isolated voice suggests: 'Improve the *morals of the people*'[40] – but immediately appends a utilitarian gloss ('a *cheap and easy* antidote against anarchy and disorder'). Predominantly the answers are secular. Partly this is contextual; this is how they construe the OSA (in other writings they wax theological). But partly it reflects a view (not universal, but frequent) of the role of the clergy; consider this minister on his parishioners:

> Several of the farmers read history, magazines and newspapers. The vulgar read almost nothing but books on religious subjects. Many of them are too fond of controversial divinity . . . To *discourage* this unhappy propensity, so common through a great part of Scotland, and to *recommend books of a more rational and instructive nature*, seems an object worthy of a clergyman.[41]

Or what this minister choses to admire in Saint Columba: 'After stripping the history of Columba of the ridiculous . . . legends with which it is disfigured . . . enough remains to convince us, that he was a *man of considerable political abilities*';[42] and what this sees as praiseworthy in his congregation: 'They are averse to long preachings, long prayers, and long psalms; their ideas of religion and morality . . . are tolerably *sound and rational*'.[43] Notice though (and we explore this further below) they are not unreflective on the social consequences of religious practice (as with this social analysis of the worst effect of the 'stool of repentance': 'it impressed on the minds of the people an idea, that there was *no other crime* great enough to deserve ecclesiastical censures, but fornication').[44]

The other 'framing' that may strike the modern reader is the repeated obsequious protestations that all are '[f]rom religious principle, *thankful and loyal* subjects of the British government'.[45] But the events of the mid-century were still vivid ('In 1746, [*our*] church, which the Highland army had converted into a [*gunpowder*] magazine, was blown up').[46] Government control continued: in 1792 the military was on the move 'to quell the riots in Ross-shire; a second time . . . on account of the disturbances in Dundee';[47] next year saw military force against the 'mob' in Inverness.[48] The war with France raised understandable security concerns (a port-town reports, with pride, its purchase of 'ten new iron cannon, 12 pounders').[49] Macleod may be right to claim that

Sociology within the *Statistical Account of Scotland*   159

likenesses between sedition trials in Scotland and England 'reflect the *common* context of panic among the political elite caused by the French Revolution';[50] but the outcomes across the two jurisdictions were very different.

The 1793 trial, in Perth, of Palmer, 'clergyman, sometime residing in Dundee', found him guilty of penning 'Seditious *Writing*, tending to inflame the minds of the people',[51] and yielded a sentence of seven years' transportation. Muir, barrister (struck off the roll without trial), 'accused of wickedly and feloniously exciting ... by means of seditious *speeches* ... a spirit of disloyalty and disaffection to the king',[52] was (in Edinburgh, 1793) sentenced to transportation for fourteen years. Watt, who may have sailed slightly (not much) closer to action – the charge being (note the dreadful pending crimes) that 'whatever was their pretence, their *real* scheme was to subvert the constitution, and introduce *Universal Suffrage* and *Annual Parliaments*, in place of that *happy* system under which we at present so securely live'[53] – received the viscerally bloody dramaturgy of this Edinburgh sentence: 'hanged by the neck, but *not* till you are dead; for you are then to be taken down ... and your bowels burned before your face ...'[54] This contrasts with a string of English acquittals and may strengthen a Scottish desire to appear 'thankful and loyal'; it may also disincline Sinclair's respondents to venture near political science.

Though, as I hope to show, they thought sociologically about aspects of their social world, what, from a modern perspective, is lacking is any sustained discussion of how accounts might be tested. The required tools are not altogether alien to them, just not deployed on social material. For example, in a discussion of tree-yield by species, we find a reasonable account of symmetric random error:

> A thousand accidental circumstances may accelerate or retard the growth of one tree ... but if the measurement is taken of many, the *hurtful and favourable* circumstances so *counterbalance* each other, as to produce a fair average result.[55]

Again, there is much discussion of agricultural and manufacturing 'experiments' (by which they mean 'trials, under differing circumstances'), with, occasionally, a more articulated model of intervention and control group; as in the 'comparative trial'[56] of two spinning-wheel designs, or the dairy farmer, who 'to try an *experiment*, bought one of Mr Bakewell's bulls. He put the half of his cows to this, the other half to a Moorland bull . . . He fed the product *equally* . . .'[57] A case might be made that this experimental mode in farming and manufacturing affected how they thought about the social ('Bigotry in farming, is more easily eradicated than bigotry in religion, as the bad consequences of a wrong system are more visible').[58] Perhaps it might be argued that their approach to matters of 'police' (that is, social policy, administration) embed these same principles. But this would be at best claimed as implicit; these principles (in regard to the social) are not rendered explicit by the ministers themselves (though Sinclair's *Analysis* comes closer: another motive to reinvestigate Sinclair-as-sociologist). For this chapter I have chosen to disregard the (important) issues of hypothesis testing and assessment, and focus on the explicit sociological narratives proffered.

Finally a word on methodology. I am, obviously, not claiming that *all* ministers thought similarly; the accounts that follow are an amalgam of *differing* voices (my citations are spread, fairly evenly, across the twenty-one volumes), so not tracing the contours of a single cognitive voice. Many of Sinclair's respondents – as indeed their remit was – report the facts as they see them without comment. But many do explore causes for actions. What follows is a presentation of *some* of these on *some* social issues. Obviously I am selective (the insightful and succinct invite citation). But I have only been selective within 'sociological' accounts (those not thinking sociologically characteristically provide *no* account; the default, for example, is rarely 'original sin'). My opening paragraph above, assigning import to such documentation, carries the (here unevidenced) assumption that 'sociological' insight would be lacking in a comparable group in the 1690s. For the present I leave that assumption untested. Minimally I seek to show that the clergy were, in the 1790s, capable of thinking sociologically. If you cede the 1690s assumption, that becomes possible ground for claiming the influence of Scottish Enlightenment thought.

In a chapter of this length, if the presentation is to provide sufficient citation detail to make meaningful reading, not all potential areas can be covered. I have chosen to focus on political unrest; religion; occupation and technology; the organisation of provision for the poor; the provision of inoculation against smallpox. Even amongst these topics, I only consider *some* of the aspects that the ministers discuss. The large themes of agricultural and manufacturing innovation, the proper role of unionisation, the state and style of education, the balance between town and country (and the proper conduct of borough administration), the interaction of Gaelic and Scots (and English) culture – all of which vividly concern them – will be sidestepped. Again, my aim is not an overview of *all* sociological thought within the OSA but ascertaining whether these ministers could think sociologically; the topics chosen illustrate a reasonable range of ways of thinking.

Political Unrest

As noted, Sinclair's respondents have an interest in disassociating themselves from the politically restive ('Such persons may assume the name of *patriots* and *friends* of the people; but they must furnish us with a new glossary before we can understand them'),[59] even whilst sometimes ascribing that virtue to the self-interest of their parishioners: *'terrified* that the French-Revolution Government should be introduced among them, for every one chooses to *keep what he has lawfully got,* and *not make an equal division* of it among his neighbours'.[60] When seeking explanation for unrest, however, their preferred – socio-economic – tools work to advantage. The minister of Campsie acknowledges the foundation of chapters of *Friends of the People* in his parish ('they met often . . . purchasing political pamphlets, and sent delegates to the different Conventions met at Edinburgh'),[61] while seeking to downplay their significance ('Notwithstanding all the bustle which was occasioned by their folly, the different Jacobin societies in this parish altogether, never contained above 60 persons').[62] He proceeds:

> Concerning the *impropriety* of such societies, the *laws* of our country hath already given ample testimony. It may not be improper, however, in the *Statistical Account* . . . to give some *description* of the people who composed the societies.[63]

A clear 'moving on from the politics, let us, in this volume, consider the sociology' step. We are told the members 'were chiefly formed from amongst the journeymen and apprentices at the different print-fields . . . mostly lads from 17 years of age to 30', with 'a few half-educated people'[64] acting as information conduits. Print-fields, in the eighteenth-century, set coloured patterns on calicos, handkerchiefs and so forth; the introduction of piece-rates (rather than day-wages) for this work had led to incipient trade unions (with closed-shop provision). As the minister from another parish expressed the contested situation:

> those illegal combinations, that are now become so common among the manufacturers [*i.e. workers*] of this country . . . they appointed a committee of their number, from the different print-fields in the west of Scotland, to . . . regulate the prices [of piece-work] . . . to allow no persons to be employed, but such as came under certain regulations which they had framed.[65]

The Jacobin *political* activism, the Campsie writer believes, occurred because three main 'causes *cooperated*':

> In the *first* place, a considerable degree of licentiousness had begun to prevail in this district, owing to high wages; and as the influx of such wealth had been rather *sudden*, due subordination of ranks was almost totally forgot.
> In the *second* place a Relief meeting [*dissenting congregation*], about 10 years ago, being erected in this parish, which had drawn off a considerable number of people . . . and rendered them, in some measure hostile to the powers that be . . .
> In the *third* place, Mr Muir, advocate [*see my Introduction, above*] . . . having some *connections* . . . in the place, was naturally induced to try the power of his eloquence upon the inhabitants . . .[66]

To that second (structural, sectarian) cause, the minister appends an (uncharitable?) accusation of direct intervention: 'I am doubtful but [*i.e. I suspect*] the spirit of innovation was *encouraged* . . . by [the dissenters'] public teachers, *with a view to increase the adherence* to their own tabernacle' (but note the attributed motive, grounded in rational self-interest). The analysis is rounded out by developing the organisational context for journeymen: 'who have abundance of *time* in the evenings to cabal together'; the characteristics for self-selection into that occupation: 'men . . . from their profession, rather given to wandering, and *fond of novelty*'; and the socialisation provided by industrial conflict in print-fields: so 'somewhat naturally addicted to *form associations* against their master's authority'.[67]

As an example of sociological reasoning this is not impercipient. The actors are defined, their characteristics linked to self-selection (to be a *first-generation* print-field worker was a particular choice). We are pointed to economic shocks (sudden high wages), to ideational predispositions (that dissenter background) and to factors enabling collective action (spare evening time, and 'unionisation' experience). We are even offered an answer to the question 'why Campsie?': the suspected actions of individual dissenter clergy and the involvement of movement leaders (Mr Muir). What of course is lacking is any specification as to how this might be tested, but that is a recurrent deficit.

Religion

Treatment of the so-called 'Cambuslang conversions' of 1742 can form a window on the ministers' willingness to think sociologically about their profession. The broad facts, as retold by the current minister of Cambuslang, are striking enough: in a crowded congregation many 'were seized all at once . . . with the most dreadful apprehensions concerning the state of their souls';[68] this *conviction* of damnation was accompanied by *'violent agitations of body . . . faintings and convulsions'* (some women reported the pain of *conviction* was greater than child-birth); *conviction* of damnation was followed by *conversion* ('as sudden and unexpected as their *conviction* . . . crying out with triumph and exultation').[69] The events 'brought vast numbers of people from all quarters' but divided contemporaneous opinion.

From an eighteenth-century perspective the '*only* extraordinary circumstance relating to this work, is the *external effects* on the bodies of men';[70] this is what requires explanation. The writer correctly reports that the 'high party' of the church saw there the influence of the Holy Spirit; the Seceders (being, he argues, despite their similar theological predispositions on the underlying issues, by then locked into opposition to the establishment) saw Satan's 'awful work upon the bodies of men';[71] whilst moderates (with whom he identifies)[72] saw 'the *influence* of fear and hope, of sympathy and example, aided by peculiar *circumstances* . . . [i.e.] the operation of *natural causes*'.[73] The *influence* came from the sermons 'addressed, not to the *understandings* of the hearers, but to their imaginations and *passions*; and especially to the passions of fear and hope'.[74] The prime aiding 'peculiar *circumstance*' being that the congregation had been – for some time – extensively primed with *verbatim* accounts of 'wonderful conversions' in New England. 'That *this preparation* gave rise to the work at Cambuslang . . . was manifest; because the persons *convicted* and *converted* there, were affected in the *same* manner, and expressed themselves in the *same* words, with those who were *convicted* and *converted* in new England.'[75] The writer also directs attention to the way in which assistant ministers individually prompted verbally echoing responses from those affected.[76]

Whether this thesis holds up is not my concern, but it could form the subject of a respectable sociological paper. The author continues – invoking the maxim that 'we are disposed to imitate the actions of others, and that we are *naturally*, and as it were mechanically, moved by seeing them' – to claim that, once started, 'the effects of *sympathy and example* sufficiently *explain* its future progress . . . Whenever anyone cried aloud . . . many others cried aloud likewise, using the *same words*, or words with the same meaning'.[77] The maxim may be closer to social-psychology than sociology (though disciplinary boundaries are permeable), but again the interest lies in whether the writers opt for socially attentive explanations.

In some ways more interesting is a contribution, in a later volume, by a minister who disagrees with this analysis. More interesting because, though disagreeing, he clearly sees the (sociological) force of the analysis, summarising succinctly:

> They have endeavoured to account for the unusual agitation and religious concern which then appeared among the people, by the influence of *natural causes alone*. They have ascribed them to the influence of passion, of hope, and fear, and sympathy, and example, or to all these causes united. They have told us, that the instruments of that work addressed the passions of men, more than their understandings; that those on whom the chief impression was made, were almost all affected in the same way, and expressed themselves in similar language; that the agitation of one was communicated to the multitude, and acted like a charm on their sympathetic feelings. This representation is *plausible*, but it is only plausible.[78]

This minister then articulates a coherent religious interpretation, ending with reference to particular individuals: '*Whatever* were the *means* . . . they experienced at that period a great and important *change*, which has formed and decided their characters through life'[79] – essentially opting for a recognition that there are two potential perspectives fitting the same observed phenomena and attempting to locate a differentiating fact (that 'change').

These are two thoughtful entries. Some present a more reductionist analysis of religious enthusiasm, as this (under the heading of '*Diseases*' in the parish):

> Convulsions were once very common . . . especially during the time of divine service; but are now quite extinct. The cure is attributed to a rough fellow of a kirk-officer, who tossed a woman in that state . . . into a ditch full of water . . .[80]

but most are keen to stress the unimportance of theological distinction:

> Men have discovered . . . that their opinions, with regard to speculative points, are *often as different as their faces*; and that the harmony of society, and the intercourse [*interactions*] of life, ought not to be interrupted by the one more than by the other.[81]

This has obvious echoes in twenty-first-century discussion of belief (and race, and gender) and, like them, opens the way to sociological discussion of the functions of distinctions. One writer suggests that, viewed contextually, even 'Papistry' might have uses:

> In this enlightened age, we can hardly think, without indignation, of that spiritual bondage in which our ancestors were held; but, perhaps, a philosopher, in viewing the state of society . . . *when* the police [*administration*] was extremely imperfect . . . would consider the great ascendancy of ecclesiastics to have been a happy circumstance for the people, seeing it was *often exerted to prevent and to redress injuries* from powerful laymen.[82]

Likewise another, seeing, *within* the Protestant tradition, the merit of checks and balances, and targeted marketing and delivery:

> The existence of Seceders . . . has perhaps no bad effect upon the manners and sentiments of the people . . . They are in some degree spies and *checks* upon the members of the established church; and the discourses of their clergy are . . . *adapted* . . . to the *capacity* and the prejudices of the *least enlightened classes*.[83]

(Sinclair was to remark, in a framing that would be recognised by much later sociologists of religion: 'It is said that in religion, as in merchandise, demand regulates the quantity manufactured'.)[84] Further, as Smith and Hume did earlier, the ministers reflect on the impact of *multiple* sects, suggesting that sectarian bitterness is in decline, partly from communicative logic, since then, given multiplicity, 'each begins to suspect, that the dictates of their own party have no better claim to *infallibility*, than those of others'[85] but also (again a social – if only superficial – mechanism) 'partly . . . from the novelty being over'.[86] They consider the *social* processes of recruitment within 'mixed-faith' marriages:

> Intermarriages with Protestant families have been frequently observed to bring over Papists, especially the female part.[87]
>
> When a Protestant man marries a Roman Catholic woman he has very little domestic peace or happiness till he professes that religion.[88]

These two accounts differ, but again my concern here is not with *what* ministers think but with the *way* in which they think about religious recruitment. Further, toleration is understood to have social consequences: 'one great reason for the *decline* of . . . sects, is the moderation with which they are treated all over this country'[89] and, though toleration is also advocated from first principles, the writers emphasise its social utility within the polity: 'The religious toleration granted [*i.e. allowed*], seems to answer, in this district, the full ends of good government and public utility'.[90] Reflecting on the persistence of sects, one writer dismisses any sustaining effect of *ideas* – 'the lower ranks are incapable of forming religious creeds, which can stand the test, *even of their own reflections*, for any length of time'[91] – and hence ties sectarian persistence to *social* forces: 'the *influence* of authority, interest, and habit'. Under this interpretation, '[i]f opposition and persecution unhappily lend their aid to that *influence* [of authority, interest, and habit] . . . the effect becomes much *stronger*'. Yet again, my concern is not with the accuracy of this analysis, but with its form: seeing religious phenomena (sects and their prevalence) as affected by social processes.

Occupation (and Technology)

A wide topic. I focus on three disparate aspects: the extent to which occupation determines character; the salience of social mobility; and the understanding of technology. Again, these topics are arbitrary and not exhaustive – the ministers talk of much else related to occupation. But they may suffice to make my argument.

Determining Character

Smith's view, that 'division of labour' engenders torpor of mind, is well known (though, as I have elsewhere argued, often over-interpreted).[92] The ministers agree with Smith's analysis; for example on mill-workers they write: 'The children . . . *confined, as it were, to the very point of the spindle*, must of course have *narrow ideas* and contracted minds'[93] or, again, lamenting 'the degradation of mind which invariably follows a minute subdivision of labour'.[94] It fits their predominant anti-urban predilections ('Farming does not require many words, but much reflection and observation').[95] But they extend the discussion more widely than Smith ever did: 'The general character of a people commonly takes its complexion from their local situation, their engagements and their pursuits'.[96] Thus they are alert to the social incentives of economic arrangements:

> The mode the farmers have of paying their rents has . . . a considerable degree of influence in forming their characters . . . as their tack-duties [*rents*] are for the most part paid in *kind*, they are anxious to conceal from their landlords . . . what the land produces.[97]

This is held to contribute to 'a sort of low cunning' the minister perceives in his flock. Another considers cattle-breeders:

> Their line of business . . . by which they are often led out into the world, and frequently into the company of gentlemen, who . . . are . . . dealers in cattle, gives an illumination to their minds, and a polish to their manners, which those in a mere grain country, are absolute strangers to.[98]

Yet another evaluates that contrast differently – 'The cattle trade is less favourable than agriculture to sobriety and honesty'[99] – but both see the impact of social context upon character and mores (as in the Campsie print-field workers, discussed earlier). A particularly striking discussion arises around the market-gardens of Inveresk, outside Edinburgh:

> The whole produce of the gardens, together with salt, and sand for washing floors, and other articles . . . were carried in baskets or creels on the backs of women to be sold in Edinburgh, where, *after they had made their market* [*negotiated their sales*], it was usual for them to return loaded with goods . . . or with dirty linens to be washed . . . This employment of women, which has certainly prevailed ever since Edinburgh became a considerable city . . . has occasioned a *reversal*

> *of the state of the sexes* in this parish, and has *formed a character and manners*, in the female sex, which seems peculiar to them, *at least in this country**. The carriers of greens, salt, *etc.* are generally the wives of *weavers, shoemakers, tailors, or sievemakers, who, being confined by their employments within doors, take charge of the children and family*, while the females trudge to Edinburgh about their several branches of business ... Their usual daily profits ... besides the *free, social, and disengaged life which they lead*, is a greater addition to the income of the family, than they could earn by any other branch of industry.[100]

This picture of the female porters is intriguing in and of itself. But for our purposes the merit is the minister's insight into the malleability of domestic arrangements, the constraints of finance and the sharing of household labour and child-care. One could see this as the prologue to a discussion of domestic roles. Admittedly he does not go on to fully write the sociological essay, but his invocation of international comparison is a good analytic move (the starred footnote invocation was to Dillon's 1780 account of women porters in Bilbao). Two points worth noting: the Dillon account forms but a small part of that book (so alert reading by the minster), and Dillon – 'they work as much as the strongest men, unload the ships, carry burdens, and do all the work of porters'[101] – only touches on part of the porters' behaviour. The comparative implication ('so similar are the manners of human creatures in similar circumstances')[102] and the exploration of familial roles are unique to Sinclair's respondent, not derivative from Dillon.

This view of character as embedded in context, extends – naturally – to reflecting on over-time changes:

> The character of a people never fails to change with their changing condition. In contemplating them at the extreme points of the period of 70 or 80 years, it would be as difficult to recognise their identity as that of Sir John Cutler's worsted stockings, when scarcely an atom of the original texture remained.[103]

This engaging metaphysical speculation – the 'Ship of Theseus' problem, twisted with substitution of substance – around the *worsted* stockings ('which his maid darned so often with silk that they become at last a pair of *silk* stockings')[104] appears memorably in the *Memoirs of ... Scriblerus* by Pope et al. The cited minister of

Kirkmichael appears to have had this satire open on his desk as he writes: he has just invoked[105] the (otherwise somewhat unusual) image of the King 'whom a fiction of the English law supposes never to die', which happens to lie on the *same* Pope page as those worsted stockings. A reminder that these ministers are subject to influences outwith the *Scottish* Enlightenment.

Social Mobility

Sinclair asked his respondents to reflect on changes over time; all are alert to price inflation, and most lament the resulting devaluation of fixed stipends, remuneration being important for recruitment of ministers (so that 'men of learning and abilities would consider the church as an object of honourable ambition')[106] and of schoolteachers: 'I think we are just on the verge of having schools remaining vacant; the office being stripped of everything that can induce a man of any capacity to accept of it'.[107] The decline of education[108] they see as an intrinsic loss ('Scotland will, ere long, be as remarkable for wealth and ignorance as it was formerly for poverty and learning');[109] concern is also linked to political stability (they consistently frame the uneducated 'vulgar' as gullible and hence discontented). But, of particular sociological interest, they also emphasise the role of village schools as an avenue for social mobility:

> In those parishes, *where . . . only ignorant, low minded schoolmasters*, unfit to teach anything but a poor smattering, *can be had*, the children of the peasantry are *doomed to perpetual . . . obscurity*. But in places, where there are teachers, liberally educated . . . persons of the *lowest birth have risen* to eminence and rank.[110]

With a decline of education, they worry that:

> those numbers, who, by means of that mediocrity [*i.e. moderate quantity*] of literature acquired in the parish schools, *rose from the lowest stations of life* to merit, wealth, and rank must be henceforth chained down, hopeless and inglorious, to the miserable sphere of their humble birth.[111]

Social mobility may be a defining Scottish myth ('a land where the road to eminence is open to all who will strive to attain it');[112] though some provide evidence ('Not a few of our most respectable farmers were once servants')[113] – indeed, one parish records a legacy, for the poor, from a businessman 'of the island of St Christopher's (who was *once a beggar boy* and educated in this parish at the public expense)'.[114] But again, the truth of this image is not, presently, my concern; their willingness to think through implications of the process of social mobility – long a sociological mainstay – is. They conceptualise the process of mobility as *structurally* significant:

> The state and manners of society *should everywhere be so formed*, that people in the *lowest stations* of life may have a foundation on which to build their *hopes of advancing their circumstances* by frugality and industry . . . This encouragement is indeed held out to mechanics [*tradesmen*] . . . but this can hardly be said to be . . . the case with respect to farming . . . [*in places*] where *large* farms are universally adopted.[115]

The point about prevalent large farms is explained by another writer:

> in these places the *distance* between master and servant is so very great, that though the latter may enjoy a present subsistence [*livelihood*], yet he can have little or no hope of *bettering his circumstances* to such a degree, as to rise to independence, and obtain possession of a farm himself.[116]

whilst yet another offers a more nuanced assessment of the position of those 'mechanics' and their changing relative status:

> The *changes* in the state of our manufactures . . . having *removed the intermediate gradations* in the scale of society, operative [*working*] people, deprived of the prospect of advancing a *step* higher, have lost that incentive to economy and industry.[117]

This is some way from Steuart's quantitative approach to *measurement* of social mobility: 'I would recommend . . . to have one [list] made out, *classing* all the inhabitants, *not only by the trades they exercise, but by those of their fathers*',[118] but it does demonstrate an awareness of social process; on this they think sociologically – mobility not just as an individual experience but as affecting the way occupations (and society) operate.

Technology

Sinclair's contributors view the OSA as a practical enterprise and are concerned to document technological progress:

> In statistical accounts, *the progress of mechanical inventions, ought not to be omitted*. The benefit of such discoveries often remains confined to corners, because the public is not made acquainted with them. The improvement of a plough, a loom, a spade, a wheel, a lever, *etc*, as well as of the more complicated machinery of a ship, or of the spinning-jenny, it is of importance to have as generally, and as quickly, known as possible.[119]

and register inventive tradesmen ('to whom the world has been more indebted than to thousands of renowned empyrics in politics, law, divinity, physic, *etc*.').[120] Their accounts display (perhaps surprising) insight into technological principles; this for example on a modified water-wheel:

> This machine is so exceedingly simple, and acts in a manner so easy, natural, and uniform, that a common observer is apt to undervalue the invention: but persons skilled in mechanics view machinery with a very different eye; for to them *simplicity* is the first recommendation a machine can possess.[121]

or this on threshing-machines:

> The public attention, with regard to those useful machines, seems to have been fixed upon a wrong point . . . *the production of the greatest quantity of work* in a given time. But . . . it would be more useful to . . . reduce them to such *simplicity* of form, and lowness of price, as would *bring them within the reach of those farmers of moderate capital*.[122]

Their accounts would provide useful grist for a study of the origins of eighteenth-century innovation, but the ministers themselves view the machinery 'merely' as economists (so social science, but not our current focus):

> A threshing machine is newly erected, which does a great deal of work; but when the *prime cost*, and *interest* thereon, tear and *wear* of every kind, the *number of hands*, and the extraordinary *waste of horses*, are all taken into account it may not be of great *profit* to the proprietor.[123]

Industrial espionage they write of with approval – again as 'simple' economists – with no moral qualms or social reflection:

> These arts [*i.e. manufactures – here weaving*] owe their introduction to the patriotism of the Lady[124] of Henry Fletcher of Salton. Animated with a desire of increasing the manufactorie of our country, *this lady travelled to Holland with two expert mechanics, in the habit of servants. Her rank procured her easy access, together with her supposed domestics, to the manufactories*; and by frequent visits, the secrets of operation were discovered; models of the various works were formed by the disguised artists [*mechanics*], and the parish became possessed of . . . discoveries which were a *wonderful saving to the nation*.[125]

There are reports of other Holland-targeted 'borrowings',[126] equally uncondemned and equally with no second-order sociological reflection.

In the drive to increased agricultural production – a continuing concern – Small's redesigned plough (reducing the requirements for horse-power and labour) is lauded by many. The minister of Small's home parish admires the yearly production of 500; 'by his acknowledged and decided superiority, such is the demand, that had he a sufficient stock, and chose to attend merely to his *personal* interest, he might make his own terms'.[127]

One minister chooses to see variation in plough design, as with induced variation in style of buttons and buckles, as an extension of the sociology of marketing:

> For some years past, the form and fashion of the plough has been perpetually changing. The wright [*joiner*] and the smith seem now to understand their [*marketing*] interest just as well as the button and buckle maker. The principles of this useful instrument seem to be but imperfectly understood as yet; and till they be understood, the operation of *taste and fashion*, and art cannot be excluded. The plough in use at present is said to be Small's, somewhat improved, *i.e.* altered.[128]

That *'improved, i.e.* altered' is a nicely supercilious touch. The writer, from my current perspective, merits credit for his perception that social mechanisms (here 'taste', 'fashion') can be drivers of technological preference and acceptance. But though I have been writing as if an accession of sociological understanding were clearly a good, this might be a counterexample. Small, in the publication of his plans, had presented his plough design as derived from, entailed by, first principles:

> Let the husbandmen once be agreed as to the state in which the ground should be left by the plough. The task which it is to perform is now a *fixed* thing, and there must be *one* manner of performing it, which is better than any other.[129]

His text deductively articulates that design (with calculated mechanics and elegant, detailed, diagrams). The problem with the 'fashion' account (as with much current sociology of science) is that it fails to engage with that text: there is a clear tension between that text ('fixed thing') and the 'taste' deconstruction – can both stand? – which requires some resolution. Fashion may be at work; but were some ploughs demonstrably better than others?

As an aside, the development of Small's plough raises an issue in the sociology of knowledge which neither the OSA nor Sir John (in his agricultural mode) address. Behind the published analysis of mechanics there lay some clever experimental work:

> [Small] contrived a device for ascertaining the best shape of the mould board [*of the plough*], by making it of *soft wood*; by means of which, it soon appeared, where the pressure was the most severe and where there was the greatest friction.[130]

That soft-wood board is a thoughtful measurement solution, locating the stress-points in a design (in an era before stress-detecting micro-sensors). But rather than invite us to admire his applied ingenuity by documenting such steps, Small himself chooses to elicit our respect through *formal* analysis and *formal* diagrams. The contrast between account and actualised endeavour may say something informative about the (possibly unhelpful?) ranking of modes-of-knowing in eighteenth-century technological development. But my focus here is on the sociological issues which the OSA respondents recognise.

Provision for the Poor

Treatment and understanding of the poor is a social policy area in which these eighteenth-century ministers (given the role of the kirk in channelling poor relief) are actively engaged, and so a sensible exploration point. Loch, using the OSA data, reckons that in non-urban parishes, the poor-roll covers around 2 per cent of the population.[131] Though the ministers are concerned to ensure that relief is targeted to the true deserving ('Charity thinketh no evil, *but charity must think the truth*'),[132] they assume – and assume that all assume – an unquestioned duty to help.

That help, they frame as a complex planning issue: 'There is no scheme respecting the poor to which objections may not be stated', observes one;[133] another remarks, 'But, "To do the *best*, (observes an eloquent writer), can seldom be the lot of man; it is sufficient if, when opportunities are presented, he is ready to do *good*"'.[134] As the maxim indicates (as cited, it comes from Dr Johnson),[135] English social policy is an active comparator but generally a negative one. Consistently the writers see the English system of poor law as deleterious: 'if such laws *provide funds* for maintaining the poor, they also *provide poor* for consuming the funds'.[136] Ministers invoke Continental observers of the English poor ('their condition, in comparison with the poor of other countries, appears truly the most miserable', observed Dr Wendeborn in 1791);[137] the ministers note also the high costs of the English scheme[138] and the dependency entailed ('trusting to these rates, the common people do not endeavour to provide anything for a time of sickness or scarcity, or for the approach of old age').[139] Some of the difference is ascribed to national culture:

> while [labourers] . . . in England have better food . . . they daily eat up their *all* . . . On the contrary, in Scotland, many half starve themselves, in order to make *savings* . . . for old age, for putting their children to apprenticeships, or for otherwise bettering their own condition, or that of their families.[140]

Dr Wendeborn's report also remarked these cultural differences: 'In Germany and other northern countries of Europe, the poor keep always in mind that it is cold in winter . . . [b]ut in England it seems as if the poor . . . never looked forward'.[141] Some of the difference the ministers ascribe to strategy: 'The English system is to support the poor, the Scotch to assist them';[142] 'By *experience*, we have found it to be a great saving of our poors funds, to aid those who are sinking into poverty, *before they fall too low*'.[143] The main difference, they argue, as that last quotation might suggest, is linked to the *administration* of resources. In

Sociology within the *Statistical Account of Scotland*   175

Scotland each kirk-session,[144] with its lifetime appointed elders, is well placed to assess social situation; Sabbath collections are 'distributed amongst the *most friendless* and deserving poor'[145] (notice the attention to *social* context, and the information-gathering required, by that 'friendless'). In England the overseers of the poor are chosen annually: 'by the time they have learnt the business, they are removed; and whatever good regulations they may have made, their successors, through ignorance, or design, either alter or neglect them'.[146] The knowledge of each kirk-session allows much local social fine tuning:[147] from the timing of payments[148] to relief in kind.[149] Customarily, the kirk-session acquired the right to recover the effects of those placed on the poor list. Most sessions see this right as a simple economic transaction; others stress the *social* leverage acquired:

> The intention of this assignation was . . . to put it in the power of the managers to regulate . . . funeral expenses . . . People of that rank have their pride and their prejudices, as well as their superiors, and it was wisely determined to make use of these . . . The desire of what is called a *decent funeral, i.e.* one to which all the inhabitants of the district are invited . . . is one of the strongest in that rank of people . . . This sum therefore every person in mean circumstances is anxious to lay up, and he will not spare it unless reduced to the greatest extremity.[150]

The ministers are alert to the social implication of this recovery of effects, and nuanced in its implementation:

> we have anxiously avoided being too strict in this particular; for, callous as the relations [*relatives*] of the pauper may be, it is still an inducement; . . . if they had *no* prospect of succeeding to the trumpery [*worthless stuff*], small as it is, the whole care of their relation would be thrown upon the parish.[151]

This image of the kirk-session acting as the informed overseer is (as they are aware) a model best suited to rural and borough parishes, not 'populous cities, where the condition of the poor cannot generally be so well known'.[152]

Respondents in urban or manufacture-rich parishes prefer to encourage the solution offered by newly emerging, occupationally based friendly societies ('each subscriber, by contributing a small sum annually, when in health and strength, is entitled, when deprived of these, to a weekly or monthly allowance'[153] – with some variation on what happens to dependents); some would advocate expanding this to effectively a *national insurance* scheme, with tax relief[154] and with graduated contributions:

> A *law* establishing ... funds of this kind in every parish, and *obliging* every person ... to become a subscriber at a certain age, would raise a sum equal to all the wants of the poor ... With regard to the lower classes of the people, such a law would seem reasonable; for if tradesmen, day labourers, and servants, while healthy and in employment, can ... enjoy the comforts of their station in a reasonable degree ... it seems equitable to make them contribute ... it gives society a security that they will not become a burden upon it ... Such a law indeed would bear hard upon such as can, [*only*] with difficulty, support themselves ... But the law ... might ... admit of *different rates* of contribution ... [and] of some exemptions altogether.[155]
>
> But perhaps the wisest measure that could be adopted would be to unite the friendly societies into *larger bodies*, and the tradesmen of the same craft throughout the kingdom into one society.[156]

The concern being to establish a more stable support fund. They are also alert to the social impact, of source of support, upon welfare recipients: 'because the delicacy of the human feelings will be less hurt, when supplies are received from a source of this kind'.[157] Such moves display a consistent 'social policy' perspective; an attention to the social mechanisms underlying need and its alleviation; their concerns – and solutions – would be recognisable to later social policy thinkers. The extension of friendly societies into other action, such as industrial tribunals – in collieries 'they hold courts ... and exact fines'[158] – is a natural progression.

They are also concerned with supply-side issues in relation to poverty. The town which imposed a sales price cap ('for the benefit of the poorer citizens')[159] on the lessee of its salmon fishery is reported with approval. Reflecting on fluctuating price and availability of grain, they suggest 'the *utility* of a public granary';[160] again, 'The Geneva granary, mentioned by ... Lord Gardenston, in his travelling memorandums, is an *excellent model*.'[161] As reported in that travelling memorandum, Geneva yields a model that is socially radical: 'The public Granaries are here [*i.e. Geneva*] rendered effectual means of *restraining monopolies, moderating the markets* and preventing the calamities of scarcity or excessive prices for bread.'¹⁶² The other interventionist organisational move recommended is towards cooperatives, utilising collective purchasing power:

> for providing coals and meal for the families concerned in them, which they are enabled to purchase at a cheap rate, by laying in large quantities at proper seasons; and they find ample credit, by the whole members being bound for the payment.¹⁶³

Relatedly, a proposal for the kirk-session to buy coal when seasonally cheap, to smooth its price for the poor: 'this would be great charity at small expense'¹⁶⁴ – again, alert to the economic framework of 'charity'. We have already noted the ministers' awareness of fossil fuel as a resource, and they are attentive to the social and economic processes at work, and the asymmetric impact. One reports:

> In no parish . . . is there coal in greater plenty . . . Very lately, however, the price of coals has been raised excessively high . . . [this] is owing entirely to their not being wrought [*worked*]. Not to mention the *inhumanity of such a conduct to the destitute poor*, proprietors of coals certainly mistake their own interest . . .¹⁶⁵

Typical is a minister who objects to 'the spirit of *monopoly*' on coal, reporting that:

> the principal proprietor of the coal mines here . . . entered into an agreement with the proprietor of an adjoining colliery, to keep his own coal-works shut till those of the other be completely exhausted; in return . . . [for] an annuity of £20 a year! Thus the poor of this parish . . . are deprived.¹⁶⁶

Such analyses lead to conclusions for a *social* fuel policy: 'Coal . . . should *not* be considered as an article of commerce, which the landlord as a merchant may speculate upon for his own advantage: it should be considered as an article of the first necessity'¹⁶⁷– effectively a proposal to nationalise coal.

These examples show a willingness to 'think through' social arrangements and substantially modify them to bring about desired ends; perhaps more social policy than mainstream sociology (but, in our present, there is debate over whether social policy is an autonomous discipline).

Lest this all seem concerned more with *subsistence* poverty than with *social disadvantage*, consider one discussion under '*Depopulation*':

> among the middling ranks, dejection of mind [*depression?*], consequent upon a change of circumstances from affluence and independence to struggling with debt and want, appear to be the principal causes of . . . distempers [*morbidity*] and mortality in this parish.[168]

This is alert to the *social* mechanisms of deprivation. The minister of one parish, where in both 1782 and 1784 'their corns were . . . destroyed by the frost', reports:

> No remarkable sickness, however, followed. [But] So great were the straits and hardships to which the people were reduced by those calamitous years, that they contracted a dull and melancholy look, which continued for several years after. Till the winter of 1788, even the curling-stone lay neglected[169]

Note the invocation of participation in structured competition (curling) as an indicator of mental health.

Inoculation

Inoculation against smallpox was an active health issue (a virulent disease, with a, not universally accepted, intervention strategy). The strategy then available (variolation) involved an unappealing, if simple, deliberate infection – as indicated in this contemporary overview: 'a light scratch is now generally made in the skin of one arm, into which a little piece of small thread *passed through pocky matter* is put, and kept there for some days by a bandage'[170] – with a fatality rate lower than natural infection, but not zero (from the same account: 'That several inoculated died, is certain').[171] Though almost all Sinclair's respondents encourage the practice, a strain of Calvinist predestinarianism amongst their congregations would oppose it. As late as 1803, the surgeons organising delivery of the then newfangled cowpox vaccine, writing for support to the ministers of the kirk, note a continuing obstacle based 'on religious prejudices . . . [which] can be removed *only* by you'.[172]

Within this context, one might expect some debate of *ideas* around the justification for, and fears of, inoculation. But amongst the clergy there is an unwillingness to engage with the beliefs of the opposers, simply dismissing them: 'Rooted *prejudices*, founded upon arguments, some of which are *trifling*, and others *absurd*, influence the minds of the people.'[173] The main perceived 'prejudice' was belief in predestination – 'blind fatality',[174] 'no person could either accelerate, or escape his *fated* death'[175] – whence 'they say [inoculation] is an encroachment upon the prerogative of providence; and it is in vain to tell them, that prudence is the gift of providence'.[176] Such religious feelings could run high: 'some of them declared, if the inoculated children had died, they would have considered it as a *just* dispensation'.[177] It may be that ministers regard the case against predestination as fought and settled; but refusal to read hesitation as a legitimate motivator remains disconcerting.

Only a couple of writers display understanding of subjective concern against 'voluntarily bringing on a [*possibly fatal*] disease which we might possibly have escaped':[178]

> The thoughts of bringing *trouble on their children*, as they call it, *with their own hands*, outweigh every argument that can be advanced in its favour.[179]
>
> it is the more difficult to overcome so unfortunate a prejudice, as, in a great degree, it has its *origin in conscience*, however erroneous and misinformed.[180]

So what is the respondents' predominant route to increasing inoculation? Unsurprisingly, given their orientation, they are attentive to *economic* constraints, suggesting people were opposed 'not so much owing to their prejudices, as to their *poverty*. A workman, with a small [*i.e. young*] family, hath very little to spare to the surgeon.'[181] It is asserted that the gentry of one parish, by paying for the inoculation of the poor, 'have done more to promote the practice, than either *reason or eloquence* could have effected'.[182] The respondents are also in favour of good example (by the clergy and gentry). Noting that some opposition is grounded in a more general medical distrust, since 'The vulgar in most parts of this country ... have an utter dislike to *all* regular physicians and surgeons',[183] there are proposals to de-medicalise (and reduce costs) by having ministers inoculate:

> it would contribute to make the practice general; which will hardly be the case while the common people consider it as a chirurgical

> [*surgical*] business ... attended with expense ... [A] plan is now in agitation, for instructing the students of divinity at the University of Edinburgh in the art of inoculation.[184]

Though one writer then frets that any resultant deaths would be reputationally damaging to the clergy.[185]

Characteristically, they do not give up on reason. There are calls for official collection of relative mortality data ('A series of *facts* ... will ... *convince* even the most ignorant and prejudiced').[186] One minister produces probability calculations comparing the chance of death through inoculation (put at 1 in 500) with the lifetime probability of death from smallpox (though, as far back as 1723, Jurin in England had produced more complex calculations).[187]

Eriksen cautions, correctly, that the 'use of numbers and proportions in eighteenth-century texts on inoculation had been too easily identified with "modern" quantitative approaches',[188] stressing the need for context. She argues that the English and French 'seem to have conceptualized this solely as a matter of *individual* lives for a long time, not as a mass population or group'.[189] If she is right about the English, then Sinclair's ministers must be seen as making innovative *Scottish* moves in the sociology of inoculation. They cast it as an issue of social policy:

> To make a *law*, obliging all persons ... to inoculate their children, would be thought inconsistent ... with the common principles of humanity. But as the prosperity ... of every country is inseparably connected with the number of its inhabitants, *something* certainly ought to be attempted, to render, if possible inoculation in Scotland more general than it is at present.[190]
>
> considering the prodigious number that Great Britain loses annually by this disease, a premium [*financial inducement*] should be given by government ... to encourage the *general practice* of inoculation, amongst the middling and lower ranks of people.[191]

The inoculated were infectious (*made* so by inoculation, as distinct from later vaccination), and the implications of this are understood, both by parishioners – 'young people ... are not much inclined to inoculation, lest they communicate the contagion to their friends in *advanced life*'[192] – and by the ministers:

> till [inoculation] *universally* prevail ... it will not be a real blessing. The infection is communicated from the inoculated to the children

of those who still retain their old prejudices; and thus we have the smallpox raging every year in a place where ... about 30 years ago, the distemper used to come only once in 4 or 5 years[193]

emphasising 'the necessity of making the practice of inoculation *as general as possible, where it is at all adopted,* otherwise it may be productive of harm, instead of good'.[194] This mode of analysis can lead to sceptical thoughts (not unfamiliar in a post-Covid era):

> It seems uncertain whether or not inoculation for the smallpox has *now* any perceptible effect upon population [*numbers*]. The ravages of the disease upon its *first introduction* into any country has always been greater than what could be compensated ... Upon its *familiarisation with the climate or condition of the inhabitants*, its annual waste would appear easily reparable by the annual propagation. In this state of the matter, though inoculation may *preserve the individual* it seems not *necessary to the preservation of the species*.[195]

Again, our concern is not with the truth or otherwise of the reflections, but with their mode. These are people thinking through the social issues of inoculation and not just, *pace* Eriksen, at the individual level.

So, they are alert to economic pressures, to expectation, to waves of infection driving acceptance ('this havoc *alarmed* the neighbourhood, and introduced inoculation with success')[196] and accepting the power structure of the society they inhabit ('Persons of superior station, could, *without difficulty*, introduce it among their dependents').[197] But there is no internal narrative of ideas; their preferred mode is rational-calculative; the following tale is told with approval:

> One surgeon in the north, presuming that self interest is a stronger hold on man than superstition, has lately opened a policy of insurance for the smallpox. If a subscriber gives him 2 guineas for inoculating his child, the surgeon, in the event of the child's death, pays 10 guineas to the parent.[198]

(And, a further twist, offering a lower *rate* of return for lower fees.)

Conclusion

Though, on inoculation, the ministers are consistently on the side of medical progress – and display a greater awareness of social issues than recent secondary literature suggests was prevalent in England – they are consistently impercipient in what might be called the sociology of ideas or perhaps, more broadly, the 'anthropological' strain within sociology. They are not given to reading ideas as, in themselves, valid motivators. A further example: we have noted their use of desire for 'a decent funeral' to motivate the poor, but they read that motivation *itself* as indefensible. They register that a rural funeral involves the whole community and takes up a day's work-time: 'But the loss of *labour*, and the loss of *time*, are not the only *evils* that follow it; it becomes oppressive to those who cannot afford the expense, but who, from *vanity* or *pride*, must continue the custom.'[199] There is no sympathy for this (uneconomic, time-costly) event, no gesture towards social roles, no recognition that community-wide involvement in mourning a death might serve a need. The family:

> often vie with those around them, in giving, as they call it, *an honourable burial* to their deceased friend. Such a custom is attended with many evils, and frequently . . . reduces to poverty many families otherwise frugal and industrious, by this piece of *useless parade* and *ill-judged expense*.[200]
>
> By exploding [*this custom*] . . . many would have it in their power to do more essential acts of kindness to their friends and relations when living . . . Nor do the deceased feel or enjoy any of the gratifications of *vanity or misplaced veneration, which prompt this custom*.[201]

Anthropologists, in the intervening years, have taught us to see 'uneconomic' displays differently. These passages on 'useless parade and ill-judged expense' are perhaps the least sociological explanations in the OSA, though one respondent (admittedly writing only about dress) is more tolerant: 'The love of show is natural, and *imaginary* wants are sometimes *no less clamorous* than those which are real'.[202]

A couple of commentators on Scottish witchcraft fall closer to Evans-Pritchard elucidating the rationality of the Zande. One, looking back at late seventeenth-century parish-records – a woman rebuked before the congregation for using apparently *trivial* (as seen from 1790) charms at Halloween – comments:

> Let not the wisdom of our fathers however be treated on such accounts lightly. The innocence or guilt of all actions depends much upon *the*

Sociology within the *Statistical Account of Scotland*   183

views which governed the actor. What may be now mere amusement, when it was performed under the *belief of incantation*, and with a *view to the agency of evil spirits*, was a proper subject of animadversion [*censure*] to those whose duty it was to watch over the moral and religious conduct of the people.[203]

Another minister takes the same analytic view, in discussing the torture of witches: 'compelling them to say *anything* which their enemies desired'.[204] He is thus clear that witchcraft is not 'real', but grasps that the accused *perceived* differently:

among those who were tried for witchcraft, we may believe that many ... were convinced, that they *were in possession* of its power. The same spirit of credulity, which led people ... to believe in witchcraft, would induce some of the weaker sort to imagine that they were *endued with the art*.[205]

The implications of this thought are left dangling, but it is clearly a thought with some analytic power.

Arguably, Sinclair's ministers are at their most assured when thinking through the very *low-level* practicalities of social administration, as on a (modern-sounding) proposal to regulate certification of new-build housing: 'it ought to be a clause in the contract, that the work is not to be judged of, nor the contract discharged, until the houses have been inhabited for twelve months'.[206] Thinking of daily activities, they are alert to social implications. Consider for example – from those parishes where the ice let it flourish – reflections on a winter sport:

Their chief amusement in winter is curling, or playing stones on smooth ice; they eagerly vie with one another ... one part of the parish against another – one description of men against another – one trade or occupation against another[207]

[They] usually conclude the game and day with a good dinner, drink, and songs[208]

This is not claimed as deep sociological analysis. But what, I think, remains noteworthy is how the ministers' natural mode of thought embeds discussion of activity within its social context (the various mappings forming teams). They reflect on its co-mingling impetus: 'Curling is a favourite diversion among the commonality; and even the gentlemen sometimes join in it'[209] – a curling co-mingling that, at first glance, can still be seen in later paintings,[210] such as on our cover, depicting the sport. They note its role in the community: 'during the severe frost last winter . . . [the curlers], more than once, played for a certain sum each, and applied the forfeited money, to purchase coals for the poor'.[211] And we saw above the use of curling as an indicator of (collective) mental health. This sport is read socially.

But these ministers are also willing to raise larger policy questions; we have already noted their openness to state control of energy supplies; another writer, thinking of Highland estate depopulation, seeks policy constraints on landowners:

> The maxim, that it is lawful for a man to do what he will with his own, has already *misled* too many; it is so far from being universally true, that it has its *limitations in every kind of property* . . . One's right to dispose of his own money, does not extend to a right of melting down the current coin.[212]

Constraining landowners would be a major policy change. But even their low-level predilection for economic-related social analysis can lead them into interesting byways. Consider this, from the minister of New Lanark, on how child labour in cotton-mills affects the marriage market:

> In most other manufactures, a woman who has a family, and becomes a widow, is generally in the most helpless situation. Here the case is very different, for the greater number of children a woman has, she lives so much the more comfortably, and upon such account alone, she is often a tempting object for a second husband.[213]

It is perhaps small instances such as this that bring to life most vividly the sense of a group of people sociologically thoughtful about the world they inhabit.

Admittedly, for not everything social do they seek explanation. Take another minor, but intriguing, example. One of their repeatedly noticed markers of social change is the proliferation of watches amongst servants and labourers ('Every stripling, as soon as he arrives at puberty, must have a watch in his pocket').[214] Implicit in the ministers' tone, but never addressed, is puzzlement as to why farm labourers have need of watches. Perhaps the fashion was sustained, as Kelly and Ó Gráda speculate, because watches 'served as convenient stores of value: a windfall could be used to buy a watch that ... could later be used as collateral'.[215] Some confirmatory 1790s report would have been welcome (unfortunately 'men are apt to overlook that which is familiar to their sight').[216]

But overall, as I hope to have evidenced, Sinclair's respondents are alert to, and given to thinking in terms of, socio-economically rational narratives for human choices. This tradition has clear affinities with what (some of us would argue) remains the most articulated and rigorous mode in contemporary sociology: empirically informed and theoretically aware. The tradition fits well with the manifest concerns of the *Scottish* Enlightenment, and Adam Smith is often in their thoughts; but notice also that these ministers have wider referents (when assessing prisons several invoke 'the benevolent Howard';[217] on agriculture Swift's Brobdingnagian king is regularly cited;[218] and the references to Pope, Dr Johnson and Dr Wendeborn – and Geneva and Bilbao – we have already met).

A final point, which is implicit in my OSA quotations throughout but which should perhaps be explicitly noted. Some scholars[219] have argued that the key thinkers of the Scottish Enlightenment identified a uniquely Scottish approach to sociological thought – *conjectural history*. Even were this analysis correct (and I have elsewhere argued that it is not),[220] no trace of this mode appears in these Scots writers at the end of the century. Within the OSA, all 194 instances of 'conjecture' appear negatively – essentially as 'under-evidenced speculation'; wisely the parish ministers hold: 'In a statistical account, as little as possible should be left to conjecture'.[221] Instead they offer empirically grounded, and often sociologically alert, accounts of their society.

Notes

1. *The Statistical Account of Scotland. Drawn up from the communications of the ministers of the different parishes by Sir John Sinclair, Bart* (Edinburgh: Creech, 1791–9) (henceforth OSA). Sinclair's most substantive editorial intervention was his insertion of Webster's comparative population data from 1755: 'Dr Webster's report was never printed. There are, however, several copies of it, in manuscript ... and the most material parts of the information it contains, will be inserted, in the course of this work' (OSA ii, p. vi). The first direct publication of Webster was not until 1952: J. G. Kyd, *Scottish Population Statistics including Webster's Analysis of*

Population 1755, Scottish History Society, third series, volume 44 (Edinburgh: Constable, 1952).
2. In an earlier paper, arguing against the conventional invocation of 'high theory' as the sociological legacy of the Scottish Enlightenment, I had suggested, in relation to the reportage within the *Statistical Account*: 'Perhaps it is at this level we should look for the sociological inheritance of the Scottish Enlightenment'. The present chapter is an attempt at making an honest proposition of that suggestion. See Kenneth Macdonald, 'Did British Sociology Begin with the Scottish Enlightenment?' in Plamena Panayotova (ed.), *The History of Sociology in Britain* (Cham: Palgrave Macmillan, 2019), pp. 37–69, at p. 66. Available online: https://link.springer.com/content/pdf/10.1007%2F978-3-030-19929-6_2.pdf
3. OSA xx, p. xiii, original emphasis. I throughout silently add italics for expositional clarity; original emphases are always noted.
4. OSA xxi, p. 405.
5. Creech's assessments of Edinburgh are poorly articulated and reveal his bookseller values: 'In 1783, a minister of Edinburgh, wrote the most admired sermons that ever were published, and *obtained the highest price that ever was given* for any work of the kind' (OSA, vi, p. 588); and his admiration of high Edinburgh culture: 'Perfumers had splendid shops in every principal street: some of them advertised the keeping of bears, *to kill occasionally*, for greasing ladies and gentlemens hair, as superior to any other animal fat' (OSA vi, p. 593).
6. M. Steven, *Parish Life in Eighteenth-Century Scotland* (Aberdeen: Scottish Cultural Press, 1995). Note that Steven's page references are to the reorganised 1970s out-of-print OSA edition edited by Withrington and Grant.
7. For example, C. Douglas, 'Enclosure and Agricultural Development in Scotland', unpublished D.Phil. thesis, University of Oxford, 2010; A. Bhattacharjee et al., 'The Spatial Development of Scotland in the First Industrial Revolution: Evidence from the Statistical Accounts', paper presented at ASREC 2017.
8. OSA iii, p. ix.
9. OSA xx, p. xiv.
10. Sir John Sinclair, *Analysis of the Statistical Account of Scotland* (Edinburgh: Tait, 1831), i, p. 5.
11. In his careful treatment of census initiation, Stephen Thompson ('Census-Taking, Political Economy and State Formation in Britain, c.1790–1840', unpublished PhD thesis, University of Cambridge, 2010, p. 42) reinstates Abbott's, as against Rickman's, standing

as the moving force behind the 1800 bill. Admittedly, Rickman, in his case for a census, had acknowledged Sinclair's work, though Thompson overstates the approbation (ibid. 46n). Rickman mentions Sinclair only in the ninth of his dozen grounds for a census, and that but tentatively: as an 'argument (*which to some may appear too refined*) ... that a specimen of the kind proposed might tend to make political economy a more general study in England (*political economy* may be defined to be the scientific application of statistical survey)' (John Rickman, 'Thoughts on the Utility and Facility of Ascertaining the Population of England', *Commercial and Agricultural Magazine* 2 (1800), pp. 391–9, at p. 395). In contrast, the successful Abbott '*jettisoned* the bulk of Rickman's arguments ... and presented the census as being about ... a short-term response to the current [grain] scarcity' (Thompson, 'Census-Taking', p. 44). Notice also – a further point against Sinclair's claim to be progenitor – that Abbott (in contrast to Sinclair's enacted, and Rickman's proposed, parish-level enumeration) wished to instruct the collectors to gather information by proceeding 'from House to House' (cited, ibid.); a very different model. Though, again muddying the narrative, note that the first four British censuses, though arguably initiated by Abbott, were overseen by Rickman.

12. Sinclair, *Analysis*, ii, p. 225.
13. Ibid. i, p. 195.
14. Smith's treatment of 'unproductive' labour, and his disagreement with Steuart, is discussed more fully in my chapter 'Adventitious Sociology: Dispassion and Insight in the Scottish Enlightenment' in the present volume.
15. Rev. John Sinclair, *Memoirs of the Life and Works of the Late Right Honourable Sir John Sinclair, bart., by His Son* (Edinburgh: Blackwood, 1837), i, p. 17.
16. After Edinburgh and Glasgow, Sinclair also attended Oxford, but like many (before and since) apparently in pursuit more of the 'likelihood of forming acquaintance with the future actors in the political drama' than of learning (ibid. p. 25).
17. Ibid. p. 18.
18. Ibid. p. 19.
19. Ibid. p. 51.
20. Sinclair, *Analysis*, i, p. 59.
21. Dugald Stewart, *Elements of the Philosophy of the Human Mind, Vol I*. (Edinburgh: Strathan, 1792), p. 215.
22. Ibid. p. 248.

23. Ibid. p. 258.
24. Sinclair, *Analysis*, i, p. 60.
25. James Steuart, *An Inquiry into the Principles of Political Oeconomy* (London: Millar & Cadel, 1767), i, pp. 72–3; Steuart's quotation is presented *in context* and discussed further in Macdonald, 'Adventitious Sociology'.
26. *Correspondence of Adam Smith*, ed. E. C. Mossner and I. S. Ross, 2nd ed. (New York: Oxford University Press, 1987), letter 150.
27. Sinclair, *Analysis*, i, pp. 55, 56.
28. Sinclair cites precursors from Spain, Sweden, France, Germany, Denmark, England, Ireland and Scotland (*Analysis*, i, pp. 64–9). The *arguments to*, as opposed to influence on (or indeed the promises of royalties to), the General Assembly ('with the leaders of which I lived on terms of intimacy and friendship', OSA xx, p. xii) are also pertinent.
29. OSA iv, p. 316.
30. OSA xix, p. 558.
31. F. A. Jonsson, *Enlightenment's Frontier: The Scottish Highlands and the Origins of Environmentalism* (New Haven, CT: Yale University Press, 2013), p. 74.
32. OSA v, p. 40.
33. OSA xvi, p. 491.
34. OSA xix, p. 585.
35. OSA ix, p. 112.
36. OSA iii, p. 142.
37. OSA v, p. 5.
38. OSA x, p. 296.
39. Ibid. p. 297
40. OSA v, p. 487.
41. OSA iv, p. 524.
42. OSA xiv, p. 200.
43. OSA xx, p. 313.
44. OSA xvi, p. 34. Though, as with this citation, the dominant tone of the respondents is against public penance, not all agree. Some would advocate a zero-tolerance policy: 'I am inclined to believe, that it would be much more the *interest of the community, in a political light*, that the laws of discipline should be more rigidly adhered to, for if once the vulgar of any country consider incontinency a venial fault they are almost ready for the commission of any crime' (OSA xv, p. 369) – a prescription that would recur in our present. Again, my concern is not with the *content* but the *form* of thinking. These writers – whether for or against – are evaluating the policy of public penance in terms of its social policy consequences.

45. OSA xvii, p. 480.
46. OSA xviii, p. 403.
47. OSA ix, p. 123.
48. OSA xxi, p. 232.
49. OSA xix, p. 164.
50. E. Macleod, 'The English and Scottish State Trials of the 1790s Compared' in M. T. Davis et al. (eds), *Political Trials in an Age of Revolutions* (Basingstoke: Palgrave Macmillan, 2019), pp. 79–107, at p. 95.
51. T. F. Palmer, *The Trial of the Rev. Thomas Fyshe Palmer* (Edinburgh: W. Skirving, 1793), p. 156.
52. Thomas Paine, *Tom Paine's Jests* (London: Ridgeway, 1793), p. 27.
53. R. Watt and D. Downie, *The Trials of Robert Watt and David Downie for High Treason* (Edinburgh: Manners and Miller, 1794), p. 61.
54. Ibid. p 83.
55. OSA xx, p. 437.
56. Ibid. p. 430.
57. OSA xv, p. 86.
58. OSA viii, p. 586.
59. OSA xvi, p. 396.
60. OSA ix, p. 324.
61. OSA xv, p. 380.
62. Ibid. p. 382.
63. Ibid. p. 380.
64. OSA xv, p. 381.
65. OSA iii, p. 448.
66. OSA xv, p. 381.
67. Ibid. p. 381.
68. OSA v, p. 268.
69. Ibid. p. 269.
70. Ibid. p. 273.
71. Ibid. p. 272.
72. The calling to Cambuslang of the writer, Dr Meek, had been contested on these grounds in the early 1770s.
73. OSA v, Ibid. p. 271.
74. Ibid. p. 273.
75. Ibid. p. 274.
76. Ibid. p. 274n.
77. Ibid. p. 274.
78. OSA xviii, p. 249.
79. Ibid. p. 251.

80. OSA xii, p. 363.
81. OSA xvii, p. 57.
82. OSA x, p. 628.
83. OSA ii, p. 282.
84. Sinclair, *Analysis*, ii, p. 3
85. OSA viii, p. 238.
86. OSA i, p. 458.
87. OSA vii, p. 365.
88. OSA vi, p. 251.
89. OSA vii, p. 365.
90. OSA i, p. 457.
91. OSA xv, p. 288.
92. Kenneth Macdonald, 'Of Shame and Poverty; and on Misreading Sen and Adam Smith', *Adam Smith Review* 11 (2019), pp. 111–262, at p. 141f. Available online: www.academia.edu/44011649
93. OSA ii, p. 164.
94. OSA xviii, p. 399.
95. OSA xix, p. 362.
96. OSA xii, p. 242. From our perspective, the *form* of Presbyterian church governance might seem to have claim to be a major determining influence on behaviour and roles in late eighteenth-century Scotland; but only one minister considers this issue: 'The *duties and privileges of the office* [of elder], tend not only to enlarge the minds of the elders, but enable them also in their intercourse with others, to extend the sphere of general information . . . The great body of the *congregation is frequently assembled* and consulted [on public business], and the habit of *thinking* acquires additional strength from the opinions which, on these occasions, are openly proposed and discussed' (OSA xviii, p. 399). Sinclair, to his credit, does mention the issue ('The popular [i.e. *of-the-people*] nature . . . of the Scotch Church Establishments, and its gradation of courts [*management bodies*], terminating in a General Assembly, must, from the collision of minds it constantly occasions, have great influence in promoting an enlargement of idea, a readiness of expression'; *Analysis*, i, p. 52), though he does not follow through on this thought in his extended discussion of the 'ecclesiastical establishment' (*Analysis*, ii, pp. 1–64).
97. OSA vii, p. 562.
98. OSA xi, p. 58.
99. OSA i, p. 175.
100. OSA xvi, p. 16–17.

101. D. T. Dillon, *Travels through Spain* (London: Robinson, 1780), p. 184.
102. OSA xvi, p. 17n.
103. OSA xii, p. 469.
104. Alexander Pope [and others], *Memoirs of . . . Martinus Scriblerus* (Dublin: Faulkner, 1741), p. 96.
105. OSA xii, p. 465.
106. OSA xix, p. 483 – clear-headed on the salience of economic incentives in pursuing a ministerial calling. Another puts it more colourfully: 'The Lord Advocate of Scotland, upon a late visit to these islands [Orkneys], arriving at this enchanted spot . . . is said to have exclaimed . . . "Happy is the clergyman who inhabits yonder [*manse*]!" "And still happier would he be," said the clergyman, "would his Lordship help him to an augmentation of stipend"' (ibid. p. 402).
107. OSA ix, p. 212.
108. They notice, interestingly, the role of private education in accelerating that decline: such 'parochial schools are but poorly endowed: the *practice of private teaching* in families has rendered the better sort too *indifferent as to this public object*' (OSA vi, p. 264) – again, a sociological awareness of the impact of an alternate private sector on elite support for 'state' education.
109. OSA vii, p. 443.
110. OSA ii, p. 381.
111. OSA ix, p. 178.
112. OSA xix, p. 126.
113. OSA xviii, p. 356.
114. OSA xii, p. 209. *St Christoper's* is St Kitts. Scotland was intimately entangled with the British empire (even east-coast Inverness records 'great influx of money from the East and West Indies'; OSA ix, p. 617); and though the ministers are against slavery (as when discussing the relicts of feudal 'services', or the emancipation of colliers, or freed slaves within Scotland) they do not address Scottish exploitation *abroad*.
115. OSA xvi, p. 507.
116. OSA xviii, p. 355.
117. OSA ii, p. 200.
118. Steuart, *Inquiry*, i, pp. 72–3.
119. OSA viii, p. 391.
120. OSA xvii, p. 123.
121. OSA xxi, p. 166.

122. OSA xiv, pp. 443–4.
123. OSA xvi, p. 236.
124. This is one of a number of instances, throughout OSA, and consistently reported on favourably, of high-status women taking effective initiatives.
125. OSA x, p. 258.
126. OSA viii, p. 525; ix, p. 75.
127. OSA xiii, p. 616.
128. Ibid. p. 126.
129. James Small, *A Treatise on Ploughs and Wheel Carriages* (Edinburgh: Creech, 1784), p. vi.
130. Sir John Sinclair, 'Account of James Small', *Scots Magazine and Edinburgh Literary Miscellany* 74 (1812), pp. 260–5, at p. 261.
131. C. S. Loch, 'Poor Relief in Scotland: Its Statistics and Development', *Journal of the Royal Statistical Society* 61 (1898), pp. 271–300, at p. 280.
132. OSA ix, p. 642.
133. OSA xiii, p. 440.
134. OSA xx, p. 338.
135. Samuel Johnson, *Introduction, Proceedings of the Committee . . . for Cloathing French Prisoners of War* (London, 1760).
136. OSA i, p. 423.
137. G. F. A. Wendeborn, *A View of England towards the Close of the Eighteenth Century; translated from the original German* (London: Robinson, 1791), i, p. 113.
138. OSA xi, p. 167.
139. OSA iv, p. 418.
140. OSA i, p. 234.
141. Wendeborn, *View of England*, i, pp. 113–14.
142. OSA xv, p. 362.
143. OSA ii, p. 510.
144. A kirk-session was (is) the lowest court in the Church of Scotland, comprising the minister and elders of an individual parish; as well as acting as a church court, kirk-sessions had important responsibilities for poor relief and education.
145. OSA xvi, p. 204.
146. OSA viii, p. 361.
147. One cannot but smile wryly at this targeted donation: 'No public charity is given to any that go about begging, except now and then a pair of *shoes*' (OSA viii, p. 479).
148. OSA vi, p. 48.

149. OSA ii, p. 395; vii, p. 115.
150. OSA vi, p. 487.
151. OSA xv, p. 362.
152. OSA xiv, p. 388.
153. OSA v, p. 168.
154. OSA viii, p. 323; xviii, p. 260. As OSA xvi, p. 43 notes, Sir George Rose's British Act of 1793 provided for this.
155. OSA v, pp. 169–70.
156. OSA xviii, p. 261.
157. OSA ii, p. 257.
158. OSA viii, p. 615.
159. OSA xi, p. 10.
160. OSA xiii, p. 611.
161. OSA ix, p. 627.
162. F. Garden, *Travelling Memorandums, Made in a Tour upon the Continent of Europe* (Edinburgh: Bell & Bradsute, 1791), p. 244.
163. OSA xii, p. 176; a similar scheme is described at OSA i, p. 363.
164. OSA ii, p. 477. Another kirk-session proposes a similar scheme in relation to a 'weekly allowance of meal, instead of money, which may ... prevent an improper use of the public bounty. Some savings may be made, also, by purchasing the meal when it is cheap' (OSA ii, p. 395) – a neat combination of social constraint and economic efficiency.
165. OSA xi, pp. 164–5.
166. Ibid. p. 367.
167. OSA xv, p. 334.
168. OSA ix, p. 563.
169. OSA vii, p. 123.
170. A. Monro, *An Account of the Inoculation of Small-Pox in Scotland* (Edinburgh: Drummond, 1765), p. 19.
171. Ibid. p. 26.
172. Vaccine Institution, *Address to the Reverend the Ministers of the Church of Scotland* (Edinburgh: Caw, 1803), p. 4.
173. OSA iii, p. 427.
174. OSA xviii, p. 173.
175. OSA xiv, p. 235.
176. OSA xii, p. 49.
177. OSA viii, p. 267.
178. OSA xx, p. 348.
179. OSA ii, p. 119.
180. OSA xvii, p. 429.

181. OSA iv, p. 335.
182. OSA xi, p. 236.
183. OSA iv, p. 208.
184. OSA ii, p. 126; also OSA xx, p. 282.
185. OSA xxi, p. 222.
186. OSA xi, p. 147.
187. A. Rusnock, *Vital Accounts: Quantifying Health and Population in Eighteenth-Century England and France* (Cambridge: Cambridge University Press, 2002), pp. 52f.
188. A. Eriksen, 'Advocating Inoculation in the Eighteenth Century: Exemplarity and Quantification', *Science in Context* 29 (2016), pp. 213–39, at p. 215.
189. Ibid. p. 237.
190. OSA xi, p. 146.
191. OSA vii, p. 279.
192. OSA xx, p. 101.
193. OSA xv, p. 114.
194. OSA ii, p. 13.
195. OSA xxi, p. 391; emphases original.
196. OSA vi, p. 92.
197. OSA iii, p. 562.
198. OSA xx, p. 349.
199. OSA ix, p. 543.
200. OSA xviii, p. 175.
201. OSA ix, p. 373.
202. OSA xvii, p. 60.
203. OSA xviii, p. 209.
204. OSA xiv, p. 373.
205. Ibid. p. 373.
206. OSA iv, p. 363.
207. OSA vii, p. 612.
208. OSA ix, p. 433; also xxi, p. 457.
209. OSA vi, p. 277.
210. The OSA under-reports curling – 'We know for certain that it was extensively practised in many of the parishes whose ministers are silent on that subject' (John Kerr, *The History of Curling* (Edinburgh: David Douglas, 1890), pp. 107–8) – but, in light of the painting on our cover, there may be some merit in exploring whether the later pictorial record supports the OSA view of curling as tending to social integration. Headgear styles in Charles Lees's earlier iconic 1849 image, of the match at Linlithgow Loch, are a mingling of tam o' shanter

and top hat, but that probably misrepresents the 'gentlemen' joining (even at a Grand Match), given that painter's habit of incorporating separately acquired portraits of the variously distinguished into his set pieces (even the apparently rustic may mislead: one gesticulating tam o' shanter wearer at the centre of the picture turns out to be an established Edinburgh haberdasher, who part-bought the finished painting; see J. Burnet, 'Who were the curlers?', *Society of Antiquaries of Scotland Newsletter* 27.2 (2015), pp. 8–9). As Lees's obituary in *The Saint Andrews Gazette and Fifeshire News* (6 March 1880) commented, his paintings 'were very remarkable for the striking likenesses they contained of *noted personages who took an interest* in the games'. The gentrification may represent a trend in reality (the Grand Caledonian Curling Club was instituted in 1838 for 'regulating the ancient Scottish game of Curling by general laws' – though note that Kerr's chapter on *Ancient Curling Societies* (*op.cit.*, p. 113f) can give detailed accounts of twenty-eight clubs already active in the eighteenth century). But the funding and ownership of paintings probably biases towards depiction of gentrification. Selectivity is an even sharper issue for the Charles Hardie 1899 *Curling at Carsbreck* painting reproduced, in part, on the cover of this volume. At first glance it appears a casual snapshot – a piece of painterly reportage – of a passing wintry event; but it is in fact a carefully curated set of formal portraits of the great and the good. The painting was commissioned by the RCC, for its Diamond Jubilee, determinedly echoing the Lees image from half a century earlier. As David Smith (2010, curlinghistory.blogspot.com/2010/06/diamond jubilee-painting.html) carefully documents, decision on inclusion was a committee matter, involving much discussion and careful selection to high criteria; the ensuing individual portraits (over sixty) greatly increasing the cost of the work. Portrayals included the First Lord of the Treasury, the Secretary for Scotland, the Lord Chamberlain, a Viceroy of India, Governors of Victoria and South Australia, the Lord Provost of Edinburgh, the Provost of Selkirk, three out of the four recent Lord High Commissioners of the Church ... and so the list continues. As the RCC *Annual* of 1899 reports: 'The Committee consider they may be congratulated on the success of the selection ... though [this] has been made from a purely curling point of view, there is no game which can boast of such a list of men among its active votaries who have distinguished themselves in other paths of life as is to be found in this short leet of curlers.' However this is to be interpreted, we have manifestly moved some way from: 'even the gentlemen sometimes join in'.

211. OSA viii, p. 85.
212. OSA xx, p. 222
213. OSA xv, p. 41.
214. OSA v, p. 404.
215. Morgan Kelly and Cormac Ó Gráda, 'Adam Smith, Watch Prices, and the Industrial Revolution', *The Quarterly Journal of Economics* 131 (2016), pp. 1727–52, at p. 1741.
216. OSA ix, p. 366.
217. Ibid. p. 623.
218. For example, 'whoever could make two ears of corn . . . grow upon a spot of ground where only one grew before, would deserve better of mankind . . . than the whole race of politicians put together' (OSA xvii, p. 174).
219. For example, H. M. Hopfl, 'From Savage to Scotsman: Conjectural History in the Scottish Enlightenment', *Journal of British Studies* 17 (1978), pp. 19–40, or J. D. Brewer, 'The Scottish Enlightenment and Scottish Social Thought, c. 1715-1915' in J. Holmwood and J. Scott (eds), *The Palgrave Handbook of Sociology in Britain* (Basingstoke: Palgrave Macmillan, 2014), p. 6.
220. Macdonald, 'Did British Sociology Begin with the Scottish Enlightenment?', p. 62f.
221. OSA xviii, p. 265.

Part III

The Sociological Afterlife of the Scottish Enlightenment

8

Hegel and the Notion of Retroactive Necessity in the Scottish Enlightenment*

Dirk Schuck

Introduction

Does Hegel postulate the inevitable historical development of the human mind in a particular direction? His idea of *Weltgeist* certainly seems to suggest as much. And does such a teleological view of history serve as the backbone for the Marxian narrative of the liberation of the proletariat? The liberation of the proletariat is imagined by Marx to be a universal liberation of humankind from oppression, with the proletariat serving as the last remaining player in a history of class, serving literally as its anti-thesis. The historical fact that neither liberation ever happened is usually taken as evidence that there is neither a *Weltgeist* nor a possible end to class history. However, there is a basic flaw in such a rejection of Hegelian Marxism. For Hegel, historical necessities only become apparent retroactively, that is after the social, political and economic process that is situated at their core has already unfolded. But this means that it is fundamentally impossible to know what the future will bring from the standpoint of the present.

What does such an insight regarding retroactive necessity[1] really mean? First, it means that, as soon as we start to think historically, the political, economic and social order of our own day becomes relative. The term 'relative' must not be read as simply a matter of contingency. We see the world in the way that we are capable of seeing it at a specific point in time, and from a specific location within that specific moment of time. Therefore, our viewpoint can only offer us relative truth insofar as 'truth' itself is a historical concept. What Hegel and Marx are trying to achieve, philosophically speaking, is an understanding of social and intellectual movement within the changing epistemological patterns which are regarded as true (or evident, as Althusser would describe it) at a specific time, and from a specific location.[2]

Hegel and Marx make their arguments from a philosophical level of historical consciousness where the bare historical fact that their imaginations did not turn into historical truth cannot be used as an argument against them, because their aim was to open up that very path of action. My aim in this chapter is to show that this historical insight into retroactive necessity does not have its origin in Hegel. Rather, Hegel already tries to rein it back in through understanding the historical imagination which gets unleashed through historical narratives of retroactive necessity as part of a larger evolutionary process in which the human mind necessarily becomes aware of itself and its formidable powers. It is only in this, more specific, sense that a critique of Hegel which regards the development of the human mind as too strong a determining factor in his philosophy of history can drive its partial point home. Hegel himself is already writing in reaction to the philosophy of history of the Scottish Enlightenment and its historical insights regarding retroactive necessity. His claim is that, although specific historic formations of human life seem to follow each other without the individual minds that are involved in this ongoing process of historical change necessarily becoming aware of it, the philosopher who has developed such a historical consciousness, nonetheless, is able to take a bird's eye view from which she can identify a transhistorical structural pattern within that process. This is symbolised in the flight of the owl of wisdom (*Minerva*): the owl only begins to set off on its journey once the development of humankind has reached a state of evening.

It is only after the long day has run its course that humankind reaches a state of awareness of its own history. For Hegel, this process carries a real historical necessity within it. The human mind must go through specific stages of development in order to become fully aware of itself and of its gradual evolution from natural determination into something freer. Although freedom is at the centre of Hegel's philosophy of history, it is notoriously hard to grasp. How far has the human mind really escaped the grip of nature? Or is human freedom 'only' signified by the self-consciousness of its natural embeddedness? And what does the mind becoming aware of itself really mean? Here, we can already see how Hegel turns the more down-to-earth, empirically grounded philosophy of history developed in the Scottish Enlightenment back into something more metaphysical. Adam Smith, in contrast, does not develop a concept of human freedom per se; rather, he puts a lot of effort into analysing the ways in which specific political, economic and social rights and liberties come about.

The common core that is shared by both Hegel's view of the development of human history and the view of that process within the Scottish Enlightenment is its historical consciousness, and I will turn to this in the following paragraph. It is possible to understand the looming idea of the historicity of the human mind which emerges within these writings as the philosophical backbone behind the revolution of mind which took place in early modernity. It reaches deep into theological discussions about the history of Christianity and its theological and historical relations to Judaism; early modern Jewish thought, in particular, questions Christian metaphysics by historical argument and by using the idea of retroactive necessity. Only from a later historical viewpoint, so the argument goes, could the prophecies of Isaiah have been read as a promise of the coming of Christ; in their own time, they instead referred to the desperate fate of the Jewish people seeking liberation from Babylonian rule.[3] The historical necessity for the coming of a saviour appears to have been read into the prophecies retroactively.

My argument in this essay will be that, even if we do not accept Hegel's metaphysical claim that human history must be read as a manifestation of the human spirit becoming aware of itself, we still need to recognise the creative power by which the human mind can narrate its own history as an essential part of a philosophy of history which seeks human emancipation.[4] This telos is the Enlightenment's shared pathos, and today we are in urgent need of such a narrative once again. This might help to explain the ongoing fascination with the Scottish Enlightenment's historical speculations regarding the economic, political and social forces which drive human progress (see the first section, 'Natural History as Conjectural History'). To regard such historical speculations as insufficient and, therefore, inferior knowledge is itself based on precarious assumptions about the criteria such knowledge must fulfil. Hegel's analysis of the opposing forces to be found within human reason can help us to see that, by denying ourselves such speculations, we fail to realise the full potential of our mind's capabilities ('The Hypothetical Status of Knowledge in Conjectural History'). For the Scots, the main historical factor which drives human progress is commerce.[5] My aim in the third section is solely to extrapolate both the speculative character of this claim and the extent to which it serves to retroactively postulate a historical narrative of human emancipation. My argument will then take a slightly psychological turn by showing that, for Hume, the imaginative power of human reasoning is a precondition for purposeful action. To conclude, I will return to the idea of retroactive necessity and demonstrate its paradoxical ability to lead us in many different directions.

Natural History as Conjectural History

The prototypical historical sociology of the Scots has its philosophical roots in a Lockean social epistemology.[6] The empirical sensualism of Locke explains how the human mind came to form a set of basic ideas, before associating these together into a cognitive web of more complex ones. This ontogenesis, which is, at the same time, a psychogenesis, has a social aspect to it. We form ideas in the way that our social environment presents them to us, with all the natural connections that entails. Adam Smith uses this kind of reasoning to explain what he calls 'natural authority'. The concept of 'natural authority' in Smith does not refer to a natural authority as such but to the way in which political authority, at a specific time and place, can appear 'natural' within a specific mindset. It is only after the social institution of property has already emerged within human society that the chieftain of a clan who owns a large herd of cattle will appear to other members of that pastoral society as having 'natural authority' over them by virtue of his ownership of that livestock.[7] From a psychological perspective, the social institution of property is upheld and maintained on the basis of a complex cognitive web of perceptions grounded in a specific set of beliefs. By contrast, in a society of hunters and gatherers in which the momentary 'possession' of objects has not yet been distinguished from lifelong 'ownership', the natural authority of this kind of pastoral arrangement has yet to come into being.[8] But what does this tell us about Smith's idea of naturalness?

For someone, like me, who is interested in the problem of ideology, it is tempting to draw a parallel between Smith's use of the concept of natural authority and Georg Lukács's later definition of ideology as a 'necessary false consciousness'.[9] The way in which Smith describes pastoral societies, it seems necessary for the members of a pastoral society to regard the person who owns the livestock as also being their political ruler because their subsistence depends on him. In its natural immediacy, this belief might also be labelled as 'false' because it is based on a contingent social arrangement which, for that reason, is not 'natural'. This, however, is not what Smith means by 'natural authority' here. Rather, the concept of natural authority derives its meaning from the Scottish idea that 'natural history' is a kind of 'conjectural history'.[10] The idea that 'natural history' can be understood in terms of 'conjectural history' centres around the claim that it is scientifically legitimate to speculate via historical reasoning about how specific stages of human development are historically interconnected. When archaeological evidence points to the existence of hunter-gatherer societies and, at the same time, to the breeding of livestock shortly thereafter in the same geographical area, it becomes legitimate to ask what political, economic and social developments took place in order for the society to pass from one stage to the other. It is also possible to deny altogether the existence of a particular qualitative moment at which the old order was transcended or at which a significant alteration took place within the society's political and social institutions.[11]

Contrary to contemporary historical anthropology, the Scots, and especially Smith, regarded the historical moment in which stockbreeding first appears as a mode of subsistence to be a significant moment of political, economic and social change, since they understood it to constitute the first historical appearance of the idea of property (as differentiated from mere possession).[12] I do not want to delve too far into the historical accuracy of such a belief because I am concerned here primarily with a methodological problem: the assumption that the formation of property signified a historical progress of a specific kind led the Scots to understand it as a major marker of human institutional development. Moreover, because Smith understands feudalism to be the next stage of development, positioning the specific despotic relation of aristocratic land ownership and primogeniture on one side of the equation and the serfdom of the people on the other, he tries to find a historical reason why this despotic understanding of property would have come about.[13] He finds this in the shift from a hunter-gatherer society to pastoral rule. The development of the human mind and its capability for abstraction plays a central role in this evolution. For the idea of property to emerge, an individual must have learned to distinguish between property and possession and must have accepted the idea that a specific object belongs to a specific person, independent of this person's empirically observable relation to that object. It may be the case that the chieftain of the Tartars has never touched any of his sheep, since his shepherds take care of them, but, nonetheless, every Tartar accepts that all the sheep belong to him. This is the 'natural' relation that Smith is most interested in. What makes this relation appear to be natural is a shared set of collective beliefs which is tied to the sensual experience of those who share it. Epistemologically speaking, the social institution of property emerges as a symbolic mediation which itself necessitates abstract forms of thinking, for example understanding a deer to be the property of an individual who has never been in physical possession of the animal.

For hunters and gatherers, however, such a development (again, we are not concerned here with the historical accuracy of Smith's description) is hard to foresee because their social institutions work perfectly well without an abstract notion of property. There is an explanatory need for a historic rupture: a moment in which a force from outside, for example, provokes a restructuring of the social realm. A tribe of hunters and gatherers might have found themselves constantly under attack from another tribe and, as a result, they might have decided to establish a caste of professional warriors which then needed to be clothed and fed. The general in charge of that army might then have claimed political power. In Smith's narrative of the emergence of the institution of property, there is a clear historical dialectic: whereas, for long periods of history, quasi-feudal or feudal property relations served as a basis for despotic power, in the modern age, the emergence of private property allows for the overcoming of feudal power. This is Smith's own historical moment, and we can now see that he constructs his narrative of the historic necessity of the social emergence of the institution of property retroactively. As a 'conjectural history', it serves as a genealogical explanation for the present moment.

In the case of the Scots, it might sometimes appear unclear to what extent they themselves were aware of their own genealogical activity in constructing such a 'conjectural history'. This is, however, more of a political than a philosophical problem, meaning that their own philosophy of history naturally served to further specific political purposes within their own time-period. Smith, for example, was clearly an advocate for the emerging 'middling sort of people' and regarded feudal rule to be one of the main hindrances to a society's commercial and civil progress.[14] Here for the first time, we explicitly touch on the problem of a clear distinction between descriptive and normative elements in historical sociology. I will, however, show that this becomes a pseudo-problem as soon as we accept the fact that philosophical narratives of history will always imply hypothetical assumptions of only relative worth, meaning that they will always rely on the construction of retroactive necessities. The next section will be concerned with why such narratives are nevertheless both of scientific value and historical necessary from the point of view of a modern philosopher.

The Hypothetical Status of Knowledge in Conjectural History

Although the owl of wisdom starts its flight late in the day, the age of the owl remains an open question and, from what we know, she appears to be quite a young owl. James C. Scott – perhaps the most prominent recent figure to disprove the Scots' philosophy of history – refers to the flight of the owl of *Minerva* in his argument that the most frequently discussed portions of human history constitute, in fact, only a tiny fraction of a much longer history[15] – the latest news, to use Nietzsche's phrase. Somehow, it seems that the natural-science paradigm of exact, unambiguous knowledge has brought historical sociology to an impasse: if it wishes to claim such knowledge for itself then it can make only very basic assumptions which appear so abstract as to be almost meaningless; the idea, for example, that all humans are social by nature because they apparently always lived in societies. On the other hand, if historical sociology accepts the fact that its knowledge is of a different kind from that of the natural sciences, that it offers no mere experimental knowledge of the mastery of nature but an essay in understanding how the development of the human species came about and the driving forces behind it, then the status of this knowledge will always be subject to doubt because it remains a hypothetical form of knowledge. At the same time, it always remains entangled with the normative viewpoint from which it forms its own assumptions. But this is what human reasoning means. In understanding the fallibility of our thoughts, we become aware of our own historical subjectivity and also, at least partially, of our own historical moment.

It might be suggested that the compelling appeal of early modern scepticism is a result of its roots in these kinds of historical insights. They are soaked into every fabric of the *ancien régime* and subvert its theological and metaphysical groundwork. A truth then, it appears, can at this stage only be a relative and historical truth. For a metaphysician, such a situation is dissatisfying since a metaphysician wants to reach indubitable knowledge. However, the modern epistemological situation also bears a risk for the moral philosopher of a mainly pragmatic conviction who is 'only' interested in bringing about political and social stability. Her historical reasoning has the potential to unfold a destructive force on society, unleashing a sceptical dynamic which tends towards moral nihilism. Whereas the Scots might be understood to share the latter concern without becoming too concerned about the former, Hegel's answer to this problem of a specifically modern political and social instability follows the pattern of Kant: only a new social and historical metaphysics will help us escape the nihilistic downward spiral of modern sceptical reasoning.[16]

It appears that human reasoning is drawn in two opposing directions. On the one hand, it aims to analyse and dissect the empirical material of the senses; on the other, it aims to recombine this dissected material into something that makes sense after all. Exactly this process can be found within Smith's conjectural history of the eventual historic emergence of private property. Although the archaeological and anthropological data of his day suggested that the institution of property had, for a long time, been tied to oppressive rule, the institution nevertheless led to the emergence of private property which, in turn, allowed for the flourishing of civil liberties. The isolated empirical data of specific historical events must be recombined into a conjectural narrative to be able to understand the process which was unfolding through this series of events.

It is possible to articulate the difference between Hegel and the Scottish Enlightenment by asking about the nature of that historical process and its ontological status. For the Scots, it is primarily a matter of historical-sociological change, capable of taking different directions, and vulnerable in principle to a substantive reversal (for example, from private property back to feudal property again). For Hegel, such a story is missing a crucial element since it fails to take into account our realisation of what this dialectical condition of opposite forces of human reasoning within us really means. For Hegel, the knowledge of the historicity of the human mind cannot be undone, but it can be transcended through a new level of philosophical consciousness in which we realise that our negative power of sceptical reasoning is able to show us the constructive potential of the positive force of human reason.[17] For Hegel, in a word, it makes us realise the formational potential of our *Geist*, or spirit.[18]

Although the Scots might not have accepted a metaphysical term such as 'spirit' as playing a central role in their social thought, the Scottish Enlightenment's philosophy of history also attributed a strong creative potential to the collective activities of the human mind. For the Scots, these activities of the mind must always be thought of as embedded within a specific practical and social arrangement, and this brings us back to Lockean sensualism and the problem of how abstract notions, from an empiricist's point of view, are able to form in the first place. What Locke wants to explain is the gradual emergence of abstract ideas out of concrete sensual experience. For Locke, the most contingent factor in this process of psychogenesis is the way in which we associate different ideas with each other, since this process relies mostly on custom.[19] Since humans are creatures of habit, it is hardly possible to overestimate society's influence on the formation of our ideas, and this societal influence on our experience can work both for the better and for the worse. The question of which political, economic and social arrangements serve the moral good was a perennial one within the Scottish Enlightenment. Notably, it is a commonly shared modern experience that virtue can emerge as a secondary effect of the prudent arrangement of these three societal spheres.[20] To put it in a nutshell, they all work best when they act as counterbalances to each other. Feudal power, for example, did not historically have a civil sphere to serve as a counterbalance and, as this civil sphere began to arise within early modern cities, the despotic quality of feudal power likewise started to vanish. In fact, early modern monarchs often legislated in favour of the early modern cities, as Smith suggests, precisely because they wanted to put a curb on local feudal powers.[21] A similar development can be seen in the early imperial dynasty's policies towards local aristocrats in early Chinese political history.[22]

There are two questions that remain to be answered before we can return to our main question and conclude our speculative findings. The first question concerns the 'spiritual substance' of the idea of historical progress within the Scottish Enlightenment. The second concerns the 'spiritual substance' of Hegel's idea of human emancipation over the course of history. Having considered these two questions, we can return to the ontological quality of the retroactive stipulation of historical necessity within the history of human societies. These three considerations will form the last three sections of this essay.

The Spirit of Commerce as a Mover of Human History

The French philosopher Montesquieu can be considered the great forebear of Hegel through his reintroduction of a specific idea of 'spirit' to early modern Enlightenment thought in his *De l'esprit des lois* (1748).[23] The concept of 'spirit' is central to Montesquieu's legal thought since, for Montesquieu, specific political, constitutional and social arrangements each embody a specific 'spirit', meaning that they aim to create and perpetuate a specific mindset within the population. A certain shared 'spirit of equality' among citizens is, for example, a necessary condition for democracy.[24] The question becomes, then, that of which constitutional and legal arrangements help this 'spirit of equality' to come about. For Montesquieu, there is one particular 'spirit' which acts transhistorically through different state formations and acts almost like a driving force behind their citizens' legal emancipation: this is the 'spirit of commerce'. Commerce, when enabled by a legislator, allows individuals to enjoy previously unknown liberties. It also – or, at least, so the story goes – makes them more socially virtuous because they step back from regarding the foreigner as an enemy but regard them instead as a potential trading partner.[25] For Montesquieu, the reason that the 'spirit of commerce' develops into the most important force of individual emancipation in early modernity is grounded in the fact that capital will always seek secure investment conditions – that is, a well-functioning separation of powers which is able to protect private property.[26] For Montesquieu, this is the reason why, historically, states which allow for individual liberty become prosperous and flourish while despotic ones do not but, rather, end in economic, social and political collapse.

While the Scots flesh out this historical narrative of *doux commerce* in more sociological and empirical detail, they very much stick to the same basic idea.[27] Indeed, by combining this narrative with the genealogy of property rights, and a corresponding history of the development of social relations, it is even possible to suggest that they turned it into a more consistent philosophy of history. Commerce, as a social and legal practice, must be understood as a source of a polity's eventual emancipation into civil society. However, we can no longer ignore the differences between the various positions within the Scottish discussion regarding commerce's progressive historical power. Ferguson, for example, is much more sceptical in this regard than Hume or Smith, largely as a result of his conviction that commercial practice can serve as an apology for the social promotion of relentless self-interest.[28] Ferguson notes that a civil polity depends on the subordination of individual self-interest, at least in part, to the interests of the community.[29] He also believes that a flourishing trade in luxury goods might eventually lead people away from the frugal lifestyle which he finds to be essential to the social perpetuation of a shared regard for equality among citizens and corresponding patterns of equity.[30] Ferguson is also sceptical about the liberating powers of commerce as a result of the growing social inequality between town and country. Whereas Smith regards the economic effect of commerce on rural areas as mainly positive in nature, Ferguson has a critical eye for the precarious effects of land enclosure and of the abandonment of the medieval commons (the institution of common pastureland which served for the subsistence of poor people).

Hume answers the quarrel regarding luxury through historical argument:[31] it might have been true in antiquity, Hume infers, that a trade in luxurious goods could easily have a devastating effect on the common interest of a polity. The ancient republican critique of luxury, therefore, has a temporal kind of truth, namely for city states that depend on a citizenry skilled in martial warfare. In such city states, a social division of labour that allows the production of luxury goods might draw necessary manpower away from the martial arts. Likewise, the enjoyment of luxury goods might soften the citizenry to a degree which has inauspicious consequences for their martial duties.[32]

Hume goes on to argue that such degenerative effects should not be expected as a result of modern trade in luxury goods. The main reason for this is that the modern state no longer depends on the martial abilities of its citizenry. On the contrary, living conditions which have the potential to soften the character are socially fruitful for the modern state because they create civility. Civility, in turn, is needed for commerce to prosper as a social practice. The social effect of luxury, therefore, in Hume's historical view, has been reversed: what was once a disintegrating force now serves to create valuable social bonds between people. As in Smith's conjectural history of the origins of property, we can observe an almost dialectical turning-point between the modern and pre-modern age. The institution of property, for Smith, has oppressive origins but it becomes a political and economic precondition for the overcoming of feudalism, manifested in the consolidation of (the institution of) private property. For Hume, the trade in luxury goods once had the power to destroy republics but in modernity its role has been reversed, bringing civility, prosperity and (self-)cultivation to the people.

Behind all these specific historic conjectures lies one central conjecture. It is the social practice of commerce which acts as a driving force in the Smithian and Humean narrative, and Ferguson also regards commercial practices to be the main factor driving historical progress although, for him, this progress appears to have a flipside as well. We have not yet given enough thought to the ontological status of 'commerce' within such narratives, however. It is possible, for example, to deny that commerce is a 'spirit' at all and argue that it is, instead, a historically specific practice. For the purposes of this essay, the most important difference between the Hegelian view and the viewpoint of the Scots is that, for the Scots, the self-regulating quality of modern commerce depends on a complex framework of political and social institutions which, from a strictly historical and empirical perspective, arose as a matter of chance. This contingency is easily revealed through cross-cultural comparison. However, such contingency does not completely rule out some element of retroactive necessity for those who are involved in the development of commerce as an ongoing historical process.

The Emancipatory Necessity of the Historical Imagination

Hegel does not attempt to deny that the formative character of the human spirit only manifests itself in social practice. Rather, he makes the claim that meaningful social practice would be unthinkable if the formative power of the human mind's collective activities was not an active possibility. The materialist turn to historical practice seems necessary in order to understand where we, as a society, or even as a species, come from and the things which constitute the human condition. We must not, however, overlook the activity of the human mind in constructing this narrative and in following this historical path. What the modern condition lets us see, for the first time, is that our most precious capability is that of thinking for ourselves. The narrative construction of retroactive necessities in conjectural history is needed in order to form a consistent history of our past and present. This might be thought of as the objective aspect of the historical need for (the construction of) retroactive necessities. There is also, however, a subjective aspect to this: purposeful action depends on the imagination of an aim towards which that action can be directed. Otherwise, human action would be meaningless and indistinguishable from animal instinct. Perhaps this truth is just the result of the human mind's need to retroactively create its own history in order to be able to project its own future.

Hume already touches on this fundamental insight when he shows, in his social epistemology, how the idea of necessity is the result of customary experience.[33] Not only do we expect the sun to rise because it fits our everyday experience but we also need to project an outcome in order for our actions to be able to follow through with those actions. It is true that the aims of our actions are sometimes subject to frustration, because the outcome of these actions is never fully in our own hands, but the point remains that we would not have started upon a course of action without some kind of imagination of its fulfilment.[34] On a meta-level, therefore, a relationship between our past and future projections is required in order for our mind to think properly. This self-conscious sense of the human mind's formative potential in dealing with the outer world is what Hegel terms self-consciousness.[35] Only when the sceptical gap between the inner and outer is bridged through imaginative projection does purposeful action become possible.[36]

From the perspective of historical philosophy, this is what might be termed the modern condition of thought, in which a level of insight regarding the need for the human mind to imagine retroactive necessities has been achieved. It is the discernment of this necessity which serves to constitute freedom of action. At first glance, it might seem that this is where Hegel departs significantly from the Scottish historical analysis of specific social conditions for human action. For the Scots, the potentialities for human freedom, as well as its obstacles, are to be found in specific political, economic, legal and social conditions and, at first sight, these do not seem to have much to do with the inner readiness of the human mind to purposefully tell its own story. But, then, what is going on here other than the narration of human progress in the face of the historical reality of human misery? Hegel is right to point out the constitutive part that creativity and imagination play in narrating a conjectural history. The metaphysical aspect is only able to return when Hegel understands the historical development of human emancipation from natural determination as a process of the human spirit becoming aware of itself. I will not discuss this metaphysical hypothesis here. What I want to ask, however, is whether the creation of imaginative histories of retroactive necessity answers a basic human need. To accept this claim would be to depart from a Hegelian understanding of 'spirit' as the substance behind the development of human history. Rather, it would point to a subjective need for telling a coherent story of ourselves and the world we live in. Humans might have a 'natural' need to reach a self-consistent 'worldview', problematic though this might be.[37]

Conclusion

In the second half of the eighteenth century, the narrative of *doux commerce*, although one-sided and written with a normative bias towards the shoring up of private property, opened up a space for speculation regarding the direction in which the historical development of human relations might eventually lead. Without it, arguments such as Kant's suggestion in his treatise *On Perpetual Peace* from 1795 that the 'power of money' (*Geldmacht*) would at last bring enduring peace to the world would not have been thinkable.[38] A vulgar Marxist critique which disregards the narrative of *doux commerce* as plain ideology misses out a critical element of this idea, and one which might be regarded as a precondition for any historical narrative's ability to project a way to global human emancipation. Historical necessity is not about the doctrinal postulation of empirical fact (or, at least, if someone makes such a claim, this might be a good moment for the subjective exercise of modern historical scepticism) but about a path of action. Even Kant, who is almost exclusively focused on the process of introspection, is aware that his speculations *On Perpetual Peace* mean nothing if they are not implemented by means of political action.

Maybe the most fascinating thing about historical speculation is its capacity to project historical necessity in a wide variety of different directions. That our historical projections have erred in the past can only serve to prove the indeterminacy of our future.

Notes

* Funded by the Deutsche Forschungsgemeinschaft (DFG, German Research Foundation) – SFB TRR 294/1-424638267.

1. I borrow the term 'retroactive necessity' from Slavoj Žižek's reading of Hegel. It is an idea which is traced by Žižek mainly for its impact on the history of Marxist political thought. However, I should not conceal that he criticises a reading of the concept of retroactive necessity as an assertion of historical indeterminacy: 'The solution is not to conceive the historical process as open, with everything depending on us, free subjects, and every objective determination a reified objectivization of our own creativity; it is also not a "balanced" combination of substantial fate and the limited space of free subjective creativity, in the sense of the famous lines from the beginning of Marx's Eighteenth Brumaire: "Men make their own history, but they do not make it as they please; they do not make it under self-selected circumstances, but under circumstances existing already, given and transmitted from the past." It is not that historical necessity provided the basic frame within which we can act freely (in the sense of Engels' notion of historical necessity which realizes itself through a complex network of individual contingencies). There is Fate, our future is predetermined, the Absolute "is already brought to completion in and for itself, without needing first to wait for us," but this very completion is our own contingent act. In short, the paradox is that the only way to assert the possibility of a radical change through subjective intervention is to accept Predestination and Fate. Historical process is thus characterized by the overlapping of necessity and contingency, the overlapping which was first explicitly formulated in the Protestant idea of predestination. It's not that a deeper necessity realizes itself through a complex set of contingent circumstances, it's that contingent circumstances decide the fate of necessity itself: once a thing (contingently) happens, its occurrence retroactively becomes necessary. Our fate is yet not decided – not in the simple sense that we have a choice, but in a more radical sense of choosing one's fate itself.' See Slavoj Žižek, 'Hegel, Retroactivity and The End of History', *Continental Thought and Theory* 2 (2019), pp. 3–10, p. 5.

2. For Althusser, the 'ideology' of a societal constellation is revealed by considering what this society regards to be 'self-evident', e. g. 'civil society' regards the individual bearer of rights as its most fundamental social entity as self-evident. See Louis Althusser, 'Ideology and Ideological State Apparatuses' in *Essays on Ideology*, transl. B. Brewster (London: Verso, 1984), pp. 36–44.
3. This example only serves to underline how historical thought principally feeds on the critique of a metaphysical stipulation of retroactive necessity. For this early modern theological critique, see Martin Mulsow, *Enlightenment Underground: Radical Germany 1680–1720*, transl. Erik Midelfort (Charlottesville, VA: University of Virginia Press, 2015), p. 45. Cf. Martin Mulsow, *Radikale Frühaufklärung in Deutschland 1680–1720 Bd. 1: Moderne aus dem Untergrund* (Göttingen: Wallstein, 2018), p. 87.
4. It must be mentioned here that Kant makes a comparable claim to the one of Hegel in his *Critique of Judgement* of 1790 and, with regard to historical thought, even more so in his later anthropological writings. Both Kant and Hegel are deeply influenced by the Scottish Enlightenment's philosophy of history in this regard. For reasons of clarity, however, I will discuss Kant's view only sporadically. One reason for this is that, for Kant, historical judgement merely serves as a mediating force to realise what he calls the 'metaphysics of morals'. Although in his later writings he underlines the 'pragmatic' character of any anthropological teleology, which contains the idea of retroactive necessity in it, his historical thought remains comparably static.
5. This is, of course, an oversimplification. The evolvement of science also contributes greatly to economic progress. It is just that the liberalisation of commerce will be regarded by the Scots as being a contingent outcome of an unintentional historical interplay that might only be explained retroactively.
6. Lockean sensualism is adapted by the Scottish Enlightenment as a theoretical groundwork for the historical development of human experience, most notably with regard to the emergence of the idea of property. Thereby, Locke's two original sources of knowledge within the human mind, 'sensation' and 'reflection', are blended into one, as the latter's level of abstraction is seen as a derivation of the former's habituation.
7. See Smith, *An Inquiry into the Nature and Causes of the Wealth of Nations* (Indianapolis, IN: Liberty Fund, 1976), V.i.b.16, pp. 717–18 (henceforth WN). Cf. Christopher Berry, *Social Theory of the Scottish*

Enlightenment (Edinburgh: Edinburgh University Press, 1997), pp. 100–2.
8. Cf. Berry, *Social Theory*, p. 95.
9. In such a reading, Smith's concept of 'natural authority' might be seen as signifying the ideology of a pastoral society in which it is accepted that a superior power owns the livestock. This might also be a deity in this regard, or an apotheosised individual. Lukács describes the 'necessary false consciousness' of a commercial society as such: 'However, if this atomisation [of the individual] is only an illusion it is a necessary one. That is to say, the immediate, practical as well as intellectual confrontation of the individual with society, the immediate production and reproduction of life – in which for the individual the commodity structure of all "things" and their obedience to "natural laws" is found to exist already in a finished form, as something immutably given – could only take place in the form of rational and isolated acts of exchange between isolated commodity owners.' See Georg Lukács, *History and Class Consciousness: Studies in Marxist Dialectics*, transl. Rodney Livingstone (Cambridge, MA: MIT Press, 1967), p. 92.
10. For a full discussion of the concept of 'natural history' as 'conjectural history' in the Scottish Enlightenment see Christopher Berry, *The Idea of Commercial Society in the Scottish Enlightenment* (Edinburgh: Edinburgh University Press, 2013), pp. 32–65. For a further hermeneutical analysis of the concept of 'conjectural history' in the eighteenth century see also Sylvana Tomaselli, 'The Role of Woman in Enlightenment Conjectural Histories' in Hans Erich Bödeker and Lieselotte Steinbrügge (eds), *Conceptualizing Women in Enlightenment Thought / Penser la femme au siècle des Lumières* (Berlin: Arno Spitz, 2001).
11. As Maurice Brown points out, Smith's conceptualisation of the four stages can be seen as a 'heuristic device' for making sense of the scattered historical data available to him. Smith developed the four stages theory out of a necessity to make the history of human societies rationally accessible for the purpose of his scholarly work, and he was well aware of this. See Maurice Brown, *Adam Smith's Economics: Its Place in the History of Economic Thought* (London: Routledge, 2013), p. 74.
12. For a substantial critique of this conjectural narrative in the face of contemporary archaeological evidence about the history of early human societies, see James C. Scott, *Against the Grain: A Deep History of the Earliest States* (New Haven, CT: Yale University Press, 2017). I argue

in a forthcoming article that Smith's historical methodology would be principally combinable with Scott's findings.
13. It is a central characteristic of the modernity of Smith's historical methodology that he sees institutions as being able to evolve in many different directions. Therefore, his historical methodology is fundamentally combinable with a non-linear idea of political, social and economic progress. These three layers of a societal structure might at times also have contradicting effects on each other. For a more elaborated picture of this early modern idea of institutional development, see also Berry's contribution to this volume.
14. Cf. Samuel Fleischacker, *On Adam Smith's Wealth of Nations: A Philosophical Companion* (Princeton: Princeton University Press, 2004), p. 111. Cf. WN II.iii.39, p. 347.
15. Cf. Scott, *Against the Grain*, p. 5.
16. In Kantian terms, to abstain from historical speculation would mean to substract historical 'judgement' from the process of historical reasoning, which is impossible. However, Kant, like Smith, would not accept this to show an evolvement of the human mind as such, as Hegel would. See Kant's introduction to the *Critique of Judgement* of 1790. Hegel's historical thought is unique in this regard in his integration of a metaphysical trajectory of 'spirit' into a historical dynamics of human evolvement. See also Note 4 above.
17. This is at least a possible interpretation of his treatment of scepticism in the *Phenomenology of Spirit* of 1807. Reason's sceptical capacity to negate at last turns into self-negation. To avoid this vicious circle, Hegel assumes that self-consciousness must bring its capacity to negate into service of its practical self-assertion. This leads him to a critical reassessment of the topic of 'mastery and servitude' along the lines of 'recognition'. See G. W. F. Hegel, *Phenomenology of Spirit*, ed. Terry Pinkard (Cambridge: Cambridge University Press, 2018), pp. 117–35. Cf. Ludwig Siep, *Hegel's Phenomenology of Spirit* (Cambridge: Cambridge University Press, 2014), pp. 87–107.
18. Cf. Christopher Berry, *Hume, Hegel and Human Nature* (The Hague: Martinus Nijhoff, 1982), p. 135.
19. See John Locke, *An Essay concerning Human Understanding*, ed. Peter Nidditch (Oxford: Clarendon Press, 1975), pp. 394–401 (2.33).
20. This thought is seen as a central insight of early political economy by a number of scholars in the history of economics. One of the most influential contributions is Albert O. Hirschman's interpretation of the notion of countervailing forces in *The Passions and the Interests* (Princeton: Princeton University Press, 1997). I want to especially

draw attention to Franz Neumann's introductory essay to Montesquieu's *Spirit of Laws* (New York: Hafner, 1949). Hirschman develops his view further in 'Der Streit um die Bewertung der Marktgesellschaft' in *Entwicklung, Markt und Moral, Abweichende Betrachtungen* (Munich: Hanser, 1989), pp. 192–225.
21. WN III.i–iv, pp. 376–427.
22. Cf. Yuri Pines, *Foundations of Confucian Thought, Intellectual Life in the Chunqiu Period 722–453 B.C.E.* (Honolulu: University of Hawaii Press, 2002), p. 198. See also Youngmin Kim, *A History of Chinese Political Thought* (Cambridge: Polity Press, 2018), pp. 94–113.
23. In the German tradition, Johann Gottfried Herder (1744–1803) is often seen as an intermediate figure between Montesquieu and Hegel because his concept of 'Volksgeist' is inspired by Montesquieu's idea of distinct 'national spirits', or 'esprit national'. It is true that Hegel adopts the concept of 'Volksgeist'. However, it is debatable if Hegel's idea of different social manifestations of collective 'spirits' is not closer to Montesquieu's original reasoning of a dependence of those national mentalities on a contingent interplay of social and material conditions, as it is to Herder's naturalised understanding of 'Volksgeister'.
24. See Montesquieu, *The Spirit of the Laws*, ed. and transl. Anne M. Cohler, Basia C. Miller and Harold Samuel Stone (Cambridge: Cambridge University Press, 1989), pp. 22–4 (1.3.3), pp. 43–8 (1.5.3–6).
25. For Montesquieu, this is not a natural effect of trade per se but only of domestic trade subject to a rule of law, which is to say that the effect of *doux commerce* is dependent on political conditions. Cf. Montesquieu, *Spirit of the Laws*, pp. 337–53 (4.20).
26. Cf. Hirschman, *The Passions and the Interests*, pp. 70–81.
27. Cf. Berry, *The Idea of Commercial Society*, pp. 26–9.
28. I thank Craig Smith for making me aware of Ferguson's concept of national spirit, and how it intersects with the early modern German discourse on the topic. I will follow up this matter in a future article.
29. See Adam Ferguson, *An Essay on the History of Civil Society*, ed. Fania Oz-Salzberger (Cambridge: Cambridge University Press, 1995), Chapter 1.6, 'On Moral Sense'.
30. See ibid. Chapter 3.6, 'On Civil Liberty'.
31. See David Hume, 'Of Commerce' in *Political Essays*, ed. Knud Haakonssen (Cambridge: Cambridge University Press, 1994), pp. 93–104.
32. It is worth noting, however, that in ancient Athens it was a matter of public debate whether or not citizen-soldiers needed an education in the liberal arts and the refinement of manners in order to counterbalance their martial impulses in the context of community

and make them fit for democracy. Cf. Paul Rahe, *Republics, Ancient and Modern, Vol. 1: The Ancien Regime in Classical Greece* (Chapel Hill, NC: North Carolina University Press, 1994), pp. 186–218. See also WN V.i.f, p. 774.
33. Cf. Hume, *A Treatise of Human Nature*, ed. David Fate Norton (Oxford: Clarendon Press, 2007), pp. 257–65, Treatise 2.3.1.
34. I analyse this aspect of Hume's theory of action in more detail in Schuck, *Die Verinnerlichung der sozialen Natur: zum Verhältnis von Freiheit und Einfühlung in der Sozialpsychologie des frühen Liberalismus* (Hamburg: Felix Meiner, 2019), pp. 81–128.
35. Cf. Berry, *Hume, Hegel and Human Nature*, p. 144.
36. In this regard, Catherine Dromelet alluded to two passages of Hume on optimism which are the following: 'A propensity to hope and joy is real riches: One to fear and sorrow, real poverty' (The Sceptic, § 22); 'These symptoms of a rising reputation gave me encouragement, as I was ever more disposed to see the favorable than unfavorable side of things; a turn of mind which it is more happy to possess, than to be born to an estate of ten thousand a year' (My Own Life, § 9).
37. The early twentieth-century German debate on the concept of 'worldview' or *Weltanschauung* might be of interest in this regard, as it is the argument of the Southwestern school of Neo-Kantianism against the early irrationalist and existentialist thinkers that an individual only eventually comes to a 'worldview' by the exercise of its teleological capacities of human reasoning. Although not something which can be characterised as scientific knowledge, a 'worldview' therefore is not 'irrational' either.
38. For Kant, the pacifying effect of the 'power of money' (*Geldmacht*) is caused by the 'spirit of commerce' (*Handelsgeist*). Although not often outlined in German Kant scholarship, Kant is a clear follower of the dictum of *doux commerce* in his philosophy of history: 'Es ist der Handelsgeist, der mit dem Kriege nicht zusammen bestehen kann, und der früher oder später sich jedes Volks bemächtigt.' See Immanuel Kant, *Schriften zur Anthropologie, Geschichtsphilosophie und Pädagogik*, ed. Wilhelm Weischedel (Darmstadt: Wissenschaftliche Buchgesellschaft, 1983), p. 226. For a critical resolution of the inherent ambiguities this creates in his overall system, see Pauline Kleingeld, 'Kant, History and the Idea of Moral Development', *History of Philosophy Quarterly* 16 (1999), pp. 59–80.

9

Traces of Hume in Sociology
Angela M. Coventry

Introduction

Sociology was formally designated an institutional discipline in the late nineteenth century with the first Department of Sociology founded in 1892 at the University of Chicago in America and the first European Sociology Department established at the University of Bordeaux in 1895. Yet reflections on society are brimming throughout the history of philosophy from ancient times to the Enlightenment of the eighteenth century. The Scottish Enlightenment era in particular is generally thought to be central to the emergence of sociology.[1] One classic source, Gladys Bryson's 1945 *Man and Society: The Scottish Inquiry of the Eighteenth Century*, connected the development of sociology to Scottish Enlightenment thinkers of the eighteenth century.[2] Twenty-five years later, Alan Swingewood examined Scotland between the years 1750 and 1790 to show that from the work of Adam Smith, Adam Ferguson, John Millar and William Robertson 'a remarkably modern sociological treatment of society and its institutions emerged'.[3] Allan Silver maintained that the liberal foundations of sociological theory about personal relations were articulated by four figures of the Scottish Enlightenment: Smith, David Hume, Francis Hutcheson and Ferguson.[4] Björn Eriksson dealt with the emergence of sociology in Scottish figures from the 1760s to the 1780s who include Smith, Ferguson, Millar, Lord Kames and William Robertson.[5]

Swingewood lamented that the Scottish Enlightenment tradition has been 'largely forgotten and ignored' in sociology.[6] Roberto Cipriani claimed that Hume's thought especially has been insufficiently studied in sociology and by historians of the social sciences.[7] More positively, recent scholarship (rightly) emphasises the role of society and social relations in Hume's philosophy.[8] The aim of this chapter is to bring the historical origins of sociology and Hume's philosophy of society a bit closer together by examining some of the ways that Hume's thought has influenced the directions of sociological thinking. I survey Humean traces in key figures in the field of sociology across the nineteenth to twenty-first centuries in Europe and the United States of America on the topics of positivism, economics, convention, custom and habit, religion, morality and the self.[9]

Positivism

Nineteenth-century French thinker Auguste Comte is usually credited as one of the earliest sociologists. Raymond Aron recently claimed that 'Comte may be considered as the first and foremost sociologist'.[10] Comte was almost certainly the first to use the term 'sociology' to designate a 'social physics' that is a scientific study of human society in the 1830 work the *Cours de la Philosophie Positive* or *Course of Positive Philosophy*.[11] Comte had many influences but he explicitly linked the origins of his own thought to eighteenth-century Scottish thinkers such as Hume and Smith.[12] In the *Course of Positive Philosophy*, Comte judged that Hume treated 'causation with great originality and boldness'.[13] He continued that Hume's work had taken 'the only major step which the human mind had ever taken towards a true and direct appreciation of nature seen in a purely relative way as befits a sound philosophy'.[14] Comte even personally expressed 'special gratitude' for the contributions of Hume (and Smith) who had proved 'very useful' to his 'early philosophical education'.[15]

Hume shaped Comte's doctrine of the law of three stages or states in the evolution of knowledge in human society: 'the Theological, or fictitious; the Metaphysical, or abstract; and the Scientific, or positive'.[16] In the first stage, religion dominates and humans explain the causes of natural phenomena by way of an imaginary God or gods. In the second metaphysical stage, abstract speculative theories prevail and obscure forces or powers behind phenomena are now posited to explain causes of nature. So we reach the third, positive stage, where Comte maintained that the proper combination of reason and observation 'are the means of this knowledge'.[17] In this stage, humans seek explanations that are restricted to the natural laws of observable phenomena by empirically oriented scientific theories. Comte's positivist vision in sociology was a systematic scientific approach to society that was grounded in observed facts. Comte thought that Hume had 'proposed the true character of positive conceptions'.[18] Hume's experience-based science of human nature revealed the illusory pursuit of first causes in religion, the shortcomings of positing obscure powers or forces in metaphysics and replaced the search for ultimate causes with the scientific study of descriptive generalisations or laws of nature. Comte may be said to extend Hume's project of a science of the mind with the positive application of the scientific method to society. Mike Gane remarked that 'Comtean sociology' emerges out of 'Humean philosophy'.[19]

Comte's positivism was influential on English social thinkers such as John Stuart Mill, Harriet Martineau and Herbert Spencer as well as the Austrian physicist-philosopher Ernst Mach. However, plenty were critical of Comte's positivism. For example, social theorist Anna J. Cooper rejected Comte's positivism in her 1892 work *A Voice from the South: By a Black Woman of the South*. *A Voice from the South* is about the racial and gender dimensions of economic and social relations in the American South. Part One makes the case for the advancement of African American women in higher education to improve the standing of the entire African American community and to aid in the progress of society. Part Two addresses how best to solve the racial tensions in American society. In the final section of Part Two, 'A Gain from Belief', Cooper briefly outlines various philosophical positions to do with positivism, agnosticism and scepticism in a survey that includes Hume, Comte, Blaise Pascal, Huxley, Mill, Spencer, G. H. Lewes and Robert Ingersoll.

Cooper's short history starts with Hume. Hume, she claimed, 'taught skepticism in England on purely metaphysical grounds'.[20] She stated that Hume 'knew little or nothing of natural science' and 'held that what we call mind consists merely of successive perceptions, and that we can have no knowledge of anything but phenomena'.[21] Next, Cooper wrote that Hume's philosophy 'passes through France, is borrowed and filtered through the brain of a half crazy French schoolmaster, Auguste Conte [sic], who thus becomes the founder of the Contist school of Positivism or Nescience or Agnosticism'.[22] What the followers of Comte's school have in common is that they do not allow 'revelation, nor a God, nor the immortality of the soul'.[23] For Cooper, the positivist system eliminates 'God and Love', and as a consequence morality is a sham, 'the precepts and sanctions of morality a lie; the sense of responsibility a disease'.[24]

Further, self-improvement is pointless and all 'hope in the grand possibilities of life are blasted'.[25] Cooper's intent is not to 'refute' positivism but to make the case for the 'one truth'.[26] The one truth is 'the fundamental need of any nation, any race . . . for heroism, devotion, sacrifice' and she thought that 'there cannot be heroism, devotion, or sacrifice in a primarily skeptical spirit'.[27] Cooper believed these values are needed to make progress in society, that 'men need to be anchored to what they *feel* to be eternal verities' so as to 'propel men into those sublime efforts of altruism which constitute the moral heroes of humanity'.[28] She found the values of heroism, devotion and sacrifice to be 'particularly urgent in a race at almost the embryonic stage of character-building'.[29]

The importance of religion for society has been emphasised by other sociologists. German sociologist Max Weber thought that religion could serve as a mechanism for social change in the classic *Protestant Ethic and the Spirit of Capitalism*, published in 1904–5. French sociologist Émile Durkheim defended that societies require and benefit from religion in the 1915 *Elementary Forms of Religious Life: A Study in Religious Sociology*. In the conclusion, he wrote that there is 'something eternal in religion which is destined to survive all the particular symbols in which religious thought has successively enveloped itself'.[30] Furthermore, Durkheim contended that religion is required for the profession and rebuilding of moral commitments: 'moral remaking can only be achieved through meetings, assemblies, and congregations in whom the individual, pressing close to one another, reaffirm in common their common sentiments'.[31]

Economics

Another of Hume's significant contributions is to the field of economics, particularly his account of money. Hume thought of money as an 'instrument which men have agreed upon to facilitate the exchange of one commodity for another'.[32] In his first work, *A Treatise of Human Nature*, he treats money as a convention like language or the rules of justice.[33] German social and economic theorist Karl Marx was influenced by Hume.[34] It is enough for Marx to quote from Hume's *Treatise on Human Nature* on the section to do with the immateriality of the soul[35] to repudiate Plutarch for bringing philosophy to the 'forum of religion' in the Appendix to his 1841 doctoral dissertation, 'The Difference between the

Democritean and Epicurean Philosophy of Nature'.[36] Eighteen years later in *A Contribution to the Critique of Political Economy* (1859), Marx singled out Hume as 'by far the most important representative' of a theory in classical political economy to do with the circulation of money in the eighteenth century.[37] Marx's *Critique of Political Economy* was later incorporated into his more famous 1867 work on political economy and society, *Das Kapital*, where the discussion of Hume is relegated to footnotes only.

Marx is critical of Hume's theory of money in Chapter 2 of the *Critique*. In classical political economy, Marx observed the 'metallic circulation as the prevailing form of circulation'.[38] Metallic money was defined as coin and metallic coin was defined as 'a mere token of value'.[39] Further, given 'the law governing the circulation of tokens of value', it was also thought that 'the prices of commodities depend on the quantity of money in circulation'.[40] Marx maintained that Hume held the view that the quantity of money in circulation determined the value of money and the price level in a particular country the total value of commodity prices to be circulated in a period of time. If the number of commodities increase, their prices will fall or the value of money increases, or if the amount of money increases, commodity prices will rise and the value of money decreases. According to Marx, Hume's theory of money circulation is a failure because he lacks two of the 'necessary' materials to understand money circulation.[41] These include a 'critical history of commodity-prices' and the 'official and continuous statistics regarding the expansion and contraction of the medium of circulation, the influx or withdrawal of precious metals, etc.'[42]

Marx allowed that it sometimes appears that a change in the quantity of tokens of money in circulation has a uniform effect on the price of commodities. The periods Hume considers are ones when changes in the price level are accompanied by corresponding changes in the quantity of tokens. Nonetheless Marx pointed out that in such times the value of money was also changing. The openings of the American gold mines during this period altered the value of money. But Hume treats gold as if it were the same as tokens of value and does not take into consideration the role of the measure of value. This means that gold enters circulation without value and derives its value from its quantity rather than from its labour content. Marx wrote that Hume 'makes commodities enter the process of circulation without price and gold and silver without value'.[43] It is as if gold enters circulation, Marx claimed, as 'non-commodities; but as soon as they appear in the form of coin, he turns them, on the contrary, into commodities, which must be exchanged for other commodities by simple barter'.[44] Hume's account of money circulation, Marx said, settles for an 'imaginary mechanical equalization process' whereby the quantity of gold and the volume of commodities balance.[45] Hume's approach is unsatisfactory to Marx because it eliminates the 'process of the movement of commodities due to the antagonism between use-value and value which commodities bear within themselves'.[46]

Marx's history of money continued that Hume's contemporary, the Scottish political economist Sir James Steuart, had also argued extensively against Hume on money along similar lines in his 1767 work *An Inquiry into the Principles of Political Economy*.[47] Marx approved of Steuart's work on money. Marx thought that Steuart had appreciated the transformation of labour and understood the difference between 'specifically social labor which is represented in exchange value, and concrete labor which produces use-values'.[48] Marx thought that Smith 'tacitly adopts' Steuart's theory whereas Hume's theory of money was 'developed to its ultimate conclusions' into the nineteenth century by the British political economist David Ricardo.[49] Ricardo 'elaborated Hume's theory' but also made Hume's mistake but instead this time about banknote, not metallic, circulation.[50] Marx claimed that Ricardo 'confounds the circulation of bank-notes, or credit money, with the circulation of mere tokens of value'.[51] Scottish political economist James Mill expands on Ricardo's view but falls again into the 'same error' as Hume, according to Marx, because he assumes that 'use-values and not commodities with a given exchange value are in circulation'.[52]

In the economic literature today, Hume is perhaps most known for holding the quantity theory of money.[53] According to the quantity theory of money, the price level of goods and services is directly proportional to the monetary supply in any given economy. This standard interpretation of Hume as a quantity money theorist has been challenged.[54] For the present purpose it is notable that Marx provided an early version of the interpretation of Hume as a money quantity theorist in his *Critique of Political Economy*. Simply put, for quantity theories of money, changes in prices correspond to changes in the monetary supply. Marx summed up

Hume's view on money circulation as follows: 'If commodities increase in quantity, their price falls or the value of money rises. If money increases in quantity, then, on the contrary, the price of commodities rises and the value of money declines.'[55] On Marx's reading, then, Hume's monetary theory is in essence that the 'rise or fall of prices depends on the quantity of money in circulation' and that for Hume, 'a change in the value of the measure of value' 'causes a rise or fall of prices and, consequently, also a change in the amount of money in circulation'.[56]

Margaret Schabas has recently related Hume on economics to Weber's *Protestant Ethic and the Spirit of Capitalism*.[57] The revival of economic sociology in the twentieth century finds James Coleman's notion of social capital linked to Hume as well as Smith and Edmund Burke.[58] And more recently, in the 2003 book *Principles of Economic Sociology*, Richard Swedberg developed a sociological theory of interest inspired by Weber and Hume.[59] Swedberg notes that, 'Several eighteenth-century philosophers, most importantly David Hume, were also fascinated by the role of interests in human affairs.'[60] Swedberg looked specifically at Hume on justice and the passions to illuminate the theory of interest in economic sociology.[61]

Convention

Annette Baier claimed that Hume's contribution on convention made him 'a glorious inventor in moral and social theory'.[62] Hume saw conventions like language, money, honesty, justice and allegiance to authority as natural products of social life. Conventions evolve gradually over time and tend in favour of public utility. He insisted that convention is not a promise, for promises 'arise from human conventions'.[63] Conventions are based on mutual interest or, more specifically, 'a general sense of common interest; which sense all the members of the society express to one another, and which induces them to regulate their conduct by certain rules'.[64] Justice, Hume thought, required 'a convention enter'd into by all the members of the society to bestow stability on the possession of those external goods'.[65] Over time the regularity of our experience of repeated observances of the rules of justice 'assures us still more, that the sense of interest has become common to all our fellows, and gives us confidence of the future regularity of their conduct'.[66]

Hume on justice and convention may be connected to Spencer. Spencer's notion of justice is the 'law of equal liberty' that holds as a necessary rule for society. Spencer's rule is the 'liberty of each, limited by the like liberty of all, is the rule in conformity with which society must be organized'.[67] In a similar manner, Hume found the establishment of justice, to 'leave every one in the peaceable enjoyment of what he may acquire by his fortune and industry' and that 'it will be for my interest to leave another in the possession of his goods, provided he will act in the same manner with regard to me'.[68] For Hume it is undoubtable that justice is fundamental for society; he said that 'the convention for the distinction of property, and for the stability of possession, is of all circumstances the most necessary to the establishment of human society'.[69] Further, like Hume, Spencer believed that conventions take place over a long period of time. Spencer thought of conventions as 'natural products of social life which have gradually evolved'.[70] In Volume 1 of *Principles of Sociology* (1873), Spencer defines what sociology is, how human beings associate with each other in communities and how institutions develop over time, and begins with an analysis of domestic institutions to do with family, marriage, women and children. Volume 2 covers ceremonial and political institutions, while Volume 3 discusses ecclesiastical institutions, professional institutions and 'industrial' (or economic) institutions. Hume's *History of England* is cited three times in support of his explanations in Volume 2.[71]

German sociologist Ferdinand Tönnies was one of the co-founders (along with Weber, amongst others) of the German Society for Sociology in 1909 and was president of the society from 1909 to 1934. In the foreword to the first edition of his influential 1887 work *Gemeinschaft und Gesellschaft* or *Community and Society*, Tönnies points to Hume as among his (many) major influences. Tönnies considered Hume one of the true inventors of sociology and drew especially from Hume on convention. Like Hume, for Tönnies conventions are the foundations of society. Tönnies treated conventions as necessarily serving a general utility to society but only on the condition that this utility is wanted and promoted by the members of society in the interests of their own utility. As shown by Niall Bond, Hume on convention is implicit in Tönnies on convention in *Community and Society*.[72] Hume understood convention to be 'common interest' combined with 'public utility' and Tönnies defined convention as necessarily being in the service of 'general utility', on the condition that this general utility is 'desired and maintained by everyone so as to promote his own utility'.[73]

In the twenty-first century, David Singh Grewal's analysis of globalisation in *Network Power: The Social Dynamics of Globalization* drew on Hume's understanding of convention. Grewal thought of globalisation as a process in which we are moved into a 'game of social coordination', where common standards allow more effective coordination.[74] Grewal understood standards as a type of convention, like money or language, a 'shared norm or practice' that facilitates cooperation in a social network.[75] Grewal's history of convention begins with Hume. Hume, Grewal claimed, is the 'most famous theorist of conventions' and 'the greatest philosopher of human sociability'.[76] Grewal found that elements of Hume's philosophy 'still echo in many contemporary debates, particularly over the role of the market'.[77] Recent trends in economic sociology include the role of conventions in the social nature of market activity and institutions.[78] Frank Dobbin has made the case for the importance of understanding how conventions and institutions come about in the study of the sociology of the economy.[79]

Custom and Habit

For Hume, custom and habit is the foundational principle of human nature that features in many aspects of his thought including abstract ideas, causality, self, external world, the passions, morality, aesthetics, justice, government, history and economics. Custom and habit occurs when the repetition of an act in human thought and behaviour produces a propensity to automatically repeat the same act.[80] Hume famously claimed that, after the repeated experience of constant conjunction of two objects, we are determined by custom and habit to expect one when the other appears. In addition to individual patterns of thought and behaviour, Hume recognised that there is a social sense of custom that has to do with social customs, conventions or regularities although he generally uses the terms 'custom' and 'habit' with no real distinction between them.[81] As shown in detail by Charles Camic, a historical investigation into the origins of habit in sociology reveals that habit was central to many of the early practitioners of sociology.[82]

Tönnies, for example, pays attention to habit and its role in human conduct. Tönnies relates the mind to action and finds that action can take on a self-propelling or habitual character. Tönnies finds this habitual character quite prevalent and he calls the human being 'a creature of habit'.[83] Habit is an important feature in the work of Durkheim. In *The Elementary Forms of Religious Life*, Durkheim defines habit as 'a tendency to repeat an act or idea automatically every time that the same circumstances appear'.[84] In Durkheim's 1893 work *The Division of Labor in Society*, he claims that primitive humans lived to a large extent by the 'force of habit' and under the 'yoke of habit'.[85] The same he thought was true for modern times when a social order based on the division of labour, Durkheim maintained, requires 'more and more intensive and assiduous work' and this 'implies an absolute regularity in habits'.[86] Durkheim also recognised the effects of the automaticity of habit in thought and action in his 1897 work *Suicide: A Study in Sociology*, particularly in the chapters on egotistical suicide.[87] He held that the 'ideas and reasons which develop in our consciousness' are 'ingrained habits of which we are unaware'.[88] Further Durkheim noted that 'habits of passive obedience, of absolute submission, of impersonalism' increased the suicide rate among military officers, whereas 'the habit of domestic solidarity' decreased the suicide rate within various other populations.[89]

Weber thought that human action is mostly 'governed by impulse or habit'.[90] He defined habit or custom 'to mean a typically uniform activity which is kept on the beaten track simply because men are "accustomed" to it and persist in it by unreflective imitation'.[91] Weber distinguishes four kinds of social action in his posthumous 1921 book *Economy and Society: An Outline of Interpretive Sociology*. Relevant is the fourth kind: traditional action that is 'determined by ingrained habituation'.[92] People engage in this type of action often unthinkingly, because it is simply always done that way. Weber writes that it is 'very often a matter of almost automatic reaction to habitual stimuli which guide behavior in a course which has been repeatedly followed' and that the 'great bulk of all everyday action to which people have become habitually accustomed approaches this type'.[93] Habit is central to any form of political legitimacy for Weber, akin to Hume's observation that it is time and custom that gives 'authority to almost all the establish'd governments of the world'.[94] In the case of legal order, according to Weber, most people follow the law 'merely as a result of unreflective habituation to a regularity of life that has engraved itself as a custom'.[95] Weber also thought that 'the existence of a mere custom' can be 'of far-reaching economic significance'.[96] In particular, Weber understood that 'the patterns of use and of relationship among economic units are determined by habit'.⁹⁷ French sociologist Pierre Bourdieu's influential notion of habitus is essentially social. Bourdieu thinks human actions are reflections of social structures and habitus refers to the social regularities that guide behaviour. Habitus is defined as the 'subjective but not individual system of internalized structures, schemes of perception, conception, and action common to all members of the same group or class'.⁹⁸

Habit proved central in the research of some of the earliest practitioners of sociology in the United States of America into the twentieth century. Charlotte Perkins Gilman in the 1898 work *Women and Economics: A Study of the Economic Relation between Men and Women as a Factor in Social Evolution* recognised the force of both individual and social habits.⁹⁹ In 1900, Franklin Henry Giddings, a former president of the American Sociological Association, stated that the task of sociology was to study the social nature of habits.¹⁰⁰ Charles Cooley, who was involved in the founding of the American Sociological Association, focused on how habit relates to the self and the modern economy in 1902.¹⁰¹ In 1905, W. I. Thomas placed group habits as among the primary interests of the social theorist,¹⁰² and in 1908, Edward Ross focused on 'habits of consumption' and 'habits of production'.¹⁰³ Edward Hayes, one of the founders and a former president of the American Sociological Association, saw habits as the decisive influencer of the human personality, in 1915. For Hayes, habits are 'definite tendencies to action ingrained in the organism' but it is not just 'overt activities alone which are subject to the law that action prepares for similar action, but thoughts and sentiments as well'.¹⁰⁴ In 1966, sociologists Peter Berger and Thomas Luckmann's book *The Social Construction of Reality: A Treatise in the Sociology of Knowledge* argued that society is created by human social interaction, and that '[a]ll human activity is subject to **habitualization**'.¹⁰⁵ Berger and Luckmann's notion of habitualisation describes how 'any action that is repeated frequently becomes cast into a pattern, which can then be ... performed again in the future in the same manner and with the same economical effort'.¹⁰⁶

Religion and Morals

Hume's 1757 essay 'The Natural History of Religion' examines the historical and causal origins of religious belief. Hume believed that religion emerges in society as a way for people to cope with uneasy feelings when they consider the future unknown events in the course of nature. Ernest Gellner described Hume's 'The Natural History of Religion' as a work in the 'sociology of religion', John Jenkins thought of Hume's essay as primarily a 'sociological inquiry' and Tamás Demeter wrote that Hume has given a 'quasi-sociological account of the origins of religion'.[107] 'The Natural History of Religion' starts with the origin of polytheism in primitive society. In primitive society, people's lives are dominated by the emotions of fear and hope, and in ignorance about the workings of nature, they invent gods, invisible intelligent powers, in charge of nature. As human society progresses, polytheism develops into monotheism as believers tend to single out one particular deity and compete to distinguish their deity as superior to all other rival deities, magnifying the deity's qualities until we at last arrive at a singular being, God, that contains all perfections. Hume further compared the positives and negatives of polytheism and monotheism and famously recommended scepticism on the entire matter at the end of the essay.

As shown by Helen De Cruz, the methodological procedure in 'The Natural History of Religion' was not unique to Hume.[108] There are other natural histories of religion as well, such as Bernard Le Bovier de Fontenelle's *Histoire des oracles* (1728) and Charles de Brosses's *Du culte des dieux fétiches* (1760). This procedure continued in sociological theories of the nineteenth and early twentieth centuries. Comte's *Système de politique positive, ou, Traité de sociologie, instituant la religion de l'humanité* in 1841 considers theological explanations of the natural world as the most primitive form to be outgrown by humanity. Weber's *Protestant Ethic and the Spirit of Capitalism* may be understood as a kind of genealogical study of religion alongside capitalist society. Durkheim's *The Elementary Forms of Religious Life* investigates the emergence of religion as a social phenomenon, looking at anthropological data of Indigenous Australians. Durkheim's primary purpose in *The Elementary Forms* was to describe and explain the earliest and most primitive religion known to humankind.[109] That distressing conditions of life in society and uncertainty about the future lead to religion has been defended by Marx and Engels.[110] Spyridon Tegos compared Hume on secular rituals, such as French highly ceremonial manners, in the sense of anxiety-soothing institutions that bind citizenry without the appeal to a civil religion, with

French sociologist Alexis de Tocqueville on rituals as 'anxiety-soothing institutions'.[111]

Hume extended the explanatory procedure to the investigation of morality. Hume famously explains the motives and circumstances that first established the conventions of justice and explains how just acts are objects of moral approval by a sense of 'sympathy with public interest'.[112] Hume also examines the origin of promising, a convention based on the need for social coordination in society.[113] Hume on morals has been shown to be influential on Spencer and Weber. Martin Stafford has argued that Spencer follows a similar method to Hume to explain how ethics evolves in the 1898 work *The Principles of Ethics*.[114] Spencer focused on how the sentiment of justice evolves when social conditions require habits of conduct and the feelings appropriate to those habits emerge. The moral sentiments, including the sentiment of justice, are passed on to future generations.[115] Further, Hume's famous statement that '[r]eason is, and ought only to be the slave of the passions'[116] was echoed by Spencer who called the emotions the 'masters' and declares that 'the intellect is the servant'.[117] Akhilesh Pathak recently claimed that the social nature of moral sentiments expressed by Hume and Smith provides sufficient ground for a parallel to be drawn between their view of human action and Weber's conceptualisation of 'consensual action'.[118]

Finally, twentieth-century Finnish sociologist Edward Westermarck was influenced by Hume on morality. Similar to Hume, Westermarck thought that morality was shaped by human psychology and attempted to describe and explain the emergence of moral beliefs.[119] G. H. von Wright argued that 'Westermarck rediscovered Hume and Smith after a century dominated first by utilitarian and then by evolutionary ethics.'[120] Von Wright found that Westermarck's views on moral objectivism and the truth-value of moral judgements, in particular, reveal 'far-reaching and often striking similarities to Hume's *Treatise of Human Nature*'.[121] Otto Pipatti in a recent book, *Morality Made Visible: Edward Westermarck's Moral and Social Theory*, emphasises Hume's influence on Westermarck's thought. One of the main aims of Pipatti's work is to illustrate 'how Westermarck's theory of moral emotions developed out of, and in response to, David Hume's and Adam Smith's study of moral sentiments'.[122] A distinctive feature of Pipatti's approach is that it takes into consideration Westermarck's unpublished lecture manuscripts and notes taken by students. Westermarck lectured on the British Enlightenment regularly in his career and his lectures on Hume, delivered in 1913 at the University of Helsinki, consist of forty typewritten pages on Hume's epistemology, philosophy of religion and moral philosophy.[123]

The Self

Hume on the self can be linked to later sociological theories of the social self. There are two aspects to Hume on the self. In Book 1 of the *Treatise*, Hume famously looked inward to the self only to discover an ever-changing series of perceptions and denied the existence of a continually existing substantial self. The self emerges through a fiction of the imagination, a psychological construction to maintain the illusion of self-continuity. In Book 2 on the passions, Hume gives an account of the social origin of passions and sympathy that allows that one can come to view oneself through the perspective of others. The 'opinions of others' affect our sentiments of pride and humility about ourselves.[124] Hume thought that in order for feelings like pride and humility to come about, the pleasant or painful object must be observable to ourselves and other people as well.[125] Given that the viewpoints of others determine our own view of ourselves, it must be that, as Jay Garfield has recently emphasised, for Hume, 'the self we represent is an essentially social self'.[126]

There is today a consensus within the discipline of sociology that the self is at some level a social construct.[127] The social construction of the self can be found in the research of the American sociologist George Herbert Mead's 1934 book *Mind, Self, and Society from the Standpoint of a Social Behaviorist*. For Mead, the self is socially constructed in the sense that it is shaped through social interaction with other people. These social experiences lead to individual behaviours that make up the social factors that create communication in society. Communication is the comprehension of another individual's gestures. In 'The Function of Imagery in Conduct', a supplementary essay to *Mind, Self, and Society*, Mead assumes the importance of the association of ideas and its role in communication. Mead writes that the role 'which the doctrine of association of ideas has played in explaining conduct finds its ground in the control over the imagery which thought exercises'.[128] He explains that, 'We speak of words as associated with things, and carry over this relation to the connections of images with each other, together with the reactions they help to mediate.'[129] Mead goes on to appeal to Hume's account of vivacity to explain imagery and 'distant stimuli'.[130] Mead also devotes a section to the role of sympathy, defined as 'taking the attitude of the other when one is assisting the other' in society.[131]

Russian social psychologist Lev Vygotsky looked at the effect of social relations on human mental development. Vygotsky claimed that learning and development is a social activity and that anything that is expressed in a child can first be detected in their environment. He wrote that any 'function in the child's cultural development appears twice, or on two planes' – first on a social plane and second on the psychological plane – which means that 'Any higher mental function was external because it was social at some point before becoming internal.'[132] For Vygotsky, 'The social dimension of consciousness is primary in time and in fact. The individual dimension of consciousness is derivative and secondary.'[133] Garfield claimed that Hume's science of the mind is a precursor to social cognitive psychology like Vygotsky's in that he understands human behaviour from 'a social level down'.[134]

Hume's philosophy may also be linked to the Canadian sociologist Erving Goffman's work on the self on at least two counts. In the introduction to his 1959 work *The Presentation of the Self in Everyday Life*, Goffman explains that in situations when an individual goes into a gathering or group situation, both the individual and the members of the group judge each other from the perspective of their own sphere, or frame.[135] The individual and the group judge each other based upon their socio-economic status, trustworthiness, pre-existing stereotypes and prejudices and those status differences that reinforce our personal and collective expectation states. Hume alluded to this in his discussion of prejudice. For Hume, prejudices are a kind of 'unphilosophical' probability. Unphilosophical probabilities are the erroneous probability judgements that humans are prone to make. Hume provides examples of prejudices as incorrect generalisations about a person's character due to their country of origin; he writes: 'An Irishman cannot have wit, and a Frenchman cannot have solidity, for which reason, tho' the conversation of the former be visibly very agreeable, and of the latter very judicious, we have entertain'd such a prejudice against them.'[136] Hume goes on to explain why these sorts of prejudices or general rules have such a strong hold on the mind despite their opposition to common sense and suggests how to correct these biases of the mind.[137]

A second point of contact has to do with Goffman's theory of impression management, also introduced in *The Presentation of the Self in Everyday Life*. Goffman used dramaturgy theory to explain the ways in which people adjust or control their communication to influence the impressions they make on other people. This is based on Goffman's idea, much like Hume's social self, that people see themselves as other people see them. The importance of a person managing the impressions one makes on those around them was also emphasised by Hume in art, taken from the short essay 'Of the Standard of Taste' in a discussion of prejudice. Hume discussed how the art critic must avoid prejudice when assessing an artwork to form a sound judgement. To overcome prejudice in artistic judgement, Hume insisted that 'every work of art . . . must be surveyed in a certain point of view'.[138] If a person's 'situation . . . is not conformable to that which is required by the performance' then the artwork will not be 'fully relished'.[139]

Relevant for overcoming prejudice when it comes to evaluating a work of art that is addressed to an audience of a different age or nation is awareness of the context of the audience for whom the artwork is created. Hume writes:

> an orator addresses himself to a particular audience, and must have a regard to their particular genius, interests, opinions, passions, and prejudices; otherwise he hopes in vain to govern their resolutions, and inflame their affections. Should they ever have entertained some prepossessions against him, however unreasonable, he must not overlook this disadvantage; but, before he enters upon the subject, must endeavour to conciliate their affection, and acquire their good graces.[140]

Given that the artist addresses their work to a particular audience, Hume thought that it was important in art criticism that the critic of a different age or nation who judges an artwork must put themselves in the situation of the designated audience. A person with prejudice 'obstinately maintains his natural position, without placing himself in that point of view, which the performance supposes'.[141] And the person that cannot be free of prejudices will have no credibility and authority when it comes to judging works of art.

Prejudice in the consumption of art can take different forms, including 'prepossessions' against the author, and the author, as Hume noted in the passage above, may in their work attempt to mitigate those prejudices against them. To consider the context helps to understand why the work of art is presented in the way that it is by the author. Part of avoiding prejudice is to be sensitive to the background of what the author is conveying to the audience as artists too are concerned to control or manage how others view them and their work. Hume attempted to influence his future readers' impressions of his own work in this passage as well. He thought that a just appraisal of his essay in the time to come required a non-prejudicial critic: 'A critic of a different age or nation, who should peruse this discourse, must have all these circumstances in his eye, and must place himself in the same situation as the audience, in order to form a true judgment of the oration.'[142]

Conclusion

Hume's experimental science of the mind engages a variety of contemporary sciences such as cognitive science, neuroscience, psychology and sociology. Hume may even have ties to the field of anthropology. Topics of convention, habit, religion, morality and the self are also of central interest to anthropologists. For example, anthropologist Philippe Bourgois incorporates Bourdieu's habitus into his work on homeless drug users in California.[143] D. W. Murray has noted that Hume on the self has ties to the work of anthropologist Katherine Ewing on the 'universal illusion of wholeness'.[144] According to Ewing's universal illusion of wholeness, individuals are constantly creating themselves a sense of self by a 'semiotic' process through which people manage inconsistency in their experiences.[145] In a like manner, Hume's account of the imagination creates the illusion of the self to disguise the continuous flow of our fragmented perceptions.

Hume had stated in the Introduction to the *Treatise of Human Nature* that all of the scientific disciplines 'have a relation, greater or less, to human nature'.[146] Further, he hoped that the findings of a science of human nature might even change and improve the other sciences.[147] Once the principles of human nature are clearly understood, we can then move to 'extend our conquests over all those sciences, which more intimately concern human life'.[148] An examination of the ways that Hume's science of human nature resonates with a variety of disciplines may serve to bolster the results of those sciences and, in turn, exploring the topics in human nature common across the disciplines brings to light the enduring features of Hume's complex intellectual legacy.[149]

Notes

1. Björn Eriksson, 'The First Formulation of Sociology: A Discursive Innovation of the 18th Century', *European Journal of Sociology* 34 (1993), pp. 251–76, p. 271.
2. Gladys Bryson, *Man and Society: The Scottish Inquiry of the Eighteenth Century* (Princeton: Princeton University Press, 1945).
3. Alan Swingewood, 'Origins of Sociology: The Case of the Scottish Enlightenment', *British Journal of Sociology* 21 (1970), pp. 164–80, p. 165. See also Steven Seidman's *Liberalism and the Origins of European Social Theory* (Berkeley, CA: University of California Press, 1983), ch. 1 and Louis Schneider (ed.), *The Scottish Moralists on Human Nature and Society* (Chicago: University of Chicago Press, 1967).
4. Allan Silver, 'Friendship in Commercial Society: Eighteenth-Century Social Theory and Modern Sociology', *American Journal of Sociology* 95 (1990), pp. 1474–504.
5. Eriksson, 'The First Formulation of Sociology', p. 252.
6. Swingewood, 'Origins of Sociology', p. 165.
7. Roberto Cipriani, *Sociology of Religion: An Historical Introduction* (London: Routledge, 2000), p. 19.
8. For example, see Jacqueline Taylor, 'Justice and the Foundations of Social Morality in Hume's *Treatise*', *Hume Studies* 24 (1998), pp. 5–30 and *Reflecting Subjects: Passion, Sympathy, and Society in Hume's Philosophy* (Oxford: Oxford University Press, 2015) and Mikko Tolonen's *Mandeville and Hume: Anatomists of Civil Society* (Oxford: The Voltaire Foundation, 2013). For Hume on society in context see Christopher Berry's *The Idea of Commercial Society in the Scottish Enlightenment* (Edinburgh: Edinburgh University Press, 2013).
9. The following abbreviations are used for David Hume: T for *A Treatise of Human Nature: Being an Attempt to Introduce the Experimental Method of Reasoning into Moral Subjects*; EH for *An Enquiry concerning Human Understanding*; and EMPL for *Essays Moral, Political, Literary*. References cite the book, chapter, section and paragraph for the *Treatise* and the *Enquiry* and a page number is provided for the *Essays*.
10. Raymond Aron, *Main Currents in Sociological Thought: Montesquieu, Comte, Marx, Tocqueville and the Sociologists and the Revolution of 1848* (London: Routledge, 2017), ch. 2.
11. See *The Positive Philosophy of Auguste Comte*, freely translated and condensed by Harriet Martineau in two volumes, 3rd ed. (London: Kegan Paul, 1893), pp. 8, 29.

12. See Mary Pickering, *Auguste Comte: An Intellectual Biography* (Cambridge: Cambridge University Press, 1993), p. 312 and C. W. Maris, 'Comte and Positivism' in *Critique of the Empiricist Explanation of Morality* (Dordrecht: Springer, 1981), p. 73.
13. *The Positive Philosophy of Auguste Comte*, p. 356.
14. Ibid. p. 356.
15. Ibid. p. 356.
16. Ibid. p. 2.
17. Ibid. p. 2.
18. Ibid. p. 356.
19. In Mike Gane, *Auguste Comte* (London: Routledge, 2006), p. 132.
20. Anna J. Cooper, *A Voice from the South: By a Black Woman of the South* (Xenia, OH: The Aldine Printing Company, 1892), p. 291.
21. Ibid. p. 291.
22. Ibid. *p.* 292.
23. Ibid. p. 292.
24. Ibid. *p.* 295.
25. Ibid. p. 295.
26. Ibid. *p.* 297.
27. Ibid. p. 297.
28. Ibid. p. 297.
29. Ibid. *p.* 298.
30. Émile Durkheim, *The Elementary Forms of Religious Life: A Study in Religious Sociology*, translated by Joseph Ward Swain (London: George Allen & Unwin Ltd, 1915), p. 427.
31. Ibid.
32. EMPL p. 281.
33. T 3.2.2.10.
34. See Ronald Meek, 'The Scottish Contribution to Marxist Sociology' in *Democracy and the Labour Movement*, ed. J. Saville (London: Lawrence & Wishart, 1954).
35. T 1.4.5.34.
36. Marx quotes from a 1790 German translation of Hume's *Treatise*: *Über die menschliche Natur aus Englischen nebst krsuchen zur Beurtheilung dieses Werks von Ludwig Heinrich Jakob, 1. Bd., Über den menschlichen Verstand* (Halle, 1790), p. 485.
37. Karl Marx, *A Contribution to the Critique of Political Economy*, translated from the Second German Edition by N. I. Stone (Chicago: Charles H. Kerr & Company, 1904), pp. 224, 219.
38. Ibid. p. 219.
39. Ibid. p. 219.
40. Ibid. p. 219.

41. Ibid. p. 222.
42. Ibid. p. 222.
43. Ibid. p. 226.
44. Ibid. p. 226.
45. Ibid. p. 227.
46. Ibid. p. 227.
47. Ibid. p. 228.
48. Ibid. p. 66.
49. Ibid. pp. 232, 260.
50. Ibid. pp. 232, 237.
51. Ibid. pp. 234–5.
52. Ibid. p. 253.
53. For an overview of the standard interpretation of Hume on money, see Carl Wennerlind, 'David Hume's Monetary Theory Revisited: Was He Really a Quantity Theorist and an Inflationist?', *Journal of Political Economy* 113 (2005), pp. 223–37, section 2. See also Margaret Schabas and Carl Wennerlind, 'Retrospectives: Hume on Money, Commerce, and the Science of Economics', *Journal of Economic Perspectives* 25 (2011), pp. 217–30.
54. See Wennerlind, 'David Hume's Monetary Theory Revisited', especially sections 3–4, and Sheila Dow, 'David Hume and Modern Economics', *Capitalism and Society* 4 (2013), pp. 1–29. For a recent work that ties Hume's economics with society see Margaret Schabas and Carl Wennerlind, *A Philosopher's Economist: Hume and the Rise of Capitalism* (Chicago: University of Chicago Press, 2020).
55. Marx, *Critique of Political Economy*, p. 222.
56. Ibid. p. 224.
57. See Margaret Schabas, 'David Hume as a Proto-Weberian: Commerce, Protestantism, and Secular Culture', *Social Philosophy and Policy* 37 (2020), pp. 190–212. See also Tamás Demeter, 'Sympathies for Common Ends: The Principles of Organization in Hume's Psychology and Political Economy' in Gábor Bíró (ed.), *Humanity and Nature in the History of Economic Thought* (London: Routledge, 2022), section 4.
58. Michael Woolcock, 'Social Capital and Economic Development: Toward a Theoretical Synthesis and Policy Framework', *Theory and Society* 27 (1998), pp. 151–208, p. 159. See also Luigino Bruni and Robert Sugden, 'Moral Canals: Trust and Social Capital in the Work of Hume, Smith and Genovesi', *Economics and Philosophy* 16 (2000), pp. 21–45.

59. See Richard Swedberg, *Principles of Economic Sociology* (Princeton: Princeton University Press, 2003), p. xii.
60. Ibid. p. 2.
61. Ibid. pp. 197, 281.
62. Annette Baier, 'Hume's Account of Social Artifice: Its Origins and Its Originality', *Ethics* 98 (1988), pp. 757–78, p. 757.
63. T 3.2.2.10.
64. T 3.2.2.10.
65. T 3.2.2.9.
66. T 3.2.2.10.
67. Herbert Spencer, *Social Statics: Or, the Conditions Essential to Human Happiness Specified, and the First of Them Developed* (London: Chapman, 1851), p. 88.
68. T 3.2.2.9–10.
69. T 3.2.2.12.
70. Herbert Spencer, *The Principles of Sociology, in Three Volumes* (New York: D. Appleton and Company, 1898), vol. 2, p. 216.
71. Spencer's *The Principles of Sociology*, vol. 2, pp. 398, 501, 502. Spencer makes frequent references to Hume in the earlier work *The Principles of Psychology* (1855) on topics such as personal identity, association, belief and the will and is critical of Hume's reduction of causality to a psychological habit based on observed regularities; see Herbert Spencer, *The Principles of Psychology* (London: Longman, Brown, Green and Longmans, 1855), vol. 2, pp. 349–54.
72. See Niall Bond, 'Ferdinand Tönnies and Enlightenment: A Friend or Foe of Reason?', *The European Legacy* 18 (2013), pp. 127–50, p. 134.
73. Ferdinand Tönnies, *Community and Civil Society*, transl. J. Harris and M. Hollis, ed. J. Harris (Cambridge: Cambridge University Press, [1887] 2001), p. 44.
74. David Singh Grewal, *Network Power: The Social Dynamics of Globalization* (New Haven, CT: Yale University Press, 2008), p. 2.
75. Ibid. pp. 32, 71.
76. Ibid. p. 59.
77. Ibid. p. 311; see also pp. 60–1, 88, 237.
78. For example, see Woolsey Biggart and Thomas D. Beamish, 'The Economic Sociology of Conventions: Habit, Custom, Practice, and Routine in Market Order', *Annual Review of Sociology* 29 (2003), pp. 443–6.
79. See Frank Dobbin, 'Introduction' in *The Sociology of the Economy* (New York: Russell Sage Foundation, 2004).

80. T 1.3.8.10–13.
81. See Jay **Garfield**'s *The Concealed Influence of Custom: Hume's Treatise from the Inside Out* (**Oxford: Oxford University Press**, 2019), p. 17 and Peter Fosl, 'Habit, Custom, History, and Hume's Critical Philosophy' in Tom Sparrow and Adam Hutchinson *(eds)*, *A History of Habit: From Aristotle to Bourdieu* (Lanham, MD: Lexington Books, 2013), pp. 133–51, p. 147n24.
82. Charles Camic, 'A Matter of Habit', *American Journal of Sociology* 91 (1986), pp. 1039–87.
83. Tönnies, *Community and Civil Society*, p. 104.
84. Durkheim, *The Elementary Forms of Religious Life*, p. 435n.
85. Émile Durkheim, *The Division of Labor in Society*, transl. George Simpson (New York: Free Press, 1933/1964), p. 159.
86. Ibid. p. 242.
87. Émile Durkheim, *Suicide: A Study in Sociology*, transl. J. A. Spaulding and G. Simpson (New York: The Free Press, 1966), pp. 158–9.
88. Ibid. p. 168.
89. Ibid. p. 238.
90. Max Weber, *Economy and Society: An Outline of Interpretive Sociology*, ed. Guenther *Roth* and Claus *Wittich* (Berkeley, CA: University of California Press, 1978), p. 21.
91. Weber, *Economy and Society*, p. 319.
92. Ibid. p. 25.
93. Ibid. p. 25.
94. T 3.2.10.4. See also Weber, *Economy and Society*, p. 215.
95. Weber, *Economy and Society*, p. 312.
96. Ibid. p. 320.
97. Ibid. p. 335.
98. Pierre Bourdieu, *Outline of a Theory of Practice* (Cambridge: Cambridge University Press, 1977), pp. 78–79, 82.
99. Charlotte Perkins Gilman, *Women and Economics: A Study of the Economic Relation between Men and Women as a Factor in Social Evolution* (Boston, MA: Small, Maynard & Company, 1898), ch. 5.
100. Franklin H. Giddings, *The Elements of Sociology* (New York: Macmillan, 1900), pp. 1, 72.
101. Charles Cooley, *Human Nature and the Social Order* (New York: Schocken, 1902), especially chs 5 and 10.
102. William I. Thomas, 'The Province of Social Psychology', *American Journal of Sociology* 10 (1905), pp. 445–55, pp. 445–7, 449–51.
103. Edward A. Ross, *Social Psychology* (New York: Macmillan, 1908), especially chs 13 and 15.

104. Edward C. Hayes, *Introduction to the Study of Sociology* (New York: Appleton, 1915), pp. 297–8.
105. Peter Berger and Thomas Luckmann, *The Social Construction of Reality: A Treatise in the Sociology of Knowledge* (Garden City, NY: Anchor Books, 1966), p. 70.
106. Ibid. pp. 70–1.
107. Ernest Gellner, *Conditions of Liberty: Civil Society and Its Rivals* (London: Penguin, 1994), p. 44; John J. Jenkins, *Understanding Hume* (Edinburgh: Edinburgh University Press, 1992), p. 8; and Tamás Demeter, 'Natural Theology as Superstition: David Hume and the Changing Ideology of Natural Inquiry' in T. Demeter, K. Murphy and C. Zittel (eds), *Conflicting Values of Inquiry: Ideologies of Epistemology in Early Modern Europe* (Leiden: Brill, 2015), ch. 7, p. 196n94.
108. Helen De Cruz, 'The Relevance of Hume's "Natural History of Religion" for Cognitive Science of Religion', *Res Philosophica* 92 (2015), pp. 653–74, section 2.
109. Anne Rawls has argued that Durkheim's *Elementary Forms of Religious Life* follows the order of Hume's *Treatise of Human Nature* in Rawls, 'Durkheim's Epistemology: The Neglected Argument', *American Journal of Sociology* 102 (1996), pp. 430–82, p. 438.
110. Karl Marx and Friedrich Engels, *On Religion* (Moscow: Progress, 1957), pp. 37–9.
111. Spyridon Tegos, 'Civility and Civil Religion before and after the French Revolution: Religious and Secular Rituals in Hume and Tocqueville', *Genealogy* 4 (2020), pp. 48–62.
112. T 3.2.2.25.
113. T 3.2.5.
114. J. Martin Stafford, 'Hume, Spencer and the Standard of Morals', *Philosophy* 58 (1983), pp. 39–55.
115. Herbert Spencer, *The Principles of Ethics in Two Volumes* (New York: Appleton, 1898), see especially vol. 2, chs 3–6.
116. T 2.3.3.4.
117. Herbert Spencer, 'Feeling versus Intellect' in *Facts and Comments* (New York: Appleton, 1902), p. 38.
118. Akhilesh Pathak, 'Max Weber and Adam Smith: Some Points of Conceptual Congruence', *IOSR Journal of Humanities and Social Science* 25 (2020), pp. 58–69, p. 62.
119. See Edward Westermarck, *The Origin and Development of the Moral Ideas* (London: Macmillan and Co., 1924).

120. See Georg Henrik von Wright, 'The Origin and Development of Westermarck's Moral Philosophy' in T. Stroup (ed.), *Edward Westermarck: Essays on His Life and Works* (Helsinki: Societas Philosophica Fennica, 1982), pp. 25–61, pp. 48–9. See also Timothy Stroup, 'Edward Westermarck: A Reappraisal', *Man* 19 (1984), pp. 575–92, p. 577.
121. Von Wright, 'The Origin and Development of Westermarck's Moral Philosophy', p. 48.
122. Otto Pipatti, *Morality Made Visible: Edward Westermarck's Moral and Social Theory* (London: Routledge, 2019), p. 1.
123. Pipatti, *Morality Made Visible*, pp. 6ff.
124. T 2.1.11.1.
125. T 2.1.6.3.
126. Garfield, *Concealed Influence of Custom*, pp. 94–5. See also Nicholas Capaldi, *David Hume: The Newtonian Philosopher* (Boston, MA: Twayne Publishers, 1975), pp. 92–3, and 'The Historical and Philosophical Significance of Hume's Theory of the Self' in A. J. Holland (ed.), *Philosophy, Its History and Historiography* (Dordrecht: Springer, 1985), p. 279; Annette Baier, *A Progress of Sentiments: Reflections on Hume's 'Treatise'* (Cambridge, MA: Harvard University Press, 1991), p. 130; and James Baillie, *Hume on Morality* (London: Routledge, 2000), p. 35.
127. Peter L. Callero, 'The Sociology of the Self', *Annual Review of Sociology* 29 (2003), pp. 115–33, p. 121. See also R. Frank Falk and Nancy B. Miller, 'The Reflexive Self: A Sociological Perspective', *Roeper Review* 20 (1998), pp. 150–3.
128. George Herbert Mead, *Mind, Self, and Society from the Standpoint of a Social Behaviorist*, ed. Charles W. Morris (Chicago: University of Chicago, 1934), p. 342.
129. Ibid. p. 342.
130. Ibid. p. 343.
131. Ibid. p. 299.
132. Lev Vygotsky, *The Mind in Society: The Development of Higher Psychological Processes* (Cambridge, MA: Harvard University Press, 1978), p. 58.
133. Lev Vygotsky, 'Consciousness as a Problem of Psychology of Behavior', *Soviet Psychology* 17 (1979), pp. 29–30.
134. Garfield, *Concealed Influence of Custom*, p. 276; see also p. 272. Siyavesi Azeri relates Hume on memory to Vygotsky's natural memory in 'Hume's Social Theory of Memory', *Journal of Scottish Philosophy* 11 (2013), pp. 53–68.

135. Erving Goffman, *The Presentation of Self in Everyday Life* (New York: Anchor Doubleday, 1959), p. 1.
136. T 1.3.13.7.
137. T 1.3.13.8–12.
138. EMPL p. 239.
139. EMPL p. 239.
140. EMPL p. 239.
141. EMPL p. 239.
142. EMPL p. 239.
143. Philippe Bourgois and Jeff Schonberg, 'Intimate Apartheid: Ethnic Dimensions of Habitus Among Homeless Heroin Injectors', *Ethnography* 8 (2007), pp. 7–31.
144. D. W. Murray, 'What is the Western Concept of the Self? On Forgetting David Hume', *Ethos: Society for Psychological Anthropology* 21 (1993), pp. 3–23, especially pp. 13–14.
145. See Katherine P. Ewing, 'The Illusion of Wholeness: Culture, Self, and the Experience of Inconsistency', *Ethos: Journal of the Society for Psychological Anthropology* 18 (1990), pp. 251–78, p. 251.
146. T Intro.4.
147. T Intro.4.
148. T Intro.6.
149. My thanks to John Hall and Tamás Demeter.

10

Hume and Durkheim: Common Views on Sociality

Catherine Dromelet

Introduction

Durkheim scholarship has already offered insights on the intellectual connections of Durkheim to the Scottish Enlightenment.[1] In particular, previous reconstructions have shown that Durkheim's methodological ideas were influenced by a specific understanding of Hume's account of causation, which Durkheim had become familiar with through his reading of Charles Renouvier and Paul Janet.[2] They were perceptive of Maine de Biran's critique of Hume and his attempt to combine Kantian categories with a spiritualist theory of internal experience.

Durkheim was unsatisfied with these responses to Hume. Hume's view, as it was then understood, suggested that the idea of causation develops in the mind as a result of one's experiences, which are made possible by the external senses. According to the received interpretation of Kant, causation was seen as an a priori category of the understanding, independent of experience. And Maine de Biran held that causal power is apprehended due to internal experience, through willed effort. For Durkheim, all these theories suggested that the origin of the idea of causation is set in the individual, and in response he introduced a sociological account of causation responding to his methodological needs. He proposed that categories underpinning language and knowledge, causation predominantly among them, are fundamentally shaped by society.[3] His account had a major impact on twentieth-century social sciences.[4]

Besides this widely discussed metaphysical–methodological debate, there is a further field, namely that of socialisation and emergence of social order, where Durkheim seems to be indebted to the Scottish Enlightenment and to Hume in particular.[5] This connection has not been paid much attention, and the present chapter intends to fill this gap. While discussing the emergence of social organisation, Durkheim puts forward ideas that strikingly resemble those featuring in Hume's account of socialisation, institutionalisation and moral practices. Although Durkheim does not invoke Hume explicitly, he refuses the idea of a social contract and the idea that society is founded on reason along very similar lines.[6] So, Durkheim's account can be read as a sociological appropriation of Hume's 'science of man' with respect to, for example, 'sympathy' as a social transmitter of emotions; to the role of social processes and structures in giving rise to moral sentiments; and to collective or public sentiments. Furthermore, there are Humean echoes in Durkheim's sociology of knowledge that serve as connective links between Hume and the Strong Programme in the Sociology of Knowledge.[7] With a combination of these Humean insights Durkheim argues for the social formation of both morality and the categories of cognition.

The following section presents the state of the art concerning the influence of Hume on Durkheim through French spiritualism and positivism, focusing on the metaphysical and methodological debates sketched above. After presenting the main nineteenth-century protagonists of the reception of Scottish and Humean ideas in France, I will focus on the passages in Hume that introduce and refine concepts – such as custom, sympathy and self-interest – that would become operative in Durkheim's account of social organisation, morality and knowledge. The last section shows how Durkheim appropriates Hume's ideas for his own scientific purposes. After discussing certain (alleged and sound) differences between the two, the chapter concludes with a summary of the major affinities between Hume and Durkheim on sociality.

Humean Echoes in Durkheim: Metaphysical and Methodological Debates

It would be audacious to hold that Hume influenced Durkheim (or that the latter drew direct inspiration from the former), since Durkheim never mentions Hume explicitly and he seemingly didn't borrow any of Hume's books from the library at the École Normale Supérieure.[8] Despite this lack of proof of direct influence, Durkheim engages in metaphysical discussions addressing the question of categories, the trigger of which can be traced back to Hume's critique of causation.[9] Most connections between the two thinkers are made in the framework of the debate on the origin of intellectual categories, including our idea of causality.

The goal of this chapter is to identify and explore the affinities between Hume and Durkheim in their account of sociality. And while it would be tempting to settle for a superficial comparison of this aspect of their works put side by side, it may prove more fruitful to depart from the reconstruction of the way Hume's ideas ended up in Durkheim's thought. Part of the puzzle has already been solved concerning the debate on the categories thanks to Schmaus and Lukes. Taking Hume's part in the debate as an entry point, this section will retrace the lineage of thinkers who have been instrumental to the transmission of his ideas in Durkheim's metaphysics and method.

The debate received special attention after Hume declared that our idea of causation does not derive from sense experiences, since there is no impression of cause.[10] As radical empiricism doesn't admit of innate ideas, causation must come from elsewhere, and Hume identifies its source in 'custom and habit' – an experience-like non-reflexive associative principle operating in the mind and in society.[11] Thomas Reid disagrees, arguing that the belief in causes and effects is so 'universal among mankind' that it can only be part of 'the constitution of the mind itself', prior to experience and reason.[12] But Reid's notions of conscience and self-reflection imply the possibility of an epistemological access to ontological facts, such as the principles of human intellect. Kant denies this epistemological access, arguing that the categories of the understanding are simply given a priori. In response to this, Durkheim contends in his 1901 essay co-authored with Marcel Mauss that the categories of the understanding, including our idea of causation, stem from social functions. Scottish and German influences thus intermingle in nineteenth-century French philosophy, and as far as Durkheim's intellectual make-up is concerned, the Scottish influence is conveyed through two opposing movements: spiritualism and positivism.

The Reception of Hume and Reid in French Spiritualism

The spiritualist tradition connecting Hume and Durkheim begins with Maine de Biran (1766–1824), whose discussion of causality runs on top of Hume's opposition to Berkeley, in the context of the debate on the nature of the mind and the notion of self.[13] On the one hand, Berkeley holds that the mind is active and can be aware of its perceiving, thinking and willing activities from the inside.[14] On the other, because Hume's radical empiricism admits no impression of self, substance, spirit or cause, the mind's awareness of its own activity and causal power cannot be demonstrated.[15] Biran strongly criticises Hume's account of causality in his *Essai sur les fondements de la psychologie*, referring to the sections on the immateriality of the soul and on personal identity in the *Treatise of Human Nature*.[16] According to him, Berkeley's views are more accurate than Hume's, which brings Biran close to Reid on the claim that the mind is not only passive but also (and mostly) active. Durkheim agrees with Biran without discrediting Hume's observations: 'In the external world, all we see are phenomena succeeding one another, not their causes. We say that movement causes heat, of course, but in reality all we see is movement preceding heat. It's only within us that we recognize a cause producing its effects'.[17]

Biran's philosophy, indebted in part to Descartes and Kant, has most affinity with eighteenth-century Scottish thinkers, and apart from disagreeing with Hume, he refers many times to Reid's *Inquiry*.[18] Biran's activist–spiritualist philosophy unfolds in France against the pervasive influence of Locke's sensationist empiricism introduced by Condillac and sustained by the *Idéologues* – the school of thought where Biran received his philosophical education. In search of a unique principle giving rise to the multiplicity of mental operations and faculties, Biran breaks up with sensationist empiricism and starts defending the existence and epistemic reliability of the inner sense or *sens intime*. The notion of inner sense is advocated by the tradition of the *méditatifs intérieurs*, including Montaigne, Descartes, Rousseau and Bergson.[19] Besides the Cartesian maxim 'I think, therefore I am', the inner sense was formulated in various manners. After a romanticist inflection with Rousseau stressing the 'I feel', Biran focused on the will or effort.[20] The inner sense of will determines our active perception of the world, and it is the same will that generates our knowledge of causation, in virtue of the causal power of physical effort. So Biran takes things one step further than Berkeley (and to some extent, Locke), reckoning the mind as *primarily* active. The free activity of the spirit, in addition to imply free will, is the condition for the primary experience of bodily effort from which our idea of causation derives. Biran's model of the active mind able to perceive itself is present in Durkheim's psychological system, but he rejects Biran's corollary notion of unconscious soul early on.[21] Instead, in the 1883–4 philosophy course, Durkheim's description of the psychological self (i.e. 'person', that is a combination of the ideas of unity, identity and causality) presupposes socially connoted notions of responsibility and human multitude. This suggests that the psychological is circumscribed in the social.

Durkheim's spiritualist orientation is also due to Victor Cousin (1792–1867), who had first-hand knowledge of Scottish thinkers on top of being a direct intellectual descendant of Biran and was an influential intellectual figure in France. Pierre Paul Royer-Collard (1763–1845), early mentor of Cousin at the École Normale Supérieure, introduced in the French education programme the 'Scot's philosophical approach' – which amounts to the philosophy of common sense.[22] Cousin develops an original interpretation of Scottish common sense. He holds that common sense is the starting point and the yardstick of scientific progress, granting to it a central position in his system. At the same time, he considers the distinction between substance and attributes, implied by sensationist empiricism, as being at odds with common sense. So, he appeals to Cartesian metaphysics to establish the reality of immaterial spirits, will and thought, thereby turning common sense against scepticism about the substances and causes, and affirming the spiritualist doctrine. Cousin goes beyond the psychological aspect of Biran's spiritualism through his own critique of Reid: he opposes Reid's conception of common sense as a psychological–subjective faculty, arguing that it exposes the mind to the risk of scepticism. Instead, Cousin introduces an impersonal, necessary common sense amounting to the intersubjective, social phenomenon of agreeableness concerning mind-dependent realities, such as the spiritual substance.[23] This aspect is prominent in Durkheim's sociology of knowledge.

Scottish Influence on Positivism and the Beginning of French Sociology

Auguste Comte (1798–1857) was familiar with Hume's 'original' and 'bold' treatment of causation. On a more general note, he holds that Hume's works represent 'the only great step that the human mind has taken towards understanding the relative character of sound philosophy, since the controversy between the Realists and the Nominalists'.[24] Together with Smith, Hume is considered by Comte as a thinker who prominently contributed to the rise of positive philosophy and proved useful for the French philosopher's own education and progression. Like Hume, Comte reckons the idea of a state of nature as chimerical;[25] he recognises the primacy of customs and manners over political institutions;[26] and he considers that beliefs are correct in virtue of their being shared by the multitude: 'I need not dwell on so clear a point as the moral tendency of the scientific elevation of the social point of view, and of the logical supremacy of collective conceptions, such as characterize the positive philosophy'.[27]

The influence of Comte's sociology on the French intellectual landscape, especially after 1870, need not be demonstrated. Durkheim himself gives him most of the credit for having established the programme and methods of the new science, acknowledging the impact of 'the master par excellence' on his own sociological enterprise.[28] Comte's authority was also conveyed by the historian Fustel de Coulanges (1830–1889) who was teaching scientific history at the École Normale Supérieure in the 1870s and 1880s. Collecting and comparing historical testimonies and anecdotes for the purpose of unveiling the fundamental principles of human nature is a method notoriously adopted by Montaigne, Bayle and Hume. Based on the same premise that human nature can be understood in the light of its own past, scientific history differs to the extent that it benefits from the development of archaeological and ethnographic studies, which provide first-hand empirical data that can be used as scientific proof.

The works of Charles Renouvier (1815–1903), which Durkheim became acquainted with during his first year at the École Normale Supérieure (1879–80), are also a vector for the sociological insights of Saint-Simon, Comte's positivism and Hume's experimental method.[29] Even though Renouvier never held a university position, he is sometimes referred to as Durkheim's teacher.[30] And the latter, being full of praise for the scientific system of the former, considered him his educator. Because of his interest for the categories of the understanding, and the analysis and limits of knowledge, Renouvier is a renowned French neo-Kantian. But his concept of reason has in fact more in common with Hume's: in the preface to his first *Essai de critique générale*, Renouvier stresses the social nature of scientific reason pertaining to general rules and the community. Reason is nothing more than 'the only and universal medium of humankind, man intelligible to man'.³¹

Besides those metaphysical and methodological debates, those who read both Hume and Durkheim cannot help but perceive a compelling constellation of concepts at work in Hume's moral philosophy and in Durkheim's social science. Lukes, for instance, highlights a Humean echo in Durkheim's idea that willpower alone cannot generate the promise to respect the law.³² Kratochwil stresses the difference in their ways of addressing the issue of the moral obligation to comply with norms.³³ Watts Miller emphasises Durkheim's engagement with Hume's *is/ought* problem.³⁴ Collins's way of laying out Durkheim's social theory highlights important common traits with Hume, such as the non-rational foundations of rationality and society, the role of sympathy in giving rise to moral feelings, the importance of customs for social order and the refutation of the hypothesis of a social contract.³⁵ Gellner claims that James Frazer, whom Durkheim directly criticises,³⁶ founds his anthropology on Hume's psychology.³⁷ Parallels were also drawn between Hume's sympathy for secular religion in his mature writings and Durkheim's anthropology of rituals.³⁸ The next two sections will bring out concepts that Hume refined in his accounts of knowledge, morality and government, and that prove to be operative in Durkheim's account of social organisation.

Hume's Articulation of Sociologically Operative Concepts

Already in the *Treatise on Human Nature* Hume is preoccupied with morality, especially with the challenge of providing its secular foundation by means of his science of man. Besides the origin of morality, the question of its authority and enforcement emerges. Hume explains that the natural laws of justice – including the stability of possession, transmission of property and promise – are inculcated in children by the parents, whose authority is restrained by natural affection.³⁹ Thus, moral law already emerges in the smallest social unit, accustoming children to obey, and this conditioning guarantees submission towards governors throughout adulthood: 'Man, born in a family, is compelled to maintain society, from necessity, from natural inclination, and from habit'.⁴⁰ However, despite the social nature of family, its analogy with other social forms has its limitations, in particular if we compare it with society where moral duty depends on a more complex mechanism.

Hume maintains that promise and allegiance have independent authorities and this distinction is salient in the comparison between a community and a society.[41] In a community where there are no given rules, promises are naturally performed as they prove useful for establishing trust in everyday affairs. When wealth increases up to the point where peace is at stake, a government emerges from the natural differences within the group and becomes established as an institution that preserves privileges. It is 'impossible for [men], of themselves, to observe those rules [of justice], in large and polish'd societies; they establish government, as a new invention to attain their ends, and preserve the old, or procure new advantages, by a more strict execution of justice'.[42] The institution of government turns the community into a society, where the performance of promises is no longer negotiable. 'There is a moral obligation to submit to government, *because every one thinks so*'.[43] In other words, with the emergence of government, the whole becomes qualitatively different from the sum of its parts: in an organised society, the collective mind takes over and individuals end up mindlessly submitting to the law of justice. The distinction between the authority of promise and that of allegiance is consistent with Hume's claim that we are aware of our own promises but not of our consent to obey the government.[44] As Hume shifts perspective from the individual to the social to explain the moral duty of obedience, he adopts sociologically operative concepts.

Hume's Psychosocial Concepts

In an attempt at providing the secular foundation of morality, Hume relies on his naturalist account of human passions, discrediting (1) the authority of popular religions because of their distorting effect on natural human drives and (2) the pretence that reason may play any role in moral action, because of its non-motivational character.[45] Reason and religion are not left out altogether, however, because reason still has a function to perform in knowledge acquisition and moral evaluation, and true religion is coextensive with moral excellence. Through his philosophical investigation Hume discovers what runs even deeper than reason and religion in human nature: custom.

'[T]he far greatest part of our reasonings with all our actions and passions, can be deriv'd from nothing but custom and habit'.[46] Custom is the principle at work in basic cognitive facts, such as the idea of necessity and the belief in causal relations.[47] It is also the social force that moulds character and makes people acquire virtuous habits by means of education.[48] Finally, custom acquaints the mind with common notions of virtue and vice, on which the evaluation of moral character is founded. Custom is a non-rational, involuntary principle of association operating both on the mind and in society. It is highly explanatory in Hume's account of knowledge and morality. On a mental level, custom or habit generates causal relations. On a social level, it determines the individual through education and peer pressure. The social meaning of custom in Hume's philosophy can be seen as corresponding to the notion of social fact in Durkheim's theory:[49] historically, custom helps to explain how things have become what they are, and sociologically, it contains at once a functional and a structural aspect. Similarly central in Durkheim's work, custom will fully take on its social meaning, and the explanation for individual beliefs and behaviours will depend entirely on social theory.

Sympathy is a fundamental factor of human socialisation for Hume. Indispensable in morality – but not sufficient on its own – it functions as a mechanism of reflection, is a motive for moral action and represents the starting point towards the sentiment of humanity. Sympathy alone, intended as a reflective mechanism and motive for moral action, cannot constitute a reliable guide for morality because of the bias or partiality naturally resulting from one's 'narrow circle'. It takes custom and experience to ascertain the utility of justice and to substantiate the moral rules that inform and refine moral evaluation.[50] With the effects of custom, sympathy develops into humanity or love of humankind, which is the most reliable guide to moral action and moral distinctions.[51] The notions of sympathy and humanity are central components of Durkheim's theory of moral obligation, as we will see in the following section.

Unlike sympathy and custom, self-interest or self-love has a more ambivalent effect on socialisation according to Hume. On the one hand it can bring the individual to satisfy their avidity beyond necessity, thereby jeopardising social bonds. On the other, when channelled to the interest of society, it induces spontaneous moral conduct. While self-interest usually involves some sort of calculus, it seems that, for Hume, public spirit or one's interest for society is not the product of a rational deliberation. Like many Scottish thinkers of the Enlightenment, Hume holds that social life organises itself in the absence of rational self-interest.[52] By claiming that reason doesn't contribute to social cohesion, Hume targets Locke's theory of the original contract.[53] Living in a society and following the law cannot be the work of rational consent, because people born in a social context are never given an option to decline the circumstances of their existence. And yet despite the hold of society on the individual through moral education and authority, the actual practice of justice is always permeated with particular motives.[54] This combination of selfish tendencies and social sentiments, conspicuous in Hume's moral theory, is also salient in Durkheim.

Secular Faith in Social Institutions

On top of psychosocial concepts Hume introduces notions that make sense only from a social perspective. Adopting a sociocentric point of view with phrases like 'public good', 'public interest', 'public utility', 'public spirit' and so on, he introduces a notion of social sentiment which opposes utilitarian individualism. He argues that selfish motives are checked by society based on two criteria of general approbation: usefulness and agreeableness.[55] Considering social sentiments, Hume's moral theory no longer rests exclusively on his psychological account of passions: it is rather sustained by the assumption that self-interest is to merge with love of humankind, as everyone individually partakes in a common sentiment of humanity.

Social sentiments regarding the utility or agreeableness of any human practice are sufficient to determine its fitness or unfitness. Thus, justice is submitted to the criterion of utility to public interest.[56] And as much as the transmission of property may have all the makings of a superstitious practice, its utility to social order earns legitimacy.[57] In fact, Hume goes as far as to consider social prerogatives as sacred and to identify certain attitudes towards government as religious.[58] The analogy between society and religion is not limited to Hume's vocabulary. Society and religion have conceptual affinities when it comes to the mechanism of moral obligation. Thus, as Hume adopts a historical approach and introduces sociologically operative concepts, he also resorts to religiously connoted vocabulary.

If human nature amounted only to its social, generous dispositions then sympathy and custom would suffice to maintain peace and order. But the spark of benevolence is 'kneaded into our frame, along with the elements of the wolf and serpent', and these antisocial features challenge the feelings inducing moral conduct.[59] So, if moral excellence is guided by the sentiment of humanity then the moral atheist is the one holding that 'all *benevolence* is mere hypocrisy, friendship a cheat, public spirit a farce, fidelity a snare to procure trust and confidence'.[60] Those who reckon humankind as mean will 'consider the common course of human affairs with too much indignation'. Hume doesn't conclude that this sentiment would lead to vice, but he holds that someone 'prepossessed with a high notion of his rank and character . . . will naturally endeavour to act up to it'.[61] Moral sentiment is more important than moral conduct per se because the latter naturally follows from the former, whereas someone acting morally without meaning it would not be partaking of the social sentiment of humanity. Threatened by its own antisocial features and aware of its own struggle to maintain peace, humankind establishes things that it deems inviolable, non-negotiable and, in that sense, sacred. Sacred human artefacts, for Hume, include positive laws, secular institutions and belief in the dignity of our species. Those social creations may be artificial and include epistemically unfounded beliefs, but they foster moral conduct. And when it comes to morality, Hume is clear about the precedence of the good over the true.

> [T]hough the philosophical truth of any proposition by no means depends on its tendency to promote the interests of society; yet a man has but a bad grace, who delivers a theory, however true, which, he must confess, leads to a practice dangerous and pernicious . . . And mankind will agree, if they cannot refute them, to sink them, at least, in eternal silence and oblivion. Truths, which as *pernicious* to society, if any such there be, will yield to errors, which are salutary and *advantageous*.[62]

The idealised, unscientific (and thereby potentially distorted) picture of reality on which morality relies to encourage good behaviour shows how close religion and morality are in Hume's philosophy. Before Durkheim and Renouvier, Hume already accounts for the emergence of sacredness in the context of social organisation.

From Literary to Scientific History

Hume attempts to discover the laws of human nature through the observation and explanation of the psychological mechanisms giving rise to human beliefs and practices. But when it comes to moral psychology, the limits of his science of man start to appear: 'those eternal immutable fitnesses and unfitnesses of things [i.e. the boundaries of right and wrong] cannot be defended by sound philosophy'.[63] Because good and evil are not qualities present in the nature of things or in their relations, only human experience can determine them. The study of history increases the pool of experience and can be used to confirm the 'reasonings of true philosophy', including concerning good and evil in politics.[64] From Book 3 of the *Treatise* onwards, Hume rather focuses on social dynamics and brings in history as testimony to illustrate and substantiate his theses concerning the fundamental principles of human, social nature.

> Mankind are so much the same, in all times and places, that history informs us of nothing new or strange in this particular. Its chief use is only to discover the constant and universal principles of human nature, by shewing men in all varieties of circumstances and situations, and furnishing us with materials, from which we may form our observations, and become acquainted with the regular springs of human action and behaviour.[65]

Like Hume, Durkheim is trying to identify the laws of human nature.

> I have made a very archaic religion the subject of my research because it seems better suited than any other to help us comprehend the religious nature of man, that is, to reveal a fundamental and permanent aspect of humanity.[66]

His approach and basic assumptions share common features with Hume's, especially when it comes to the value of history in the knowledge of human practices, and the role of sympathy and custom in the self-organisation of the social body. By contrast, Durkheim benefits from the advancement of ethnographic studies and Comte's establishment of sociology as a scientific discipline. Based on actual data and by means of comparative method and systematic analysis, his social theory is supported by the rigour of scientific history. Despite the recasting of sociological concepts through French spiritualism and positivism, central notions and concerns that are at work in Durkheim's account of social organisation still bear Hume's stamp, as we will see in the next section.

Appropriation of Humean Ideas in Durkheim's Social Theory

Recounting the history of French sociology, Durkheim attributes to Henri de Saint-Simon and Comte – admirers of Hume and Smith – the establishment of this discipline as a science.[67] Saint-Simon put forward the notion of social physics and it was Comte who coined the term *sociologie*. Downstream of Comte (and Herbert Spencer) was Alfred Espinas, a social realist who elaborated the analogy between social organisation and biological organisms, highlighting the complexity of psychological ties within a group compared with the simplicity of its material ties.[68]

Durkheim stresses the representative nature of society, which he conceives as an organisation of collective representations. He brings out the similarity between psychology and sociology and holds that social and individual consciousness can be understood in similar terms. The multiplicity of impressions and representations mingle in a self – which in this case is a plural self, 'we' or *le nous social*. Society is conceived of as a life form whose distinctive characteristic, compared with other life forms, is that its components are more apparent.[69]

Enthusiastic about the programme outlined by Comte for the new science, Durkheim takes up the project where it had been left thirty years prior. His method and empirical research in sociology substantiates claims that resonate with Hume's ideas on sociality, moral obligation and social epistemology.

Sympathy and the Non-rational Basis of Social Solidarity

There is no such thing as an original contract, for Durkheim, because every contract depends on a pre-contractual, implicit agreement rooted in human sociality. A contract is an explicit agreement between two parties and its pre-contractual basis is the unspoken promise, from both parties, that they will in fact respect the explicit agreement. This original promise indicates the non-rational character of social engagements. Truly rational individuals would be aware, of course, that cheating on their contractual partners will grant them more gain as well as diminish their chances of losing a great deal in the case where they are the one who is being cheated on.[70] 'Self-interest is indeed the least constant thing in the world ... Thus such a cause can give rise only to transitory links and associations of a fleeting kind'.[71] So contracts must be based on non-contractual relationships.

Non-contractual elements of contracts are the basic agreements that are not supposed to be negotiated. They amount to an organic kinship that represents the moral basis of social organisation, because it pertains to shared feelings and similarities that bring human beings to seek each other out and associate.[72] This 'mechanical' solidarity based on similarities has no political connotations. Like Hume, Durkheim recognises the difference between social organisation 'truly grounded in the nature of things' and a façade system surviving by 'administrative artifice'.[73] Genuine organisation emerges from horizontal interactions, through social rituals, contagious emotions and the development of collective consciousness. Artificial organisation is imposed from above by a tyrannical government (such as imperial despotism during the Second Republic) or from the outside because of war.[74] It should not be concluded that administration and institutions would necessarily lead to weaker social sentiments: for Durkheim, through the establishment of authorities, contracts and judges, solidarity becomes 'organic', in the sense that setting up a political commonwealth gives rise to social organs, or institutions, with which individuals maintain vertical ties on top of remaining 'mechanically' solidary to one another, thereby expanding collective consciousness. Non-contractual agreements thus permeate traditional communities as well as modern societies.[75] Their foundational role in contracts and social engagements is enforced by the sentiment of moral duty.

It has been argued that Durkheim subscribes to Kant's concept of moral obligation, especially when it comes to the compelling nature of moral duty.[76] In the essay on 'Individualism and the Intellectuals', however, Durkheim defends a nuanced view that is partly opposed to Kant's and brings him close to Hume. In this essay Durkheim identifies two individualistic stances: utilitarian and idealist. The first consists in the 'utilitarian egoism of Spencer and the economists';[77] it argues that one is entitled to seek the satisfaction of one's private needs, but this selfish tendency is easily counteracted by the other goal of utilitarianism, which is to contribute to the well-being of society. Public utility may thus justify the sacrifice of individuals.[78] According to Durkheim, idealists like Kant defend the view that everyone should act morally based on their rational understanding of universal moral principles. This implies a belief in the notion of 'humanity in the abstract' and in universal moral good.[79] In virtue of its universal character, moral duty is compelling as if it had religious authority.[80] Durkheim partly agrees with both views. Like utilitarians, he conceives of moral behaviour and evaluation as oriented by feelings of pleasure and pain in the moral agent or bystander, rather than by general maxims and abstract ideas concerning good and virtue. Like idealists, he believes in the compelling authority of moral principles. At the same time, Durkheim is unsatisfied with both views as well because they focus on the individual and ignore the value of social bonds. Utilitarianism can be interpreted as a selfish theory supporting the precedence of ends over means, which is also desacralising for the human person. And idealism mobilises generalised maxims based on general notions, instead of feelings, suggesting a discontinuity or a gap between the nature of things and the elaboration of moral distinctions. Durkheim, therefore, opposes both forms of individualism – in particular, the idealist one – which he qualifies as 'the catalyst of moral dissolution' by virtue of 'its antisocial essence'.[81]

In his criticism of idealist individualism, Durkheim sees potential in the religious aspect of moral obligation. Instead of adopting a vocabulary alluding to the transcendental nature of universal moral maxims, he emphasises the human, intersubjective foundation of religious authority. He highlights the relatable feeling of belonging to a community, where a sense of humanity is shared and sacralised through social rituals. 'If [a man] has a right to this religious respect, it is because he partakes of humanity. It is humanity which is worthy of respect and sacred'.[82] So, unlike Kant, who conceives of moral duty as the rational, impersonal understanding and following of given moral principles, Durkheim considers that the feelings shared via sympathy have more authority than reason, because their impact on the group is such that it spontaneously gives rise to solidarity and common interest, with no need for people to put their mind to it.

> For ours is not naturally a wise and pure reason which, purged of all personal motives, would legislate in the abstract its own conduct. Doubtless, if the dignity of the individual came from his personal characteristics, from the peculiarities which distinguish him from others, we might fear that it would shut him off in a sort of moral egoism which would make any solidarity impossible. But in reality he receives

dignity from a higher source, one which he shares with all men ... After all, individualism thus extended is the glorification not of the self but of the individual in general. It springs not from egoism but from sympathy for all that is human.[83]

In his account of moral obligation, Durkheim thus gives a Scottish turn to idealist individualism by placing at its centre the notion of sympathy. He derives morality from sympathy rather than from reason or truth. This move brings him close to Hume's account of self-love and humanity, which can conflate with the passion of pride in a virtuous character.[84] However, unlike Hume, for whom moral character and behaviour are mostly a matter of pride and social esteem, Durkheim emphasises the strong moral constraint of social institutions over the mind of the individual, whose value as a person depends on her/his participation in the religion of humanity. Humanity intended as a sacred entity stems from sympathy and solidarity taking place at the profane level of inter-individual relations. In other words, Durkheim explains the genealogy of moral institutions, a dignified sphere of human life in modern society, by appealing to mechanisms operating already at an underlying level of human activity which can be observed in communities and traditional societies.

Sociology of Knowledge

In the essay co-authored with Marcel Mauss, Durkheim presents the observations made on traditional societies that demonstrate the social origin of mental classifications or 'collective representations'. The classification of natural objects and animals in Australian tribes is a secondary result of the human need to gather in different groups maintaining specific relationships with one another. They resort to totems: a symbolic use of nature that simultaneously projects society-made order and hierarchy onto nature itself.[85] The notion of space and its division depends entirely on social organisation, on the specific functions within a group, and therefore differs from tribe to tribe.[86] Various systems of classification can overlap to meet the representational and divinatory needs of a growing society, as Durkheim and Mauss illustrate with the Taoist system in the Far East. In addition to the notions related to space, those of time and causation are being articulated in association with specific rituals.[87] The essay concludes with the claim that these abstract classifications are the conceptual result of religious affective states spread among the members of a tribe or society by means of sympathy. From a sociocentric perspective, things, beings and facts are perceived as 'sacred or profane, pure or impure, friendly or unfriendly' and so on. When social affectivity progressively decreases, and as social structures solidify, this system of emotions leaves cognitive traces or 'mental habits' consisting in a powerful logical system of conceptual divisions and categories.[88] 'Reason, which is none other than the fundamental categories taken together, is vested with an authority that we cannot escape at will'.[89]

Durkheim's interpretation of the observations made on traditional models of social organisation emphasises the influence of the social on the individual mind, in which the only operating psychological functions are of the affective kind. The sentimental, non-rational foundation of belief and knowledge indicates a salient affinity with Hume, even though accurate and just reasoning on the part of the philosopher is presented as more respectable than popular superstition in Hume's normative epistemology,[90] while in Durkheim's social relativism logical thinking is always the work of the community.[91] Despite this nuance, Hume's psychosocial notion of custom can be understood as anticipating some of the ideas at work in the Strong Programme in the Sociology of Knowledge.[92] According to the Strong Programme, knowledge is not concerned with justification because it is created by a network of sociological causes. Focusing on the community, the goal is to investigate the social causes by which systems of belief emerge. Rationality, truth, clarity and other epistemological normative categories are not at play. This sociocentric view on knowledge is already adopted by Hume and common-sense philosophers, for whom science and morality cannot be valid, ultimately, without general approbation – which is as close as they can get to objectivity.

In society, where knowledge is one of the highest forms of human creation, 'sociology of knowledge . . . poses a threat' by exposing its non-rational origins.[93] But Durkheim didn't mean to desacralise reason and science with his conclusions. 'If philosophy and the sciences were born in religion, it is because religion itself began by serving as science and philosophy'.[94] His sociological science of human nature rather connects knowledge and practice at the root. Durkheim emphasises the bridges between natural and human sciences and contributes, in the footsteps of the encyclopedists, to induce 'a lively feeling for the unity of human knowledge'.[95]

Conclusion

Proving that Durkheim read Hume is just as difficult as ignoring the distracting number of affinities between their accounts of sociality. Besides Durkheim's probable acquaintance with Humean psychology through his reading of James Frazer and Hume's critique of causality via Renouvier and Janet, it may be argued that he inherited his Scottish ideas on sociality from Smith and Hutcheson, whom he mentions when discussing the role of benevolence and sympathy in the foundation of moral law.[96] But then one should explain why Durkheim gives such a Humean turn to his critique of sentimentalist morality by highlighting the need for a self-standing and socially shared moral law exerting its authority on the mind from the outside.

Before compiling a list of common views, it is worth noting the main purported difference between Hume and Durkheim, besides the already mentioned reliance on literary versus scientific history.[97] It has been argued that Durkheim's concept of moral obligation is inspired from Kant's categorical imperative.[98] And Durkheim subscribes indeed to the irrational character of the 'faith and submission' with respect to moral law in Kant's ethics. In Durkheim's own system, moral authority is secured by the imperative dictates – conveyed through command, justification and emotion – of the 'religion of humanity'.[99] But Durkheim disagrees with the 'exaggerated ... autonomy of reason' in Kant's account of moral duty; instead, it is 'sympathy' or the ability to 'relate' to one's fellow human beings that dignifies any individual partaking of morality and social rituals. 'Sympathy for all that is human' is the foundation of solidarity among peers, and the resulting faith in humanity compels people into submission to common good, thereby urging them to accomplish their social–moral duties.[100] Durkheim's alleged affinity with Kant would then emphasise his disagreement with Hume, who claims instead that '[i]f we consider the ordinary course of human actions, we shall find, that the mind restrains not itself by any general and universal rules; but acts on most occasions as it is determin'd by its present motives and inclinations'.[101] Kratochwil argues in this direction. He interprets Hume, based on his position in Book 3 of the *Treatise*, as a 'rule-utilitarian' and reads Durkheim as an idealist, based on his self-proclaimed remoteness from utilitarian ethics.[102] But this difference depends on a caricatural reading of Hume that focuses on the *Treatise* and ceases to be valid once we consider his moral enquiry and subsequent writings.

The tendency to overlook Hume's later works may also inaccurately suggest that his position towards religion is more critical than Durkheim's. This point has already been dismissed (see 'Secular Faith in Social Institutions', above) but a further nuance can be mentioned concerning their takes on religion. For Hume, religion and morality derive from human nature while, for Durkheim, society, religion and morality are simultaneous phenomena. They meet eventually on the idea that certain moral things are sacred in human society and, as such, society is intended as a secular religion.

An important difference, however, between the two thinkers reflects in part their distance in time. An advocate of commercial development, Hume condemns religious superstition in so far as it hinders civility, arts and the sciences. He conceives of the division of labour as resulting from the rise of modern societies. On his part, witnessing the social impact of the industrial revolution, Durkheim is more seriously concerned with the condition of the poor as well as more openly sympathetic to religion. Adopting a rigorous sociological mindset, he holds that organic solidarity characterising modern societies is rather a consequence of the division of labour resulting from demographic growth.

Despite the dissimilarity, I have tried to show in this chapter that Hume and Durkheim hold fundamental common views on sociality. Durkheim has affinities with the Scots' political theory in general, concerning the invalidity of the notion of social contract and the importance of social cohesion for the establishment and legitimacy of political authority. He adopts, through Janet, Hume's idea that good is more important than truth.[103] Both Hume and Durkheim think that morality is coextensive with human society. They derive the dignified spheres of human activity (such as knowledge and morality) from the lower spheres (passions and sympathy), and consequently their notions of reason are alike. They see a continuity between sympathy and humanity and consider that the sentiment of humanity is fundamental for moral conduct. They have a similar understanding of the difference between a community and a modern society. And, despite Comte's influence, Durkheim considers like Hume that humankind consists in multiple societies rather than in one global society-species.

Notes

I want to thank John Hall, Kenneth Macdonald, Tamás Demeter, Dirk Schuck and Spyridon Tegos, whose insightful comments on a previous version of this chapter helped me to improve its content and quality. This chapter is part of a project (1254721N) funded by FWO (Belgium).

1. Steven Lukes, *Émile Durkheim: His Life and Work*, 2nd ed. (Harmondsworth: Penguin Books, 1973); Warren Schmaus, *Rethinking Durkheim and His Tradition* (New York: Cambridge University Press, 2004).
2. Charles Renouvier, *Essai de Critique générale: Premier essai. Analyse générale de la connaissance. Bornes de la connaissance* (Paris: Ladrange, 1854), pp. 222–3; Paul Janet, *Traité Elémentaire de Philosophie à l'usage des classes* (Paris: Delagrave, 1889), §187, pp. 198–202.
3. Emile Durkheim and Marcel Mauss, 'De quelques formes primitives de classification: contribution à l'étude des représentations collectives', *L'Année sociologique* (1901–2), pp. 1–72.
4. Schmaus, *Rethinking Durkheim and His Tradition*.
5. On Hume's contribution to the social sciences, see Angela Coventry, Alex Sager and Tom Seppäläinen, 'A Humean Social Ontology' in Angela Coventry and Alexander Sager (eds), *The Humean Mind* (Abingdon: Routledge, 2019), pp. 446–57.
6. Randall Collins, *Sociological Insight: An Introduction to Non-Obvious Sociology*, 2nd ed (New York: Oxford University Press, 1992).
7. David Bloor, *Knowledge and Social Imagery*, 2nd ed. (London: University of Chicago Press, 1991).
8. Warren Schmaus, 'Rawls, Durkheim, and Causality: A Critical Discussion', *American Journal of Sociology* 104 (1998), pp. 872–86, at pp. 873, 877–8, and *Durkheim's Philosophy of Science and the Sociology of Knowledge: Creating an Intellectual Niche* (Chicago: University of Chicago Press, 1994), p. 17.
9. Durkheim and Mauss, 'De quelques formes primitives de classification'.
10. David Hume, *A Treatise of Human Nature*, ed. David Fate Norton and Mary J. Norton (Oxford: Clarendon Press, [1739–40] 2007) (hereafter: T), 1.3.14.15. For a classic introduction to the debate on causation starting with Hume, see John L. Mackie, *Cement of the Universe: A Study of Causation* (New York: Oxford University Press, 1980). The discussion is still going on up to this day as reflected in Rani Lill Anjum and Stephen Mumford, *Causation in*

Science and the Methods of Scientific Discovery (New York: Oxford University Press, 2018).

11. T 1.3.11.4; Hume, *An Enquiry concerning Human Understanding*, ed. Tom L. Beauchamp (Oxford: Clarendon Press, [1748] 2006) (hereafter: EHU), 5.5–6. See also Catherine Dromelet and Marco Piazza, 'Habit and Custom in the History of Early Modern Philosophy' in D. Jalobeanu and C. T. Wolfe (eds), *Encyclopedia of Early Modern Philosophy and the Sciences* (Cham: Springer, 2020), pp. 1–9.
12. Thomas Reid, *Essays on the Intellectual Powers of Man*, ed. Derek R. Brookes (Edinburgh: Edinburgh University Press, [1785] 2002), 6.5.11, p. 490.
13. Philip P. Hallie, 'Maine de Biran and the méditatifs intérieurs', *Journal of the History of Ideas* 18 (3) (1957), pp. 295–312, at pp. 304–5.
14. George Berkeley, *Principles of Human Knowledge and Three Dialogues*, ed. Howard Robinson, 2nd ed. (New York: Oxford University Press, [1710] 1999), part 1, §27, §135.
15. T 1.4.6.
16. Maine de Biran, *Essai sur les fondements de la psychologie*, ed. F. C. T. Moore, vol. 2 in *Œuvres de Maine de Biran*, ed. François Azouvi, vol. VII/2 (Paris: Vrin, [1812] 2001), p. 277.
17. André Lalande, *Durkheim's Philosophy Lectures: Notes from the Lycée de Sens Course, 1883–1884*, ed. and transl. Neil Gross and Robert Alun Jones (New York: Cambridge University Press 2004), Lecture 17 on 'Consciousness. On the Nature of the Self', p. 93.
18. Daniel Schulthess, 'Maine de Biran, interprète et critique de Thomas Reid' in Elisabetta Arosio and Michel Malherbe (eds), *Philosophie française et philosophie écossaise 1750–1850* (Paris: Vrin, 2007), pp. 39–51, at pp. 44–5, 51. On Biran's connection to the Scottish Enlightenment, see also Marco Piazza, 'On Sympathy and Attention: Maine de Biran, Reader of Adam Smith and Dugald Stewart' in Manfred Milz (ed.), *Posteriorities of Maine de Biran's Physio-Spiritualism* (Leiden: Brill, forthcoming) and 'Maine de Biran e l'Illuminismo Scozzese', *Rivista di storia della filosofia* 1 (2005), pp. 23–59.
19. Hallie, 'Maine de Biran and the méditatifs intérieurs'.
20. Ibid. p. 300.
21. In his philosophy course at the Lycée de Sens (1883–4) Durkheim argues that the mind has direct access to itself; self-perception is the source of the idea of self. He raises the possibility that the idea may not per se imply the reality of the self, but in virtue of the necessity that 'we're unable to assume its nonexistence', the question is

settled. Lalande, *Durkheim's Philosophy Lectures*, Lecture 17 on 'Consciousness. On the Origin of the Idea of Self', pp. 89–91.
22. James W. Manns and Edwards H. Madden, 'Victor Cousin: Commonsense and the Absolute', *The Review of Metaphysics* 43 (3) (1990), pp. 569–89, at p. 569.
23. Claire Etchegaray, 'Sens commun et philosophie écossaise chez Victor Cousin' in Elisabetta Arosio and Michel Malherbe (eds), *Philosophie française et philosophie écossaise 1750–1850* (Paris: Vrin, 2007), pp. 95–114.
24. Auguste Comte, *The Positive Philosophy of Auguste Comte* (New York: Cambridge University Press, [1853] 2009), vol. 2, p. 428.
25. Ibid. pp. 76–7.
26. Ibid. p. 38.
27. Ibid. p. 552.
28. Émile Durkheim, 'Sociology in France in the Nineteenth Century' in *On Morality and Society; Selected Writings*, ed. R. N. Bellah (Chicago: University of Chicago Press, 1973), pp. 3–22, 10.
29. Ibid. p. xii.
30. Schmaus, *Rethinking Durkheim and His Tradition*, p. 94; Émile Durkheim, *The Elementary Forms of Religious Life*, transl. Karen E. Fields (New York: The Free Press, [1912] 1995), p. lxix.
31. Renouvier, *Essai de Critique générale: Premier essai*, p. ix.
32. Lukes, *Émile Durkheim: His Life and Work*, p. 274.
33. Friedrich V. Kratochwil, *Rules, Norms, and Decisions: On the Conditions of Practical and Legal Reasoning in International Relations and Domestic Affairs* (New York: Cambridge University Press, 1991), pp. 95–129.
34. William Watts Miller, *Durkheim, Morals and Modernity* (London: Routledge, 1996), p. 1.
35. Collins, *Sociological Insight*.
36. Durkheim, *The Elementary Forms of Religious Life*, pp. 182–6.
37. Ernest Gellner, *Reason and Culture: The Historic Role of Rationality and Rationalism* (Oxford: Blackwell, 1992), pp. 35–6.
38. Catherine Dromelet, 'Dual Minds: Lessons from the French Context of Hume's Social Theory', *Journal of Scottish Philosophy* 19 (2021), pp. 203–17.
39. T 3.2.2.4. 'Men are necessarily born in a family-society, at least; and are trained up by their parents to some rule of conduct and behaviour'. See also David Hume, *An Enquiry concerning the Principles of Morals*, ed. Tom L. Beauchamp (Oxford: Clarendon Press, [1751] 2006) (hereafter: EPM), 3.16.

40. David Hume, Essay V, 'Of the Origin of Government [1777]' in *Essays, Moral, Political, and Literary*, ed. Eugene F. Miller (Indianapolis, IN: Liberty Fund, 1985–7), pp. 37–41, §1.
41. T 3.2.8.6.
42. T 3.2.8.5.
43. T 3.2.8.8; our emphasis.
44. T 3.2.8.9.
45. T 3.1.2.7; David Hume, *A Dissertation on the Passions; The Natural History of Religion*, ed. Tom L. Beauchamp (Oxford: Oxford University Press, [1757] 2007) (hereafter: NHR), 14: 81–4; T 3.1.1.
46. T 1.3.10.1.
47. EHU 8.5
48. EHU 8.11.
49. Peristiany refers to custom as a moral fact in Durkheim's social theory (Émile Durkheim, *Sociology and Philosophy*, transl. D. F. Pocock, intr. J. G. Peristiany (Abingdon: Routledge Revivals, 2010), p. xiii), and Lukes claims that Durkheim's notion of social facts amounts to the facts of moral life (Durkheim, *The Division of Labour in Society*, transl. W. D. Halls, ed. Steven Lukes, 2nd ed. (Basingstoke: Palgrave Macmillan, 2013), p. xxvi).
50. '*The practice of the world* goes farther in teaching us the degrees of our duty, than the most subtile philosophy, which was ever yet invented. And this may serve as a convincing proof, that *all men have an implicit notion* of the foundation of those moral rules concerning natural and civil justice, and are sensible, that they *arise merely from human conventions*, and from the interest, which we have in the preservation of peace and order' (T 3.2.11.5; our emphasis). It is clear from this passage that Hume conceives of a social mind.
51. EPM 5.39. See Anthony E. Pitson, 'Sympathy, Humanity, and the Foundation of Morals' in Jacqueline Taylor (ed.), *Reading Hume on the Principles of Morals* (Oxford: Oxford University Press, 2020), pp. 95–117.
52. On the self-organisation of political life in Hume, see Tamás Demeter, 'Sympathies for Common Ends: The Principles of Organization in Hume's Psychology and Political Economy' in Gábor Bíró (ed.), *Humanity and Nature in Economic Thought: Searching for the Organic Origins of the Economy* (London: Routledge, 2022), pp. 3–23. See also Christopher J. Berry, 'Sociality and Socialisation' in *Essays on Hume, Smith, and the Scottish Enlightenment* (Edinburgh: Edinburgh University Press, 2019), pp. 75–87.

53. Christopher Berry, *Social Theory of the Scottish Enlightenment* (Edinburgh: Edinburgh University Press, 1997), pp. 30–2.
54. T 3.2.6.9.
55. EPM 9.13.
56. EPM 3.1, 3.47–8.
57. EPM 3.35–48.
58. '[S]trict adherence to any general rules, and the rigid loyalty to particular persons and families, on which some people set so high a value, are virtues that hold less of reason, than of bigotry and superstition . . . 'tis certain, that the concurrence of all those titles, original contract, long possession, present possession, succession, and positive laws, forms the strongest title to sovereignty, and is justly regarded as sacred and inviolable' (T 3.2.10.15).
59. EPM 9.4.
60. EPM App. 2.1.
61. David Hume, 'Of the Dignity or Meanness of Human Nature' in *Selected Essays* [1741/1777], ed. Stephen Copley and Andrew Edgar (New York: Oxford University Press, 1998), pp. 43–8, at §2, pp. 43–4.
62. EPM 9.14.
63. T 3.1.1.17.
64. T 3.2.10.15; EHU 8.7
65. EHU 8.7.
66. Durkheim, *The Elementary Forms of Religious Life*, p. 1.
67. Durkheim, 'Sociology in France in the Nineteenth Century', pp. 3–12.
68. Lukes, *Émile Durkheim: His Life and Work*, pp. 79, 84.
69. Durkheim, 'Sociology in France in the Nineteenth Century', p. 13.
70. Durkheim, *The Division of Labour in Society*, pp. 160–1; see also Collins, *Sociological Insight*, pp. 9–11.
71. Durkheim, *The Division of Labour in Society*, p. 161.
72. Ibid. pp. 17–18.
73. Durkheim, 'Sociology in France in the Nineteenth Century', p. 12.
74. Ibid. p. 11.
75. The structural distinction between community and society is analogous in Hume and Durkheim: they both describe modern society as having institutions, unlike communities or traditional societies.
76. Émile Durkheim, *On Morality and Society: Selected Writings*, intr. Robert N. Bellah (Chicago: University of Chicago Press, 1975), p. xii.
77. Durkheim, 'Individualism and the Intellectuals [1898],' in *On Morality and Society*, pp. 43–57, at p. 44.

78. Ibid. p. 46.
79. Ibid. p. 45.
80. Ibid. p. 46.
81. Ibid. p. 46.
82. Ibid. p. 48.
83. Ibid. pp. 48–9.
84. Willem Lemmens, 'The Pride of Pericles, Hume on Self-Love, Benevolence, and the Enjoyment of Our Humanity' in Esther E. Kroeker and Willem Lemmens (eds), *Hume's* An Enquiry concerning the Principles of Morals, *A Critical Guide* (Cambridge: Cambridge University Press, 2020), pp. 33–52.
85. Durkheim and Mauss, 'De quelques formes primitives de classification', pp. 7–34.
86. Ibid. pp. 34–55.
87. Ibid. pp. 55–62.
88. Ibid. pp. 66–72.
89. Durkheim, *The Elementary Forms of Religious Life*, p. 13.
90. EHU 1.12.
91. Durkheim, *The Elementary Forms of Religious Life*, pp. 434–5.
92. Bloor, *Knowledge and Social Imagery*, pp. 3–23.
93. Ibid. p. 48.
94. Durkheim, *The Elementary Forms of Religious Life*, p. 8.
95. Durkheim, 'Sociology in France in the Nineteenth Century', p. 5.
96. Lalande, *Durkheim's Philosophy Lectures*, Lecture 58 on 'Critique of Utilitarianism. The Morality of Sentiment', pp. 237–8.
97. This methodological difference may explain why Hume thought that religion started out in polytheism (NHR 1, 34–6), while Durkheim observed the precedence of rites over beliefs, in primitive religions, where divinity worship is not always de rigueur (*The Elementary Forms of Religious Life*, p. 33).
98. Durkheim, *On Morality and Society*, p. xii.
99. Ibid. pp. 47–8.
100. Ibid. pp. 47–9.
101. T 3.2.6.9.
102. Kratochwil, *Rules, Norms, and Decisions*, pp. 95–129.
103. Quoting Janet, Durkheim (*The Division of Labour in Society*, p. 56n2) subscribes to the idea that 'The essential characteristic of the good, as compared with the true, is therefore to be obligatory. Taken by itself, the true does not possess this characteristic.'

11

Westermarckian Evolutionary Perspective on Scottish Moral Sentimentalism

Otto Pipatti

The Finnish sociologist Edward Westermarck (1862–1939) has a peculiar position in the history of sociology. At the turn of the twentieth century, Westermarck was better known and more widely read than many of the now celebrated classics of sociology.[1] His first book, *The History of Human Marriage* (1891), was a critical success and a bestseller in Britain, and it was quickly translated into French, German, Spanish, Italian, Russian and Japanese, among others. Westermarck's second book, the monumental 1,500-page study *The Origin and Development of the Moral Ideas* (1906–8), was also praised by most critics.[2] In 1907, Westermarck became Britain's first professor of sociology.[3] Westermarck received invitations to lecture at several American universities, and Harvard offered him a full professorship.[4] It seemed that '[s]uch a success for a single man's gigantic work put a whole school – Durkheim's – in the shade'.[5]

However, Westermarck's fame declined in the 1920s and 1930s, and after the Second World War he was identified as 'one of those nineteenth century evolutionists, whose work was no longer of interest to anybody'.[6] Westermarck does not appear in the literature on classical sociology, let alone in textbooks.[7] Contemporary sociologists dealing with Westermarck's key research topics such as morality and emotions are unaware of his legacy. Simply put, sociology as we know it today, with its many theoretical traditions, developed as if Westermarck never existed.

Today, Westermarck is best known for his theories of incest avoidance ('Westermarck effect') and the incest taboo, which provide the foundation for the current anthropological, psychological and biological study on the subject.[8] Westermarck's theory of incest is often referred to as one of the first sociobiological and evolutionary psychological hypotheses on human behaviour. However, only a few evolutionary scholars are aware that it is only a small part of his work on moral emotions.

In addition to sociology, Westermarck holds a central but largely ignored role in the history of British moral thought. One may even say that 'Westermarck rediscovered Hume and Smith after a century dominated first by utilitarian and then by evolutionary ethics'.[9] Westermarck presented his 'general theory of the nature of moral consciousness' in the first thirteen chapters of *The Origin and Development of the Moral Ideas*.[10] Later on, Westermarck summarised his theoretical views in his main philosophical work, *Ethical Relativity*.[11] Westermarck's moral theory provides a detailed account of human moral psychology, expanding into an in-depth analysis of the emotional foundations of social life. In addition, *The Origin and Development of the Moral Ideas* contains a huge array of more restricted hypotheses of moral phenomena Westermarck studied, with the aim to 'discover the principle which lies at the bottom of the moral judgement in each particular case'.[12]

Westermarck built his theory of moral emotions by combining eighteenth-century Scottish moral sentimentalism, Darwinian evolutionary theory and comparisons of anthropological data available in his time. Above all, Westermarck emphasised his debt to 'the moralists of the emotional school', and especially Adam Smith.[13] He acknowledged that 'of all moral philosophers or moral psychologists there is none from whom I have learned anything like as much as from Adam Smith'.[14]

The aim of this chapter is to outline an overview of the Scottish roots of Westermarck's theory of morality. I will begin by taking a brief look at Westermarck's life and career. Then I will discuss Westermarck's conception of sociology and its relation to his study of morality. The rest of the chapter focuses on the Humean and Smithian elements of his thought. While I avoid the exegetical disagreements of Hume's and Smith's texts, my focus is on how Westermarck read and understood their ideas and developed them further in his own theory of moral emotions.

Life and Career

Westermarck grew up in a wealthy, Swedish-speaking family in Helsinki, the capital of Finland, which was until 1918 an autonomous part of the Russian Empire. During his studies at the Imperial

Alexander University of Finland (University of Helsinki), Westermarck was drawn to British empiricist philosophers and especially Darwin's *The Descent of Man* (1871). Darwin's attempt to show that the psychological and emotional differences between humans and animals are differences in degree, not in kind, became the guiding principle of Westermarck's theory formation.

Westermarck received his doctorate in 1889, and a year later he was appointed docent (lecturer) of sociology. This position was one of the first lectureships of sociology in the world. Between 1906 and 1918, Westermarck held the chair in practical (moral and social) philosophy in Helsinki, and much of his teaching focused on sociology and social anthropology. From 1918, he served as a professor of philosophy at the Åbo Akademi University in Turku. During his career, Westermarck held teaching positions simultaneously in Finland and England. Beginning in 1904, Westermarck lectured at LSE and three years later he was appointed professor of sociology. Westermarck held the Martin White Chair of Sociology at LSE until his retirement in 1930.[15]

Besides being a theoretical and comparative scholar, Westermarck was one of the pioneers of ethnographic fieldwork.[16] Between 1898 and 1914, he spent a total of six years in Morocco, including a continuous two-year period at the beginning of the century. Fluent in Arabic and Berber dialects, Westermarck published ethnographic works on Moroccan religious and magical beliefs and practices.[17] In the mid-1920s, he bought a villa in the outskirts of Tangier and spent a part of his time in Morocco for the rest of his life.

Due to his possible homosexuality, Westermarck never married. He was a strong critic of the societal influence of religion, and politically he was a liberal reformist. In his scholarly work and social activities, Westermarck promoted legal reforms relating to the liberalisation of divorce laws, the juridical equality of spouses, the position of unmarried women and adulterine children, animal rights and the decriminalisation of homosexuality.[18] In Britain, he was well integrated into many networks of liberal intellectuals – for example, members of the Fabian Society belonged to his circle of friends.[19]

Sociology as the Study of the Causes of Social Phenomena

Most of the founding figures of sociology such as Durkheim, Weber, Simmel and Tönnies were Westermarck's contemporaries.

In broad terms, these canonised classical sociologists shared an interest in the study of modern society and the changes in social relations caused by the division of labour, industrialisation and urbanisation. For Westermarck, the subject of sociology was much broader. He defined sociology as 'the science of social phenomena in the widest sense of the word'.[20] This shows that his sociological works on morality and marriage deal largely with phenomena that may be observed and explored in all human societies.

Westermarck defined social phenomena in terms of human action. 'By a social phenomenon I understand a mode of conduct which is related to an association of individuals – either joint acts of associates, or conduct toward an associate or associates'.[21] In other words, by social phenomena Westermarck meant how human beings respond and react to each other. Central to this are *human emotions*, and Westermarck linked sociology specifically to the study of the manifestation of emotions in human action and social interaction.[22] In addition, he analysed the role of emotions in the emergence and maintenance of moral norms and rules regulating human behaviour.

More specifically, for Westermarck, sociology is the study of the *causes* of social phenomena: 'The object of sociology is to explain social phenomena, to find their causes, to show how and why they have come into existence'.[23] In his view, social phenomena arise from a combination of biological, psychological and social causes. Westermarck's theory formation is characterised by combining these perspectives and levels of explanation. He strongly rejected biological organismic analogies that were popular among classical sociologists and subsequent functionalist theorists in sociology and social anthropology. For Westermarck, evolutionary and biological explanations meant the application of Darwin's theory of evolution by natural selection to the human emotions and sociality.

As a sociologist, Westermarck was above all a scholar of the *origins* of social phenomena and institutions. By the origin of morality, Westermarck meant the emotional tendencies on which moral ideas and judgements are based and which maintain them in all social environments. Similarly, the origin of marriage refers to emotions such as maternal and paternal affection, pair-bond attachment and sexual jealousy that give rise to and structure family formation among humans. Westermarck's third major research subject was religion, and in his view religious beliefs emerge and persist in human societies ultimately for emotional reasons.[24] Westermarck uses the terms 'origin' and 'cause' interchangeably. In other words, origins serve as reasons for why certain kinds of social phenomena and institutions exist. The study of *emotional origins* forms the very essence of Westermarck's sociology.

The Scottish Roots of Westermarck's Study of Morality

Westermarck developed his theory of moral emotions during the 1890s.[25] It was only then that he became truly fascinated by the 'clearness and a sense of reality' that he found in the moral philosophy of David Hume and Adam Smith. 'Even if [their] hypotheses were not unfailingly true', Westermarck writes, 'in every case it seemed possible that they could be corrected by a deeper search into the facts of experience'.[26]

Westermarck continued the legacy of Hume and Smith in many ways. First, he regarded Hume and Smith as the chief ancestors of his research programme of morality. For Westermarck, the task of ethics is not to formulate normative rules for human action but to study how and why human beings make moral judgements.[27] In this sense, ethics is a 'psychological' and 'sociological' discipline.[28] In his lectures and published writings, Westermarck calls Hume and Smith specifically 'moral psychologists'. This means that they represented ethics as a descriptive enterprise and sought to 'explain and understand [moral] phenomena as shaped by human psychological nature'.[29] In Westermarck's view, such a study falls within the field of sociology.[30]

Second, like Hume and Smith, Westermarck explored the emotional basis of moral judgements and the nature and characteristics of the emotions moral judgements are based on. Hume and Smith called these emotions 'moral sentiments' and for Westermarck they were 'moral emotions'. Here, they were all theorists of sympathy, emphasising its role in how moral sentiments or emotions arise. As we shall see, Westermarck's analysis of the different ways in which the moral emotions may arise offers a broader and more explanatory description of the whole spectrum of morally relevant phenomena.

Third, Westermarck was very interested in the moral psychology of responsibility, devoting six chapters in *The Origin and Development of the Moral Ideas* to the subject. Westermarck's detailed analysis of 'conduct and character' – that is, which components of human behaviour people pay attention to when making moral judgements – combines Hume's and Smith's perspectives on moral responsibility. Westermarck's theory of how moral judgements are directed towards settled character traits is derived directly from Hume, but it also goes much further than Hume in analysing the differences between 'innate' and 'acquired' character. Adam Smith in turn provided the solution to the fundamental moral psychological problem: namely, *why* it is that moral judgements centre around volition and intentionality.[31] In Westermarck's view, Smith's theory of moral sentiments 'throws light on the deepest shafts of the moral consciousness, and that is mainly why I appreciate Smith's work so high'.[32]

Fourth, Westermarck was impressed by Hume's and Smith's attempts to trace similarities in the emotional structure between humans and other animals. All of them established their theories of morality on emotional dispositions humans share with many animals. Whereas Smith considered these sentiments to be given to us by the author of nature for 'self-preservation, and the propagation of the species',[33] Westermarck compared the behavioural traits of humans and animals from the perspective of Darwinian evolutionary theory and pondered on how natural selection may have favoured the underlying emotional tendencies. In this regard, Smith's way of linking morality to resentment and gratitude 'took moral psychology a long step forward',[34] because 'anger towards an ill-doer and friendliness towards a well-doer are mental facts easily explicable as results of natural selection'.[35]

Finally, Westermarck follows Hume in his moral subjectivism. At the heart of Westermarck's philosophical writings is his critique of moral objectivism and normative ethics. By moral objectivism, Westermarck meant ethical theories which assume that there exist universally valid moral principles that are discernible through reason or some other human faculty. A key part of Westermarck's moral philosophy is to demonstrate the emotional background of objectivist ethical theories. As we shall see, central to this is Hume's argument on objectification of emotions as a major element in moral experiences.

The Emotional Basis of Morality

By morality, Westermarck meant people's ideas of right and wrong, good and bad, which are expressed in moral judgements we make about each other and events in our surroundings. Moral ideas and judgements are based on the special kind of emotions Westermarck calls *moral approval* and *moral disapproval or indignation*. Moral approval is akin to *gratitude*, and both include a 'desire to produce pleasure in return for pleasure received'. Moral disapproval is a form of *resentment* and akin to *anger* and *desire for revenge*. While positive retributive emotions motivate people to return good for good, negative retributive emotions motivate punishment, characterised by a 'desire to inflict pain in return for pain inflicted'.[36]

These emotions are retributive in nature, a term used by Westermarck to denote both a 'hostile attitude of mind towards a cause of pain' and a 'friendly attitude of mind towards a cause of pleasure'. Retributive emotions express a 'mental constitution which has been acquired through the influence of natural selection' because they have a 'tendency to promote the interests of the individuals who feel them'. Retributive emotions are adaptive traits because 'by resentment evils are averted, by retributive kindliness benefits are secured'.[37] Establishing his moral and social theory on retributive emotions also makes Westermarck a theorist of reciprocity.

It was Adam Smith's insight on 'the retributive character of the moral emotions' that makes *The Theory of Moral Sentiments* 'the most important contribution to moral psychology made by any British thinker'.[38] Westermarck refers here to Smith's way of grounding a theory of moral judgement on the sentiments of gratitude and resentment. Gratitude is, for Smith, the 'sentiment which most immediately and directly prompts us to reward, or to do good to another'. Resentment, in turn, is the 'sentiment which most immediately and directly prompts us to punish, or to inflict evil upon another'.[39] According to Westermarck, Hume described moral approval and disapproval merely as feelings of pleasure and pain, failing to 'analyse the moral emotions with sufficient sharpness or profundity to discover their retributive nature, which at once throws light on many of the otherwise dark corners of the moral consciousness'.[40]

Westermarck did not represent the kind of pure emotivism which identifies moral judgements with emotional expressions. He emphasises that his 'theory of the emotional origin of moral judgements ... does not imply that such a judgement affirms the existence of a moral emotion in the mind of the person who utters it'. People may express moral judgements 'without feeling any emotion at all', although in his view completely non-emotional mental states do not exist.⁴¹ Nor does he claim that only the emotions of moral approval and disapproval would lead people into making moral judgements.

Instead, Westermarck analyses the origin of morality in a much broader and more general sense. The fundamental point is 'whether there are any specific emotions that have led to the formation of the concepts of right and wrong, good and bad, and all other moral concepts, and therefore may be appropriately named moral emotions'.⁴² The concepts people use when talking about moral issues may differ in different cultures but the *underlying moral emotions* are universal to human nature, and there is no doubt that all ethnic groups 'give expressions to those emotions in their speech'.⁴³ As Westermarck puts it, 'it is the instinctive desire to inflict counter-pain' – whether mental or physical – 'that gives to moral indignation its most important characteristic'. Without the retributive nature of moral emotions, '*moral condemnation and the ideas of right and wrong would never have come into existence*'.⁴⁴ Westermarck's interest focused on the special kind of emotions that generate human species-typical moral reality. In his view, it is impossible to imagine morality as we know it without these evolved emotional dispositions.

The Characteristics of Moral Emotions

One of the key questions in Westermarck's moral theory is what distinguishes the moral emotions from other retributive emotions – moral disapproval from anger and revenge, and moral approval from gratitude. This question is also at the heart of Westermarck's perspective on Hume and Smith. All of them recognised something essential about human social reality when proposing that the moral sentiments or emotions have their special observable characteristics that distinguish them from other emotions.

Following Hume, Westermarck describes moral approval and disapproval as 'disinterested'. This means that they appear to be independent of our personal interests.⁴⁵ When a person experiences moral disapproval or indignation, he or she feels that 'his condemnation is not due to the particular circumstance that it is he himself who is the sufferer, that his judgment would be the same if *anybody else* in similar circumstances had been the victim'.⁴⁶ Secondly, according to Westermarck, moral emotions are characterised by the appearance of 'impartiality'. This refers to our experience that we would react in the same way regardless of who is the agent and to whom the action we observe is directed.[47] As Frans de Waal puts it, Westermarck suggests that the moral emotions are connected to more 'general judgments of how *anyone* ought to be treated'.[48] Otherwise our emotions are not moral approval or disapproval but more like personal anger or gratitude.

It was Adam Smith's description of the gratitude and resentment of the 'impartial spectator' that helped Westermarck to formulate his theory of moral emotions. The gist of Westermarck's interpretation of the impartial spectator is that it is by examining the retributive emotions people feel when they observe the actions of others from the position of a non-involved bystander that we can best understand and describe the nature of the moral emotions. Simply put, when we observe morally relevant social interactions without being personally involved, 'we pass our judgements as impartial spectators'.[49] Westermarck also uses the impartial spectator in his theory of self-evaluation, stating that 'almost inseparable from the moral judgments which we pass on our own conduct seems to be the image of an impartial outsider who acts as our judge'.[50]

It is important to notice that for Westermarck the moral emotions and behaviours motivated by them are not necessarily disinterested and impartial in any larger sense.[51] Moral judgements may well reflect our own personal interests, yet we tend to experience our approval and disapproval as disinterested. Similarly, impartiality can be 'real or apparent'.[52] In reality, our moral emotions are often biased in favour of one party over another, but we are not usually aware of such partialities.

The third characteristic of moral emotions is 'a certain flavour of generality'. When people make moral judgements, they rarely feel that they are expressing merely their personal viewpoints. Very often, moral judgements also refer directly or indirectly to the emotions of others. Moral approval and disapproval include a 'vague assumption' that most people in our reference group would respond the same way in a similar situation.[53] This generalising feature is attached to moral emotions even when a person is aware that his viewpoint is not shared by others: 'He then feels that it *would be shared* if other people knew the act and all its attendant circumstances as well as he does himself, and if, at the same time, their emotions were as refined as are his own'.[54]

Westermarck's idea of generality overlaps to some extent with Hume's conception of a 'general point of view' as a characteristic of moral judgements, but he refers in this context especially to Smith. Whether we feel moral emotions on behalf of others or because we are the recipients of good or bad deeds ourselves, our retributive emotions derive their moral character from the fact that 'we assume that *any impartial judge* would share our views'.[55]

Disinterestedness, impartiality and the flavour of generality characterise moral emotions as 'public emotions' that are shared in a given society or social group as regards certain acts. These essential characteristics of moral emotions may be summed up by stating that when our indignation is moral indignation, we feel our reaction is justified. We feel that *anyone* in a similar situation would respond with similar righteous anger.

The Origin of Moral Emotions: Sympathy, Emotional Contagion, and Likings and Aversions

Westermarck explored in detail the mediating psychological, especially emotional, mechanisms through which the moral emotions arise. First, according to Westermarck, we feel moral approval and disapproval when we sympathise with the pleasure and pain of others. By sympathy or sympathetic emotions, Westermarck denotes feelings and emotions that we feel as reactions to similar feelings and emotions in others. In the first place, this may be the result of the 'close association that exists between these feelings and their outward expressions'. Accordingly, 'The sight of a happy face tends to produce some degree of pleasure in him who sees it; the sight of the bodily signs of suffering tends to produce a feeling of pain'. In addition, sympathetic emotions may arise from observing acts and situations: 'Sympathetic pain or pleasure may be the result of an association between cause and effect, between the cognition of a certain act or situation and the feeling generally produced by this act or situation'.[56] It is through perceiving the situational context that we may feel sympathetic emotions without observing similar emotions in the person concerned.

The details of Westermarck's analysis reveal far-reaching similarities to Hume's associationist account of sympathy in the *Treatise of Human Nature*.[57] Although Westermarck highly valued Smith's 'extraordinarily fine observations' on the causes and effects of sympathy, he was critical of Smith's key notion that sympathetic emotions are founded upon the imaginative process, where we put ourselves in the other person's place and reproduce the act with ourselves as either the agent or the recipient in the situation. In any case, Westermarck gave Hume and Smith much credit for being the first to ground moral sentiments in our capacity to sympathise with others.[58]

Next, Westermarck observes that we may be aroused to moral emotions when observing retributive emotions in other people. Westermarck distinguishes this kind of transfer of emotions, or emotional contagion, from sympathy, which concerns our affective responses to benefits and injuries caused to others. As 'a group of chimpanzees may be thrown into a state of blind fury by the angry cries of one of its members', a human individual may be sucked into the anger of a crowd without being aware of its cause.[59] Retributive emotions that are transmitted from one individual to another and that spread within groups are 'of considerable importance both as an originator and a communicator of moral ideas'.[60] As a result, acts and human characteristics may elicit moral disapproval in a society without anyone quite knowing why. The original causes of moral condemnation 'may have been ignorance, superstition, prejudice, or sheer selfishness in those who once laid down the rules of conduct, and their prescriptions may nevertheless be indiscriminately and thoughtlessly accepted by succeeding generations'.[61]

Third, moral emotions may manifest themselves via emotional 'likings' and 'aversions' or 'antipathies', which are independent of our sympathy with the emotions of others. In this respect, Westermarck's theory of moral judgements differs clearly from Hume and Smith. Westermarck emphasises that people often feel hostile and judgemental emotions towards persons who inflict no injury on anybody. Emotional disgust that leads to moral disapproval very often concerns 'differences of taste, habit, and opinion'[62] and, more broadly, anything which is 'unusual, new, or foreign'.[63] Similarly, in many situations people react with emotional likings that lead to moral approval without the influence of sympathy. Qualities like courage may arouse admiration and esteem regardless of the purpose of the action, and moral approval may also be directed to acts that concern only the agent's own interests. Here too, Westermarck emphasises the importance of the social environment, because our likings and aversions increase when we observe similar emotions in others.

Finally, people have a strong tendency to disapprove of actions that deviate from customs prevalent in a society or social group.

Customs are for Westermarck 'public habits' – that is, 'the habits of a certain group of men, a racial or national community, a class or rank of society'.[64] A breach of custom is closely linked to the causes of moral emotions discussed above, because acts that evoke sympathetic moral disapproval or emotional disgust usually also deviate from social customs. According to Westermarck, people tend to experience their retributive emotions as disinterested, impartial, shared by others and justified, when they are in congruence with established social customs. The central importance given to sympathy, emotional contagion and customs shows that Westermarck links moral emotions inextricably to their social contexts: 'Society is the school in which we learn to distinguish between right and wrong. The headmaster is Custom, and the lessons are the same for all the members of the community'.[65]

Besides describing the nature and characteristics of the moral emotions, Westermarck asks *why* these emotions are part of human nature. This is an evolutionary question. His solution is that 'society is the birthplace of the moral consciousness'.[66] By this Westermarck refers to the *social environment* in which the uniquely human moral emotions evolved and became part of our biological inheritance.

Society is, for Westermarck, 'an association of individuals of the same species characterised by some kind of cooperation'.[67] In his view, the tendency to feel retributive moral emotions evolved in the close-knit societies of early humans, where individuals were united by 'the solidarity of interests'. These emotions gave selective advantage because, in such circumstances, 'acts which are beneficial to the agent are at the same time beneficial to his companions, and the distinction between *ego* and *alter* loses much of its importance'.[68] In Westermarck's view, in the course of human evolution, natural selection has favoured individuals who responded with moral approval to behaviours that were beneficial to themselves and others, and with moral indignation to behaviours that were threatening and harmful to them. Westermarck emphasises that 'the first moral judgments expressed, not the private emotions of isolated individuals, but emotions felt by the society at large'.[69]

The Emergence and Maintenance of Moral Norms

Westermarck's theory of moral emotions expands into an account of the origin of moral norms. Westermarck analyses moral norms as customs, whose breach has a tendency to arouse moral disapproval that is shared in a society or social group. In his writings, Westermarck traces the origin of moral norms or customs to many different sources, of which sympathy and emotional aversion are very important.

According to Westermarck, 'sympathy is the primary basis for many customs and laws that regulate relationships between members of the same society'.[70] He analyses in detail many moral rules that, although varying in their cultural-contextual details, arguably exist in an identifiable form in all known human societies. They concern infliction of physical harm and injury, killing, theft, offences against honour and reputation, impoliteness, lying and cheating, reciprocation in a social relationship where this is expected, the neglect of basic parental duties, and self-neglect and self-harm. In addition, sympathy is involved in influencing moral rules concerning the treatment of the dead and insulting the gods.[71]

In all these cases, moral condemnation arises from 'the principle of sympathetic resentment':[72] namely, that 'other members of the society sympathise with the sufferer, resent injustice, and feel indignation towards the wrongdoer'.[73] It is in this sense that moral emotions are 'public emotions' which given acts tend to arouse in society. In Westermarck's moral and social theory, society simply represents the continuous presence of other people as spectators of human actions and social interactions.

The importance of emotional disgust, in turn, shows that 'aversions which are generally felt readily lead to moral disapproval and prohibitory customs or laws'.[74] These emotional tendencies play a crucial role in Westermarck's account of incest taboo, but in his view they have also shaped attitudes towards homosexuality and the formation of moral rules concerning food, hygiene and cleanliness, bestiality and cannibalism.[75]

However, according to Westermarck, moral customs or norms are to a large extent arbitrary and variable, being caused by the fact that a 'habit may develop into a genuine custom simply because men are inclined to disapprove of anything which is unusual'.[76] When a habit, 'however trivial it may be', has developed into a social custom, it constitutes a moral rule, and 'the unreflecting mind has a tendency to disapprove of any deviation from it'.[77] For this reason, customary practices uphold the moral condemnation of acts which would not, without the influence of custom, arouse moral disapproval.

Objectified Moral Reality

The last centrepiece of Westermarck's moral theory which has its roots in Scottish moral philosophy is his thesis of objectification. It is also a crucial factor underlying the disinterested, impartial and general nature of moral emotions. By objectification, Westermarck means our tendency to interpret subjective experiences as external, objective facts. Just as people call 'sunshine warm and ice cold on account of certain sensations which they experienced', they also consider 'certain acts to be good or bad on account of the emotions those acts aroused in their minds'.[78] According to Westermarck, human beings have a strong tendency to reflect or project their moral emotions as qualities of acts and objects that evoke them. Thus,

> It is only because our emotions have been set in motion that we call anything good or evil. The moral qualities such as good and evil are thus valid only from the standpoint of sentient beings, just as sense perceptions only possess validity from the standpoint of sensing creatures.[79]

These arguments have their origin in Hume's moral philosophy.[80] Hume argued famously that 'the mind has a great propensity to spread itself on external objects'[81] and that we 'gild' and 'stain' acts and character traits 'with the colours borrowed from internal sentiment'.[82] According to Hume,

> when you pronounce any action or character to be vicious, you mean nothing, but that from the constitution of your nature you have a feeling or sentiment of blame from the contemplation of it. Vice and virtue, therefore, may be compared to sounds, colours, heat and cold, which, according to modern philosophy, are not qualities in objects, but perceptions in the mind.[83]

An essential part of Westermarck's moral subjectivism is that the lack of mind-independent moral facts does not deprive morality of its importance to the human condition. Westermarck emphasises that, just as the human mind is structured so that we hear sounds, see colours and perceive the temperature, we have evolved as biological organisms to experience human behaviour and social interaction in moral terms:

> Our moral consciousness belongs to our mental constitution, which we cannot change as we please. We approve and we disapprove because we cannot do otherwise. Can we help feeling pain when the fire burns

us? Can we help sympathising with our friends? Are these phenomena less necessary, less powerful in their consequences, because they fall within the subjective sphere of experience?[84]

Extinct Classical Legacy

In this chapter, I have focused on some of the key elements of Westermarck's theory of morality, all of which reveal his close indebtedness to David Hume and Adam Smith, both as a successor and a grateful critic. These connections are also visible in many other contexts, such as Westermarck's description of self-directed moral emotions and siding with Smith on the debate on the role of social utility in moral judgements. In a way, Scottish connections are manifested throughout Westermarck's oeuvre because his theory of moral emotions provides the wider background to his works on marriage and family, religion and Moroccan ethnography.

First, Westermarck argued that culturally varied customs and norms that regulate marriage practices and relationships between family members and kin are morally structured, meaning that deviation from them arouses moral emotions that are typically shared in a society or social group. Moreover, Westermarck's theory of the incest taboo is based on emotional aversion and collective moral disapproval, discussed in his work on moral emotions. Second, Westermarck emphasised 'the enormous influence' which religious beliefs have 'exercised upon the moral ideas of mankind', as well as 'how exceedingly varied this influence has been'.[85] His last major work, *Christianity and Morals,* is an attempt to show how the key Christian doctrines of morals and salvation can be analysed with the help of his concepts, especially the retributive nature of moral emotions, sympathy and emotional disgust. In addition, the work examines 'the influence which Christianity has exercised in concrete cases upon ideas and behaviour within different branches of morality'.[86] Finally, Westermarck's fieldwork focuses largely on the relationship between religion, magic and morality. Although Westermarck does not deal with his theory of moral emotions in his ethnographic works, this broader framework helps us to understand his ethnographic observations.

Westermarck taught at LSE for a quarter century, and his lectures and seminars were popular and much liked among students.[87] One of Westermarck's students, and later a colleague and friend, was Bronislaw Malinowski (1884–1942), who acknowledged him as a scholar 'to whose personal teaching and to whose work I owe more than any other scientific influence'.[88] Westermarck's relation to Malinowski has been an ill-charted territory in the history of sociology and social anthropology, but David Shankland is undoubtedly right when stating that 'the topics taught and discussed by Westermarck, such as the analysis of social institutions or the relationship between the social and the biological basis of behaviour, later were to become fundamental to Malinowski's vision'.[89] There are also many traces of Westermarck's teaching and research in the works of LSE sociologist Morris Ginsberg (1889–1970).

Although Westermarck never became an originator of a sociological tradition in Britain, the situation was different in early twentieth-century Finland, a small and remote country with a population of less than three million. There, a group of disciples shared his evolutionary interest in the human mind and the comparative study of the origins of social phenomena. Like Westermarck, most of them understood origins as the ever-present causes of social phenomena and institutions, and analysed origins as a combination of biological, psychological and social factors. Many of them became internationally renowned scholars who published their main works through leading British publishers. Yrjö Hirn (1870–1952) dealt with art, Gunnar Landtman (1878–1940) studied social inequality and social classes, and Rafael Karsten (1879–1956) focused on religion. Rudolf Holsti (1881–1945) dealt with warfare and state formation, and Ragnar Numelin (1890–1972) studied migration and diplomacy.[90] Of these scholars, Hirn is of particular interest to the topic of this chapter because his magnum opus, *The Origins of Art*, combines Adam Smith's theories of sympathy and the impartial spectator with Westermarckian evolutionism.[91]

Encouraged and guided by Westermarck, many of these disciples also conducted extensive, years-long ethnographic fieldwork in the 1910s and 1920s. Landtman worked among Kiwai Papuans of New Guinea, Karsten among the Indian tribes of Western Amazonia and Gran Chaco lowlands in South America and Hilma Granqvist (1890–1972) devoted herself to a methodologically pioneering study of a single Palestinian village.[92]

The Westermarckian school dominated Finnish social sciences for half a century from the 1890s to the 1940s, but after the Second World War Finnish sociology was reshaped along American lines with no trace of Westermarck's existence. Internationally, we can only guess in which direction some branches of sociology would have developed if Westermarck's evolutionary sociology had generated theoretical and empirical successors to continue his legacy to the present day.

Notes

1. J. P. Roos, 'Emile Durkheim versus Edward Westermarck: An Uneven Match' in Heinz-Jurgen Niedenzu and Tamás Meleghy (eds), *The New Evolutionary Social Science: Human Nature, Social Behavior, and Social Change* (Boulder, CO: Paradigm Publishers, 2008), p. 135.
2. Edward Westermarck, *The History of Human Marriage* (London: Macmillan, 1891); *The Origin and Development of the Moral Ideas*, 2 vols (London: Macmillan, 1906–8). *The History of Human Marriage* was published in 1921 as a fully updated edition, *The History of Human Marriage*, 3 vols (London: Macmillan).
3. Christopher Husbands, *Sociology at the London School of Economics and Political Science, 1904–2015* (London: Palgrave Macmillan, 2019), pp. xvi, 18.
4. Edward Westermarck, *Memories of My Life* (New York: Macaulay Company, 1929), pp. 247–8.
5. Rolf Lagerborg, 'The Essence of Morals: Fifty Years (1895–1945) of Rivalry between French and English Sociology', *Transactions of the Westermarck Society* 2 (1953), p. 17.
6. Knut Pipping, 'Who Reads Westermarck Today?', *The British Journal of Sociology* 35 (1984), p. 317.
7. For exceptions, see Otto Pipatti, *Morality Made Visible: Edward Westermarck's Moral and Social Theory* (London: Routledge, 2019); Otto Pipatti, *The Origins of Human Social Nature: Westermarckian Sociology and Social Anthropology* (London: Palgrave Macmillan, in press); Salla Tuomivaara, *Animals in the Sociologies of Westermarck and Durkheim* (Cham: Palgrave Macmillan, 2019); Stephen Sanderson, 'Edward Westermarck: The First Sociobiologist' in Rosemary Hopcroft (ed.), *Oxford Handbook of Evolution, Biology, and Society* (Oxford: Oxford University Press, 2018), pp. 63–86.
8. See, for example, Arthur P. Wolf and William Durham (eds), *Inbreeding, Incest, and the Incest Taboo: The State of Knowledge at the Turn of the Century* (Stanford, CA: Stanford University Press, 2004).
9. Georg Henrik von Wright, 'The Origin and Development of Westermarck's Moral Philosophy' in Timothy Stroup (ed.), *Edward Westermarck: Essays on His Life and Works* (Helsinki: Societas Philosophica Fennica, 1982), p. 48. See also Knud Haakonssen and Donald Winch, 'The Legacy of Adam Smith' in Knud Haakonssen (ed.), *The Cambridge Companion to Adam Smith* (Cambridge: Cambridge University Press, 2006), p. 382.
10. Westermarck, *Memories*, p. 232.
11. Edward Westermarck, *Ethical Relativity* (London: Paul Kegan, 1932).

12. Westermarck, *Moral Ideas*, pp. 327–8.
13. Westermarck, *Ethical Relativity*, pp. 71, 117–18.
14. Edward Westermarck, 'Lectures on Adam Smith', in Otto Pipatti, 'Edward Westermarck's Lectures on Adam Smith', *Econ Journal Watch* 20 (2023), p. 157.
15. Husbands, *Sociology*, pp. 12, 22.
16. David Shankland, 'Edward Westermarck, a Master Ethnographer, and his Monograph *Ritual and Belief in Morocco*' in Frederico Delgado Rosa and Han Vermeulen (eds), *Other Argonauts: Ethnographers before Malinowski, 1870–1922* (New York: Berghahn, 2022); Pipatti, *Origins of Human Social Nature*, ch. 7.
17. Edward Westermarck, *Marriage Ceremonies in Morocco* (London: Macmillan, 1914); *Ritual and Belief in Morocco*, 2 vols (London: Macmillan, 1926).
18. Niina Timosaari, *Edvard Westermarck: totuuden etsijä* [A Seeker of Truth] (Helsinki: Gaudeamus, 2017).
19. Olli Lagerspetz and Kirsti Suolinna, *Edward Westermarck: Intellectual Networks, Philosophy and Social Anthropology* (Helsinki: The Finnish Society of Science and Letters, 2014), ch. 2.
20. Westermarck, 'Sociology as a University Study' in *Inauguration of the Martin White Professorships of Sociology* (London: Murray, 1908), p. 27.
21. Westermarck, 'On the Relation between Sociology and Ethics' in *Sociological Papers Vol. II* (London: Macmillan, 1906), p. 192.
22. H. A. Lake Barnett, 'Notebook: Social institutions – Professor Westermarck, Summer Term 1911' (British Library of Political and Economic Science: Small LSE deposits/135/4: Notes on LSE Lectures by Mrs H A Lake Barnett), p. 1. Ragnar Numelin, 'Prof. E. A. Westermarcks föreläsningar i Sociologi' [Lectures on sociology] (Åbo Akademi University Library: Ragnar Numelin Collection, Box 44, 1911–1912), p. 2.
23. Westermarck, 'Sociology as a University Study', pp. 24–5. Social anthropology was for Westermarck 'only a branch of sociology' which studies 'the cultures of non-European peoples and particularly of those who have no written history' (Westermarck, 'Methods in Social Anthropology', *The Journal of the Royal Anthropological Institute of Great Britain and Ireland* 66 (1936), p. 226). Westermarck did not consider his works on marriage and morality as anthropological studies, but instead used anthropological data as a foundation for his theories.
24. Edward Westermarck, *Ritual and Belief*, pp. 16–23, 32–4 and passim; *Christianity and Morals* (London: Paul Kegan, 1939), pp. 1–6.

25. See Pipatti, *Morality Made Visible*, pp. 22–36.
26. Westermarck, *Memories*, p. 30. The details of Westermarck's interpretation of Hume and Smith are revealed in his lectures on the philosophy of British Enlightenment. These lectures are in Swedish and were delivered in 1913–14 at the University of Helsinki. His lectures on Hume consist of forty typewritten pages and cover Hume's epistemology, philosophy of religion and moral philosophy. The first part of Westermarck's 24-page lecture manuscript of Smith focuses on his life and works and the rest on *The Theory of Moral Sentiments* (Pipatti, 'Edward Westermarck's Lectures on Adam Smith'). For descriptions of Westermarck's lectures on Hume's and Smith's moral philosophy, see Timothy Stroup, *Westermarck's Ethics* (Åbo: Åbo Akademi, 1982), pp. 134–46 and Pipatti, *Morality Made Visible*, chs 7 and 8. Also Westermarck's lectures on Shaftesbury and Hutcheson have survived, as well as his lecture on the Scottish school of common sense. The way Westermarck's lectures are constructed says a lot about his approach to the history of British moral philosophy. Westermarck read the works of Shaftesbury, Hutcheson, Butler, Hume and Smith, seeking empirical claims and hypotheses on moral psychology and behaviour which could be exposed to critical examination and further development.
27. Edward Westermarck, 'Normative and Psychological Ethics' in Leila Haaparanta and Ilkka Niiniluoto (eds), *Analytic Philosophy in Finland* (Amsterdam: Rodopi, 2003), pp. 43–7.
28. Westermarck, *Memories*, p. 218.
29. Westermarck, 'Hume' (Åbo Akademi University Library: Westermarck Collection Box 78, Lectures, 1913), p. 74.
30. Westermarck, 'On the Relation between Sociology and Ethics', p. 192.
31. See Pipatti, *Morality Made Visible*, ch. 6.
32. Westermarck, Westermarck, 'Lectures on Adam Smith', p. 156.
33. Adam Smith, *The Theory of Moral Sentiments* (Indianapolis, IN: Liberty Fund, 1982), pp. 77–8 (henceforth TMS).
34. Westermarck, 'Upplysningstidevarvets filosofi' ['Philosophy of the Enlightenment'] (Åbo Akademi University Library: Westermarck Collection Box 79, Lectures, 1931), p. 193.
35. Westermarck, 'Remarks on the Predicates of Moral Judgments', *Mind* 9 (1900), p. 185.
36. Westermarck, *Moral Ideas*, vol. 1, p. 94.
37. Ibid. pp. 41, 93–5. For Westermarck's evolutionism in the light of modern gene-centred view of evolution, see Pipatti, *Morality Made Visible*, pp. 16–17, 143–5.

38. Westermarck, *Ethical Relativity*, p. 71. For Smith's analysis of gratitude and resentment as retributive emotions, see Pipatti, *Morality Made Visible*, pp. 129–31.
39. TMS pp. 67–8.
40. Westermarck, 'Hume', p. 83.
41. Westermarck, *Ethical Relativity*, p. 114. See also Westermarck, *Moral Ideas*, vol. 1, p. 4.
42. Westermarck, *Ethical Relativity*, p. 62.
43. Westermarck, *Moral Ideas*, vol. 1, p. 131.
44. Ibid. p. 92.
45. Westermarck, *Moral Ideas*, vol. 1, p. 101; Westermarck, 'Hume', pp. 76–7.
46. Westermarck, *Ethical Relativity*, p. 90; emphasis added.
47. Westermarck, *Moral Ideas*, pp. 103–4.
48. Frans de Waal, *Primates and Philosophers: How Morality Evolved* (Princeton: Princeton University Press, 2006), p. 20.
49. Westermarck, 'Lectures on Adam Smith', p. 156. Westermarck refers to Smith's impartial spectator in *Moral Ideas*, vol. 1, p. 43 and *Ethical Relativity*, p. 70. There is also a clear normative dimension to Westermarck's ethics. In the *Moral Ideas*, he postulates a kind of an ideal observer position, which he refers to as a 'scrupulous judge', 'conscientious and intelligent judge' and 'scrutinising and enlightened judge'. Westermarck makes proposals for legal reforms from such a position. Niina Timosaari, 'Moralrebellen Edvard Westermarck' ['Westermarck as a Moral Rebel'] in Otto Pipatti and Petteri Pietikäinen (eds), *Moral, evolution och samhälle: Edvard Westermarck och hans närmaste krets* [Morality, Evolution, and Society: Edward Westermarck and His Circle] (Helsinki and Stockholm: Svenska litteratursällskapet i Finland & Appell Förlag, 2021), pp. 132, 140.
50. Westermarck, *Moral Ideas*, vol. 1, p. 107.
51. Arthur P. Wolf, 'Edward Westermarck and the Meaning of "Moral"' in Walter Sinnott-Armstrong (ed.), *Moral Psychology, Vol. 1: The Evolution of Morality: Adaptations and Innateness* (Cambridge, MA: MIT Press, 2008), p. 193.
52. Westermarck, *Ethical Relativity*, p. 93. See also *Moral Ideas*, vol. 1, p. 104.
53. Westermarck, *Moral Ideas*, vol. 1, pp. 104–5.
54. Ibid. pp. 104–5.
55. Westermarck, *Ethical Relativity*, pp. 93; emphasis added.

56. Westermarck, *Moral Ideas*, vol. 1, p. 109.
57. See Pipatti, *Morality Made Visible*, pp. 46–7, 110–11, 126–8.
58. Westermarck, 'Hume', p. 81; Westermarck, 'Lectures on Adam Smith', pp. 152–3, 157.
59. Westermarck, *Ethical Relativity*, p. 106.
60. Westermarck, *Moral Ideas*, vol. 1, p. 114.
61. Westermarck, *The Future of Marriage in Western Civilisation* (New York: Macmillan, 1936), p. 239.
62. Westermarck, *Moral Ideas*, vol. 1, p. 116.
63. Westermarck, *Ethical Relativity*, p. 107.
64. Westermarck, *Moral Ideas*, vol. 1, p. 118.
65. Westermarck, *Ethical Relativity*, p. 50; see also *Moral Ideas*, vol. 1, p. 9.
66. Westermarck, *Moral Ideas*, vol. 1, p. 117.
67. Lake Barnett, 'Social institutions', p. 4; David Mitrany, 'Social institutions – Westermarck' (British Library of Political and Economic Science: Mitrany/1: Lecture Notes BSc 1912-ff., 1916), p. 6.
68. Westermarck, *Moral Ideas*, vol. 2, p. 197.
69. Westermarck, *Moral Ideas*, vol. 1, pp. 117–18.
70. Westermarck, *Ur sedernas historia. Föredrag hållna i Åbo hösten 1911* [On the History of Customs: Lectures Delivered in Åbo in Autumn 1911] (Helsinki: Söderström, 1912), p. 61.
71. See Pipatti, *Morality Made Visible*, pp. 72–82.
72. Westermarck, *Moral Ideas*, vol. 1, p. 524.
73. Westermarck, *Ur sedernas historia*, pp. 61–2.
74. Westermarck, *History of Human Marriage*, vol. 2, p. 198; *Ethical Relativity*, p. 249.
75. Westermarck, *Moral Ideas*, vol. 2, pp. 324–6, 332, 346, 351–2, 483–4, 576–7, 580.
76. Westermarck, *History of Human Marriage*, vol. 1, pp. 69–70.
77. Westermarck, *Moral Ideas*, vol. 1, p. 159.
78. Ibid. p. 4.
79. Westermarck, 'Hume', pp. 75–6.
80. Timothy Stroup, 'In Defense of Westermarck', *Journal of the History of Philosophy* 19 (1981), p. 226. For Westermarck's account of objectification, see *Moral Ideas*, vol. 1, pp. 4, 8; *Ethical Relativity*, pp. 49–51, 114–15. For commentaries, see Stroup, *Westermarck's Ethics*, pp. 144–5, 179–80, 221–2; Pipatti, *Morality Made Visible*, pp. 56–8, 107–9.
81. David Hume, *A Treatise of Human Nature* (Oxford: Clarendon Press, 1978), p. 167.

82. David Hume, *Enquiries concerning Human Understanding and Concerning the Principles of Morals* (Oxford: Clarendon Press, 1978), p. 294.
83. Hume, *Treatise*, p. 46.
84. Westermarck, *Moral Ideas*, vol. 1, p. 19.
85. Westermarck, *Moral Ideas*, vol. 2, p. 745.
86. Westermarck, *Christianity and Morals*, p. 214.
87. Ashley Montagu, 'Recollections of an Old Student in Young Age' in Stroup, *Edward Westermarck: Essays on His Life and Works*, pp. 63–70; Geoffrey May, 'Obituary Notice. Edward Alexander Westermarck (1862–1939)', *American Sociological Review* 5 (1940), pp. 122–5.
88. Bronislaw Malinowski, 'Foreword' in Ashley Montagu, *Coming into Being among the Australian Aborigines* (London: Routledge, 1937), pp. xix–xxxv. See also Bronislaw Malinowski, 'Anthropology of the Westernmost Orient. Ritual and Belief in Morocco. By Edward Westermarck. In 2 vols', *Nature* 120 (1927), pp. 867–8.
89. David Shankland, 'Westermarck, Moral Behaviour and Ethical Relativity' in Nigel Rapport and Huon Wardle (eds), *An Anthropology of the Enlightenment: Moral Social Relations Then and Today* (London: Bloomsbury Academic, 2018), p. 70. For Westermarck's influence on Malinowski, see Pipatti, *Origins of Human Social Nature*, ch. 9.
90. Yrjö Hirn, *The Origins of Art: A Psychological and Sociological Inquiry* (London: Macmillan, 1900); Gunnar Landtman, *The Origin of the Inequality of the Social Classes* (London: Paul Kegan, 1927); Rafael Karsten, *The Civilization of the South American Indians, with Special Reference to Magic and Religion* (London: Paul Kegan, 1926); Rafael Karsten, *The Origins of Religion* (London: Paul Kegan, 1935); Rudolf Holsti, *The Relation of War to the Origin of the State* (Helsinki: Finnish Academy of Science and Letters, 1913); Ragnar Numelin, *The Wandering Spirit: A Study of Human Migration* (London: Macmillan, 1937); Ragnar Numelin, *The Beginnings of Diplomacy: A Sociological Study of Intertribal and International Relations* (Oxford: Oxford University Press, 1950).
91. Pipatti, *Origins of Human Social Nature*, ch. 4.
92. Gunnar Landtman, *The Kiwai Papuans of British New Guinea: A Nature-Born Instance of Rousseau's Ideal Community* (London: Macmillan, 1927); Rafael Karsten, *Indian Tribes of the Argentine and Bolivian Chaco* (Helsinki: Societas Scientiarum Fennica, 1932); Rafael Karsten, *The Head-Hunters of Western Amazonas: The Life and Culture of the Jibaro Indians of Eastern Ecuador and Peru*

(Helsinki: Societas Scientiarum Fennica, 1935); Hilma Granqvist, *Marriage Conditions in a Palestinian Village*, 2 vols (Helsinki: Societas Scientiarum Fennica, 1931–5). For commentaries, see David Lawrence, *Gunnar Landtman in Papua: 1910 to 1912* (Canberra: The Australian National University Press, 2010); Christer Lindberg, 'It Takes More Than Fieldwork to Become a Culture Hero of Anthropology: The Story of Rafael Karsten', *Anthropos* 90 (1995), pp. 525–31; Christer Lindberg, 'Anthropology on the Periphery: The Early Schools of Nordic Anthropology' in Henrika Kuklick (ed.), *New History of Anthropology* (Malden, MA: Blackwell Publishing, 2008), pp. 161–72; Kirsti Suolinna, 'Hilma Granqvist: A Scholar of the Westermarck School in its Decline', *Acta Sociologica* 43 (2000), pp. 317–23; Pipatti, *Origins of Human Social Nature*, ch. 8.

12

In Praise of Adam Smith, or, The Workings of Commercial Sociability

John A. Hall

The presence of an accepted canon of thought carries such weight that it deserves periodic re-evaluation. This chapter urges sociologists to consider the state of sociological theory – that is, the basic guiding assumptions that we need for our research and, in consequence, those that we must teach our students. For there has been something of a canon of sociological theory. The most striking expression of this situation has been Anthony Giddens's *Capitalism and Modern Social Theory*, the clearest analysis of the thought of 'the holy trinity' of Marx, Durkheim and Weber.[1] Of course, that book never had the field all to itself. Talcott Parsons had sought to include Pareto and Alfred Marshall whilst omitting Marx.[2] Raymond Aron's brilliant volumes added Montesquieu, Comte and Tocqueville, whilst omitting Marshall.[3] Jeffrey Alexander's huge treatise sought to add Parsons to Giddens's trinity, whilst omitting the other thinkers mentioned.[4] It is noticeable that the sales of Aron and Giddens outstripped those of Parsons and Alexander – which is not to say, for instance, that much attention was given to Aron's discussions of Montesquieu, Comte and Pareto.

Looking at the matter from a different angle shows something else about canonical matters. The *Times Higher Educational Supplement*'s top fifty universities in the United States and top twenty-eight universities in Canada all teach sociological theory, at undergraduate and usually at graduate levels. It has been possible to gain a clear view of what is taught.[5] Cursory analysis of the syllabi in question makes it abundantly clear the canon has been extended – or perhaps destroyed – in a wholly welcome if slightly bewildering manner. Though the famous trinity is always present, syllabi now include W. E. B. Du Bois; Continental philosopher-sociologists such as Foucault, Habermas and Agamben; and various figures, from the past as well as from the present, bringing gender considerations to the fore.

The purpose of this chapter is not to add further modern names but rather to go in the other direction, to suggest including in our teaching and research a figure from an earlier period. Systematic study of the syllabi mentioned make it clear that Adam Smith has no salience for sociologists.[6] Smith's most obviously sociological book (and the one that he loved the most), *The Theory of Moral Sentiments* (hereafter TMS), appears in a serious way (that is, students are asked to read at least a few of its pages) on only three of 141 syllabi.[7] *An Inquiry into the Nature and Causes of the Wealth of Nations* (hereafter WN) does better: twelve teachers ask their students to read pages they have selected, and a further eight ask for some of the pages taken from WN included in the reader on theory edited by Craig Calhoun and his colleagues to be read.[8,9] There are further mentions of him as a theorist, but these do not ask for anything by Smith to be read. This chapter can thus usefully be seen as a romantic but serious intervention, seeking to praise Smith: the contention is that the neglect of Smith is a terrible mistake as his ideas are essential for sociology.[10]

That last comment suggests an initial and obvious justification for the case to be made here. By and large, some of the main concepts of Marx, Durkheim and Weber – alienation, anomie and disenchantment – can usefully be seen as anti-capitalist in spirit, though they are of course much more than that. Accordingly, to write a book on *Capitalism and Modern Social Theory* without Smith is to imagine Hamlet without the prince. It seems very likely that the omission was and is caused by taking Smith to be some sort of pure economist, an ideologue of individualism and self-interest: some of the syllabi examined, for instance, mention him almost as a foe to be opposed.[11] It is worth engaging in a little sociology of such ignorance so as to understand this baneful state of affairs. The most important feature is surely the replacement of a more general political economy by separate social science disciplines, with Smith thereby being ensconced within economics. This is a category mistake: Smith is a key sociological figure, and we need to take him back – especially given the misunderstandings about his work so often made by economists.[12] The canon of sociological theory was decisively influenced by Parsons, and this despite an extant native tradition that was put largely to one side.[13] This had a great deal to do with the impact of the 1930s, to the New Deal and to the discovery of thinkers able to help understanding of the European crises of the twentieth century. But the canon was more fully formed a little later. It was heavily influenced by Marx's critique of political economy, in part because Marx was describing industrial rather than the commercial society, with a corresponding emphasis on production rather than consumption. Although Marx most often criticised minor figures in British political economy, he did know Smith rather well and was indebted to him at key points; but this mattered less to sociology than the moments at which he claims Smith to have been a naive supporter of a capitalist order.[14] Finally, there is a rather different factor at work. Far too little attention has been given to Scotland, as compared to France and Germany, in accounts of the Enlightenment. Perhaps the political stability in the former is less interesting than the revolutions present in the latter cases; perhaps too there is difficulty in coming to terms with the brilliant but uncomfortable scepticism of David Hume, the leading figure in the Scottish case.

It is easy and pleasurable to provide the necessary rectification, given the revolution in Smith scholarship resting on the 'Glasgow' critical edition of his works used here, together with the brilliant studies that have resulted.[15] But there is a problem here. Smith was a polymath, with original ideas on a wide range of topics from the origin of language to the philosophy of science, from the functions of art to the evolution of law and, of course, from human nature to political economy. Further, he admired system in intellectual matters and certainly provided it himself, creating a conceptual architecture – albeit one that was not fully completed – seamlessly binding these topics together. This system was always aware of opposing positions, and thereby filled at times with subtle ambivalences, and its intent was normative as well as descriptive.

This chapter deals with the problem created by such extraordinary range by extracting, as much as is possible, one element of his work from the larger system. Concentration is on Smith's political economy because it is of most obvious interest to sociology, although occasional comments are made about the larger system in which it is embedded – in part so its range can at least be indicated. The central contention can be specified immediately: Smith offers us the best available account both of the workings of capitalism and of the ills to which it can succumb, both placed within a liberal political theory. Highlighting is in order here: the contention is that Smith is the crucial interpreter of the character of the modern social formation in which more and more people live. Note, however, that no claim is being made that Smith should replace thinkers and theories on whom we have relied, as is made clear in the conclusion.

The Scottish Enlightenment

The fact that eighteenth-century Scotland was one of the greatest sites of the Enlightenment should be obvious immediately when we think of Smith and his close friend Hume, not altogether falsely seen as almost the creators of the theory of capitalism and that of empiricism, the core of modern epistemology. Both lived in an exceedingly interesting social world. The aristocracy of England and Lowland Scotland was far from traditional, in contrast to that of the Highlands and of the Continental aristocracies of their own time: it was an improving, commercial class.[16] Glasgow was an outstanding example of such early capitalism – that is, of a commercial revolution that preceded the industrial revolution, a point worth noting as Smith's example of a pin factory is often taken to be part of the later breakthrough made possible by the widespread use of fossil fuels.[17] The character of this world was at the forefront of attention because in 1745 the retainers of the Highlands clans had marched through Edinburgh in an attempt to restore the Stuart monarchy.[18] Both Hume and Smith regarded themselves as 'North Britons' wishing to participate in and to extend what they felt to be an emerging civil society. The world they inhabited and endorsed was polite and polished, free from civil war and indeed from great viciousness in the interstate arena.

Scotland's Calvinist background had encouraged high levels of literacy, seen particularly in the fact that Scotland had five universities compared to England's two. This played some part in creating quite fabulous intellectual ferment, in science as much as in the humanities. The genius of Hume lay in showing that our knowledge rests on habit and convention rather than on reason. We can only learn through sensation, Hume demonstrated conclusively, and this necessarily undermined every claim made by rationalist metaphysics about the world and our life within it. Sensationalism allows no proof, for instance, that the sun will come up tomorrow; we take for granted that it will and proceed to live accordingly. Hume's whole position was summed up with characteristic acerbity in *A Treatise of Human Nature*: 'Reason is, and ought only to be the slave of the passions, and can never pretend to any other office than to serve and obey them'.[19] That might suggest the world of Friedrich Nietzsche, but such a supposition would be far from the truth.[20] The passions at the heart of the naturalism of the Scottish Enlightenment were not the dark, dangerous and devious ones of the later naturalism of Nietzsche and his follower Sigmund Freud but altogether civil ones – we are, as it were, in the world of Jane Austen, who may in fact have been influenced by Smith.[21] For this was not in fact a world of uncertainty at all, despite the scepticism entailed in sensationalism: custom provided regularity and stability. Knowledge and social life were held more precisely to rest on the 'imagination', with sympathy as the key sentiment that linked humans to one another. It was on this basis that Hume and Smith sought to create a science of man, one to complement in the humanities Newton's achievement in natural science. Two particular points are worth noting about it. First, these thinkers had no time for the social contract theories of such Whig predecessors as John Locke: society had always been present; it was not the result of an act of will.[22] Second, the great admiration shown for Montesquieu was limited by an insistence that his views were not soundly based on a systematic understanding of human nature.[23]

Smith was born outside Edinburgh in 1723; he attended university in Glasgow from the age of fourteen. Six years of independent study followed, largely in Oxford, allowing him to suddenly gain reputation from 1748 as the result of public lectures in Edinburgh on rhetoric and on jurisprudence.[24] He was appointed Professor of Logic at Glasgow University in 1751, switching the next year to becoming Professor of Moral Philosophy. His first substantial public intervention in 1775–6 was a comment on the similarity between Bernard Mandeville's *Fable of the Bees* and Rousseau's second discourse on the origin of inequality.[25] Both thinkers saw misery in society, Smith noted, as neither had a sense of human sociability – though Rousseau insisted that pity was present in simple societies, arguing in consequence that commercial society was likely to cause unhappiness by removing the unitary and stable sense of self that had then existed. Smith made clear his disagreements, and his worries, about this position in 1759 in TMS. A more general point can be made here. Rousseau was suspicious of wealth at all times but attempted to control its evil effects when speaking about life in commercial society – rather than about the benefit of simpler societies. His prescriptions then drew on the tradition of civic virtue, of the simplicity and discipline he admired in Sparta. Smith had no time for that tradition. For one thing, classical Greece was based on slavery, which he abhorred at all times. For another, civil society, with commerce at its core, need not cause psychic distress nor diminish human welfare. His work can be seen as endorsing a world based on wealth rather than one focused on virtue.[26]

We possess students' notes on his lectures on jurisprudence given in 1762–3 and 1763–4.[27] Both rest on a developmental scheme, from hunters and foragers to the domestication of animals to agrarian conditions before the emergence of the commercial society that he sought to understand.[28] These lectures considered justice, seen as the foundation of civilised society, and 'police' – that is, policy concerning government, revenue and arms, held to vary according to the development stages identified in his conjectural history.[29] It seems that Smith had drafted a book on the state by this time, a part of which became Book III of WN. But his lectures on jurisprudence in 1763–4 show that he had discovered the importance of the division of labour before he left the university in 1764, and that led to his second great book. He then served as tutor to the son of the Duke of Buccleuch in the ensuing years, thereby allowing him to spend time in Paris where he came into contact with French economists, before devoting himself to the private study that resulted in WN. In the years that followed he revised his two major treatises and worked on two books: the one on the state, the other on the arts and the philosophy of science. These were not completed and the manuscripts were burnt according to his wishes just before he died in 1790. The essays on the histories of astronomy, ancient physics and ancient logic and metaphysics offered a philosophy of science that clearly mattered to him, as they were published as he wished soon after he died.[30]

The Sociology of Political Economy

Smith was a very forceful writer, and this description of the central tenets of his political economy pays particular attention to some of his own formulations – they are exceptionally striking, able immediately to remove misconceptions held about his views.

Commercial Sociability

Smith's very particular achievement was to develop a particular view of human nature on which a general theory of commerce is based.[31] This can be put differently: it is not a question of capitalism providing an economic mechanism for society, much more that we live in capitalist society. The logical steps in the argument are essentially simple, although extracting them in this way gives a false impression of Smith's work in one respect – namely, his constant concern with empirical evidence, demonstration and indeed proof.

The very first sentences of TMS warn us that Smith does not – as so many falsely believe – view human nature for a moment in terms of the maximising of self-interest:

> How selfish soever man may be supposed, there are evidently some principles in his nature, which interest him in the fortune of others, and render their happiness necessary to him, though he derives nothing from it except the pleasure of seeing it. Of this kind is pity or compassion, the emotion which we feel for the misery of others, when we either see it, or are made to conceive it in a very lively manner.[32]

The emphasis on pity immediately distinguishes Smith from Rousseau: this sentiment – better described in Smith's view as sympathy – exists and has power within advanced society.[33] Whilst it is certainly the case, as we shall see, that Smith has a far more favourable view of life within commercial society than does Rousseau, it would be a grave mistake to consider sympathy in moral terms, as something sweet and light. Smith's sympathy – and Rousseau's pity – is best seen as empathy, the ability of the imagination to understand all sorts of human passions. The difference between the two is simple. Rousseau feels that empathy declines in modern society: hypocrisy and vanity lead to a loss of fellow feeling. Smith stresses the opposite. Empathy is limited in simpler societies, as poverty and scarcity necessarily diminish this feeling; in contrast, commercial society increases empathy, allowing greater interest in the lives of one's fellows. And this is a good point at which to specify the character of TMS: it is one of the greatest treatises in the sociology of emotions, although we will see that it contains even more than this.[34]

We do not actually feel the pain of someone being tortured, Smith insisted in a famous example, but we are able to imagine how it feels – indeed, our mind naturally wants to engage in this feeling. From this simple opening a whole view of the world follows, in the most straightforward manner. I do not like seeing pain or any other form of behaviour that disturbs me. By an act of imagination, I realise that others equally shy away from any disturbance that I might cause – and so take care to act with consideration for them, because of the pleasures of what Smith terms 'mutual sympathy'. Life in this world is other-directed; we constantly think of others, as they think of us. 'We examine our persons limb by limb, and by placing ourselves before a looking-glass . . . endeavour, as much as possible, to view ourselves at the distance and with the eyes of other people'.[35] We learn to act as if before 'an impartial spectator' and thereby create rules that can guide us. This is accordingly not just a theory of our own behaviour but one of morality in society. We do not just follow the whims of the crowd but act with principles in mind. One is reminded both of Durkheim's 'conscience collective' and of Freud's notion of the superego.[36]

This is the world of 'propriety', the title of the first part of TMS. Interestingly, it is the absolute opposite of the view proposed by David Riesman and his colleagues in *The Lonely Crowd*.[37] The thesis of that book by and large saw a decline in American character as inner-directed puritan values were being replaced by a flaccid other-directed mentality. Smith admires what Riesman loathed. It is not irrelevant to note that the language employed by Smith and his friends and colleagues certainly derided passionate conviction, disliking enthusiasm of all sorts. One is reminded of the work of Erving Goffman, perhaps above all that on the ways in which something like mutual sympathy is at work when maintaining interaction.[38]

Hume claimed – in a letter to Smith of 28 July 1759 – that there was a hinge to his whole system.[39] Wishing to do well in the eyes of others means that riches are taken more seriously than poverty; that, in other words, our desire to emulate success is central to most human behaviour. Smith insists that the stomach of a rich man can hold no more than that of someone who is poor and goes on to say that the rich sometimes sleep worse in their palaces than the poor in their cottages.

> From whence, then, arises that emulation which runs through all the different ranks of men, and what are the advantages which we propose by that great purpose of human life which we call bettering our condition? To be observed, to be attended to, to be taken notice of with sympathy, complacency and approbation, are all the advantages which we can propose to derive from it. It is the vanity, not the ease, or the pleasure, which interests us. But vanity is always founded upon the belief of our being the object of attention and approbation. The rich man glories in his riches, because he feels that they naturally draw upon him the attention of the world . . .[40]

What we have here is Smith's account of the origin of rank or, to put it in contemporary terms, of social class. It is as well to underline what is being said here. Bluntly, the most important sentiment that drives human beings is that of the desire to be loved; in Smith's words, 'the chief part of human happiness arises from the consciousness of being beloved'.[41] Making money is but a means to this end.[42] This is a very particular world, not just of the permanent trait of sociability but of its expression through commerce, that is commercial sociability, a world of competitive consumption. For many years it was believed that there was an 'Adam Smith problem'; that is, the apparent contradiction between the emphasis on sympathy in TMS contrasted so much with the role given to self-interest in WN that it seemed to suggest that Smith had changed his mind.[43] But Smith was an exceptionally sophisticated thinker, always aware of the purpose of his work and able to offer a system of thought in which the various parts fitted smoothly together. There is no 'Adam Smith problem'.[44]

It is important not to misrepresent Smith at this point. He was not naive. People could act in vicious as well as in benign ways. Commercial sociability exists only in a world in which basic justice is present, one in which the protection of property is assured.[45] Nonetheless, there is something to be said for the view that Smith is too much an eighteenth-century thinker taking deference for granted when he discusses rank. He is aware that envy is an alternative to emulation, but he dismisses it.

> But we never have occasion to makes this opposition to our sympathy with joy. If there is any envy in the case, we never feel the least propensity towards it . . . we are always ashamed of our own envy, we often pretend, and sometimes really wish to sympathize with the joy of others, when by that disagreeable sentiment we are disqualified from doing so. We are glad, we say, on account of our neighbour's good fortune, when in our hearts, perhaps, we are really sorry. We often feel a sympathy with sorrow when we would wish to be rid of it . . .[46]

Nietzsche and Freud surely saw things differently, as suggested, most notably in Freud's account of the pleasure to be gained by seeing someone have an accident that one had oneself avoided.[47]

To gain the most complete sense of what Smith is arguing it is worth seeing what follows from this stress on emulation. Smith rarely goes against David Hume but does so in this matter. Hume stressed the utility of any contrivance, noting the pleasure that can be gained from seeing how well it serves its purpose. Smith will have none of it. He excoriates those who sew larger pockets into their clothes so that they can fill them with ever great quantities of trinkets and baubles.[48] But he goes much further:

> in the languor of disease and the weariness of old age, the pleasures of the vain and empty distinctions of greatness disappear . . . Power and riches appear then to be, what they are, enormous and operose machines contrived to produce a few trifling conveniences to the body, consisting of springs, the most nice and delicate, which must be kept in order with the most anxious attention, and which in spite of all our care are ready every moment to burst into pieces, and to crush in their ruins their unfortunate possessor. They are immense fabrics, which it requires the labour of a life to raise, which threaten every moment to overwhelm the person that dwells in them, and which, while they stand, though they may save him from some smaller inconveniences, can protect him from none of the severer inclemencies of the season. They keep off the summer shower, not the winter storm, but leave him always as much, and sometimes more exposed than before, to anxiety, to fear, and to sorrow; to diseases, to danger, and to death.[49]

Anyone imagining Smith to be some sort of straightforward economist, concerned only with rationally maximising utilities, must be severely jolted by reading this passage. What this passage implies is – to use a metaphor drawn from later technology – an ascending escalator, one without end, where people are aware of each other, constantly trying to catch up with those above them, running and running until their death. The poor do not attack the rich because they imagine that they might themselves yet rise. That had been Rousseau's point in his second discourse: always imagining the grass to be greener on the other side of the fence, always longing for what one can see but does not possess, will cause psychic distress as one's identity will no longer be secure. The French moralist was always in Smith's mind, and it is no accident that Smith noted that 'man is an anxious animal'.[50] Smith nonetheless accepts what Rousseau loathes, in effect turning the French moralist on his head. Social cohesion comes accidentally, without intention or planning: we run and run until we die, never asking the reason why. This is the central, as it were foundational, explanation that Smith offers for the workings of capitalism. The picture is scarcely morally admirable, as we will see Smith stress towards the end of his life, but it provided sufficient cement to hold society together.

Natural Liberty and its Enemies

The passage immediately above is followed by Smith claiming that: 'it is well that nature imposes upon us in this manner. It is this deception which rouses and keeps in continual motion the industry of mankind'.[51] This is the link or bridge to WN, where Smith expands on this admiration for commercial society, moving from the functions of commerce to something altogether more basic. The start of the book claims that commercial society can provide better accommodation for an industrious labourer than was available to many an African king.[52] This was a crucial statement: a society was to be judged by its ability to provide plenty for all. The fact that a decent living standard was desirable in and of itself was made particularly clearly in his comments on the horrors of the stationary state in China.[53] But the book adds something else to what has already been said about the workings of capitalism. It offers a smaller, more technical account of the conditions that allow for the creation of universal opulence and of those that may destroy it. Differently put, we are offered an account of wealth on which competitive emulation is based.

The first two books of WN sought to explain the nature of the natural liberty that creates universal opulence. The basic contours of his argument here are well known. Smith's famous example was a pin factory: when the task of manufacturing pins was broken down into its component steps and each step was assigned to a different worker, pin manufacturing became much more effective: a solitary worker might produce only one pin a day, but in a team his share in a team of ten might well amount to 4,800. Smith was absolutely correct; prosperity does indeed rest on increasing productivity. The details of the explanation stress three things. First, Smith shows great sympathy for labour, seeing it as the fundamental source of value – although, unlike Marx, he drew a distinction between this and market price.[54] Crucially, the division of labour causes improvement because of the expertise, dexterity and specialisation of workers; that is, from high levels of human capital. He makes clear in this connection that the

> difference of talents in different men is, in reality, much less than we are aware of; and the very different genius which appears to distinguish men of different professions, when grown up to maturity, is not upon many occasions so much the cause, as the effect of the division

of labour. The difference ... between a philosopher and a common street porter, for example, seems to arise not so much from nature, as from habit, custom, and education.⁵⁵

In this world it will not be necessary for humans to suck up to those above them.⁵⁶ All sorts of controls over labour will be removed, allowing contract to replace dependence. Second, the division of labour increases in tandem with the size of the market. Here we have the seeds of the theory of comparative advantage. It makes no sense for England to produce wine as well as wool; far better to specialise in the latter, so as to send it to Portugal in order to receive their wine in return. Finally, self-interest drives the world of exchange. 'It is not from the benevolence of the butcher, the brewer, or the baker, that we expect our dinner, but from their regard to their own interest. We address ourselves, not to their humanity, but to their self-love ...'⁵⁷ It is scarcely necessary to say that this is not a claim about the fundamental need of human beings, merely a claim about the 'higgling and bargaining' of the marketplace.

Misconceptions would abound were we to leave matters here. In what way is it reasonable to imagine that we are all part of the same society – that, to put matters differently, we all have a step on the societal escalator? The formal and abstract model of natural liberty that Smith presents at the start of WN clearly identifies factors on which the system depends, noting as well the dangers that may beset it. He holds that social stratification rests on labour, landlords and merchants, with the relations between them establishing price. His sympathy for labour, noted above but often ignored by commentators, is clearly expressed: high wages are vital, as they increase skill levels and occasion population growth. But labour is threatened by merchants, keener 'to lower [wages] than to raise them' and likely to be able to do so because their smaller number allows them to combine effectively.⁵⁸ Smith goes much further. 'People of the same trade seldom meet together, even for merriment and diversion, but [when they do] the conversation ends in a conspiracy against the publick, or in some contrivance to raise prices' – another statement sure to remove the misconception that Smith was some sort of naive supporter of every form of unregulated self-interest.⁵⁹ He stresses in this regard that 'the rate of profit does not, like rent and wages, rise with prosperity, and fall with the declension of society. On the contrary, it is naturally low in rich, and high in poor countries, and it is always highest in countries which are going fastest to ruin'.⁶⁰ Landlords tend to be too lazy to think carefully about the state of the political economy, whilst workers lack time to work out their best interests. The situation of merchants is wholly different.

> The interest of the dealers, however, in any particular branch of trade or manufactures, is always in some respects different from, and even in opposition to that of the publick. To widen the market and to narrow the competition, is always the interest of the dealers. To widen the market may frequently be agreeable enough to the interest of the public; but to narrow the competition must always be against it, and can serve only to enable the dealers, by raising their profits above what they naturally would be, to levy, for their own benefit, an absurd tax upon their fellow citizens. The proposal of any new law or regulation of commerce which comes from this order, ought always to be listened to with great precaution, and ought never to be adopted till after having been long and carefully examined, not only with the most scrupulous, but with the most suspicious attention.⁶¹

All sorts of restraints need to be removed in order for a system of 'natural liberty' to work properly, notably apprenticeship rules that favour merchants far more than workers.

It is as well to pause for a moment. Smith has provided us with a theory that faces both ways. On the one hand, the system of natural liberty can provide wealth, with the societal escalator thereby creating social cohesion; on the other hand, this mechanism is constantly threatened by merchants, always keen to look after themselves in a way that hurts their fellow citizens, with the risk that follows of sending society into ruin. The implication that follows is obvious. Merchants must be treated with suspicion, even made to behave decently. Government is needed.

Commerce and Liberty

Smith's account of the 'causes' – that is, the origins – of commercial society in Book III of WN gives us vital clues about his work as a whole. For one thing, it explains the importance of commerce as an agent of social change. For another, it allows us to understand his values; that is, the key political preference behind his whole system.

Smith begins by noting what he calls the natural order of things: growth in agrarian conditions is needed in order to support urban life. There are many reasons for this, above all the fact that it is dangerous and so unattractive to trade at great distances given obvious insecurities. The second step in the argument reveals a good deal about Smith's political views. Feudal Europe was the least likely of all agrarian regimes to produce any sort of progress. Smith here offers a powerful Enlightenment view of the Dark Ages. Feudal lords are only interested in fighting and so have no interest in improvement – indeed they love to domineer and so prefer slaves even to serfs. Furthermore, in this world tenants lacked basic security so they too did not encourage economic development. Smith holds the way in which land descends only to eldest sons to be ridiculous: '[great estates] are founded upon the most absurd of all suppositions, the supposition that every successive generation of men have not an equal right to the earth, and all that it possesses'.[62] This is an appropriate moment to begin to make it clear that Smith favoured policies that would prevent inequality becoming excessive.[63] He was well aware that the highest measure of opulence would result when stock was widespread. The natural tendency of those possessing a great deal to waste it over time helped in this regard. But he was insistent, as we shall see, that government had a major role in attacking inequality, not least through taxation. Again, the hand of government was not to be hidden.

Smith then explains how commercial society in fact came to the fore, wholly against the natural order identified. The key of the explanation lies in the surprising rise of cities and towns during this miserable feudal period. Three sets of actors were involved. Kings were weak, endlessly bullied by their overmighty subjects – and thereby unable to enforce the rule of law. Townsmen were equally at the mercy of the feudal lords. From this followed a political bargain:

> The burghers naturally hated and feared the lords. The king hated and feared them too; but though perhaps he might despise, he had no reason either to hate or fear the burghers. Mutual interest, therefore, disposed them to support the king, and the king to support them against the lords. They were the enemies of his enemies, and it was his interest to render them as secure and independent on those enemies as he could.[64]

The granting of charters by the king made towns and cities islands in a feudal sea, allowing them to become reliable centres of production. Everything then changed. In feudal circumstances there was no option for the great lords but to spend their surplus on retainers, by – literally – feeding and supporting these hired hands. For as soon as the great landlords could buy the luxuries produced by the newly autonomous cities they did so:

> All for ourselves, and nothing for other people, seems, in every age of the world, to have been the vile maxim of the masters of mankind. As soon, therefore, as they could find a method of consuming the whole value of their rents themselves, they had no disposition to share them with any other persons. For a pair of diamond buckles perhaps or for something as frivolous and useless, they exchanged the maintenance, or what is the same thing, the price of the maintenance of a thousand men for a year, and with it the whole weight and authority which it could give them.[65]

Kings had been unable to establish the rule of law given their weakness in the face of their powerful barons. The loss of lordly power meant that they were at last able to do so. This mattered enormously. Smith had noted that disorder encouraged people to bury their stock to preserve it from predation.[66] Order allowed stock to be used and universal opulence established.

Reflection on several points within this account deserve highlighting. First, this account should not be taken to mean that Smith somehow favours commerce over agriculture. To the contrary, the natural emergence of cities follows the improvement of agriculture – and we will note below further comments about the room for improvement in the countryside.[67] Second, we can see here that Smith is most certainly not an economic determinist; rather, his argument centres on the interaction between politics and economics. The parcellisation of sovereignty after the Fall of Rome (a political condition) allows autonomous cities to produce luxuries (an economic consideration) and this thereby undermines the power of the lords (a political variable) allowing the order that then serves as the background condition to universal opulence (the economic result).[68] Third, the emergence of commercial society was not planned in any way:

> A revolution of the greatest importance to the publick happiness, was in this manner brought about by two different orders of people, who

had not the least intention to serve the public. To gratify the most childish vanity was the sole motive of the great proprietors. The merchants and artificers, much less ridiculous, acted merely from a view to their own interest ... Neither of them had either knowledge or foresight of that great revolution which the folly of the one, and the industry of the other, was gradually bringing about.[69]

There could be no clearer statement of the unintended consequences of human action.

But there is something of the greatest importance that needs to be highlighted. Commerce of course brings wealth, but just as importantly it brings order by undermining political power. But it is not just order. His loathing of the brutish feudal aristocracy makes something else clear. His greatest allegiance was to a softer, more liberal world. Capitalism was desirable most of all as an instrument to that end. Smith's equation is 'commerce and liberty'. This is the thesis of *'le doux commerce'*: the view that, in the words of his friend Samuel Johnson, 'a man is never so innocently employed as when he is making money'. This is a political argument in favour of capitalism, a position to which our attention was drawn by Albert Hirschman.[70] But it must be stressed that this is not a nineteenth-century position calling, for instance, for equal voting rights. It is a proto-liberal position, stressing the benefits of decent, softer politics.

Legislators

Let us turn from the history of government to the functions Smith assigns it in Book V of WN. The provision of defence for the country and the protection of private property from the arbitrary depredations of power are absolutely basic. But much more is involved. He insisted that the state should provide public works and infrastructure necessary for society. Crucially, basic education should be generally available because both economy and society would benefit from a well-trained population. There was yet another function Smith saw for the state. He disliked monopolies, including those of the Anglican and the Presbyterian establishments, and proposed instead controlling religious extremism by means of pluralism – that is, by allowing the proliferation of radical, enthusiastic and intolerant sects so as to ensure that none could dominate society as a whole. It would be a mistake to leave these matters without noting that Smith had very particular views about the funding of these services. Local services were best provided at the locality, and as many services as possible should be funded from fees rather than from central revenues. He felt this to be true of much of education, noting that the Scottish system thrived on subscriptions rather than central revenue – teachers had to perform in order to make their living. Smith took great interest in fiscal sociology. He offered a detailed and careful analysis of where state revenues came from, together with interesting principles laid down on which taxation should be based. Smith favoured progressive tax regimes that recognised the limited incomes of the poor and avoided taxes on necessities like food and clothing, whilst calling for high levels of taxation of luxuries. He maintained that the rich should contribute to taxation not only 'in proportion to their revenue' but also 'something more than in proportion'.[71] He had very progressive views about inheritance, particularly disliking entails, as noted, and he was sympathetic to the abolition of heritable jurisdictions in the Highlands so as to curtail a repeat of the rising of 1745. He had equally interesting views on debt: Ireland and the North American colonies had occasioned so much that prosperity had been put in question.

At this point we can begin to transition to Smith's immediate practical politics. Scotland had benefited from being incorporated with England, and he certainly felt that the same would be true of Ireland – suffering then from an imposed and brutal Protestant Ascendancy together with trade restrictions that hurt their economy. He is best described as a unionist. Then, he had spent the years before the publication of WN in London and had studied the situation in the Thirteen Colonies in North America closely, leading him to come to very similar conclusions. But much more important was his general view of empire:

> The rulers of Great Britain have, for more than a century past, amused the people with the imagination that they possessed a great empire on the west side of the Atlantic. This empire, however, has hitherto existed in imagination only. It has hitherto been, not an empire, but the project of an empire; not a gold mine, but the project of a gold mine; a project which has cost, which continues to cost, and which, if pursued in the same was as it has been hitherto, is likely to cost immense expence, without being likely to bring any profit; for the effects of the monopoly of the colony trade, it has been shown, are,

to the great body of the people, mere loss instead of profit... If the project cannot be completed, it ought to be given up. If any of the provinces of the British empire cannot be made to contribute towards the support of the whole empire, it is surely time that Great Britain should free herself from the expence of defending these provinces in time of war, and of supporting any part of their civil or military establishments in time of peace, and endeavour to accommodate her future views and designs to the real mediocrity of her circumstances.[72]

This view is part of a much more sustained political intervention.

Smith confided to his friend Dugald Stewart that WN was nothing less than 'a complete attack on the whole commercial system of Great Britain'.[73] The fundamental problem lay in the mercantilist doctrine that a state would prosper most if it could attract gold and silver, and prevent such specie leaving the country.[74] This was to mistake the character of money, to see it solely as a source of value rather as a medium of exchange. But this notion then embedded itself in the view that the balance of trade with any country always had to be in surplus. Smith opposed this in the strongest possible terms, taking as an example the prohibition on exporting wool. 'To hurt in any degree the interest of any order of citizens, for no other purpose but to promote that of some other, is evidently contrary to that justice and equality of treatment which the sovereign owes to all the different orders of his subjects. But the prohibition certainly hurts, in some degree, the interest of the growers of wool, for no other purpose but to promote that of manufacturers'.[75] He described at length a long list of policies designed to help those engaged in foreign trade, judging them harshly.

> The inland or home trade, the most important of all, the trade in which an equal capital affords the greatest revenue, and creates the greatest employment to the people of the country, was considered as subsidiary only to foreign trade. It neither brought money into the country, it was said, nor carried any out of it. The country therefore could never become either richer or poorer by means of it, except so far as its prosperity or decay might influence the state of foreign trade.[76]

It is the presence of favours of all sorts that are given to merchants that leads to the world of high profits and low wages which Smith feared diminishes the benefits that capitalism can bring. He is particularly interesting when dealing with colonies, noting the distorting effects of monopolies given to particular companies. And something further is involved. The free trade in the Americas, especially between the West Indies and the Thirteen Colonies, was a great success. The situation with their trade with the metropole was very different:[77]

> The industry of Great Britain, instead of being accommodated to a great number of small markets, has been principally suited to one great market . . . But the whole system of her industry and commerce has thereby been rendered less secure . . . Great Britain resembles one of those unwholesome bodies in which some of the vital organs are overgrown . . . The expectation of a rupture with the colonies, accordingly, has struck the people of Great Britain with more terror than they ever felt for a Spanish armada, or a French invasion.[78]

Finally, there is another side to mercantilism, one that further enlightens us about Smith's politics. The traditional European attitude of the early modern period had been to see economic affairs in zero-sum terms, with the gain for one state coming at the expense of a rival. This was a reason for war – something that should and could be avoided. David Hume had welcomed the economic success of neighbouring states in 1758 on the grounds that an increase in the size of their economies would provide markets for the produce of his own country.[79] Smith made this case even more forcefully. It is not much of a stretch to infer from Smith that trade based on comparative advantage was a form of international social cohesion through which all capitalist nations could prosper, thereby not just removing occasions for war but providing cement for peace between nations. The 1790 revisions to TMS sought to revise his earlier view, that our affections are engaged most powerfully when relations with our immediate others are involved. Smith was far from happy with this and argued in his late revision to TMS that the wise would and should reflect on this situation, becoming better people by extending the range of their sympathies.[80] This view had resonance for international economic competition: it should be a matter of competitive emulation rather than any sort of zero-sum contest.[81]

It is time to pull the strands of the argument concerning the state together, and it is necessary to do so as there is obvious tension in these last paragraphs between the need for state power and the fear that the state can be suborned or captured by merchants.

There is in fact no logical conflict here: Smith's system depends on autonomous state actors being able to resist the importuning of factions. But how was the latter to be avoided – or, to put the matter differently, for whom was Smith writing? We can best approach the answer by returning to TMS, or more particularly to the additions he made to it in 1790. He inserted a chapter immediately after the earlier description of the origin of rank in which he describes the way in which admiration of the rich can corrupt our moral sentiments. Smith claims that there are two forms of life in front of us, one that is corrupted, the other wholly different:

> the wise and the virtuous chiefly, a select, though, I am afraid, but a small party, who are the real and steady admirers of wisdom and virtue. The great mob of mankind are the admirers and worshippers, and, what may seem more extraordinary, most frequently the disinterested admirers of worshippers, of wealth and greatness.[82]

TMS is in very large part a social psychology describing the accumulation of trinkets and the longing for still more that drives most people. But anyone who writes a book is engaged in the exercise of reason; one makes an argument hoping to convince. That is true here, and it thereby tells us a great deal about the audience that Smith had in mind.[83] 'The great mob of mankind' will not listen to his arguments, and the fact that they do not is perfectly acceptable as it keeps the machinery of society running smoothly. But Smith hoped that his intended readers, his 'small party', were wise enough to see through this deception; indeed, his intent was that the wise reader would realise that a decent material existence, together with the consolations of philosophy, is all that life can offer. But he also hoped that the wise would be politically sophisticated enough to appreciate the unconscious working of society without necessarily being caught up in the illusion themselves. The state needed to be strong in key areas, as noted, above all in the provision of justice and education, so that the decentralised workings of the market could work their magic. Smith wrote then for a very particular audience, offering them in WN a political economy seen as 'a branch of the science of a statesman or legislator'.[84] His books were expensive when first published, certainly in comparison to those of Thomas Paine, and so were most likely to be purchased by the elite, whose composition included the improving commercial aristocracy of England and the Lowlands, as well as the growing educated civil society of which he was a part. But it also included at least some politicians, not least William Pitt, the prime minister. One possibly apocryphal biographical detail describes the first meeting with Pitt at a private dinner whose members included such key members of the establishment as William Wilberforce. Pitt insisted that 'we will stand till you are first seated, for we are all your scholars'.[85] He met Pitt on further occasions and saw some of his proposals about taxation adopted. In a nutshell, Smith was something of an insider. He knew full well that politicians were often not to be trusted, but his aim was surely to make an autonomous elite both less corrupt and more intelligent.[86]

Advocacy

Any description has at its back a particular stance, and that is certainly so here. This account of Smith's political economy may have dispelled obvious misconceptions because of the forcefulness of his own formulations, but it is unlikely that description by itself will convince sociologists to take Smith seriously. Accordingly, advocacy for his position is offered in two stages.

Three Considerations

Two preliminary points are in order. Though simplistic, it is not entirely wrong to suggest that theorists have assumptions about the nature of human beings; that is, to use a rather pompous expression, they all possess their own philosophical anthropologies. For example, the problem of theodicy stands at the heart of Weber's work, with the emphasis on meaning following directly from it; in contrast, the need for discipline, integration and cohesion matter most for Durkheim. These are powerful points, but so too is Smith's: we do much in our life to gain recognition and respect. The second preliminary point is simply to highlight the certain fact that one element of the general view is quite simply correct. Prosperity does depend upon productivity.

It is as well to highlight the emphasis that has been given to the '*doux commerce*' thesis; that is, to the notion that wealth can help provide a decent world by replacing violent passions with those associated with money-making and consumption. The tradition as a whole is usefully summarised by a later thinker, Maynard Keynes, to whom it meant everything at a moment when liberalism seemed so ineffective in the face of the two revolutions of the twentieth century:

> There are valuable human activities which require the motive of money-making and the environment of private wealth-ownership for their full fruition. Moreover, dangerous human proclivities can be canalised into comparatively harmless channels by the existence of opportunities for money-making and private wealth, which, if they cannot be satisfied in this way, may find their outlet in cruelty, the reckless pursuit of personal power and authority, and other forms of self-aggrandisement. It is better that a man should tyrannise over his bank balance than over his fellow-citizens; and whilst the former is sometimes denounced as being but a means to the latter, sometimes at least it is an alternative.[87]

The fundamental reason for advocating wealth over the republican tradition of civic virtue remains that given by Smith himself: the political economies of Greece and Rome were based on slavery. But we can add a second reason: wealth papers over the cracks in society. Redistribution is very hard to achieve; social peace has resulted in large part through the increasing size of an unequal share of the societal pie.

Secondly, consider how strange is the extraordinary success of capitalism within advanced liberal democracy. A system of social inequality in which those at the bottom have the right to vote ought to be plagued with conflict, putatively leading to a different social order. But this has not proved to be the case: liberal democracies, once established, have been stable. One general theory – effectively that of Talcott Parsons – suggested that shared belief in the universal values underlying the system holds this type of society together. There is little evidence for that view.[88] Several factors explain this stability, for sure, including the capacity of political liberalism to diffuse rather than to concentrate conflict throughout society. But a crucial part of any explanation must surely be the fundamental one offered by Smith, encapsulated here in the image of the societal escalator on which we run likes rats on a treadmill, amusing ourselves to death. Others have since recognised this crucial mechanism. Pierre Bourdieu made exactly this point in *Distinction*.[89] The purpose of consumption is not, he stressed in line with Smith, utilitarian; if it were, the upper classes would have IKEA furniture. Rather the purpose of consumption is the desire for status, the desire to mark oneself off from those below.⁹⁰ Of course, this world is full of traps. At the very top of the escalator, for instance, tired and faded clothes matter more than anything new and glossy, easily dismissed as the symbol of vulgarity – albeit the older clothes had best be well cut.⁹¹ All of this is to say that Smith endorsed the core practice of the commercial world – namely, our belief that the grass is greener on the other side of the fence. The illusion or deception that keeps the wheels of industry at work may not be morally admirable or even sensible, but it ensures social cohesion. This general point is much better expressed in a very different way. Sociological theory in general – and especially that of Marx – leads us to expect capitalism to be unstable. Smith suggests that we start from the other end, expecting capitalism to have considerable elements leading to stability.

Finally, Smith's account of what have been referred to as the technical matters to do with the more precise conditions of wealth creation is equally brilliant. Sometimes striking features of contemporary capitalism – above all the seeming division between high technology skills and the limitations of much other work – suggest that we live in an entirely new world, one in which generalised human capital may matter less than the genius of the few. There are reasons to doubt this. It is worth noting the very striking resemblance between Smith's attack on high profits and low wages and Thomas Philippon's recent analysis of the economy of the United States. Philippon makes exactly Smith's point about the way in which low wages and high profits can hurt an economy.⁹² Competition, he explains, has declined, profits have risen and the share of those profits going to labour has declined thereby pushing capitalism into dangerous and unstable waters. Both thinkers stress that innovation – the root of capitalist growth – often comes from below, from talented people with easy entry into the market, and this view seems to be supported by recent evidence from Scandinavia.⁹³ Smith's and Philippon's argument that the reduction of competition and the diminution of labour's share of the economic pie leads to the stalling of innovation and the blocking of market access for newcomers carries great force.⁹⁴ It is worth noting some of Philippon's figures. He estimates that the decline of competition in recent years has raised profits by 4 per cent but diminished labour's share of national income by 6 per cent. As a result, he calculates that American workers have lost something like $1.5 trillion, 'more than the entire cumulative growth of real compensation between 2012 and 2018'.⁹⁵ The point to be made here is simple: the economy has underperformed, to the tune of 5 per cent. That is striking in and of itself. But there is a second point to be made regarding Smith's notion of ruin. We live in an increasingly global economy because capitalist operations can now escape state boundaries and move about the world with great ease. So it is entirely possible, although by no means inevitable, that capitalists can make great profits while their nation states decline. It is worth remembering that Smith had claimed with great clarity that 'a merchant . . . is not necessarily the citizen of any particular country. It is in a great measure indifferent to him from what place he carries on his trade . . .'⁹⁶

Comparisons

When making comparisons with other thinkers it is as well to remember that sociological theory resides within the larger sphere of social theory. Smith is an exemplar of one interesting and subtle school of social theory, endorsing commercial society in large part because of the soft politics that it brings in its wake. Equally importantly, he stands apart from any purely individualist theory, from any sort of methodological individualism; he offers a sociology, something effectively denied to purely individualist accounts. Comments have been offered about the virtues of his approach. Let us now see how his thought stands up in comparison with the ideas of some other major sociological thinkers, whose thought can best be understood in relation to two rather different trends in social theory, those derived from Rousseau and from Nietzsche.⁹⁷ At this point it is worth reiterating the warning given above: no claim is being made that Smith should somehow displace the thinkers to be considered – rather, he adds to their contributions, not least by allowing them to be more clearly understood.

Durkheim's enormous contribution to sociology is not in question. Perhaps his greatest contribution is to have shown the way in which society lends compulsion to the concepts with which we think, though he is best known for his concern with the breakdown of social cohesion. Here of course he is the descendant of Rousseau, whom he much admired: we are likely to be unhappy, indeed moral monsters, if we constantly dream that the grass is greener on the other side of the fence. There is much to criticise all the same. At the descriptive level, the contrast between mechanical and organic societies is far too bold, certainly less sophisticated than Smith's use of stadial theory, and awfully inaccurate in one crucial regard – namely, that the great agrarian civilisations were based on extremely specialised divisions of labour. Greater problems arise at the normative level. Rousseau argued that the psychic misery of commercial society could be managed either by a retreat into simplicity or by the creation of a shared morality, perhaps backed by religion, which would keep us to our better, more unified selves – that would force us, as he put it, to be free. Durkheim of course had not time for the retreat to a simpler world, although he analysed the nature of such retreat with unparalleled power. But he certainly argued for a cohesive and unitary moral code for his own time, albeit one that recognised a measure of difference within a common frame. In this he stands far from Smith. Three objections can be made. First, is there sufficient sociological evidence available to convince us that most lives in commercial society are as miserable as this tradition imagines? Second, how desirable is this return to moral unity? The absence of self-control is certainly horrible but so too can be enforced and regimented identity. The contrast is with liberal societies at their best, worlds in which people can try on different fronts until they create an identity all their own.[98] Furthermore, one remembers at this point Raymond Aron's comment to Léon Brunchsvicg on his return from a year in Weimar Germany, namely that the Nuremburg rallies were religion according to Durkheim, society worshipping itself. What guarantee is there that any new social identity will be morally attractive? Surely any such morality is likely to be tinged with nationalism, an uncertain source of virtue. Perhaps we are better off without. Finally, one wonders about the extent to which a shared identity is possible in a world marked by the complex division of labour.

There is a great deal to be said for placing Marx within the tradition best exemplified by Durkheim. For his earliest work shows a similar concern with the loss of self-identity, with 'splits' and divisions of all sorts within state, economy and society.[99] In this whole area Marx is of course, absurd, completely naive compared to the Durkheimian insistence on the regulated control of appetite. We can return to our species being with ease, bereft of central authority once exploitation of one class by another comes to an end. All of us can be Renaissance people, skilled in everything rather than specialised in one or two. But there are very great links beyond this between Smith and Durkheim. For one thing, Marx's account of historical development in *The German Ideology* follows Smith very closely, particularly in the role it gives to the autonomy of cities in the Occident – although Marx's account is as deterministic as a piece of German machinery, in that being far removed from Smith's sense of a fortuitous opening to commercial society. For another, Marx adopts Smith's labour theory of value, albeit in an excessively rigorous manner which does not allow for the way in which Smith's 'higgling and bargaining' in the marketplace establishes actual price. Beyond this there is a crucial difference. Smith does not believe that there is any necessary logic that will lead to the demise of capitalism; to the contrary, the image of the escalator does a very great deal to explain why it has worked so well. The point can be made in a different way. Social theories encourage us to look for empirical evidence likely to support them. Marxist theorists and those influenced by Marx accordingly look for class conflict, tending to suggest false consciousness of one type or another when it cannot be found. A whole literature in this regard has been that seeking to explain how working-class Tories – or Trump supporters – can be so misguided, voting against their own material interests. Class conflict does exist, although its causes may have more to do with political exclusion than material interests, but the whole approach may be mistaken. A Smithian approach has a great deal to be said in contrast: those at the bottom wish to succeed in a system which they may not like but which they have no desire to destroy. This is not, as noted, to say that Smith has no fears for the future capitalism. But his fears centre on the ability of capitalists to capture the state and not on any inevitable logic of the declining rate of profit leading to revolution from below. Smith gives us the concepts most appropriate to our world.

The simplest way in which the thought of Max Weber can be understood is as an attempt to combine, or to stand between, the ideas of Marx and Nietzsche – making Weber belong in part to the different intellectual tradition already noted. His interest in the economy produced the wonderful distinctions made in *Economy and Society*. But his own theory of historical development is at once worse and better than that of Smith. It is certainly worse in that 'traditional' societies have very great variety that is better captured in stadial theory. But it is also better. Weber resembles Smith in seeing the breakthrough to the modern world as fortuitous, but he adds to something to this lacking in Smith – drawn from his Nietzschean, existentialist proclivities. The puritans acted upon the world and made a new one for non-rational reasons. Weber's account of the rise of the West may of course not be true, but there is everything to be said for his insistence – so opposed to Smith – that human personality is not the same throughout the historical record. Linked to this is Weber's great sociology of religion, and to the key thesis related to it – that we must now live without God, in a disenchanted world. This latter position is subject to the same sort of critique just directed against Durkheim. How enchanted were we really in a world in which life expectancy was short and pains of every sort the stuff of daily life? Is it really true that the modern world is cold, as he imagined – somehow seen in the image of assembly line production? Surely a distinction can be drawn: coldness in design and production but ease and warmth in use – as in that marvel of engineering, the cell phone, whose contents we do not understand but whose capacities amaze and whose pleasures delight continuously. And there is a more serious point. Weber at times sought to escape disenchantment with a call for vision in politics, based on allowing room for the emergence of charismatic leaders. But what if it is the wrong vision? Perhaps we do not need another hero. Again, maybe the dull world of Smith is better. Thomas Macaulay, the nineteenth-century English historian and public intellectual, once saw human progress in the laying of new drains in South Wales. There may be something to this.

Conclusion

Smith's work has many further virtues that have not been mentioned, notably its concern with social change and its sympathy for matters to do with gender.[100] But there are clearly weaknesses. He has little to say about race. Tocqueville is more striking in this regard, as he is in two other ways. For one thing, Tocqueville stresses the importance of countervailing forces within society; in direct contrast to Smith, he notes the importance of an aristocracy as the initial guarantor of liberties, especially when its role is seen in the workings of regional assemblies.[101] Then he offers something that is simply more noble, a view of actors making their world with consciousness: differently put, Tocqueville offers a different theory of the source of public virtue, namely that daily exercise of liberty that cements it in political culture. Most importantly, Smith's work fails, as does most of classical sociological theory, to give serious attention to nationalism. Smith was aware of different national interests, and one merit of his work is to see that states influence history as much as does capital. But there are two significant weaknesses. The immediate critique of his work was that of Alexander Hamilton and Friedrich List. The leaders of peripheral states rapidly realised that the most powerful capitalist economy had the capacity to overwhelm their industries due to its highly developed industrial structure, thereby condemning their states to backwardness. Alexander Hamilton realised this and so wrote his 'Report on Manufactures', making the initial case for tariff walls behind which infant industries could grow. This view was systematised by Friedrich List, and it has most certainly affected social development thereafter – with the maximal policy seemingly being that of protecting, before then escorting one's industries onto the world market. Secondly, crucially but not surprisingly, he has little sense that society has come to mean national society: a crucial background element to the societal escalator, its sense that one is within the system, is the sense of national belonging.[102]

But Smith does help us to understand capitalism. On the one hand, the image of the societal escalator does most to explain the marked stability of liberal capitalism in the advanced world during the postwar period. On the other hand, his warnings about the predatory behaviour of capitalists themselves is stark and powerful: exactly such behaviour is now hurting the leading state in capitalist society. We must and can take Smith a little further in connection with the latter point. Smith had a fundamental commitment to creating a society in which those at the bottom of society would still, so to speak, be within it, possessed of a place on the escalator. The two world wars did a great deal to create such conditions within the advanced world. It is worth digressing for a moment to ask why capitalism was performing so much better in the immediate postwar years. Thomas Piketty and Walter Scheidel have reminded us that war has done most – via destruction, taxation and the need to motivate conscription armies – to establish basic levels of equality – levels that Smith took for granted.[103] The two world wars established a relatively consensual system based on full employment and welfare rights that allowed capitalism to become more successful and so more stable. That world may now have gone. There is a sense in which we need republican civic virtue in order to equalise social conditions; but we have no way of getting it. This is dreadful given the large amount of research suggesting that many are left out and feel left out, and so are prone to act against cosmopolitan elites able to swim in international capitalist society whilst they remain caged within their nation states. The theorist who has given us the most suggestive tools to deal with this development is Karl Polanyi: the notion that society might seek to protect itself has daily resonance. And this brings us to the final consideration. Smith sought autonomy for political leaders so that they could follow the precepts of political economy. He was followed in this by Maynard Keynes, trying to do exactly the same thing, absolutely prone to consider politicians as stupid but himself with almost complete access to the higher levels of government. Where is such an elite, autonomous, incorruptible and wise, to be found today, able to equalise social conditions sufficiently to create some sort of new social contract?

Notes

1. Anthony Giddens, *Capitalism and Modern Social Theory: An Analysis of the Writings of Marx, Durkheim and Weber* (Cambridge: Cambridge University Press, 1971).
2. Talcott Parsons, *The Structure of Social Action: A Study in Social Theory with Special Reference to a Group of Recent European Writers* (New York: McGraw Hill, 1937).
3. Raymond Aron, *Main Currents of Sociological Thought*, 2 vols (New York: Basic Books, 1965).
4. Jeffrey Alexander, *Theoretical Logic in Sociology*, 4 vols (Berkeley, CA: University of California Press, 1982–3).
5. The syllabi of 141 of 207 sociological theory courses were located and analysed. The procedure began by looking at the website of the university, and more particularly that of the relevant sociology departments. This did not yield many results. Accordingly, the code of the course and the name of the instructor was then used for further searches on Google. Sometimes the teacher put their syllabus onto a personal site, such as ResearchGate or Academia.edu. However, the site that was, by far, the most helpful was Course Hero, a website where students share class resources. It should also be noted that any syllabus taught was used, as long as it was given after 2010 – with the most recent iteration always being the one considered. I am very grateful to Charlotte Gaudreau for her very able research assistance.
6. There are exceptions, but none succeeded in changing the general picture presented here. See Gladys Bryson, *Man and Society: The*

Scottish Inquiry of the Eighteenth Century (Princeton: Princeton University Press, 1945); Alan Swingewood, 'Origins of Sociology: The Case of the Scottish Enlightenment', *British Journal of Sociology* 21 (1970), pp. 164–80; and B. Eriksson, 'The First Formulation of Sociology: A Discursive Innovation of the 18th Century', *European Journal of Sociology* 34.2 (1993), pp. 251–76.
7. Adam Smith, *The Theory of Moral Sentiments*, ed. A. I. Macfie and D. D. Raphael (Oxford: Oxford University Press, [1759] 1979), henceforth TMS.
8. Adam Smith, *An Inquiry into the Nature and Causes of the Wealth of Nations*, ed. R. H. Campbell, A. S. Skinner and W. B. Todd, 2 vols (Oxford: Oxford University Press, [1766] 1979), henceforth WN.
9. Craig Calhoun, J. Gerteis, J. Moody, S. Pfaff, K. Schmidt and I. Virk (eds), *Classical Sociological Theory* (Oxford: Basil Blackwell, 2007).
10. It is worth noting an oddity. Smith was once very much present in American sociology, above all in Chicago in the early years of the twentieth century. Some of the work discussing Smith at that time was not terribly sophisticated, and a good deal of it was dominated by pressing concerns to do with social reform. See Christopher Lasch, *The New Radicalism in America, 1889–1963: The Intellectual as a Social Type* (New York: Alfred Knopf, 1965) and Dorothy Ross, *The Origins of American Social Science* (Cambridge: Cambridge University Press, 1991). This is true, for example, of Albion Small's *Adam Smith and Modern Sociology* (1907), which curiously has nothing substantial to say about TMS. There is, however, one exception to this judgement. Charles Cooley's looking-glass view of the self comes directly from Smith, and this conception has stayed within American sociology through the development of symbolic interactionism. See Charles Cooley's *Charles Cooley on Self and Social Organization*, ed. Hans-Joachim Schubert (Chicago: University of Chicago Press, 1998) and Paul Rock's *The Making of Symbolic Interactionism* (London: Macmillan, 1979). Hence the title of this chapter could stress the importance of 'bringing Smith back in'. However, Cooley's was a limited if important use of Smith, taking from him a crucial element of social psychology without paying attention to the role that it played within a larger comparative historical sociology. The case is then for a much more complete inclusion, for taking Smith seriously.
11. It is easy to understand this sentiment. In Britain, Margaret Thatcher referred to him as 'a jolly good Scot', whilst the key intellectual figure in her cabinet, Sir Keith Joseph, asked his civil servants to read Smith's work; both were close to the free-market Adam Smith Institute. During

the Reagan administration in the United States the Adam Smith necktie became the symbol of conservative Washington.
12. Milton Friedman's 'The Role of Government in a Free Society', Lecture delivered at the Hoover Institution, Stanford University, February 9, in *Milton Friedman Speaks* [videotape publication] (New York: Harcourt Brace Jovanovich, 1978) is a classic example. However, some contemporary economists have begun to appreciate his work and to incorporate his ideas into their own: Amartya Sen's *The Idea of Justice* (Cambridge, MA: Harvard University Press, 2009) is the outstanding exemplar.
13. Dorothy Ross, *The Origins of American Social Science* (Cambridge: Cambridge University Press, 1991).
14. Spencer Pack, 'Adam Smith and Marx' in Christopher Berry, Maria Pia Paganelli and Craig Smith (eds), *The Oxford Handbook of Adam Smith* (Oxford: Oxford University Press, 2013), pp. 523–38.
15. The Glasgow critical editions remain key. Recent monographs of great power include Ronald Meek, *Smith, Marx and After* (London: Chapman and Hall, 1977); Donald Winch, *Adam Smith's Politics: An Essay in Historiographic Revision* (Cambridge: Cambridge University Press, 1978); Knud Haakonssen, *The Science of a Legislator: The Natural Jurisprudence of David Hume & Adam Smith* (Cambridge: Cambridge University Press, 1981); D. D. Raphael, *Adam Smith* (Oxford: Oxford University Press, 1985); Charles Griswold, *Adam Smith and the Virtues of Enlightenment* (Cambridge: Cambridge University Press, 1999); Istvan Hont, *The Jealousy of Trade: International Competition and the Nation-State in Historical Perspective* (Cambridge, MA: Harvard University Press, 2005); Michael Frazer, *The Enlightenment of Sympathy: Justice and Moral Sentiments in the Eighteenth Century and Today* (Oxford: Oxford University Press, 2010); Fonna Forman-Barzilai, *Adam Smith and the Circles of Sympathy: Cosmopolitanism and Moral Theory* (Cambridge: Cambridge University Press, 2010); Nicholas Phillipson, *Adam Smith: An Enlightened Life* (London: Penguin, 2011); Istvan Hont, *Politics in Commercial Society: Jean-Jacques Rousseau and Adam Smith* (Cambridge, MA: Harvard University Press, 2015); and Craig Smith, *Adam Smith* (Cambridge: Polity Press, 2020).
16. Dietrich Rueschemeyer, Evelyne Stephens and John Stephens, *Capitalist Development and Democracy* (Chicago: University of Chicago Press, 1992).
17. That breakthrough was instigated by James Watt, one of Smith's closest friends. Anthony Wrigley, *Continuity, Chance and Change: The Character of the Industrial Revolution in England* (Cambridge:

Cambridge University Press, 1990) provides essential background information.
18. Hume's comment is revealing: '... eight Millions of People' might 'have been subdued and reduced to Slavery by five Thousand, the bravest, but still the most worthless among them', in Ernest Mossner, *The Life of David Hume* (Oxford: Oxford University Press, 1980), p. 177.
19. David Hume, *A Treatise of Human Nature* (London: Penguin, [1739 and 1740] 1985), p. 462.
20. Ernest Gellner, *The Psychoanalytic Movement: The Cunning of Unreason* (Chicago: Northwestern University Press, 1996), ch. 1.
21. See Peter Knox-Shaw's *Jane Austen and the Enlightenment* (Cambridge: Cambridge University Press, 2004); also see Cecil Bohannon and Michelle Vachris's *Pride and Profit: The Intersection of Jane Austen and Adam Smith* (Lanham, MD: Lexington Books, 2015).
22. Bertrand Russell, the great inheritor of Hume's work, was wont to note that contract theories suggesting that a sudden decision would make or ameliorate society were ridiculous for the most obvious of reasons: only the socialised and the moral would have made the contracts in question.
23. Phillipson, *Adam Smith: An Enlightened Life*, pp. 102–5.
24. The student notes of his lectures on rhetoric, given in 1762–3 – *Lectures on Rhetoric and Belles Lettres* (Oxford: Oxford University Press, 1983) – develop an original view of the nature and development of language. Smith clearly thought his view to be important as he published one of the lectures, 'Considerations Concerning the First Formation of Languages and the Different Genius of Original and Compounded Languages', as an article in his lifetime (1761, now in the volume cited in this note, pp. 201–26). Language is seen as a response to the human need to understand each other better – thereby making Smith stress the importance of clarity and approachability. The emphasis on mutual understanding is the beginning of his concern with propriety. For the context of Smith's view, see Charles Taylor, *The Language Animal: The Full Shape of the Human Linguistic Capacity* (Cambridge, MA: Harvard University Press, 2016).
25. Adam Smith, 'A Letter to the Authors of the *Edinburgh Review*' in *Essays on Philosophical Subjects*, ed. W. P. D. Wightman (Oxford: Oxford University Press, [1755–6] 1980), pp. 242–54.
26. Istvan Hont and Michael Ignatieff (eds), *Wealth and Virtue: The Shaping of Political Economy in the Scottish Enlightenment* (Cambridge: Cambridge University Press, 1983) and Dennis C. Rasmussen, *The*

Problems and Promise of Commercial Society: Adam Smith's Response to Rousseau (University Park, PA: Pennsylvania State University Press, 2008).
27. Adam Smith, *Lectures on Jurisprudence*, ed. R. L. Meek, D. D. Raphael and P. Stein (Oxford: Oxford University Press, 1978).
28. Meek, *Smith, Marx and After*.
29. Haakonssen, *The Science of a Legislator*.
30. Adam Smith, *Essays on Philosophical Subjects*, ed. W. P. D. Wightman (Oxford: Oxford University Press [1795] 1980). Smith offers an emotivist theory of knowledge. Scientific development is driven by anxiety, whilst theories gain credence for the way in which their elegance pleases our aesthetic sense. See Jack Barbalet, *Emotion, Social Theory and Social Structure: A Macrosociological Approach* (Cambridge: Cambridge University Press, 1998) and C. Smith, *Adam Smith*, ch. 2.
31. Phillipson, *Adam Smith: An Enlightened Life*, p. 149.
32. TMS I.1.1.1.
33. TMS I.1.1.5.
34. Smith's contribution to the sociology of emotions is potentially enormous, but it has as yet barely been tapped, despite the excellent contribution of Barbalet, *Emotion, Social Theory and Social Structure*. Smith's analysis of self-hatred is especially striking, as it shows, somewhat as Durkheim was to do later, how moral standards are internalised (see TMS II.ii.2.2). It is worth noting that Smith's view of emotions powerfully links feelings with actions, something that is not always true of recent work in this field.
35. TMS III.1.4.
36. See Raphael, *Adam Smith*, pp. 41–3, and Sule Ozler and Paul Gambrinetti, *Psychoanalytic Studies of the Work of Adam Smith: Towards a Theory of Moral Development and Social Relations* (London: Routledge, 2018).
37. David Riesman, with Nathan Glazer and Rueul Denney, *The Lonely Crowd: A Study of the Changing American Character* (New Haven, CT: Yale University Press, 1950).
38. See Erving Goffman, 'On Face Work' in *Interaction Ritual: Essays on Face-to-Face Interaction* (Harmondsworth: Penguin, 1967), pp. 5–45, and John A. Hall, *The Importance of Being Civil: The Struggle for Political Decency* (Princeton: Princeton University Press, 2013), ch. 4.
39. David Hume 'Letter to Adam Smith, 28 July 1759' in E. C. Mossner and I. S. Ross (eds), *The Correspondence of Adam Smith* (Oxford: Oxford University Press, [1759] 1987), p. 43.

40. TMS I.iii.2.1.
41. TMS I.ii.5.i. The final revision of TMS addressed ethical worries, leading Smith to claim that 'Man naturally desires, not only to be loved, but to be lovely' (TMS III.2.2).
42. Smith noted later that humans constantly wish to improve their situation, but what matters is the desire to prosper in the eyes of their fellows, in WN II.iii.
43. August Oncken, 'Das Adam Smith-Problem', *Zeitschrift für Sozialwissenshaften* 1 (1898), pp. 25–33.
44. A crucial piece of evidence here is the fact that the 1790 revision of TMS, noted below, was designed not to question or deny his earlier statement but to restate and reinforce it in clearer terms.
45. The lectures on jurisprudence offer an account of the origins of the state, and of its history and forms interpreted by means of a history of property relations. The part of the argument most concerned with the character of early modern European states appears in Book III of WN, discussed below.
46. TMS I.iii.4.
47. Envy is of course the most negative sentiment of all, seeking to destroy what it cannot possess. A dreadful mistake of most right-wing thinkers has been to see calls from below in this light. There is little to this claim, with calls for redistribution in the name of justice being a desire to share in the benefits of society rather than to destroy it. It is worth insisting that jealousy differs completely from envy: it is the desire to catch up and to improve. The central point about Smith's view of the motivation of most of mankind is that it is based on jealousy – the desire to work hard so as to copy the lifestyles of those higher in the social echelon. This highlights the difference between the naturalism of Smith and Hume in contrast to that of Nietzsche and Freud.
48. TMS IV.i.6.
49. TMS IV.i.8.
50. Smith, *Lectures on Jurisprudence*, p. 497.
51. TMS IV.i.10.
52. WN I.1.
53. WN I.viii.24.
54. WN I.vii.
55. WN I.ii.4.
56. WN I.ii.2.
57. WN I.ii.2.
58. TMS I.ii.5.i.

59. WN I.x.c.27.
60. WN I.xi.p.10.
61. WN I.xi.p.10.
62. WN III.ii.6.
63. An initial version of this chapter suggested – following Deborah Boucoyannis's excellent 'The Equalizing Hand: Why Adam Smith Thought the Market Should Produce Wealth without Steep Inequality', *Perspectives on Politics* 11 (2013), pp. 1051–70 – that Smith favoured policies that 'equalized' social conditions. This was not wrong insofar as it meant that he proposed policies that would prevent inequality becoming too steep, not least by opposing the ability of merchants to capture the state. But 'equalizing' is certainly wrong insofar as it might suggest that he sought to establish an egalitarian society. That was not Smith's intention. He did not think that rank could ever be abolished, nor that the societal escalator would cease its functioning. I am grateful at this point for comments made by Kenneth Macdonald, in the first of his chapters in this volume and in comments made at the seminar which formed part of the preparation for this volume. He is unquestionably right to insist that we place Smith in his time rather than projecting on to him contemporary social democratic values. Nonetheless, I am firmly opposed to his general view. Whilst Smith was trying to understand the society of which he was a part, he most certainly had normative views as to how it could be made to work best. These views most definitely included a measure of sympathy for labour, and more generally an insistence that excessive levels of inequality would undermine the commercial sociability he so firmly endorsed.
64. WN III.iii.8.
65. WN III.iv.10.
66. WN II.i.31.
67. WN III.iii.20.
68. Exactly the same point can be made about his conjectural history of the state. See Smith, *Lectures on Rhetoric and Belles Lettres*.
69. WN III.iv.17.
70. Albert Hirschman, *The Passions and the Interests: Political Arguments for Capitalism before Its Triumph* (Princeton: Princeton University Press, 1977).
71. WN V.ii.e.6.
72. WN V.iii.92.
73. Dugald Stewart, 'Account of the Life and Writings of Adam Smith, LL.D' in *Essays on Philosophical Subjects*, ed. W. P. D. Wightman (Oxford: Oxford University Press, [1794] 1982), pp. 269–332.

74. He also devoted a chapter to another error. The Physiocrats were wrong to insist that prosperity had to be based on agriculture alone, rather than on a combination of agricultural and commercial prosperity. Further, these French economists were dangerous, too keen on imposing their own system from above (see WN IV.ix).
75. WN IV.viii.32.
76. WN IV.i.10.
77. Smith realised that complete change was unlikely. Rulers disliked giving up territory, so 'To expect, indeed, that the freedom of trade should ever be entirely restored in Great Britain, is as absurd as to expect that an Oceana or Utopia should ever be established in it' (WN IV.ii). As a result, he offered many suggestions for reform, including finding ways in which colonies could pay towards the costs of their maintenance.
78. WN IV.vii.c.43. Recent history lends much support to Smith at this point. Foreign policy is often bent so as to support particular markets, thereby ignoring the speed with which capital, left to itself, can adapt to changing circumstances – as was so noticeable in the way in which Finland turned its whole economy away from Russia towards the rest in a very few years when the socialist bloc collapsed.
79. David Hume, 'Of the Jealousy of Trade' in *Hume: Political Essays*, ed. K. Haakonssen (Cambridge: Cambridge University Press, [1758] 1994), pp. 150–3. Cf. Istvan Hont, *The Jealousy of Trade: International Competition and the Nation-State in Historical Perspective* (Cambridge, MA: Harvard University Press, 2005).
80. Forman-Barzilai, *Adam Smith and the Circles of Sympathy*.
81. Hont, *Politics in Commercial Society*, ch. 6.
82. TMS I.iii.3.2.
83. A good deal more was involved in the revisions made in 1790. Smith chose to respond to Thomas Reid's earlier criticism of the book as but 'a Refinement of the selfish system' (see Phillipson, *Adam Smith: An Enlightened Life*, p. 163). Smith had always rejected this view, believing that following the rules created by the fiction of the impartial spectator led to behaviour that was principled rather than immediately self-serving. But he remained worried on this point and added a whole new part – 'Of the Character of Virtue' – to the revised edition of the book in 1790. Here the discussion of virtue centres on the notion of self-command, making it absolutely clear that a principled actor should and would stand out against the immediate social pressure of his fellows. To the degree that this is so, Smith is trying to move somewhat beyond a totally other-directed view of social life – away, as it were, from a purely descriptive social psychology to a genuine ethical theory.

84. WN IV.Introduction.
85. Phillipson, *Adam Smith: An Enlightened Life*, pp. 267–8. This is slightly misleading in that Smith's views generally lent to the left, to the Whigs rather than to the Tories.
86. Winch, *Adam Smith's Politics*. Hirschman's *The Passions and the Interests* claimed that Smith destroyed the tradition he described in his famous treatise on the passions and the interests because he had reduced everything to self-interest. That is not correct, even though Smith has no fully developed theory explaining why politicians would place the general interest above their own.
87. John Maynard Keynes, *The General Theory of Employment, Interest and Money* (London: Macmillan, [1936] 1973), p. 374.
88. Michael Mann, 'The Social Cohesion of Liberal Democracies', *American Sociological Review* 35 (1970), pp. 423–39.
89. Pierre Bourdieu, *Distinction: A Social Critique of the Judgement of Taste* (Cambridge, MA: Harvard University Press, 1979).
90. This makes Smith a notable theorist of fashion; see Craig Smith's 'Adam Smith's "Collateral" Inquiry: Fashion and Morality in the Theory of Moral Sentiments and the Wealth of Nations', *History of Political Economy* 45 (2013), pp. 505–22.
91. Thorstein Veblen, *The Theory of the Leisure Class* (Oxford: Oxford University Press, [1899] 2007). There is of course a difference: Veblen differed from Smith in seeing such consumption as wasteful.
92. Thomas Philippon, *The Great Reversal: How America Gave Up on Free Markets* (Cambridge, MA: Harvard University Press, 2019).
93. See Darius Ornston, *When Small States Make Big Leaps: Institutional Innovation and High-Tech Competition in Western Europe* (Ithaca, NY: Cornell University Press, 2012) and John Campbell and John A. Hall, *The Paradox of Vulnerability: States, Nationalism and the Financial Crisis* (Princeton: Princeton University Press, 2017). Smith's emphasis on imagination tells us a great deal about new innovations, a point supporting the view that consumption matters quite as much as production; see Frank Trentmann, *The Empire of Things: How We Became a World of Consumers from the Fifteenth Century to the Twenty-First* (London: Harper Collins, 2016).
94. Philippon, *The Great Reversal*.
95. Ibid. p. 293.
96. WN III.iv.24. See also II.v.14–17.
97. John A. Hall, 'The Grammar of Social Theory, or, Negotiations in Hell', *Irish Sociological Review* 28 (2019), pp. 29–43.

98. Smith is equally open to criticism here. The 'civility' he admires can be highly constraining, so suffocating as to make it impossible for alternative voices to he heard. See J. M. Cuddihy, *The Ordeal of Civility: Freud, Marx, Levi-Strauss and the Jewish Struggle with Modernity* (Boston, MA: Beacon Press, 1974) and Hall, *The Importance of Being Civil*, ch. 4.
99. Leszek Kolakowski, 'The Myth of Human Self-Identity: Unity of Civil and Political Society in Socialist Thought' in S. Hampshire and L. Kolakowski (eds), *The Socialist Idea: A Reappraisal* (New York: Basic Books, 1985), pp. 41–58.
100. Smith's follower John Millar's *Origin of the Distinction of Ranks* is pioneering in this regard; see R. Olson, 'Sex and Status in the Scottish Enlightenment Social Science: John Millar and the Origin of Gender Roles', *History of the Human Sciences* 11 (1998) pp. 73–100.
101. Daniel Ziblatt, *Conservative Parties and the Birth of Democracy* (Cambridge: Cambridge University Press, 2017) offers a rather different mechanism pointing in the same direction.
102. Ernest Gellner, *Nations and Nationalism* (Oxford: Basil Blackwell, 1983).
103. Thomas Piketty, *Capital in the Twenty-First Century* (Cambridge, MA: Harvard University Press 2014) and Walter Scheidel, *The Great Leveler: Violence and the History of Inequality from the Stone Age to the Twenty-First Century* (Princeton: Princeton University Press, 2017). A final point can be made here. The escalator view of social cohesion would fail to work should a general rejection of consumerism come to the fore, a public distaste for its nonsensical waste. This possibility has been suggested in Krzysztof Pelc's brilliant *Beyond Self-Interest: Why the Market Rewards Those Who Reject It* (London: Bloomsbury, 2022). Bluntly, I cannot believe this, but suggest that we remain aware of this future possibility.

13

John Millar and Sociology: Disciplinary History and its Discontents

Nicholas B. Miller

Introduction: How Did Millar Attain a Sociological Legacy?

In recent decades, John Millar, Professor of Civil Law at the University of Glasgow from 1761 to 1800, has become a canonical figure of the Scottish Enlightenment in view of his practice of stadial history with an eye to topics of property, politics, household relations, marriage and gender. Millar is now widely recognised as Adam Smith's finest student, who served as a junior counterpart to his mentor as well as Adam Ferguson in authoring the type of 'natural history of society' inspired by Montesquieu and propounded by Hume. Core to this recovery was William C. Lehmann's nomination of Millar and Ferguson as sociological pioneers in 1930.[1] Lehmann's book, the first and only monograph-length study on Millar to be authored during the twentieth century, promised the recovery of 'His Contributions to Sociological Analysis' in its title.[2] Since the 1960s, reference to Millar's *Origin of the Distinction of Ranks* (1771) has become standard within disciplinary histories of sociology.[3] Consistent with the practice of intellectual history since Pocock and Skinner, intellectual historians of Millar have shied away from disciplinary labels for his inquiry, though the themes of property, inequality and gender upon which they have brought Millar to bear reflect a clear affinity to what became core concerns of sociology.

Evincing the enduring impact of Lehmann's disciplinary biography, a curious footnote has circulated within modern and contemporary scholarship on Millar, attributing the earliest call for Millar's intellectual recovery to the early twentieth-century German sociologist Werner Sombart.[4] Following Lehmann, a great number of scholars have highlighted how Sombart commended

Millar's *Ranks* as 'an astonishing [*stauenswert*] book', one that, despite having 'been completely forgotten' contained 'one of the best and complete sociologies we have'.⁵ The weaponised character of Sombart's animated praise, contained in an essay on the historical origins of sociology contributed to the Festschrift for Max Weber in 1923, has, however, escaped notice. In this essay, Sombart claimed that Millar's *Ranks* contained the kernel of 'the technological-economic theory of society', his rendition of what elsewhere had been 'described unfortunately as the Materialist Theory of History'. To Millar's account, 'the nineteenth century' – that is, Marx – 'added nothing but details'. 'His sociology of marriage, conducted through a technological-economic perspective to history, is such a complete treatment of the matter that F. Engels in his treatise on the origin of the family did not develop a single new idea.' Further, 'One must admit that Millar's formulation of the economic theory of society is superior to Marx's in completeness and clarity.'⁶ Sombart's commendation of Millar was thus a pregnant one. Filling a void emergent through his intellectual distancing from Marxist socialism in the aftermath of the Russian Revolution, and ultimately culminating in his embrace of national socialism in the late 1920s, Sombart found in Millar a replacement for Marx.

Sombart's claim that Millar had 'been completely forgotten' by the early twentieth century was a rhetorical flourish that has been sustained for nearly a century. The question of how Sombart learned of Millar remains essentially unexplored. The standing account provided by Lehmann is that Millar's memory 'completely faded out' amidst the French Revolution, with his legacy restricted to intermittent commendations by John Mill, John Rae and John Stuart Mill.⁷ Further, Lehmann – quoting Sombart – contended that Millar had become completely forgotten – '*gänzlich verschollen*' – by the time sociology emerged as a discipline.⁸ This briefest of reception histories has circulated across many of the modern schools of interpreting Millar, including Marxist, disciplinary history of sociology, Cambridge school and the history of philosophy and social theory.⁹

As a contribution to this volume's objective of reassessing the sociological heritage of the Scottish Enlightenment, this chapter recounts the neglected history of how Millar became first perceived as a pioneer of sociological inquiry around the turn of the twentieth century. Drawing on the possibilities of *longue durée* research opened by the digitisation of much of the printed corpus of the nineteenth and twentieth centuries, this chapter synthesises a wide range of literature in which Millar was discussed, making use of the ability to search for relevant keywords including 'Millar' and 'Ranks'. Accidents of spelling, poor quality digitisation and misrendering of past typographies all deny any search claim to exhaustiveness, yet digitised search permits contemporary researchers unprecedented scope for targeted and discrete readings, including, in this case, Millar's forgotten late nineteenth- and early twentieth-century reception.

This chapter offers a sustained reassessment of Millar's legacy and reception history through the recognition that John Millar should be understood above all as a historian, whose social analysis came to be construed as more systematic than it really was through Sombart's weaponisation of his intellectual heritage. Here, I develop Michael Ignatieff's halting commendation on Millar's practice of social theory, namely that his 'synoptic integration of family, economy, and state spheres ... makes the *Ranks* such subversive reading for anyone whose mental categories are bounded by the sociology, economics, and political science which descend from the original Scottish project'.[10] As past scholars have intuited for well over a century, Millar's principal relevance for thinkers today, including sociologists, is the historical perspective he casts on two key enduring themes: inequality and gender in early history and the run-up to modernity.

Barring Sombart's weaponisation of Millar as a substitute for Marx – more recently indulged by George Watson – I suggest his greatest utility for contemporary social scientists, including historical sociologists, might be reduced to four points developed at length in my monograph on Millar.[11] First, social inequality (implicitly if not explicitly) is endemic to any complex society but particularly aggravated by disparities of property.[12] Second, market-induced individualism possessed undesirable outcomes and required certain responses via mechanisms of collective support beyond individual charity, including the state (such as poor laws).[13] Third, as advanced in his methodological introduction, repeated observation of practices at odds with deductive reasoning demand to be treated complexly, rather than rejected as a failure of observation (in other words, a defence of inductive reason).[14] Fourth, and connected with this latter point, a practice of universalist social inquiry should be adopted that when mapped onto history does not eliminate inconvenient testimony for the sake of analytical consistency.[15]

As Ignatieff pointedly argued, Millar did not produce any enduring philosophical system. Yet Millar's lack of system should be appraised less as an intellectual failing than as revealing his own methodological frustrations with the confines of stadial history. Readers since Herder have taken Millar's stadial edifice at face value, rather than pondering the dissonances within. As I will demonstrate below, the most prominent reputation Millar would hold prior to Sombart was as an eighteenth-century thinker uncommonly sensitive to the divergent streams of early history perceptible within his sources. While many of Millar's contemporaries skipped over the challenge of reconciling travellers' reports of matrifocal arrangements with the contention that women's status in society generally improved through civilisation, Millar built upon Hobbes to offer a unique analysis focusing on dynamics of parental affection prior to the institutionalisation of patrifocal marriage. This did little to advance the case of a materialist philosophy of history or, less anachronistically, a stadial approach to histories of marriage and inequality. This is because it was not meant to.

While multiple streams of Millar's 'rediscovery' since the mid-nineteenth century can be identified, there were two of greatest significance in configuring Millar as a (proto-)sociological thinker. The first was an enduring discussion of the history of marriage, which gained new vigour with the publication of Bachofen's *Mutterrecht* in 1861 and crossed emerging disciplinary distinctions between sociology, anthropology and history. It was through this line of inquiry that Millar was initially named as an early or proto-sociologist between 1890 and 1910. The second, principally occurring in Continental Europe after the turn of the twentieth century, was an emerging interest among twentieth-century Marxist sociologists in Germany in charting Millar's place in Marx's intellectual genealogy. It was here that Werner Sombart constructed the image of Millar as a pioneering sociological thinker who not merely anticipated Marx but offered an alternative basis for historical materialism, or what Sombart rendered as the technological-economic theory of society. Below, I discuss each in turn, before concluding with a proposal that Millar's nuanced practice towards the interpretation of historical evidence, first identified by Scottish folklorist Andrew Lang in 1897 as anticipating cultural anthropologist Edward Burnett Tylor's 'test of recurrences', serves as his principal claim for contemporary theoretical relevance by sociologists and other social scientists today. By evidencing the

European scope of Millar's reception prior to Sombart, this chapter confirms the importance of taking a transnational approach to appraising the diverse legacies of the Scottish Enlightenment up to World War II, before which Millar was rarely nationalised as Scottish and his most pronounced impact was in Germany.[16]

Millar's Initial 'Rediscovery': From the Enlightenment Natural History of Marriage to the Victorian Debate on Matriarchy

Millar's written corpus is relatively modest. He authored only one major work besides the *Ranks*, his voluminous and incomplete *Historical View on the English Government*, which, like the *Ranks*, was published in multiple English editions, in addition to contemporary translations into French and German. From a sociological perspective, the *Ranks* is Millar's work of greater import. The reception history of Millar's two treatises, however, exhibited a dynamic inverse to his own intellectual trajectory. Millar's turn to the history of the English constitution in his *Historical View* betrayed a sense that the *Ranks*, emblematic of the vogue of natural histories of mankind authored in the 1760s and 1770s across Scotland and elsewhere in Europe, had become outmoded, even before Dugald Stewart would confer upon them the dismissive label of conjectural history in his *Life of Smith* of 1791. While modern scholars have praised Millar's comparatively 'minute' practice of source footnoting in his *Ranks*, his German contemporaries, who sustained his interest in the type of *longue durée* historical questions relating to the household, already found his work underwhelming in this regard by the 1780s. Christoph Meiners, in his 1786 history of mankind, mentioned Millar along with Ferguson, Dunbar and Pagano as offering 'valuable commentaries on the origin of civil society, on the emergence of the various ranks, and on the relations and rights of these ranks as well as the two sexes with each other', though without sufficient rigour to attain a truly global perspective.[17] Meiners, who elevated race to be the main factor in human history, engaged little with their theoretical insights, instead using their treatises as repositories of interesting sources. Millar conversely, after authoring the *Ranks*, increasingly shied away from global comparison, preferring the specificity of the British context in his subsequent historical work.

The first half of the nineteenth century witnessed perhaps the greatest reception Millar's *Historical View* would ever have. Embodying a distinctly Whiggish approach to English constitutional history, it engaged directly with Hume's history of Britain, shearing it of its Tory sympathies while retaining Hume's secular approach to historical explanation. James Mill celebrated Millar's *Historical View* as a work of great value, though Mill's conceit that his ignorance of Indian realities made his *History of India* even more credible betrayed a methodologic chasm from Millar's own practice of national history. The elder Mill would go on to advocate Millar's *Historical View* to his son John Stuart Mill, who likewise wrote of it fondly to his Continental correspondents. A high estimation of Millar's historical contributions would endure to the mid-century. In 1842, Louis Raymond Véricour remarkably placed Millar on the level of Gibbon when describing English-language works in the philosophy of history: 'the most remarkable are the *Decline and Fall* of Gibbon and Mr. Millar's works'.[18]

Two shifts in Millar's reception occurred in the mid-nineteenth century. The first of these emphasised Millar's teaching of law, closely engaging with his celebrated practice as the rejuvenator of Glasgow's legal faculty during his nearly forty-year occupation of the Chair of Civil Law from 1761 to 1800.[19] James Reddie in 1840 commended his 'truly philosophic lectures on general jurisprudence, and on government' that embodied a historical approach to the study of law closer to the subsequently emergent German Historical School than the Benthamian analytical school that grew across Britain.[20] As recently observed by Cairns, Romanticist endorsers of the German Historical School in Scotland later 'viewed the Germans as continuing a historical traditional developed by eighteenth-century Scottish thinkers such as Lord Kames and John Millar'.[21] The second and more pivotal shift was the emergence of a decades-long debate on the history of marriage, set off by the publication of Jung's *Geschichte der Frauen* in 1850, in which Millar's *Ranks* was read initially as a source for primary evidence, and later as a theorist.

It was on the topic of the history of marriage that Karl Marx read Millar's *Ranks* during the summer of 1852. He took extensive reading notes on the *Ranks* along with a set of nine other texts at the British Library in German, French and English united by their focus on the history of gender.[22] Millar's *Ranks* was amongst the oldest of the nine, tied with Antoine-Leonard Thomas's *Essai sur la caractère, les moeurs, et l'esprit des femmes dans les differens siècles* (1771). The other Enlightenment-era works on the topic read by Marx were *The History of Women* (1782) by Millar's fellow Scotsman William Alexander, Eichhorn's *Allgemeine Geschichte* (1796) and Christoph Meiner's *Geschichte der weiblichen Geschlechts* (1788–1800). Marx read these works in view of the discussion of the history of marriage in several recent German cultural histories, including Drumann's *Grundriss der Culturgeschichte* (1847), Wachsmuth's *Allgemeine Culturgeschichte* (1850–1) and Jung's *Geschichte der Frauen* (1850). Marx's notes on Millar constituted the lengthiest in the volume, comprising 10.5 pages of tight citations in the 57-page-long notebook.

While Marx read Millar closely, he was primarily interested in his use and discussion of sources on the history of gender. The bulk of his notes were lengthy transcriptions of passages from the *Ranks*. Two scholars, Danga Vileisis and Sam Stark, have explored Marx's notes on Millar in depth. Stark notes that Marx deployed his reading to undercut his German American rival Karl Heinzen, but Millar was not included among the authors mentioned in Marx's published retorts.[23] Further, Marx began his survey of the history of marriage prior to the publication of Heinzen's article, evidencing his interest in the topic during the early 1850s. Vileisis closely studied Marx's hard-to-decipher notes, written in nineteenth-century script in a distinct version of 'Dinglish'. The few editorial asides within the morass of transcription are mocking in tenor, with Marx finding Millar's analysis quaintly moralising.[24] Vileisis makes much of Marx's inversion of Millar's argumentation when extracting from Millar's chapter on 'changes in the condition of women, arising from the improvement of useful arts and manufactures'. This of course may have been merely human error. Marx does not appear to have been impressed by Millar's theoretical achievements and made no mention of him in any of his subsequent work.

In the 1860s, Bachofen's *Mutterrecht* oriented discussion of the history of marriage upon the question of matriarchy. It was as part of this debate that Millar's *Ranks* was seriously engaged with intellectually for the first time in decades. In the second section of the *Ranks*, Millar discussed the question of maternal power in societies lacking patrifocal marriage – or what he rendered as 'the influence acquired by the mother of a family, before marriage is completely established'. While Scottish ethnologist and anthropologist James McLennan professed to have been ignorant of Millar's *Ranks* when first authoring his *Primitive Marriage* of 1865, he noted in the revised second edition of 1876 that Millar had 'almost anticipated' Bachofen's concept of *Mutterrecht* in his discussion of 'ancient gynaikocracy'.[25] Over the next fifteen years, when Finnish sociologist Edward Westermarck would publish the *History of Human Marriage* in 1891, Millar's *Ranks* became a fixed feature of the research bibliography on the topic of the history of gender.

Millar figured prominently in debates during the 1890s to define the intellectual precedents to the emergent disciplines of sociology and anthropology. Herbert Spencer in his multivolume 1876 *Principles of Sociology* did not discuss Millar, but an anonymous critical review drew on Millar to expand upon the former's account of the divine origins of kings. 'An important worker in the field [who] is almost forgotten', Millar admirably synthesised divergent testimony to indicate 'the earliest form of authority in human society', that of parents, proceeding in stages to transition to that of chiefs. Millar 'anticipated a great deal of what has since been advanced as original', although failed in the reviewer's estimation to have sufficiently considered the factor of religious superstition as a political legitimising device in early society.[26] Herbert Spencer's former assistant James Collier later described Millar as an almost-sociologist; freethinker John Mackinson Robertson named him, alongside several other Enlightenment Scots, as one of the first British sociologists. Conversely, Andrew Lang and John Hepburn Millar described Millar as an early anthropologist. The most important late nineteenth-century discussants of Millar were two Scotsmen, the Fabian folklorist John Stuart-Glennie (1841–1910) and radical liberal John Mackinson Robertson (1856–1933), both of whom were intimately engaged in debates on the interpretation of folklore and antiquity.

Stuart-Glennie applied Millar to the crossing of two major intellectual trajectories of the period: first, during the 1890s, the historical question of matriarchy, and second, after the turn of the twentieth century, social Darwinism. Stuart-Glennie developed a radical stance on human diversity informed by a racialised approach to history, culminating in a racial theory of folklore. In an 1891 treatise asserting that certain racial groups were originally matriarchal, Stuart-Glennie advanced a two-part refutation of Millar's universalist account of maternal power in primitive societies prior to the invention of marriage, developed in the second section of the *Ranks*. First was his notion of hataerism, of 'an original promiscuity of human sexual intercourse', which endured through the work of McLennan, Giraud-Teulon, Morgan and Lubbock but was more recently critiqued by Spencer, Starcke and Letourneau.[27] Second was Millar's contractualist explanation of primitive maternal power deriving from bonds of filial obligation preceding the configuration of androcentric marriage.[28] Drawing instead on an evolutionary approach, Stuart-Glennie contended that such promiscuity was to be found nowhere among mankind's nearest primate relations.[29]

Later, in an editorial in *Nature* in 1901, Stuart-Glennie adopted a more sympathetic appraisal of Millar, naming him alongside Smith and Hume as 'among the foremost workers and discoverers' leading to the recognition of 'history as science', the 'most complex of the sciences of evolution'.[30] Smith and Millar, departing from Turgot and Hume, inaugurated an 'analytical and inductive' approach to history that was strengthened by Darwin through the fashioning of evolutionary models of change. Stuart-Glennie praised Millar for his early contributions to analysing 'ethnological discoveries, which have resulted in a theory of the origins of civilization in a conflict of higher and lower races' and 'the folklorist discoveries, generalized in a theory of primitive conceptions of nature as conceptions of its solidarity through the interaction and limitless transformation of its parts'.[31]

In 1891, when reviewing Westermarck's *History*, conservative French historian René de Kerallain (1849–1928) noted that Millar had a century prior argued that the family was the basis of political society and that marriage was a natural outgrowth of human social development. On this latter point, Kerallain underlined how Millar confronted – through 'language that testified to his fervent faith' – the possible challenge that 'orthodox Christians' might pose to this type of analysis, which rendered redundant the role of Christian providence in regulating marriage. Kerallain cited the first English language edition of the *Ranks* of 1771 and thanked Paul Marie Viollet (1840–1914), who had just been appointed in the year prior as Professor of Civil and Canon Law at what is now the École Nationale des Chartes, for first bringing Millar to his attention.[32]

The assessment of Millar as an almost-sociologist was first made by James Collier (1846–1925), Herbert Spencer's eventual memorialist.

Collier was a Scotsman who migrated to New Zealand after serving as Spencer's assistant for ten years, from 1871 to 1882. Once in New Zealand, Collier exhibited great interest in the interconnections between history, nature and society and became a theorist of colonisation. His work was characterised by the use of biological terminology and the conviction that indigenous populations were doomed for extinction, though he expressed a degree of sympathy for the plight of these groups. In an account of the historical development of sociology within a popular piece on the history of colonisation, Collier suggested that

> Prof. John Millar's Origin of Ranks, of which the third edition was published so long ago as 1781, shows how near a man may be to a discovery without making it. Only after eighty years did his inchoate speculation issue in the most finished piece of inductive research that sociology has to show – McLennan's *Primitive Marriage*.[33]

Oxford folklorist Andrew Lang, on the other hand, described Millar as a thinker possessing a principally historical and anthropological legacy, both of which disciplines were likewise indicated by John Hepburn Millar in his 1903 literary history of Scotland.[34] Counter to the notion of complete oblivion by the early twentieth century, John Hepburn Millar contended that the *Ranks* 'is a work which has won high praise from modern experts in anthropology on account of its comparatively full discussion of the position of woman in primitive and savage communities, and it may still be read by the layman with profit'.[35]

In 1897 and 1900, in his critiques of the epistemology of Max Müller, Lang praised Millar for anticipating Tylor's 'Test of Recurrences' for the evaluation of travellers' tales for anthropological inquiry. The contention here was that if similar practices were reported by radically different observers across time and space, then 'it becomes difficult or impossible to set down such correspondence to accident or willful fraud'.[36] Some years earlier, Lang had engaged with Millar's account on the history of early marriage while authoring his entry on the 'Family' for the *Encyclopædia Britannica*. Lang's entry adopted an anthropological approach to the topic that revealed, like Collier and Stuart-Glennie, the growing prominence of racialised categories of human difference. Millar's primary analytical point of note, according to Lang, was that he 'distinctly' expressed the notion that 'the looser relations of savages may not have been the material out of which the modern family was gradually fashioned'. Additionally, Lang brought Millar to bear on the question of matrilineality, namely his discussion of the inheritance of citizenship in classical antiquity.[37]

John Mackinson Robertson likewise praised Millar's analytical legacy while eviscerating Stuart-Glennie's racial history of folklore. Prior to entering politics as the Liberal MP for Tyneside from 1906 to 1918, Robertson was a prolific exponent of freethinking and is perhaps best known as an advocate of the Christ myth theory. As early as 1895, Robertson suggested Millar's place in the sociological canon by dint of his discussion of early gender relations, which placed him in the school of thought most recently advanced by McLennan versus Buckle.[38] During an interview in 1898 by Frederick James Gould in his personal library, Robertson named Millar as one of a cohort of early Scottish sociologists who foreshadowed Darwin and Spencer. Besides Millar, these were Dunbar, Stuart and Ferguson. According to Robertson, an 'absolute breach occurred in the development of the science', after their ideas were articulated in the 1770s and 1780s, with a new movement set forth by Hallam, who insisted on concrete historical facts and shied away from generalisation and theory, especially about primitive societies. A return to theory waited until Spencer applied evolutionary analysis to the question of social development.[39] Robertson offered a more elaborate articulation of this disciplinary history in 1905, wherein he noted that 'a history or survey of British sociology in the eighteenth century has still to be written'. Scotland would loom large in this history; besides Gibbon, Robertson nominated Smith, Hume, Ferguson, Dunbar and Millar for inclusion.[40]

The evident revisiting of Millar's work in the 1890s was not restricted to questions of disciplinary legacy. Readers who first became familiar with Millar as part of the question of matriarchy and marriage remembered him to later discuss other themes. One example was that of abolitionism. Kerallain provided multiple footnotes to Millar in his review of James Ingram's *History of Slavery* in 1895.[41] Ingram had included Millar in a list of eighteenth-century abolitionists, drawing on early nineteenth-century abolitionist Thomas Clarkson's commendations of Adam Smith, James Beattie and Francis Hutcheson as persons who 'denounced' the slave trade 'when the nature of [it] began to be understood by the public'.[42]

A second and sustained lens through which Millar was increasingly read was that of the history of inequality. Here, Swedish Finnish historical anthropologist Gunnar Landtman, a pupil of Edvard Westermarck, marked an important transition. In 1909, Landtman engaged Millar at the intersection of anthropological work on gender and family life and sociological discussion of the history of inequality.[43] Particularly evident was his use of Millar's notion of rank and his decision to structure an account of social inequality through the prism of evolving household relationships. Skewering Rousseau's account of the natural state, Landtman declared 'the earliest history of mankind was the history of an utter barbarism'.[44] While free from masters, 'the savage . . . is bound hand and foot by custom', yet 'among the most primitive peoples there is found an equality of rank' which may be perceived as commendable.[45] Landtman proceeded to document this through diverse examples taken from late nineteenth-century anthropological research, reflecting the extent to which Enlightenment-era categories of stadial history – and the conceit that evidence of the 'earliest history of mankind' could be sourced from the contemporary lifestyles of 'primitive' peoples – had become naturalised components of intercultural comparison. Moving on to advance the contention that women were generally subjected to men in early history, he drew heavily on Westermarck's discussion of the topic, including Millar as one of its four main discussants since antiquity (the others were Aristotle, Albert Hermann Post and Ernst Grosse).[46]

Later in Landtman's *Primary Causes of Social Inequality*, Millar was brought to bear on the topics of parental authority over children and a chapter on 'Social Differentiation through Personal Qualities', wherein it was noted that in Millar's *Ranks* 'we read that in the rudest and most barbarous age "there are no distinctions among individuals, but those which arise from their age and experience, from their strength, courage, and other personal qualities"', Landtman citing from the 1803 edition.[47] In a discussion on the historical formation of classes, Landtman drew on Millar to develop a claim that growing and reproduced inequality of property between different families works in tandem with tradition to create social deference. That is, when the same families, over generations, have held a material superiority over others, this preeminence, based on wealth, comes to be a more influential factor in their distinction from others than purely personal characteristics.[48]

Through this inquiry, Landtman configured Millar as a discussant of note for the history of social inequality, the topic on which he would be most discussed during the early twentieth century.

Millar's Socialist 'Rediscovery:' From Enlightenment Stadial Theory to Historical Materialism

About two decades after disciplinary histories of sociology emerged in the 1890s, Marxist sociologists in Germany began the more discrete chronicling of the intellectual genealogy of Marx's materialist philosophy of history. Confronting Marx's literary remains, these scholars encountered a scarcity of footnotes amidst a sea of manuscripts. While they believed that the materialistic philosophy of history constituted perhaps the most important interpretative innovation in the history of historiography, they practised a type of analysis that placed emphasis on individual genius rather than social-cultural conditions. Falling under the umbrella term *Dogmengeschichte*, or the history of dogma, these works were much more philosophies of history than they were instances of Marxist sociology in practice. It was upon this emerging scholarship that Werner Sombart drew in 1923 to commend Millar as the eighteenth-century progenitor of historical materialism, or what he renamed the 'technological-economic theory of history'.

Following Friedrich Engels's death in 1895, Marxist scholars became interested in tracing the intellectual genealogy of historical materialism back to the eighteenth century. Léon Cahen in 1906 proposed that the basis of the idea of class war was to be found among Bolingbroke, Holbach, Quesnay, Turgot and Smith.[49] Friedrich Muckle, in a doctoral dissertation submitted that same year on the influence of Saint-Simon upon Marx, briefly suggested that the quartet of Vico, Montesquieu, Rousseau and Ferguson set forth the basic principles of historical materialism.[50] Five years later, Walter Sulzbach would be the first to bring Millar into consideration on this topic when he attempted to extend and partially correct Muckle's analysis in his dissertation at the University of Freiburg in 1911. Sulzbach proposed an eclectic quartet of eighteenth-century thinkers of greatest importance in contributing to an incipient historical materialism *avant la lettre*: the German philologist Johann Adelung, the German historian and statistician August Ferdinand Lueder, the Feuillant revolutionary Antoine Barnave and John Millar. Of these, Sulzbach judged Millar and Barnave to have been the most important.[51]

Marking a turn in the history of Millar's reception, Sulzbach emphasised Millar's practice of stadialism but dedicated in the process almost no attention to his account of gender relations and marriage practices. Sulzbach contended that Millar constituted a 'significant advance' beyond Ferguson and James Steuart in appraising the historical effects of 'the rise of the middle class' (*Bürgerstand*), developing through the prism of rank an account of the pastoral roots of class-based economic dependence.⁵² Sulzbach's two-page-long discussion of Millar's ideas emphasised the latter's notion of how political and economic distinctions reinforced one another: for instance, through the process by which feudal lords signalled status through luxury good accumulation in medieval society or, more recently, how a transfer of power from aristocrats to men of commerce was effected through servicing this continued – and ultimately antiquated – taste for luxury.⁵³ Sulzbach also praised Millar's putatively class-based understanding of the Glorious Revolution as a singular episode of the 'greater wars of the Bürgerturms against feudalism', confirming the ascendancy of men of commerce.⁵⁴ Through this account, Sulzbach thus judged Millar as anticipating two dimensions of Marxist historical materialism: the notion of class war and the appraisal of the primacy of economic factors in history. While Sulzbach did not manage to convince all his readers that Millar and Barnave were the two key intellectual predecessors of Saint-Simon, he certainly expanded the scope of scholarly awareness of Millar's potential utility.

Heinrich Cunow, in a multivolume survey on Marxist sociology in 1920, dismissed Millar's importance, judging him a marginal figure compared to his own eighteenth-century hero, the revolutionary-era French journalist Simon-Nicholas Henri Linguet. For Cunow, Millar's *Ranks* was merely a *Werkchen* (little work) that had little place in the emerging canon of pre-Marxist social thought, let alone the history of the discipline of sociology.

> Millar was completely unaware of any concept of social classes [*Gesellschaftsklasse*]. He only knows of differences of rank and title [*Rang- und Standesunterschieden*] and fell back upon the older model of the physical superiority of the stronger versus the weaker members of society, despite occasional consideration of the influence of wealth on the ordering of rank. He did not perceive the economic foundations of class formation.⁵⁵

It was against this background that Werner Sombart authored his well-known veneration of Millar's *Ranks* in his 1923 contribution to the Festschrift for Max Weber. Sombart's admiration of Millar was part of a broader claim that sociology originated amongst a cohort of 'English thinkers', 1670–1770, who refuted natural law and contract theory through an embrace of natural sociability and statistical knowledge.[56] Sombart was apparently unaware that the three 'English' stars whom, he proposed, first deserved the title of sociologist – Ferguson, Smith and Millar – were all Scots. After discussing Ferguson briefly and encouraging study of Smith's lectures, Sombart turned to venerate Millar, starting by proposing a revised (and rather anachronistic) title for Millar's *Ranks* that would 'render it sensibly into German': the *Sociology of Authority* (*Soziologie der Herrschaft*). 'While it has been completely lost, it contains one of the best and complete sociologies that we have.'[57]

Sombart encouraged his readers to contemplate Millar and Marx side by side, beginning by reproducing the third paragraph of Millar's *Ranks* in its entirety, and then assigning a putative counterpart in Marxist terminology for each of Millar's points:

> **Millar, 1:** In searching for the causes of those peculiar systems of law and government which have appeared in the world, we must undoubtedly resort, first of all, to the differences of situation, which have suggested different views and motives of action to the inhabitants of particular countries. Of this kind, are the fertility or barrenness of the soil, the nature of its productions, the species of labour requisite for procuring subsistence, the number of individuals collected together in one community, their proficiency in arts, the advantages which they enjoy for entering into mutual transactions, and for maintaining an intimate correspondence.[58]
>
> **Marx (via Sombart), 1:** The State of Productive Forces (Stand der Produktivkräfte) and the Configuration of the Modes of Production (Gestaltung der Produktionsweise)
>
> **Millar, 2:** The variety that frequently occurs in these, and such other particulars, must have a prodigious influence upon the great body of a people; as, by giving a peculiar direction to their inclinations and pursuits, it must be productive of correspondent habits, dispositions, and ways of thinking.[59]

Marx (via Sombart), 2: Institutional and Cultural Superstructure ('institutionelle und geistige Überbau')

Summarising this comparison, Sombart contended:

> One will admit that this formulation of economic social theory surpasses that of Marx in completeness and clarity. The content of this book, in not being made up of incomprehensible phrasing, thus offers, to my knowledge, the most complete application we have of the 'materialist theory of history' to the various domains of culture.[60]

Sombart's use of Millar, that is, was to undermine Marx through a retrenchment of Sulzbach's position versus the withering critique of Cunow, supplemented by a stylistic preference for Millar's descriptive language opposed to Marxist jargon.

Sombart continued celebrating Millar's intellectual merits in a 1924 piece on the theory of class war, in which he covered much the same ground as Sulzbach to argue Millar's originality prior to Saint-Simon, though positioning Millar as part of a clearer trajectory of intellectual development approximating the Enlightenment.[61] The theory of class war, for Sombart, depended upon three principles: those of interest, class and power. Millar had contributed to conceptualising the former, identifying 'wealth, power, and well being' (*Rigdom, magt, vellevnet*) as the primary motives of human behaviour and interest, together with Ferguson, Smith and Barnave, as a constitutive element of society.[62] Millar, like these thinkers, in Sombart's argument achieved an awareness of social stratification in its connection with historical and economic stages. Here, Sombart drew on a mix of Marxist and Enlightenment-era stadial renderings, including nomadism, primitive communism, pastoral slavery, agricultural feudalism, industry and commercial democracy.[63] Once again naming Millar as one of the first sociologists, Sombart was, however, somewhat more reserved in this piece in his praise of his status relative to Marx: ultimately it was Saint-Simon, not Millar (nor Marx), who first perceived European history to be principally defined by processes of economic change.

Sombart's proposal of Millar over Marx quickly occasioned a scholarly controversy amongst Marxist scholars, including the founding editor of the Marx-Engels-Institute in the Soviet Union, David Riazanov. In a literature review on Marx and Engels's relationship to Feuerbach published in the first issue of the Marx-Engels-Institute's in-house journal, Riazanov skewered Sombart's praise of Millar:

> After a long search, a happy accident helped Sombart to determine the author who already in 1771 demonstrated that 'there was no need in the nineteenth century to discover the materialistic philosophy of history.' (!?) [sic] Yes, even more! According to him, the content of this book, which Sombart had finally found, presents 'the most complete application of the materialistic philosophy of history that we have to various spheres of culture.'[64]

As indicated by the tone of this extract, Riazanov dismissed these claims as ridiculous. To Riazanov, Millar was merely 'one of the numerous "cultural historians" of the second half of the eighteenth century who continued in the school of Montesquieu'.[65] Reiterating Cunow, he emphasised that the fundamental difference between Millar and Marx was the notion of the economic basis of class formation. To exhibit his points more clearly, he returned to the only primary source we have of any potential reception of Millar by Marx: his 1852 reading notes from the British Library on the history of women and cultural history. Riazanov went on to summarise the content of Millar's *Ranks*: the status of women in different eras, paternal authority, chiefly authority, sovereign authority and the situation of slaves and villeins.[66] While all interesting, he did not fully 'explain' these institutions: rather, he described all of them as 'a violation of the natural rights and liberties of mankind'. Reiterating Marx's attitude to Millar, Riazanov cast him more as a moralist than a sociologist.[67]

As the 1920s wore on, Millar's status as an early sociologist became fixed in pointed opposition to Marxist scholarship. Marxist thinkers like Friedrich Pollock reiterated Riazanov's and Cunow's dismissal of his significance. Anti-Marxist thinkers, however, gravitated towards Sombart's interpretation as a means of delimiting Marx's originality in the history of sociology. Pitirim A. Sorokin, a Russian American anti-communist sociologist who had fled to the US after the Russian Revolution and gained faculty positions at Minnesota and Harvard, included Millar in a source book on rural sociology, grouping him with Kames, Meiners, Linguet and Turgot as early theorists of 'the problem of the origin and development of social inequality'.[68] Sorokin extracted from Millar's discussion of the effects of the rise of agriculture on women's status in society. In

Germany, Sombart's argument that Millar constituted a definitive proponent of the 'English sociology of the eighteenth century' was reiterated in conservative thinker Hans Freyer's 1931 textbook on sociology and Sombart's overview of the fascist uses of sociology in 1936.[69]

Sombart's celebration of Millar as an early sociologist was thus anything but a straightforwardly Marxist appropriation of his legacy. Rather, his praise of Millar was part and parcel of his intellectual renunciation of Marx and socialism during the 1910s and 1920s. His basic appraisal of Millar was picked up by William C. Lehmann who, decades before offering a systematic monograph advancing the position, had already described Millar as remarkable from 'a sociological point of view' in 1930 in his dissertation on Adam Ferguson's putative contributions to sociology.[70] Further, the intellectual profile of the thinker typically thought in literature on the Scottish Enlightenment to have originated a Marxist interpretation of Smith, Millar and Ferguson's stadialism, Roy Pascal, was anything but a sociologist. Pascal was a specialist in German literature at the University of Birmingham and proposed that the Scots had attained instead a type of 'historical school' that influenced Marx via political economy; in his 1938 piece, he did not engage directly with the post-Sombartian Marxist sidelining of Millar.[71] There is an irony in this history of reception. If Millar's moralist invectives against commercial society in the *Ranks* and particularly in the *Historical View* led to his immediate marginalisation around 1800, as advanced by Ignatieff, it simultaneously included the seeds of its putative rediscovery. In the late 1910s, with the memory of Millar sustained through decades of scholars interested primarily in the question of the history of women, Millar had found a latter-day reader for whom his unique blending of Enlightenment stadialism and Commonwealthman politics finally had something to say.

Conclusion

Intellectual historians of the late twentieth century robustly critiqued disciplinary history on grounds of presentism and anachronism. As classically advanced by Collini, Winch and Burrow, it 'in essence consists in writing history backward . . . Past authors are inducted into the canon of the discipline as precursors or forebearers, and passed in review as thought by a general distributing medals – and sometimes reprimands – at the end of a successful campaign'.[72] Besides anachronism, there is also a causal paradox when situating the Scots as disciplinary forebears of modern social scientific disciplines including sociology. If it were true that eighteenth-century Scottish thinkers including Millar could be said to, in Lehmann's words, 'lay the foundations of what was later to become the science of sociology', then why, as admitted by his disciplinary historian counterpart Swingewood, 'did the school have virtually no influence in the nineteenth century'?[73] In pointed ripostes to this disciplinary conundrum, Duncan Forbes and Michael Ignatieff instead emphasised Millar's location within historical streams of political thought: the former nominating the label 'scientific Whig', the latter, drawing on Pocock's study of civic republicanism, Enlightenment Commonwealthman.[74] As Ignatieff argued, Millar's 'syncretic view was possible, not because he "anticipated" our disciplines but precisely because he was *not* working within their precincts, but instead within a jurisprudential and civic humanist mode which treated private and public spheres together, which unified "oeconomics" and "politics" in one historical synthesis'.[75] The turn to explaining Millar and his counterparts' social thinking as the product of converging intellectual traditions certainly permitted a more historically robust account of the particularities of their thought. It did not, however, reconsider the dubious claim of sociological 'rediscovery' upon which the novelty of Lehmann's and Swingewood's postwar disciplinary histories rested.

Revisiting the interpretative legacies of disciplinary history yields new insights upon not merely Millar's reception history but, moreover, the question of how the Enlightenment first became configured as a coherent field of scholarly inquiry during the early twentieth century. At issue here is the methodological character of intellectual historians' critique of disciplinary history during the 1970s and 1980s. Missing from their analysis is how disciplinary history and the field of Enlightenment studies were in part co-produced. Sombart in this regard is exemplary. While the term 'Enlightenment' does not appear in his 1923 contribution to the Festschrift for Max Weber, his temporalisation of an 'Anglo-French sociological literature' from 1670 to 1770 stretched across Paul Hazard's *Crise de la conscience européene* (1680–1715) and Ernst Cassirer's *Philosophie der Aufklärung* (second half of the eighteenth century). While the anachronistic character of the concept of Enlightenment has been abundantly recognised in contemporary scholarship, relatively little attention has been paid to how its designated luminaries were studied in the second half of the nineteenth century. Previous scholars' lack of attention to Millar's reception between, say, Mill and Sombart mirrors the ambiguous place of the nineteenth century in the historiography of the Enlightenment, particularly in Scotland. The neglect of this reception can be attributed principally to factors at the intersection of discipline, language and interpretation. Postwar English-language scholarship on Millar has neglected to pursue his weighty German-language reception, not merely in the late eighteenth and early nineteenth century – which I will pursue at another place – but, as demonstrated in this chapter, thereafter. Likewise, a stereotyped understanding of Marxist scholarship among British intellectual historians has long left unexplored the question of how and why Millar received such glowing commendations by Sombart, impeding the recognition that Millar's twentieth-century recovery was distinctly polemical and occurred transnationally.[76]

To shift towards disciplinary reflections, Millar's lingering contribution to sociological analysis may be his hesitation of system, or a universalism couched by accident. This does not align easily within the facile notion of the Enlightenment as a universalist project. Yet there are more than just intellectual historical merits to a more nuanced characterisation of John Millar as thinker. Like most of his Enlightenment-era counterparts, the universalist conceits of his stadial arguments were fractured by an implicit Eurocentrism; staked crucially not by a limited imagination but rather by the specific moral and political concerns of its practitioner. Emblematically, core to Millar's account of the history of marriage was the appraisal that the monogamous practices of the 'commercial society' of contemporary (that is, eighteenth-century) Europe emerged only through the historical conjuncture of the fall of the Roman Empire and Christian morality; polygamy, on the other hand, was what within Millar's stadial analysis was judged the typical outcome of the increase of wealth and luxury in a society.[77] Millar's indulgence in exceptions in both early and contemporary history was coherent with his methodology as set forth in the introduction to the *Ranks*, wherein he noted that variety of accidents which gave rise to differences between societies occupying the same level of stadial development. The stages were merely the guide, not the destination. As practised within the *Ranks*, Millar gave substantial hearing to discordant testimony rather than rejecting them out-of-hand for the sake of analytical consistency. This should be appraised as something other than self-defeating; rather, the space it suggested for nuance and sensitivity to detail – which Millar did not always achieve – continued to impress latter-day readers on the question of gender.

Studying stadial history as practice – rather than theory – reveals how it contained the seeds of a historicist approach. In showcasing multiple forms of social order in early society, Millar was less universalistic than often assumed, recognising historical specificity amidst global and universal comparison. There is still perhaps a disciplinarily legacy for sociology here, particularly in view of David Graeber and David Wengrow's recent contention of cooperative rather than strictly hierarchical forms of community governance in early history. Millar's conviction that different groups in early history, in different situations, might have achieved different arrangements for organising social and political life offers an alternative to the model of state dominion that has prevailed in anthropological, sociological, historical and archaeological analysis since Millar's time.[78] Millar's practice as a historian offers diverse and nuanced perspectives for historical sociological analysis which deserve to be more thoroughly engaged.

Notes

1. William C. Lehmann, *Adam Ferguson and the Beginnings of Modern Sociology: An Analysis of the Sociological Elements in His Writings with Some Suggestions as to His Place in the History of Social Theory* (New York: Columbia University Press, 1930). Lehmann developed these claims in reference to Millar over the next two decades. William C. Lehmann, 'John Millar, Historical Sociologist: Some Remarkable Anticipations of Modern Sociology', *The British Journal of Sociology* 3 (1952), pp. 30–46.
2. William C. Lehmann, *John Millar of Glasgow: His Life and Thought and His Contributions to Sociological Analysis* (Cambridge: Cambridge University Press, 1960).
3. Heinz Maus, *A Short History of Sociology* (London: Routledge, 1962), p. 6. Alan Swingewood, *A Short History of Sociological Thought*, 2nd ed. (London: Macmillan, 1991), pp. 21–4. Mario A. Toscano, *Introduzione alla sociologia* (Milan: Franco Angeli, 2006), p. 45. Alan Sica, 'Classical Sociological Theory' in George Ritzer (ed.), *The Wiley-Blackwell Companion to Sociology* (Hoboken, NJ: John Wiley, 2016), p. 88.

4. Sombart is perhaps best known for his earlier contributions to the sociology of capitalism, including coining the concepts of 'late capitalism' and 'creative destruction'. F. X. Sutton, 'The Social and Economic Philosophy of Werner Sombart: The Sociology of Capitalism' in Harry Elmer Barnes (ed.), *An Introduction to the History of Sociology* (Chicago: University of Chicago Press, 1961), pp. 316–31.
5. Note that all translations from German, French and Norwegian included in this chapter are my own. Werner Sombart, 'Die Anfänge der Soziologie' in *Hauptprobleme der Soziologie: Erinnerungsgabe für Max Weber*, ed. Melchior Palyi (Munich and Leipzig: Dunckler & Humblot, 1923), vol. 1, pp. 9–10.
6. Sombart, 'Anfänge der Soziologie', pp. 9–10.
7. Lehmann, *John Millar*, p. xiii.
8. Ibid. p. 145.
9. Roy Pascal, 'Property or Society: The Scottish Historical School of the Eighteenth Century', *Modern Quarterly* 1, no. 2 (1938), p. 178. Ronald L. Meek, 'The Scottish Contribution to Marxist Sociology' in John Saville (ed.), *Democracy and the Labour Movement: Essays in Honour of Dona Torr* (London: Lawrence & Wishart, 1954), p. 93. Alan William Swingewood, 'The Scottish Enlightenment and the Rise of Sociology: With Special Reference to the Social Theories of Adam Ferguson, John Millar, and William Robertson' (PhD diss., University of London, 1969), pp. 13, 241, 255. Michael Ignatieff, 'John Millar and Individualism' in Istvan Hont and Michael Ignatieff (eds), *Wealth and Virtue: The Shaping of Political Economy in the Scottish Enlightenment* (Cambridge: Cambridge University Press, 1983), p. 317. Louis Schneider, 'Tension in the Thought of John Millar' in Jay Weinstein (ed.), *The Grammar of Social Relations: The Major Essays of Louis Schneider* (New Brunswick, NJ: Transaction Books, 1984), p. 97. Paul Smith, 'The Materialist Interpretation of John Millar's Philosophical History: Towards a Critical Appraisal' (PhD diss., University of Glasgow, 1998), pp. 45, 76, 313. Christopher J. Berry, *Essays on Hume, Smith and the Scottish Enlightenment* (Edinburgh: Edinburgh University Press, 2018), p. 8.
10. Ignatieff, 'John Millar and Individualism', p. 321.
11. George Watson, *The Lost Literatures of Socialism* (Cambridge: Lutterworth Press, 1998), p. 28.
12. Nicholas B. Miller, *John Millar and the Scottish Enlightenment: Family Life and World History* (Oxford: Voltaire Foundation, 2017), pp. 179–208.
13. Ibid. pp. 179–208.

14. Ibid. pp. 23–7.
15. Ibid. pp. 23–7.
16. Fania Oz-Salzberger, *Translating the Enlightenment: Scottish Civic Discourse in Eighteenth-Century Germany* (Oxford: Clarendon Press, 1995), p. 23.
17. Christoph Meiners, *Grundriß der Geschichte der Menschehit* (Lemgo: Meyersche Buchhandlung, 1785), preface (Vorrede).
18. Louis Raymond Véricour, *Modern French Literature* (Edinburgh: William and Robert Chambers, 1842), pp. 18–19.
19. N. A., 'Cultivation and Progress of Law in Scotland, Part Third', *The Law Review, and Quarterly Journal of British and Foreign Jurisprudence* 14 (1851), p. 257.
20. James Reddie, *Inquiries Elementary and Historical in the Science of Law* (London: Longman, 1840), pp. 50–2.
21. John W. Cairns, 'Intellectual History and Legal History' in Richard Whatmore and Brian Young (eds), *A Companion to Intellectual History* (Chichester: John Wiley, 2016), p. 215.
22. International Institute of Social History, Karl Marx / Friedrich Engels Papers 171, Excerpts of Karl Marx, Volume 59 (VIII. 1852), Inv. Nr. B 61, ARCH00860.
23. Sam Stark, 'Marx und die Frauenfrage', *Zeitschrift für Ideengeschichte* 9, no. 3 (2017), pp. 55–66.
24. Danaga Vilesis, 'Geschlechterverhältnisse und gesellschaftliche Reproduktion. Zur markschen Rezeption von John Millar' in Urs Lindner, Jürg Nowak and Pia Paust-Lassen (eds), *Philosophieren unter anderen* (Münster: Westfälisches Dampfboot, 2008), pp. 106–18.
25. James McLennan, *Studies in Ancient History* (London, 1876), p. 420.
26. 'The Origin of Rank', *The Saturday Review*, 10 March 1877.
27. John S. Stuart-Glennie, 'The Origins of Matriarchy' in *The Women of Turkey and Their Folk-Lore* (London: David Nutt, 1891), p. 597.
28. Ibid. p. 600.
29. Ibid. p. 373.
30. J. S. Stuart-Glennie, 'History as Science', *Nature* 64, no. 1657 (August 1901), p. 327.
31. Ibid. pp. 326–7.
32. René de Kerallain, Review of Edward Westermarck, *The History of Human Marriage* (London: Macmillan, 1891), *Revue générale du droit, de la législation et de la jurisprudence en France et à l'étranger* 17 (1893), pp. 280–5.
33. James Collier, 'The Evolution of Colonies, III. Immigrants and Indigenes', *Popular Science Monthly* 53 (May–October 1898), p. 632.

34. John Hepburn Millar, *A Literary History of Scotland* (New York: Charles Scribner's Sons, 1903), pp. 367–8.
35. Ibid. p. 367.
36. Andrew Lang, *The Making of Religion*, 2nd ed. (London: Longmans, Green, and Co., 1900), p. 41. Andrew Lang, *Modern Mythology* (London: Longmans, Green, and Co., 1897), vol. 6, pp. 100–1.
37. Andrew Lang, 'Family', *Encyclopædia Britannica*, 9th ed., vol. 9 (American reprint: Philadelphia: Maxwell Somerville, 1894), pp. 18–19.
38. John Mackinson Robertson, *Buckle and His Critics: A Study in Sociology* (London: Swann Sonnenschein and Co., 1895).
39. John Mackinson Roberston in Frederick James Gould, *Chats with Pioneers of Modern Thoughts* (London: Watts & Co., 1898).
40. John Mackinson Robertson, *Course of Study* (London: Watts & Co., 1904), pp. 346–8.
41. René de Kerallain, Review of John Kelly Ingram, *A History of Slavery and Serfdom* (London: Adam and Charles Black, 1895), *Revue historique* 62 (1896), pp. 154–9.
42. James Kells Ingram, *A History of Slavery and Serfdom* (London: Adam and Charles Black, 1895), p. 154.
43. Gunnar Landtman, *The Primary Causes of Social Inequality* (Helsinki, 1909).
44. Ibid. p. 1.
45. Ibid. p. 2.
46. Ibid. p. 8.
47. Ibid. pp. 11, 33.
48. Ibid. p. 85.
49. Léon Cahen, 'L'idée de lutte de classes au XVIIIe siècle', *Revue de synthèse historique* 12 (1906), pp. 44–56.
50. Friedrich Muckle, *Die Geschichte der sozialistischen Ideen im 19. Jahrhundert*, 2 vols (Leipzig: Teubner, 1909).
51. Walter Sulzbach, *Die Anfänge der materialistischen Geschichtsauffassung* (Karlsruhe: G. Braunsche, 1911), vol. 5, pp. 80–2.
52. Ibid. pp. 64–6.
53. Ibid. pp. 66–8.
54. Ibid. p. 70.
55. Heinrich Cunow, *Die Marxsche Geschichts-, Gesellschafts- und Staatstheorie: Grundzüge der Marxschen Soziologie* (Berlin: Buchhandlung Vorwärts, 1920), vol. 1, p. 119.
56. Sombart, 'Die Anfänge der Soziologie', p. 10.
57. Ibid. p. 10.

58. John Millar, *The Origin of the Distinction of Ranks*, ed. Aaron Garett (Indianapolis, IN: Liberty Fund, 2006), pp. 83–4.
59. Ibid. p. 84.
60. Sombart, 'Die Anfänge der Soziologie', p. 14.
61. Werner Sombart, 'Klassekampens Teori', *Samtiden: tidsskrift for politikk, litteratur og samfundsspørsmål* 35 (1924), pp. 37–54.
62. Ibid. p. 37.
63. Ibid. p. 46.
64. David Riazanov, 'Aus dem literarischen Nachlass von Marx und Engels: Marx und Engels über Feuerbach', *Marx-Engels-Archiv* 1 (1926), pp. 214–15.
65. Ibid. p. 214.
66. Ibid. p. 215.
67. Ibid. p. 215.
68. Pitirim A. Sorokin, Carlze C. Zimmemann and Charles J. Galpin (eds), *A Systematic Source Book in Rural Sociology* (Minneapolis: University of Minnesota Press, 1930), vol. 1, pp. 127–8.
69. Hans Freyer, *Einleitung in der Soziologie* (Leipzig: Quelle und Meyer, 1931), p. 40. Werner Sombart, *Soziologie: Was Sie ist und Was Sie sein sollte* (Berlin: De Gruyter, 1936), p. 14.
70. Lehmann, *Adam Ferguson and the Beginnings of Modern Sociology*.
71. Pascal, 'Property or Society', pp. 167–79.
72. Stefan Collini, Donald Winch and John Burrow, *The Noble Science of Politics: A Study in Nineteenth-Century Intellectual History* (Cambridge: Cambridge University Press, 1983), pp. 1–2.
73. Lehmann, *John Millar*, book flap. Swingewood, 'The Scottish Enlightenment and the Rise of Sociology', p. 372.
74. Ignatieff, 'John Millar and Individualism', p. 323.
75. Ibid. p. 321.
76. Ibid. p. 317.
77. Miller, *John Millar*, pp. 29–70.
78. David Graeber and David Wengrow, *The Dawn of Everything* (New York: Macmillan, 2021), ch. 2. Millar is mentioned twice, both times in relation to an alleged 'indigenous' critique of European inequality that was advanced by Lafitau. Particularly in Chapter 2, Millar is presented as part of a European response to this critique via Turgot and in parallel to Graffigny's *Letters of a Peruvian Woman*.

'Das Adam Smith Problem': A Sociological Reassessment

Aldo Mascareño and Leonidas Montes

Introduction

'Das Adam Smith Problem' has occupied Smith scholarship for over a century. In brief, the problem consists of an apparent contradiction between the central arguments of his two major works, *The Theory of Moral Sentiments* (TMS) and *An Inquiry into the Nature and Causes of the Wealth of Nations* (WN).[1] While the former conceives of sympathy – the human capacity of comprehending and internalising others' sentiments and acting accordingly – as the basis of his moral theory on human interactions, the latter introduces self-interest – namely, acting according to one's own concerns and preferences – as a central motivation in social affairs, particularly in the economic realm. Correspondingly, the problem is read as an inconsistency, an irreconcilable difference between both works.

Currently, there is more agreement concerning the consistency of both works and the fact that they are part of an incomplete theoretical system. The apparent contradiction between both concepts can only derive from a narrow and socially decontextualised understanding of them. If we observe the terms in their intellectual context and pay attention to the social processes they refer to, we notice that they may even presuppose each other. Sympathy implies the individuality of agents and an internal effort to adopt others' positions, and self-interest presupposes the active acknowledgement that there are multiple individuals in social interaction with different and even diverging interests and personal projects. Thus, sympathy and self-interest would be complementary motivations in social life.

This socially embedded character of sympathy and self-interest is crucial for a broader understanding of both concepts and, particularly, for the social processes they trigger and support. For example, while reassessing Das Adam Smith Problem, James R. Otteson argues that behind TMS and WN there is a model of functioning of social institutions in which individuals 'pursuing their own interests give rise over time to an unintended system of order'.[2] Dogan Göçmen contends that in both works Smith develops a theory of social individuality which is originally advanced in TMS and then applied in WN to the social facts emerging from commercial society.[3] In a similar vein, Risto Kangas claims that commercial society weakens social ties, yet the permanent interaction among individuals produces social order.[4] And Leonidas Montes concludes that sympathy takes place in a complex social environment of reciprocal interactions in which individuals are led to establish rules that bring about social order. Therefore, sympathy and self-interest are not isolated or contradictory principles.[5] When we consider their performance in society, a complementary picture does emerge that fits contemporary sociological accounts of modern society and the major trends of its complex dynamics.

In this chapter, we argue that sympathy and self-interest refer to two central and complementary processes explaining contemporary modern society's emergence and decentralised coordination. While self-interest stresses the engagement in one's own activity and personal project (whatever the nature of this project, either commercial, scientific, artistic, or political), sympathy moves individuals and groups to stabilise reciprocal expectations (both cognitive and normative) concerning activities and projects, so we can anticipate what to expect from others' self-interest. Society is thus the result of decentralised self-interested contributions coordinated by sympathetic reciprocal expectations.

We develop this theoretical argument based on the work of the German sociologist Niklas Luhmann. His theory considers motivation as a critical factor for the functioning of social systems (economy, politics, science, arts, law, among others).[6] Motivation triggers social selectivity: namely, the engagement of individuals in multiple activities offered by social systems. Yet this engagement does not depend only on the autopoietic (self-interested in Smith's language) operations of individuals and systems but also on the construction of socially embedded reciprocal expectations among individuals (sympathy). These expectations work as a procedure to stabilise and generalise social norms and meanings that may motivate individuals to pursue autonomous goals within recognisable limits and symbolically shared structures.[7] At the same time, they monitor the risks of too much autonomy and too little interdependence, or too much cohesion and scarce autonomy, for this may lead to a breakdown of social order over time.[8] The work of a differentiated complex society depends, therefore, on the act of balance between autonomy and interdependence or, in Smithian language, between self-interest and sympathy. Consequently, we also contend that a cross-fertilisation between both theories is helpful for analytical purposes. A view on Smith's understanding of self-interest and sympathy may illuminate Luhmann's theory and the connection of individual motivational factors for social selectivity. And Luhmann's model may update Smith's conception of modern society as a complex interplay between autonomy and interdependence of individuals and systems.

To unfold this connection, we begin with a reconstruction of Adam Smith's concepts of sympathy and self-interest in which we give particular attention to their interplay and the social processes they put into motion: the construction of stabilised social norms (sympathy) and the intrinsic motivation to engage in the division of labour (self-interest). Next, we describe Niklas Luhmann's theory of self-referential social systems, attending to the interrelation between autonomy and mutual expectations. Then, after a brief review of the influence of Smith in modern sociology, we proceed to articulate Smith's and Luhmann's approaches considering sympathy as a social expectation and the embeddedness of self-interest within the sympathetic process. Finally, we draw some conclusions.

The Mutual Reinforcement of Self-interest and Sympathy in Adam Smith

The Smith Problem

The pervasive and controversial 'Adam Smith Problem' was put forward by the German Historical School.[9] The Problem as such states that there is an irreconcilable inconsistency between TMS, with its sympathy-based concept of human nature, and WN, founded on an egoistic theory of self-interest. If self-interest is an important motive in both works, it is also true that nowhere in WN Smith does refer to sympathy, the foundational concept of TMS. The simple explanation for this absence that one book is on ethics and the other about political economy does not surmount the Problem. As we will see, a proper understanding of both concepts as part of a complex social system allows a possible alternative that also sheds light on Luhmann's circularity of expectations.

The Smith Problem rests upon a particular historical and intellectual context during the second half of the nineteenth century. This context is still relevant for our understanding of sympathy and self-interest. As has been already argued, TMS presents a solid defence of self-interest, and morality plays a pervasive role throughout WN. But before delving into this issue, let us briefly summarise the origins and shaping of the classic Adam Smith Problem.

On 10 March 1777, only a year after the publication of WN in English, Johann Georg Heinrich Feder (1740–1821) wrote in the *Göttingische gelehrte Anzeigen* that 'Many of his propositions [Adam Smith] cannot be accepted as principles of universal policy; they are adapted only to a particular stage of industry, wealth, and civilization'.[10] This very early and almost forgotten assessment of WN set the stage for over a hundred years.

More than fifteen years later, Christian Garve's popular translation of WN into German (published in two parts in 1792 and 1794) brought back a renewed interest in Smith's WN. And the main protagonist was Friedrich List (1789–1846) who put forward a serious and influential nationalistic critique:

> It is a very common clever device that when anyone has attained the summit of greatness, he kicks away the ladder by which he has climbed up, in order to deprive others of the means of climbing up after him. In this lies the secret of the cosmopolitical doctrine of Adam Smith . . . and all his successors.[11]

List considered that laissez-faire would benefit Great Britain but not the developing economies. For the latter, he proposed protective tariffs and an infant industry promotion strategy. The ground for how the German Historical School would receive Adam Smith was delineated. Its main exponents –Wilhelm Roscher (1817–1894), Bruno Hildebrand (1812–1878), Karl Knies (1821–1898) and Lujo Brentano (1844–1931) – would take part in this debate. This was the beginning of Smithianismus and the so-called *Umschwungstheorie*, the idea that there was a radical change from TMS to WN, from morality to selfish political economy, from sympathy to egoism.

But the fiercest attack came from a Polish nobleman. In more than 450 pages Witold von Skaŕzyński (1850–1910) attempted to prove that Adam Smith was neither an original philosopher nor the creator of political economy but simply 'a vain teacher and an honest man'.[12] And he gave this simple but deadly wrong verdict:

> Smith was an Idealist, as long as he lived in England under the influence of Hutcheson and Hume. After living in France for three years and coming into close contact with the Materialism that prevailed there, he returned to England a Materialist. This is the simple explanation of the contrast between his Theory (1759), written before his journey to France, and his Wealth of Nations (1776), written after his return.[13]

Only in 1896, when Smith's *Lectures on Jurisprudence* were found and published, there was evidence that many of Smith's ideas in WN, especially his notion of self-interest, were quite clear before his grand tour to the Continent. In brief, the historical origins of the supposed Adam Smith Problem are linked to an intellectual context hostile to the British laissez-faire doctrine and the Manchester school.

At the turn of the century there are some scattered references to the Problem.[14] But it was Jacob Viner's classic and seminal paper 'Adam Smith and Laissez Faire' that challenged the traditional view of Smith as a precursor of economic laissez-faire and revived the tensions between TMS and WN. Viner complains that when Smith worked on the extensive revisions and additions to TMS 'he was elderly and unwell'.[15] And he restressed the conflict between both books declaring that: 'there are divergences between them [TMS and WN] which are impossible of reconciliation'.[16]

For the bicentenary of WN, the editors of the Glasgow Edition of TMS categorically dismissed the Problem as 'a pseudo-problem based on ignorance and misunderstanding'.[17] Although they were quite right in denouncing how sympathy and self-interest had been misinterpreted, they immediately argued that 'Sympathy is the core of Smith's explanation of moral judgement. The motive to action is an entirely different matter'.[18] Later, David Raphael argued that 'the role of sympathy in his book [TMS] is to explain the origin and the nature of moral judgement, of approval and disapproval'.[19] In our opinion it is a mistake to confine the broader sense of Smithian sympathy to moral judgement alone. Socially, sympathy is much more than a faculty that allows us to approve or disapprove. It is, as we will argue in this chapter, a process that foreshadows Luhmann's account of society.

Smith's Sympathy

Following Aristotle's classic idea of *zoon politikón*, Smith's sympathy requires human beings to be naturally social. Ethics is a social phenomenon with no room for Robinson Crusoes. As we are not born with the notions of good and bad, we learn what it means to be good or bad:

> Were it possible that a human creature could grow up to manhood in some solitary place, without any communication with his own species, he could no more think of his own character . . . Bring him into society, and he is immediately provided with the mirror which he wanted before. It is placed in the countenance and behaviour of those he lives with . . . and it is here that he first views the propriety and impropriety of his own passions.[20]

Human nature is predominantly social, and sympathy, underpinned by the relevance of the impartial spectator, is the core of moral judgement. As human conduct is fundamentally moral – we live and learn our mores in society – social interaction shapes moral approbation. In a way, the original etymology of ethics that distinguishes ethos with epsilon from ethos with eta – one ethos related to character and the other to habit – represents another Aristotelian virtuous interaction that helps our understanding of sympathy. For Smith the experience of conduct – that is, the exercise of sympathy – shapes our habits and our moral character as well. Both kinds of ethos – character and habit – interact within the sympathetic process.

The first, and very well-known, sentence in TMS – '[h]ow selfish soever man may be supposed, there are evidently some principles in his nature, which interest him in the fortune of others, and render their happiness necessary to him, though he derives nothing from it except the pleasure of seeing it'[21] – already defines sympathy as an inner principle in human nature. Smith is aware that common language might mislead readers as to what he actually means by sympathy:

> Pity and compassion are words appropriated to signify our fellow-feeling with the sorrows of others. Sympathy, though its meaning

was, perhaps, originally the same, may now, however, without much impropriety, be made use of to denote our fellow-feeling with any passion whatever.[22]

After stating that sympathy is not simply fellow-feeling related to pity – it pertains to 'any passion whatever' – Smith reiterates that it has to do with 'joy and grief'.[23] Smith stresses the importance of the causes of the passions, concluding that '[s]ympathy, therefore, does not arise so much from the view of the passion, as from that of the situation which excites it'.[24] Therefore, sympathy is different from its literal etymological sense (*syn-pathos*) – that is, simply fellow-feeling. Smith's sympathy implies not only being in the person's shoes but also knowing where those shoes are standing (*en-pathos*, or modern empathy – that is, feeling 'in' the other). Of course, I will have fellow-feeling with any passion, but I cannot sympathise 'till informed of its cause'.[25] Using the etymology of sympathy as fellow-feeling, I can sympathise with you if you start crying, regardless the cause. But according to Smith, I cannot sympathise with you if you start crying bitterly because you cannot find your pencil to underline this passage. In other words, I can feel and share your passion but that does not necessarily mean that I can sympathise with you.

But Smith is very aware that there is another side to sympathy as well, so he carefully explains its broader meaning. In this sense, the causes that motivate the passions are fundamental. Sympathy is not only related to feelings but also requires a process of deliberation. He concludes that '[s]ympathy, therefore, does not arise so much from the view of the passion, as from that of the situation which excites it'.[26] As we have already pointed out, sympathy goes beyond its literal etymological meaning, as it implies not only being in the person's shoes but also knowing or assessing where those shoes are standing. I can feel and share your passion, but that does not necessarily mean that I can sympathise with it. Smith's sympathy also requires a rational assessment of the circumstances, which implies a reflexive process. Therefore, Smith's sympathetic process has both moral and intellectual components. Simply stated, the attainment of mutual sympathy requires both heart and head. And as we will see, the interaction of the individual within society through self-interest and sympathy also combines fairness with deliberation.

Progress, Division of Labour and Self-interest

Already in the Introduction and Plan of the Work, on the first page of WN, Smith refers to the 'savage nations of hunters and fishers' that are 'miserably poor'.[27] They have 'the necessity sometimes of directly destroying, and sometimes of abandoning their infants, their old people, and those afflicted with lingering diseases, to perish with hunger, or to be devoured by wild beasts'.[28] And he follows on comparing this situation with 'the civilized and thriving nations' in which 'the produce of the whole labour of society is so great, that all are often abundantly supplied'.[29] Smith, as an early visionary of modernity, was predicting the positive consequences of progress and commercial society compared to the 'savage nations of hunters and fishers' of our ancestors. The almost visual image of the kids and elderly abandoned – 'with lingering diseases, to perish with hunger, or to be devoured by wild beasts'[30] – is as eloquent as the morality of the comparison. Thus, the road to progress is morally delineated.

The first chapter of Book I of WN is about the division of labour. Smith analyses and explains the exponential productive impact in a 'very trifling manufacture',[31] the pin factory that he had seen in Kirkcaldy. He observes how 'great multiplication of the productions of all the different arts' promotes the 'universal opulence which extends itself to the lowest ranks of the people'.[32] And he closes the first chapter comparing, in a suggestive Rawlsian manner, the 'extremely simple and easy' condition of a poor workman with a European prince 'that does not always so much exceed that of an industrious and frugal peasant as the accommodation of the latter exceeds that of many an African king, the absolute master of the lives and liberties of ten thousand naked savages'.[33] But Smith's defence of commercial progress demands to go deeper.

The second chapter, the most important of WN, is about the principles of the division of labour. This fundamental and rather short chapter is the main pillar of Smith's political economy. The first paragraph, worth reproducing, beautifully refers to the causes and unintended consequences of the division of labour:

> This division of labour, from which so many advantages are derived, is not originally the effect of any human wisdom, which foresees and intends that general opulence to which it gives occasion. It is the necessary, though very slow and gradual consequence of a certain propensity

in human nature which has in view no such extensive utility; the propensity to truck, barter, and exchange one thing for another.[34]

Our propensity to exchange – the foundation of political economy – is 'the necessary consequence of the faculties of reason and speech'. It belongs to human beings. But it relates to ethics. That is why Smith, in an apparently crude way, puts forward this simple comparison: 'Nobody ever saw a dog make a fair and deliberate exchange of one bone for another with another dog'.[35] But this sentence hides a moral complexity. Smith uses the word fair. Its importance is enormous. This unique Anglo-Saxon concept has a social and moral sense.[36] Its meaning goes beyond reason and rational deliberation. It appeals to the notion of a fair game, to social rules and not only laws, to what is socially approved but not necessarily demanded. To behave or act following the morality of fairness also requires mutual sympathy. If the word sympathy does not appear in WN, it is present in the moral foundations of commercial society. Exchange, as the first cause for WN, rests upon sympathetic fairness, upon the social interaction of sympathy.

Then follows the famous and traditionally misinterpreted sentence: 'It is not from the benevolence of the butcher, the brewer, or the baker, that we expect our dinner, but from their regard to their own interest'.[37] It is worth noting that Smith uses 'the butcher, the brewer, or the baker', a representation or an image that during the eighteenth century made much sense to common people. Meat, beer and bread were the main necessities for the people. Expensive books were luxury goods for intellectuals like Adam Smith. And the main aim of WN, as we know, is to improve the condition of the poor. So, this trilogy of 'the butcher, the brewer, or the baker' is also socially and morally charged.

Regard to our own interest is not necessarily selfish behaviour. It is a realistic account of human nature that has moral foundations and is strongly defended in TMS. It is prudence in its classical sense.

Adam Smith shares, particularly with David Hume, a realistic and pragmatic view of human nature. Even if we try to attain moral perfection, as human beings we must necessarily fall short of any absolute perfection. For example, Smith distinguishes between inferior and superior prudence:

> Wise and judicious conduct, when directed to greater and nobler purposes than the care of the health, the rank and reputation of the individual, is

frequently and very properly called prudence ... superior prudence ... necessarily supposes the utmost perfection of all intellectual and of all the moral virtues. It is the best head joined to the best heart. It is the most perfect wisdom combined with the most perfect virtue. It constitutes very nearly the character of the Academical or Peripatetic sage, as inferior prudence does that of the Epicurean.[38]

Superior prudence requires the 'most exact propriety'. But our eclectic philosopher concentrates on inferior prudence, following the more practical concept of prudence developed by the Epicureans. With an emphasis on 'a steady perseverance in the practice of frugality, industry and application',[39] prudence represents the pragmatic and worldly face of this virtue which is present in TMS and WN. In this sense, prudence is the cardinal virtue of Smith's moral system that most clearly serves to promote self-interest and commercial society.

In fact, Smith restricts prudence to 'our own happiness ... originally recommended to us by our selfish ... affections'.[40] His understanding of prudence is worth reproducing:

The care of the health, of the fortune, of the rank and reputation of the individual, the objects upon which his comfort and happiness in this life are supposed principally to depend, is considered as the proper business of that virtue which is commonly called Prudence ... Security, therefore, is the first and the principal object of prudence.[41]

The virtue of prudence is clearly related to self-interest. It is a self-regarding virtue that fosters Smith's recurrent defence of the right of all people to pursue the 'bettering of our condition'. The latter does not entail the cold individualism of the *homo œconomicus* as a socially detached acquisitive individual or a Robinson Crusoe detached from society. Prudence demands the approval of the impartial spectator and the supposed impartial spectator within each of us.[42] In short, self-interest is a motivation behind prudence, but prudence is not the blind pursuit of one's own wishes, wants or desires regardless of others. It also demands sympathy.

Therefore, prudence is not possessive individualism *à la* McPherson[43] nor an atomistic account of society that fosters utility maximisation. Adam Smith was not a proto-utilitarian. He knew that riches and money can be problematic. Just remember the story of the poor man's son who admires the rich and 'labours night and day to acquire talents superior to all his competitors' but does not realise that 'wealth and greatness are mere trinkets of frivolous utility' that 'gratify that love of distinction so natural to man' but bring 'no real satisfaction'. The moral, with an underlying Aristotelian sense of *eudaimonia* and human flourishing, is obvious: 'power and riches' can lead 'to anxiety, to fear, and to sorrow'.[44]

Prudence is related to well-being and society as 'the habits of *oeconomy*, industry, discretion, attention, and application of thought, are generally supposed to be cultivated from self-interested motives, and at the same time are apprehended to be very praiseworthy qualities, which deserve the esteem and approbation of everybody'.[45] But it is a self-regarding virtue rather than a manifestation of selfishness. And, as a virtue, it needs social approval within the sympathetic process. In sum, prudence relates to self-interest and sympathy.

Self-interest and sympathy are not incompatible as it has been supposed. They both relate to the individual within the social system, and they both inform and relate to Luhmann's system theory. Self-interest is autonomy within interdependent social relations. And sympathy is interdependence for autonomy. This idea of looking at the interaction between Smith's sympathy as a circularity of expectations between one and the other allows an understanding of self-interest as part of that system. This connection certainly recovers Andrew S. Skinner's view of Smith as a 'system builder',[46] a precursor of modern social science, and Schliesser's recent unfolding of Smith as a systematic philosopher.[47]

Autonomy and Interdependence in Niklas Luhmann

Niklas Luhmann's systems theory is currently sociology's most interdisciplinary approach. By combining elements from the sociological tradition, phenomenological philosophy, theoretical biology, second-order cybernetics and complexity sciences, Luhmann's theory offers an overarching approach to modern society. His theory is characterised by autonomous levels of systems (both psychic and social) that work interdependently. In this section, we aim to explain the functioning of Luhmann's rather counterintuitive articulation of autonomy and interdependence of systems that resembles the allegedly contradictory combination of self-interest and sympathy in the Smithian approach.

In contrast to the ontological tradition, which produces definitions that attribute a substance to an entity and define it by listing its components, Luhmann departs from a difference to build his theory. This is the difference between system (*System*) and environment (*Umwelt*).⁴⁸ The original insight is that we cannot understand the system in a vacuum or isolated from its surroundings, that is, as an *autarchic monad without windows* in the sense of Leibniz.⁴⁹ In connection with cybernetics, Luhmann understands the relationship between system and environment as a difference in levels of complexity: the environment is far more complex than the system.

Considering human affairs, Luhmann suggests the concept of *meaning* as the fundamental category for processing and reducing complexity. Meaning refers to the different ways humans order their experiences and actions. Making sense of something integrates a new experience or action into a major web of interrelated symbols that organise the meaningful world. This is done by the system (either psychic or social) in an autonomous way, namely, according to its own history and expectations. Yet this cannot happen in isolation. Instead, individuals and social systems must recognise themselves as part of the meaningful world to experience and act in. Thus, they are, at the same time, autonomous and interdependent.

As Luhmann argues: 'This referring-beyond-itself, this immanent transcendence of experience, is not a matter of choice; rather, it is the condition on the basis of which all freedom to choose must be first constituted'.⁵⁰ In other words, autonomy is gained through the recognition of a shared meaningful social structure (interdependence) in which there are multiple possibilities. Hence, meaning, as a basic category, presupposes the interplay of autonomy and interdependence in the constitution of human experiences and actions.

Although psychic and social systems share the meaningful structure of the world, they function in different operational modes. For the psychic system (individuals), *intentionality* is the central operation. The flux of consciousness intentionally connects one thought to another, producing the meaningful web of *motives*. On the other hand, communication is the fundamental operation of social systems (interactions, organisations, major functional systems, societies). It connects one event of communication to another through acceptances or rejections and produces different autonomous social systems, such as the economy, politics and law.⁵¹ However, despite all operative autonomy of both individuals and social systems, there is a fundamental relation between them which is called *interpenetration*:

We speak of 'penetration' if a system makes its own complexity (and, with it, indeterminacy, contingency, and the pressure to select) available for constructing another system ... Accordingly, interpenetration exists when this occurs reciprocally ... This means that greater degrees of freedom are possible in spite (better: because!) of increased dependencies.[52]

For the existence of society, the interdependence of individuals and social systems is therefore crucial. Autonomous individual motives, such as the interaction between self-interest and sympathy, are distributed in different social systems through communication,[53] thus producing what Luhmann calls *expectations of expectations*. Given the unrestrained behaviour of individuals, their future selections cannot be taken for granted. Rather, future behaviour must be expected as a possibility. Those possibilities depend, however, on individual autonomy and the autonomy of social systems. As Luhmann argues:

It is necessary, therefore, not simply to be able to expect the behavior, but also the expectations of others in order to find solutions to problems that can be both integrated and tested. It is not simply necessary in order to control the context of social interactions that everyone experiences, but also that everyone can anticipate what the other expects from him.[54]

In other words, to accomplish our own goals in social interaction, or more technically, to coordinate present selectivity with future behaviour, one has to be open to the meaningful world of others. This Luhmannian concept resembles Smith's sympathy.

Expectations can certainly be disappointed, and one can react to the disappointments by confirming the expectation (a normative reaction) or learning from the disappointment and consequently changing the expectation (a cognitive reaction).[55] When individuals recognise these expectations, they can act with autonomy and, at the same time, be acquainted with others' expectations of their own behaviour. They know they can engage in reciprocal interactions without having to resolve at every step what comes next because they act in systems composed by expectations of expectations. And they also know what to expect if they autonomously decide to interrupt or defraud others' expectations, because the system provides alternatives.

Autonomy and interdependence work together in the construction of social interactions. Interdependence provides both individuals and systems with multiple possibilities of selection, thereby preventing them from falling into autarchy and solipsism. And autonomy is the basis upon which individuals and systems choose their own options, avoiding the homogenisation that interdependence may entail. As in the case of the Smithian concept of sympathy, individuals remain autonomous entities but can connect with others' feelings in interdependent relationships.

Connecting Smith and Luhmann: An Intellectual Sympathy

Cross-fertilisation efforts between theoretical approaches should not be read as a purely intellectual exercise. Instead, they are helpful to illuminate either blind spots or underdeveloped segments of conceptual architecture that produce a connection between a phenomenon and our explanations.[56]

When connecting Adam Smith and Niklas Luhmann, we can expand our comprehension of the sympathetic process with contemporary theoretical tools and offer a sociologically grounded view on the compatibilisation of self-interest and sympathy not in a *narrow* but in a *fundamental* sense. We argue that the Luhmannian category of *expectations of expectations* helps us to recognise the reflexivity, the shared common meanings, among autonomous individuals and the openness to others involved in the sympathetic process. Consequently, in this section, we begin with a brief review of sociological approaches to Smith's theory; next, we reconstruct the concept of sympathy as expectation of expectation in a Luhmannian sense; then, we analyse the embeddedness of self-interest in sympathy; and finally, we consider the impartial spectator as a second-order observer, namely, as a double-sided process of mutual observation and recognition.

Adam Smith in Contemporary Sociology

The reception of Adam Smith in sociology might be divided into two categories: (a) the examination of Smithian topics such as division of labour, exchange and evolution in different sociological analyses of secondary literature, and (b) the engagement with

Smith's arguments in major sociological works. We offer a brief overview of both.

In the secondary sociological literature, one of the addressed issues is whether the division of labour is the fundamental force behind the expansion of markets. Slim Rashid, for example, argues that Smith's original contribution to the analysis of the division of labour is limited by the extent of the market, so that the more complex the market, the more complex the division of labour in society.[57] On the contrary, for Ramesh Chandra, Smith's main contribution lies in the analysis of the institutions that promote market exchange and division of labour.[58] He concludes that division of labour is a self-reinforcing evolutionary process that defines the extent of the market – an argument also put forward by Henry Clark.[59] Other sociological aspects discussed concerning this topic are, for example, the difference between social and organisational division of labour,[60] the sexual division of labour[61] and its relationship with demography and population growth.[62]

An important strand of the literature refers to different concepts and topics advanced by Smith, which were fundamental for the rise of modern sociology. To that extent, Smith is considered an early founding figure of sociology. Walter Nord, for example, argues that the keys of modern exchange theory should not be attributed to Georg Homans or Marcel Mauss, but to Smith.[63] Torben Nielsen contends that Smith's theory contributes to a reconsideration of social organisation as a form of self-government, beyond the roles that state and market may play in this regard.[64] And authors such as Tony Aspromourgos, David Thacher and Francesca Dal Degan agree on the fundamental sociological insight that Smith put forward: namely, that individuals cannot be considered in isolation.[65] Individuals must be rather comprehended in a milieu of moral sentiments that historically change depending on the interactions and experiences of individuals in society.

Major sociological works have also made use of Smithian concepts and arguments. Well known is Karl Marx's recognition and critique of Smith's theory of value.[66] Also familiar is Émile Durkheim's assessment of the consequences of the division of labour on the autonomy of the individual and the cohesion of modern society.[67] Less known, however, are the relevance that Niklas Luhmann attributes to Adam Smith regarding the origins of modernity and the differentiation of the economic system, on the one hand,[68] and the use of Smith's writings for a canonical description of the market polity in the pragmatic sociology of Luc Boltanski and Laurent Thévenot, on the other.[69]

Niklas Luhmann considers Adam Smith's theory as the first approach to a new evolutionary process consisting in the differentiation of an autonomous economic system guided by money and prices but in which sympathy plays a central role.[70] As Luhmann argues:

> Each participant is expected to attend the expectations of the others (which does not necessarily mean to meet them). Adam Smith called this 'sympathy', Mead called it 'taking the role of the other'. By means of such expectations, the participants put themselves under pressure to make decisions'.[71]

Expectations of expectations – or sympathy in Smithian terms – are thus the engine of social interaction. It is the reflexivity of the interaction that counts.

Boltanski and Thévenot also consider that WN sets the underpinnings of economics as a discipline, and TMS reflects on the more fundamental level of the social bond or a *grammar* – a concept also suggested by Smith: 'the rules of justice may be compared to the rules of grammar'.[72] This grammar includes several elements: the capacity to reach an agreement in market exchanges, the common identification of external goods, an affective disposition to other persons and things, and the liberation from domestic bonds. There is a passion towards the possession of goods (self-interest), but at the same time 'persons have to be detached enough from themselves and from domestic subordinations to get along with all the other individuals in a marketplace that serves as the higher common principle, and to agree about the goods exchanged, which express their desires'.[73] Therefore, self-interest presupposes a grammar of sympathy in the market polity. And that grammar delineates the meaning of self-interest. While sympathy allows for self-detachment and capacities for interaction, the metaphor of the impartial spectator establishes the independence from domestic ties that may favour selfishness.

Contemporary sociology agrees on the relevance of Smith's theory for the construction of the discipline and, at the same time, it allows us to interpret 'Das Adam Smith Problem' as an example of the relational constitution of modern society. We elaborate this argument in the following sections.

Sympathy as a Social Expectation: The Basis of Social Order

As previously discussed, sympathy in Smith's view not only refers to a fellow feeling (pity, joy or grief) through which an individual can share with another her feelings in any given situation (narrow sense).[74] A second and more basic meaning of sympathy refers to the reflexive process underlying every affection or passion. At this fundamental level, sympathy entails a moral grammar for social relations, which in Luhmannian terms can be called a dynamic process of construction of social expectations (fundamental sense of sympathy).

The apparently simple and rather natural expression of a fellow feeling in everyday life (joy for the success of members of our family or friends, grief because of a loss, compassion with the suffering of people in the narrow sense) is always full of presuppositions that must be met to identify the fundamental sense of sympathy. Drawing on Niklas Luhmann's approach, we reconstruct these presuppositions as follows:

- First, two individuals (we call them *alter* and *ego*) should be reflexive entities that recognise themselves with psychic, emotional and agential capacities. In Luhmannian terms, they must be self-referential systems that 'must have the freedom to speak, to do this or not'.[75] Thus, sympathy requires reflexivity.
- Second, both *alter* and *ego* must recognise that they construct their relationships upon symbols and structures already made in the past.[76] They can reproduce or change them through present actions and communications but cannot fully control them because the others are as autonomous as they are, so that unintended consequences of every action always may follow. Thus, sympathy requires sharing a meaningful world.
- And third, as entities of a shared, meaningful world, both *alter* and *ego* must recognise its contingency. The world is contingent because the selections are neither necessary nor impossible.[77] Hence, reciprocal expectations could be disappointed. Thus, sympathy requires cognitive openness to the changing sensibility of others.

Therefore, the construction of reciprocal expectations (sympathy in a fundamental sense) is far from simply expressing desires or emotions (sympathy in the narrow sense). Just the opposite: because of the former, we have access to the latter. To develop sympathy, individuals require reflexivity, sharing a meaningful world and being open to the sensibility of others. To that extent, the sympathetic process becomes reciprocal and complex: (a) *alter* expects *ego*'s behaviour and vice versa, and (b) *alter* also expects that *ego* expects *alter*'s behaviour and vice versa. It is thus a process of anticipation of expectations, which is called by Luhmann *expectation of expectation*,[78] or sympathy by Smith.

Considering this, when Smith contends that sympathy refers to a passion (narrow sense) and 'the situation which excites it' (fundamental sense),[79] he has in mind a moral order in the eighteenth-century language that is well described in Luhmann's account of a social order of expectations. A relevant implication of this is that sympathy as a process presupposes an operation (reflexivity), a grammar (a structure of shared meanings) and the recognition of others (the cognitive openness to their changing sensibility).

The Embeddedness of Self-interest in Sympathy

As we have argued, self-interest does not mean selfish behaviour. Considering the three above-described presuppositions of social order (fundamental sympathy), self-interest can be understood as the autonomy of individuals (*alter* and *ego*) to manage their cognitive, emotional and behavioural capacities (reflexivity). They must recognise the meaningful world in which they and other individuals also live, including the autonomy of others as a legitimate situation no one can fully control (a shared meaningful world). And they also must acknowledge that expectations can be disappointed (cognitive openness to the changing sensibility of others). In other words, there is no autonomy without interdependence, no meaningful social relationships without sympathy.

Considering these presuppositions in the context of market relations, production for the exchange must have a view on the interactions beyond the domestic unit and demands – as Boltanski and Thévenot argue – the consideration of the needs of others as well as their recognition as entities capable of their own selectivity. Since we can meaningfully interact with them (in terms of price, quantities or regularity of services), we presuppose a common world in which what we communicate, agree and exchange can be stabilised as a social expectation. To that extent, self-interest is embedded in sympathy; that is, for every self-interested behaviour in the division of labour, others' expectations must be considered and even anticipated in the form of expectations of expectations.

Similarly, Adam Smith argues that the habits of industry stem from self-interested motives, yet industrious behaviour deserves esteem from everybody. The care of the self that emerges from prudence elicits approbation from others so that self-interest should not be regarded as a solipsistic motive but comprehended within the perspective of social welfare. These apparently contradictory attitudes become articulated in the division of labour: individual motives and abilities spontaneously combined produce the wealth of nations, not only in material but also in civilisational terms. In Smith's words:

> the most dissimilar geniuses are of use to one another; the different produces of their respective talents, by the general disposition to truck, barter, and exchange, being brought, as it were, into a common stock, where every man may purchase whatever part of the produce of other men's talents he has occasion for.[80]

This is a significant outcome of the division of labour in Smith's account, which is not possible at all without comprehending the visible manifestations of self-interest and the process of sympathy.

The Impartial Spectator as a Second-order Observer

We cannot sympathise or even understand others without knowing and assessing why they do what they do. To avoid misconceptions and misunderstandings, we need – in Smith's account – to imagine how a third party (freed from partiality and prejudice) would judge our own and others' behaviour. The *impartial spectator* accomplishes this task.

In Luhmann's system theory we find an equivalent: the second-order observer. Every system (including individuals) is provided with the capacity of observation, and we observe by selecting and applying distinctions to the meaningful world. While the first-order observer directly observes facts in the world (objects, processes and problems), the second-order observer observes how others observe.

Through *second-order observation*, we can internalise the Smithian impartial spectator and consider her point of view as a socially situated stance. Furthermore, by knowing it, we can assess and initiate the reflexive process of mutual understanding, share the meaningful world of others and be cognitively open to his or her sensibility. The crucial contribution of the second-order observer to the sympathetic process is thus twofold. On the one hand, we can see the distinctions others apply to observe and understand the world and have access to his or her justifications and blind spots. On the other, through second-order observation, we can also recognise that others can do the same with us, namely, assess our justifications and blind spots. Being conscious of our own justifications and blind spots allows us to acknowledge that we are *the other of others* and that we need the cognitive openness of an impartial spectator to observe others and see how they see us. The success of the sympathetic process lies in this double-sided possibility of mutual observation and recognition.

In this vein, the second-order observer has a broader view of the meaningful world. As Luhmann argued: 'Second-order observation conveys universal access to the world'.[81] This is crucial for the sympathetic process. Thus, the second-order observer becomes an impartial spectator that invites us to a fine tuning of expectations, which embeds self-interest within sympathy.

Conclusions

Much has been written about the famous Adam Smith Problem that questions the relationship between *The Theory of Moral Sentiments* and *An Inquiry into the Nature and Causes of the Wealth of Nations*. Although there is general agreement that both works are part of an incomplete system of ethics, politics and jurisprudence that Smith promised but could not complete (see his promise in the Advertisement and at the final words of TMS), the Problem is still relevant for anyone attracted to Smith scholarship. It is historically and philosophically fascinating. Moreover, as we have attempted to show, it has implications for the modern social theory debate.

Since the rise of sociology as an academic discipline, Smithian arguments have been discussed and reconstructed. He has even been considered an early figure of modern sociology. Classical sociologists such as Émile Durkheim emphasised the analysis of the division of labour, while contemporary sociology has become more interested in his work on sympathy and moral sentiments. As we have argued, TMS and WN should not be considered in isolation. Our own reconstruction and association with the work of Niklas Luhmann were aimed at presenting this connection: self-interest is embedded in sympathy, as it recognises that the autonomy of individuals takes place in a shared meaningful world in which they reflexively agree on constructing social expectations that open up to the others.

The theoretical association with Niklas Luhmann was thus helpful in a twofold sense. On the one hand, Luhmann provides Smith's approach with a robust theory of the circular formation of social expectations in which autonomy (self-interest) presupposes sociability (sympathy). On the other, Smith's theory contributes with relevant insights for a theory of the psychic system and its orientation to society in the Luhmannian framework. This theory has not been systematically developed yet. However, Adam Smith's insights into social interaction contribute to our modern understanding of the role of individuals in systems theory.

Notes

1. Adam Smith, *The Theory of Moral Sentiments* (Oxford: Clarendon Press, [1759] 1976), henceforth TMS, and Adam Smith, *An Inquiry into the Nature and Causes of the Wealth of Nations*, vols 1 and 2 (Oxford: Clarendon Press, [1776] 1976), henceforth WN.
2. James R. Otteson, 'The Recurring "Adam Smith Problem"', *History of Philosophy Quarterly* 17 (2000), pp. 51–74, p. 70.
3. Dogan Göçmen, *The Adam Smith Problem* (London: Tauris Academic Studies, 2007).
4. Risto Kangas, 'The Market, Values and Coordination of Actions: From Value Integration to *Libertas Indifferentiae*', *Journal of Classical Sociology* 9 (2009), pp. 291–318.
5. Leonidas Montes, 'The Origins of *Das Adam Smith Problem* and Our Understanding of Sympathy', in Sandra Peart and David M. Levy (eds), *The Street Porter and the Philosopher: Conversations on Analytical Egalitarianism* (Ann Arbor, MI: The University of Michigan Press, 2011), pp. 158–78.
6. Niklas Luhmann, *Theory of Society*, vols 1 and 2 (Stanford, CA: Stanford University Press, 2013).
7. Niklas Luhmann, *A Sociological Theory of Law* (London: Routledge, 2014).

8. See Aldo Mascareño, Eric Goles and Gonzalo A. Ruz, 'Crisis in Complex Social Systems: A Social Theory View Illustrated with the Chilean Case', *Complexity* 21:S2 (2016), pp. 13–23; and Aldo Mascareño, 'Critical Transitions in Ecosystems and Society: The Contribution of Sociological Systems Theory to the Analysis of Socio-Environmental Transformations', *Frontiers in Sociology* 6:763453 (2022).
9. For a brief historical account of *Das Adam Smith Problem* see TMS, intr. pp. 20–5, and David Raphael, *Adam Smith* (Oxford: Oxford University Press, 1985), pp. 87–90. Other classic sources are August Oncken, 'The Consistency of Adam Smith', *Economic Journal* 7 (1897), pp. 443–50; and August Oncken, 'The Adam Smith Problem' [1898], in Hiroshi Mizuta (ed.), *Adam Smith: Critical Responses* (London: Routledge, 2000), pp. 84–105. See also Glen R. Morrow, *Ethical and Economic Theories of Adam Smith* (New York: Augustus M. Kelley Publishers, [1923] 1969); Glen R. Morrow, 'Adam Smith: Moralist and Philosopher', *Journal of Political Economy* 35 (1927), pp. 321–42; Russell Nieli, 'Spheres of Intimacy and the Adam Smith Problem', *Journal of the History of Ideas* 47 (1986), pp. 611–24; and James R. Otteson, *Adam Smith's Marketplace of Life* (Cambridge: Cambridge University Press, 2002), pp. 134–6. On the emergence of the *Problem*, see Keith Tribe and Hiroshi Mizuta, *A Critical Bibliography of Adam Smith* (London: Pickering & Chatto, 2002); and Ingrid Peters-Fransen, 'The Canon in the History of the Adam Smith Problem', in Evelyn L. Forget and Sandra Peart (eds), *Reflections on the Classical Canon of Economics: Essays in Honour of Samuel Hollander* (London: Routledge, 2001), pp. 168–84.
10. Quoted in Gustav Cohn, 'The History and Present State of Political Economy in Germany' [1873], in Mizuta (ed.), *Adam Smith: Critical Responses*, vol. 1, p. 64; emphasis in the original.
11. Friedrich List, *The National System of Political Economy* (London: Longmans, Green, [1841] 1904), p. 295.
12. Witold Skarżyński, *Adam Smith als Moralphilosoph und Schoepfer der Nationaloekonomie. Ein Beitrag zur Geschichte der Nationaloekonomie* (Berlin: Theobald Grieben, 1878), p. xvii.
13. Skarżyński, *Adam Smith als Moralphilosoph und Schoepfer der Nationaloekonomie*, p. 183.
14. See Leonidas Montes, *Adam Smith in Context: A Critical Reassessment of Some Central Components of His Thought* (New York: Palgrave Macmillan, 2004), pp. 73–8.
15. Jacob Viner, 'Adam Smith and Laissez Faire', *Journal of Political Economy* 35:2 (1927), pp. 198–232, p. 217.

16. Viner, 'Adam Smith and Laissez Faire', p. 201.
17. TMS intr. p. 20.
18. TMS pp. 21–2; emphasis in the original.
19. Raphael, *Adam Smith*, p. 29.
20. TMS III.1.3, p. 110.
21. TMS I.i.1.1, p. 9.
22. TMS I.i.1.5, p. 10.
23. Smith's debt to his friend David Hume is enormous, especially regarding the use and improvement of the concept of sympathy. After the first edition of TMS was published, Hume wrote a letter to Smith arguing 'I wish you had more particularly and fully prov'd, that all kinds of Sympathy are necessarily Agreeable. This is the Hinge of your System . . . Now it would appear that there is a disagreeable Sympathy, as well as an agreeable . . . A Hospital would be a more entertaining Place than a Ball' (Adam Smith, *Correspondence of Adam Smith* (Indianapolis, IN: Liberty Fund, 1987), p. 43). Hume had detected the difference, but for this point Smith's sympathy was philosophically broader and even more precise. For example, see Samuel Fleischacker, *Being Me Being You: Adam Smith and Empathy* (Chicago: University of Chicago Press, 2019), pp. 15–17 and pp. 23–7; and Samuel Fleischacker, *Adam Smith* (London: Routledge, 2021), ch. 4.
24. TMS I.i.1.10, p. 12.
25. TMS I.i.1.8, p. 11.
26. TMS I.i.1.10, p. 12.
27. WN intr. p. 10.
28. WN intr. p. 10.
29. WN p. 10.
30. WN p. 10.
31. WN I.i.3, p. 14.
32. WN I.i.10, p. 22.
33. WN I.i.11, p. 24.
34. WN I.ii.1, p. 25.
35. WN I.ii.2, p. 25; emphasis added.
36. See Anna Wierzbicka, *English: Meaning and Culture* (Oxford: Oxford University Press, 2006), pp. 141–4; and Leonidas Montes, 'Adam Smith's Foundational Idea of Sympathetic Persuasion', *Cambridge Journal of Economics* 43 (2019), pp. 1–15, pp. 8–9.
37. WN I.ii.2, pp. 26–7.
38. TMS VI.i.14, p. 216.
39. TMS IV.2.6, pp. 189–90.
40. TMS VI.concl.1, p. 262.

41. TMS VI.i.5 and 6, p. 213.
42. See TMS VI.i.11, p. 215.
43. C. B. McPherson, *The Political Theory of Possessive Individualism: Hobbes to Locke* (Oxford: Oxford University Press, 1962).
44. TMS IV.I.7, pp. 181–3.
45. TMS VII.ii.3.16, p. 304.
46. See Andrew S. Skinner, 'Adam Smith: The Development of a System', *Scottish Journal of Political Economy* 23 (1976), pp. 111–32; and Andrew S. Skinner, *A System of Social Science Papers Relating to Adam Smith* (Oxford: Clarendon Press, 1979).
47. Eric Schliesser, *Adam Smith: Systematic Philosopher and Public Thinker* (Oxford: Oxford University Press, 2017).
48. Niklas Luhmann, *Social Systems* (Stanford, CA: Stanford University Press, 1995).
49. Gottfried W. Leibniz, 'The Monadology' in *Leibniz's Monadology: A New Translation and Guide*, ed. Lloyd Strickland (Edinburgh: Edinburgh University Press, 2014), pp. 14–33.
50. Niklas Luhmann, 'Meaning as Sociology's Basic Concept', in Niklas Luhmann, *Essays on Self-Reference* (New York: Columbia University Press, 1990), pp. 21–79, p. 25.
51. Luhmann, *Theory of Society*, vol. 1, ch. 4.
52. Luhmann, *Social Systems*, p. 213.
53. See Aldo Mascareño, 'The Function of Ethics from the Perspective of the Individuals', *Soziale Systeme* 17 (2011), pp. 186–210.
54. Luhmann, *A Sociological Theory of Law*, p. 26.
55. Different social systems deal with both types of expectations. Law, for example, concentrates on the stabilisation of normative expectations. It develops rules and courts to re-establish disappointed normative expectations, but also develops procedures in coordination with politics and legislation to change norms when they become obsolete because of the dynamics of social reality. Thus, law can also cognitively learn from the disappointment. See Niklas Luhmann, *Law as a Social System* (Oxford: Oxford University Press, 2004). Science, on the other hand, works mainly with cognitive expectations; it learns from empirical and theoretical research that the world is other than expected and consequently changes its methods and theories to develop new strategies and provisional knowledge. This idea of provisional knowledge resembles Smith's own view of philosophy of science which is much influenced by Newton. On this issue see Leonidas Montes, 'Smith and Newton: Some Methodological Issues concerning General Economic Equilibrium Theory', *Cambridge Journal*

of Economics 27 (2003), pp. 723–47; and Eric Schliesser, 'Some Principles of Adam Smith's Newtonian Methods in *The Wealth of Nations*', *Research in the History of Economic Thought and Methodology* 23 (2005), pp. 33–74. Yet, science also preserves normative expectations as principles of its functioning, such as the rejection of plagiarism, the privacy of research subjects and the restrictions to the experimentation with humans. They guide research agendas as well as the cognitive search for knowledge. See Niklas Luhmann, *Die Wissenschaft der Gesellschaft* (Berlin: Suhrkamp, 2018).

56. Humberto Maturana, 'Science and Daily Life: The Ontology of Scientific Explanations', in Wolfgang Krohn, Gunter Küppers and Helga Nowotny (eds), *Selforganization: Portrait of a Scientific Revolution* (Dordrecht: Kluwer Academic Publishers, 1990), pp. 12–35.
57. Slim Rashid, 'Adam Smith and the Division of Labour: A Historical View', *Scottish Journal of Political Economy* 33 (1986), pp. 292–7.
58. Ramesh Chandra, 'Adam Smith, Allyn Young, and the Division of Labor', *Journal of Economic Issues* 38 (2004), pp. 787–805.
59. Henry C. Clark, 'Conversation and Moderate Virtue in Adam Smith's "Theory of Moral Sentiments"', *The Review of Politics* 54 (1992), pp. 185–210.
60. Stéphan Vincent-Lancrin, 'Adam Smith and the Division of Labour: Is there a Difference between Organisation and Market?', *Cambridge Journal of Economics* 27 (2003), pp. 209–24.
61. Sumitra Shah, 'Sexual Division of Labor in Adam Smith's Work', *Journal of the History of Economic Thought* 28 (2006), pp. 221–41.
62. Philip Kreager, 'Adam Smith, the Division of Labor, and the Renewal of Population Heterogeneity', *Population and Development Review* 43:3 (2017), pp. 513–39.
63. Walter Nord, 'Adam Smith and Contemporary Social Exchange Theory', *American Journal of Economics and Sociology* 32 (1973), pp. 421–36.
64. Torben H. Nielsen, 'The State, the Market and the Individual: Politics, Economy and the Idea of Man in the Works of Thomas Hobbes, Adam Smith and in Renaissance Humanism', *Acta Sociologica* 29 (1986), pp. 283–302.
65. Tony Aspromourgos, 'Adam Smith and the Division of Labour among the Social Sciences', *Review of Political Economy* 23:1 (2011), pp. 81–94; David Thacher, 'The Perception of Value: Adam Smith on the Moral Role of Social Research', *European Journal of Social Theory* 19 (2016), pp. 94–110; and Francesca Dal Degan, 'Beyond Virtues and Vices: Antonio Genovesi's and Adam Smith's

"Science of Relationships"', *The European Journal of the History of Economic Thought* 25 (2018), pp. 562–81.
66. Karl Marx, *Capital: A Critique of Political Economy* (New York: International Publishers, 1967).
67. Émile Durkheim, *The Division of Labour in Society* (New York: Palgrave Macmillan, [1902] 2013).
68. Niklas Luhmann, *Die Wirtschaft der Gesellschaft* (Frankfurt: Suhrkamp, 1996).
69. Luc Boltanski and Laurent Thévenot, *On Justification* (Princeton: Princeton University Press, 2006). Rather minor but significant references to Smith can also be found in the symbolic interactionism of Erving Goffman regarding the description of habits in *The Presentation of the Self in Everyday Life* (Edinburgh: University of Edinburgh, 1956), as well as in Talcott Parsons, *The Structure of Social Action* (New York: The Free Press, 1937) and Jürgen Habermas, *Theory of Communicative Action, Volume Two: Lifeworld and System: A Critique of Functionalist Reason* (Boston, MA: Beacon Press, 1987) concerning the rise of modern economy.
70. Luhmann, *Die Wirtschaft der Gesellschaft*, ch. 1.
71. Ibid. p. 294.
72. TMS III.6.11, p. 175.
73. Boltanski and Thévenot, *On Justification*, p. 52.
74. We use the Luhmannian figure of *alter* and *ego* to express the basic components in a situation of communication. See Luhmann, *Social Systems*, ch. 4.
75. Luhmann, *Social Systems*, p. 141.
76. Luhmann, *Theory of Society*, vol. 1, ch. 2, particularly sections 2.9 and ff.
77. Niklas Luhmann, *Beobachtung der Moderne* (Opladen: Westdeutscher Verlag, 1992).
78. Luhmann, *A Sociological Theory of Law*, p. 26.
79. TMS I.i.1.10, p. 12.
80. WN I.ii.5, p. 30.
81. Niklas Luhmann, *Soziologische Aufklärung 5. Die Soziologie und der Mensch* (Wiesbaden: VS Verlag, 2005), p. 16.

15

The Foundational Document of the Sociology of Knowledge

Tamás Demeter

Knowledge as a Natural Phenomenon

Much of Scottish Enlightenment thinking about nature and human nature is aptly characterised by the term 'providential naturalism': the view that phenomena are providentially ordered, so the laws and principles one can read from these phenomena reflect the purposes of providence.[1] Nature is thus conceived with an intrinsic teleological-cum-theological meaning: when studying phenomena with descriptive and explanatory intentions we inevitably reach insights with normative and transcendent significance. This commitment is well reflected in David Fordyce's 1754 philosophical programme:

> We discover the *Office*, *Use* or *Destination* of any Work, whether *natural* or *artificial*, by observing its Structure, the Parts of which it consists, their Connection or joint Action. It is thus we understand the *Office* and *Use* of a Watch, a Plant, an Eye, or Hand. It is the same with a *Living Creature*, of the *Rational*, or *Brute Kind*. Therefore to determine the *Office*, *Duty*, or *Destination* of *Man*, or in other words what his *Business* is, or what *Conduct* he is obliged to pursue, we must inspect his *Constitution*.[2]

It is easy to find ample illustrations of this widely shared stance in contemporary Scottish texts. George Turnbull in 1740 similarly holds that by 'examining the structure and fabrick of the mind . . . we can ascertain the end and purpose of our being'.[3] Hutcheson in his 1742 introduction to moral philosophy also proclaims that the wisdom of Deity has formed human nature, so we 'must expect to find in our structure and frame some clear evidences, shewing the proper business of mankind' and 'what character God our Creator requires us to maintain'.[4]

As an alternative, one can discern a much less outspoken orientation of philosophical inquiry. It can be characterised as 'agnostic naturalism',[5] which severs the connections of inquiry into human nature from providential considerations. Hume expresses this stance in his famous letter to Hutcheson in September 1739:

> I cannot agree to your sense of Natural. 'Tis founded on final Causes; which is a Consideration, that appears to me pretty uncertain & unphilosophical. For pray, what is the End of Man? Is he created for Happiness or for Virtue? For this Life or for the next? For himself or for his Maker? Your Definition of Natural depends upon solving these Questions, which are endless, & quite wide of my Purpose.[6]

Here Hume deprives 'natural' from its then common normatively loaded meaning. While phenomena of nature and human nature had been widely conceptualised as being intrinsically theological and normative, Hume expelled this normativity, steering towards an ideal of value-free inquiry into causal mechanisms that would become characteristic to cognitive psychology and much of the social sciences. This aspiration is transparent in Hume's programme for *A Treatise of Human Nature*. Founded on 'the experimental method of reasoning', as its subtitle announces, Hume here explores the psychological and social mechanisms underlying a wide range of human phenomena from perception and belief formation to affective functioning and socialisation. The search for causal mechanisms, rather than epistemic norms and ideals of inquiry, is distinctive of the epistemology in Hume's *Treatise*.

Situating Hume's theory of knowledge in the context of early modern enterprises, Gary Hatfield argues that for Hume belief-forming mechanisms are truth-neutral: in Hume's construal, not even the proper operation of these mechanisms can ensure the production of true beliefs – nor can they provide the standards by which to judge whether a belief is true or false. Hume thus diverges from the main thrust of early modern epistemology that, following Descartes and Aristotle, agreed to posit a faculty (reason, or the intellect) whose proper functioning provided the standards for, and aimed to ensure by them, the formation of true beliefs.[7] In contrast, Hume's theory of belief formation deflates the role of epistemic norms if compared to the epistemological projects driven by some vision of what ideal knowledge should meet.[8] This deflation is at the core of Hume's naturalised epistemology: instead of advocating constitutive norms for the production of objective knowledge (such as clear and distinct insight, or rationality), he suggests we should 'cultivate habits of imagination that will prove useful in the course of experience' – despite their lack of rational justification. The epistemic norms Hume provides are in this reading 'recommendations for how one should guide the development of one's cognitive habits' and 'for training based on what has been successful'.[9]

Consequently, as Jerry Fodor puts it, 'Hume rather clearly didn't believe that justification is all that interesting a notion'[10] – as far as at least the general thrust of the *Treatise* is concerned.[11] Rather than justificatory reasons underpinning beliefs or epistemic ideals to be pursued, Hume looks for the causal mechanisms producing and sustaining beliefs, and he thereby transforms epistemology from a normative into an empirical inquiry. Hume's turn to empirical inquiry is a characteristically Newtonian move towards naturalisation. As Howard Stein has argued, Newton's philosophical strategy involved turning traditional metaphysical questions – like, for example, those concerning space or God – into empirical ones, and so they are effectively transferred from the field of metaphysics to natural philosophy.[12] This is the core of Hume's empiricism, too, that is frequently exhibited in his analysis of, for example, our belief in an external world, causation, free will or the self.

This strategy, congruently with Hume's famous ban on an a priori deduction of 'ought' from 'is',[13] constrains the prospects of a normative a priori epistemology. Prescribing epistemic 'ought' from cognitive 'is', the normative from the natural, seems possible only derivatively, even for Hume's own rules of experimental reasoning.[14] Hume's naturalistic epistemology can deliver the principles of psychological and social processes underlying normative and evaluative practices based on a descriptive and explanatory inquiry into human functioning. Reflecting on the social and psychological mechanisms of cognition based on this inquiry can reveal their function, and it can also reveal the ways of perfecting these mechanisms and protecting them from going astray. But it must be emphasised that these 'philosophical decisions are nothing but the reflections of common life, methodized and corrected'.[15]

The emphasis on the natural and empirical is not only Hume's crucial step away from normative epistemology but it is also the first step towards the socialisation of knowledge – depending on one's willingness to acknowledge social factors among the relevant causes of belief formation.[16] Hume is willing to do so. He is aware that our belief-forming mechanisms are naturalistic not only because they depend on our psychology but also because they are partly yet profoundly culturally conditioned and social. These social mechanisms are also naturalistic in that they fit into a network of mundane causes and effects which equally includes mental states and institutions – but with no reference to sources of normativity that transcend that network of causes and effects. Our cognitive and affective endowments are as natural as the conceptual and inferential practices we are socialised into: the latter are partly fostered and maintained by structural pressures arising from relations among individuals and the institutional environment.

This conviction is already manifested in Hume's dictum that 'all the sciences' are 'dependent on' the 'science of human nature' because 'they lie under the cognizance of man'.[17] To find out the limits and prospects of our cognitive enterprises we must be 'acquainted with the extent and force of human understanding' and 'explain the nature of the ideas we employ, and of the operations we perform in our reasonings'. This knowledge can only be gained by the experimental method of reasoning 'from a cautious observation of human life and take them as they appear in the common course of the world, by men's behaviour in company, in affairs, and in their pleasures'. Even the exploration of individual cognitive capacities must take a social route through public behaviour and observable interactions.[18]

Hume, just like several other central figures of the Scottish Enlightenment, contributes to the emergence of a discipline that later would be called sociology. As he stands at the beginning of this process, the tools available for sociological inquiry and theory construction are naturally rudimentary, and this prevents the formulation of self-conscious sociological programmes.[19] But it does not prevent the formulation of sociological visions. This is what Hume provides for later projects in socialising knowledge in the form of *philosophical genealogies* couched in terms of the social mechanisms of belief formation. As Bernard Williams defines it: 'A genealogy is a narrative that tries to explain a cultural phenomenon by describing a way in which it came about, or could have come about, or might be imagined to have come about.'[20] Hume provides several such naturalistic narratives with respect to religion, morality, politics and art – but his method is similarly genealogical with respect to fundamental concepts and beliefs.[21]

Following Miranda Fricker's terminology, the epistemological product of Hume's genealogical method can be aptly called an 'abstracted social conception' of knowledge that acknowledges social processes as constitutive in the elevation of individual beliefs to the status of knowledge.[22] This programme is not built on the foundation of empirical research into actual cases of knowledge production; it draws more generally on history, the observation of common life and insights from Hume's own science of human nature. Hume's genealogy of knowledge provides a theoretical framework to conceive broadly of the social mechanisms and the psychological underpinning of our epistemic interdependencies, from the transmission of beliefs to the processes through which beliefs reach the highest epistemic status they can reach – given the human condition. Hume thus provides conceptual resources and an outlook for naturalising epistemology in both social and psychological directions.

This genealogy has non-accidental congruences with the Edinburgh Programme for a Sociology of Scientific Knowledge, particularly as represented by David Bloor. Bloor considers Hume as a predecessor who was 'laying the foundation for a scientific sociology of knowledge',[23] and recurrently invokes him as the 'Edinburgh historian and sociologist'[24] whose views are in opposition to those of philosophers that are apparently normativists, absolutists and non-naturalists with respect to some knowledge claims. Bloor emphasises the convergences of non-naturalistic views of knowledge and religious doctrines: those claiming that knowledge rests on 'a supernatural foundation', embodied, for example, in epistemic norms, rationality and so on, build their argument on 'quasi-theological premises'.[25] This group includes the overwhelming majority of Scottish Enlightenment philosophers, who (as we have seen above) 'devoted their energy to portraying our natural cognitive equipment as a gift from God. They have treated this machinery and its output not as a product of nature but as part of a divine plan, and underwritten by divine guarantees.'[26] Bloor frequently contrasts Hume's views in this respect with those of Thomas Reid: he considers Reid a forerunner of present-day critiques of sociology of knowledge with their commitment to the non-natural sources of normativity and justification, and aspirations for knowledge whose validity transcends the world of psychological, social and historical causes and effects from which it emerges.[27]

For Bloor, 'knowledge' is just 'whatever men take to be knowledge' or, a bit more technically, a 'collectively accepted system of belief'.[28] 'Knowledge' so understood is insensitive to transcendent epistemic norms and ideals of justification, but it is sensitive to the *causes* that elevate belief systems to the status of knowledge in a given community. This interest in causal explanations is the core of Bloor's naturalism – as well as Hume's – and this is the core of their relativism, too:[29]

> What is scientific knowledge supposed to be relative to? The answer is that it is relative to whatever causes determine it. There are as many 'relativities' as there are causes. That is the point: knowledge is part of the causal nexus, not something that transcends it. Knowledge is not a supernatural phenomenon, as it would have to be if it were to earn the title of 'absolute.' Knowledge is a natural phenomenon and must be studied as such by historians, sociologists, and psychologists.[30]

Relativism and naturalism thus go hand in hand: they are both rooted in the denial that there is an elevated level of cognition where the network of causes and effects is transcended, and where knowledge, truth or justification resides. 'Knowledge', 'truth' and 'justification' can mean anything only as parts of this empirically accessible causal network, and there is nothing outside and beyond our knowledge-making practices that could lend epistemic authority to the fruits of our inquiry.

The sociological categories of this causal analysis include institutions, traditions, conventions, education, identity and interest. Invoking Fricker's terminology again,[31] they constitute a 'situated social conception' of knowledge to be deployed as tools for empirical analysis in particular instances of knowledge production. Bloor provides an impressive illustration of a situated conception: *The Enigma of the Aerofoil* presents the history of two rival approaches – one dominant in Britain, the other in Germany – to the question of how to design the wing of an aircraft. Focusing on the period between 1909 and 1930, Bloor shows that these alternative approaches and the divergent results they produced were rooted in different institutional settings, the consequently different values and identities of the protagonists and a different understanding of relations among disciplines.

In Britain, the questions of design were pursued by physicists and applied mathematicians whose education and ensuing theoretical commitments were informed by the Cambridge mathematical tripos, and it made them immune to otherwise productive but mathematically less refined ideas coming from engineering. In the early decades of aircraft design, the British insisted on considering every aeroplane 'as a collection of unsolved mathematical problems',[32] whose analysis was expected to deliver the most realistic mathematical modelling – the basis from which aerodynamic design was to be deduced. This approach was combined with experiments in sophisticated wind tunnels in which mathematical models were tested – and would be shown to be problematic. Yet the prospects of mathematical analysis were not considered bleak; instead, the observations were reinterpreted so that theoretical analysis would require revisions only. Until the interwar period, the British insisted on this 'ideal mathematics'–driven approach and gave it up when they could not get the mathematics right.[33]

In Germany, by contrast, those attending the problems of aerodynamic design came from the system of *technische Hochschulen* and consequently had a practical take on the issues. At the initial stages of aircraft design, and during World War I, German designers used their intuition, tested their insights in the wind-tunnel and only then provided a mathematical and theoretical analysis. The resulting theoretical advances would begin to play a role in design only at the later stages, in the interwar period, when theory started to guide practice. They could easily adopt insights from British engineering, and they were content with 'only' manageable calculation instead of mathematical perfection. A crucial lesson is that the causes explaining why knowledge production took a more or a less successful path are of the same *kind* in both cases: institutions, traditions, identities, values and commitments.

Although Hume would not provide detailed empirical case studies, his social epistemology does provide conceptual tools for similar analyses: Bloor's approach couched in terms of institutions, traditions, identities, values and commitments can be read as echoing Hume's analysis of the social roots of belief and sentiment.[34] One central function of Hume's *sympathy* is to transfer beliefs and sentiments among members of a community. The practices and institutions of education serve as the ways of ensuring group cohesion by ensuring the convergence of values, commitments and attitudes. They also facilitate our adherence to convergent 'general rules' that regulate both our understanding and our passions.[35] They play a role in determining social identities and help ascribe cognitive and affective realities to ourselves and others according to the identities so established. Due to customs arising from repeated exposure to such sympathetic transmissions, education turns out to be responsible for 'more than one half of those opinions, that prevail among mankind' and also for 'the principles, which are thus implicitly embrac'd' – that is, rules for the regulation of our cognitive, affective and social lives. Hume's views on custom, sympathy and education are indeed conformable to a central lesson that Bloor's *Enigma* provides: the constitutive 'maxims' of inquiry that education conveys 'are frequently contrary to reason, and even to themselves in different times and places'.[36]

Humean Tools for a Sociology of Knowledge

Naturalism and relativism are both consequences of the aspiration for a causal explanation of knowledge. The commitment to search for *causality* is the first pillar of Bloor's programme for the sociology of knowledge – and it is also the central element of the 'experimental method of reasoning' that Hume, according to the subtitle of the *Treatise*, aims to introduce into moral subjects, that is into the study of phenomena pertaining to moral agents qua moral agents.

The requirement of causal explanation has further consequences. As Bloor summarises the methodological core of the Strong Programme in the Sociology of Knowledge, the commitment to causality is accompanied by the commitments to *impartiality* and *symmetry* claiming that sociological explanations should proceed irrespective of the truth or falsity of the beliefs to be explained and, consequently, that the explanations should invoke the same kinds of causes while explaining beliefs. True beliefs do not constitute a privileged class; they have their mundane causes just like their false relatives. And this applies to sociological beliefs as well, hence Bloor's commitment to *reflexivity*: beliefs inculcated by sociological inquiry are subject to causal determination by the same kinds of causes as any other belief.[37]

The causal commitment entails the denial that knowledge can have validity transcending the causes that determine epistemic status in a community. It denies that there can be forms of justification elevating beliefs to an epistemic status whose nature is different from the nature of the causes of its acceptance. It cannot be universal and objective in an *absolute* sense because the causes are particular, partly subjective, and partly intersubjective – that is, they are constrained by human nature and condition.[38] Our cognitive procedures and faculties, just like our moral ones, can justify themselves only by reflecting on and approving themselves. As there is no superior faculty or procedure that could justify the others, the only source of justification that we can reach out to in order to transcend reflection and self-approval is society: common approbation and consensus.[39]

It is maybe not surprising that one can find the traces of similar commitments in 'the sociologically minded David Hume'.[40] As Hume's experimental reasoning reveals,[41] there is nothing in human nature and condition that could provide justification for our beliefs beyond that limit. Reason, empirical or a priori, is just a 'kind of cause' whose 'principles and operations' are the subject of the science of human nature – an empirical discipline situating the mind's functioning within the network of psychological and social causes, and not in a realm of logical necessities that obtain independently from the empirical reality of these causes.[42] Epistemic evaluation and justification of our cognitive engagements cannot but rely on principles that are 'themselves integral to the forms of engagement they were used to justify';[43] reason, being a part of this engagement, cannot get us outside of the intricate network of causes and effects. Even if the natural effect of reason is 'truth', its actual effects cannot be evaluated outside this network of influences[44] and independently of the fact that, being a human faculty, it is intrinsically fallible. Consequently, we are destined to scepticism that we can only mitigate by feeding our need for justification with causal genealogies of how we come to conceptualise phenomena, come to believe things and believe that we know things.

The lack of extra-causal reason is clearly reflected in Hume's concept of belief and his account of the mechanisms of belief formation. For Hume, 'belief consists merely in a certain feeling or sentiment; in something that depends not on the will, but must arise from certain determinate causes and principles, of which we are not masters'.[45] This summary reflects two crucial features of Hume's theory of belief. His *doxastic sentimentalism* locates the mark of belief in a specific feeling that distinguishes it from other ideas that we might entertain without believing them. From this angle, it is the phenomenal aspect of an idea that defines its cognitive status in the inferential processes of reason and imagination. These processes have their own logic, but 'logic' for Hume does not designate a normative discipline of inferential rules but an empirical discipline whose 'sole end ... is to explain the principles and operations of our reasoning faculty, and the nature of our ideas'.[46] Hume's logic concerns the causal processes behind the generation of doxastic sentiments: it is about affective psychology rather than norms of rationality.[47]

The other crucial feature is *doxastic involuntarism*. What we believe lies largely outside our rational control, but there are regular causal mechanisms behind belief formation and revision. They bestow stability on belief, and this stability distinguishes belief from mere fantasy.[48] Most of our beliefs are inevitable, not because of the compulsion of extra-causal and immutable rationality or logic but because there is no escape from the principles of human nature. The products of the involuntary processes of belief formation are ideas that have a distinguished causal role in our cognitive architecture. A belief 'renders realities more present to us than fictions, causes them to weigh more in the thought and gives them a superior influence on the passions and imagination'.[49]

The causes of belief are of two kinds: natural and artificial. Our natural beliefs are due to our psychological constitution: they arise from the 'permanent, irresistible and universal principles' of our faculties – that is, the senses, memory, imagination and reason. These principles belong to the innate, natural cognitive endowment of individuals.[50] Our cognitive and affective functioning arises from their intricate interaction; perhaps most important among them in the present context is the influence of the understanding on the senses and the imagination on reason. They explain our perceptual and inferential capacities, which present us with 'systems of reality'.[51] The constituents of these systems are perceptions as presented by memory or the senses, or as connected by the relation of causation. Perceptions in either of these systems are suitable objects of belief.[52]

But the principles of understanding and the imagination are not exclusively of the 'permanent, irresistible and universal' kind; some of them are 'changeable, weak and irregular', conditioned by contingent or even idiosyncratic circumstances. And most of our beliefs are 'deriv'd from principles, which, however common, are neither universal nor unavoidable in human nature'.[53] These beliefs are typically due to education and inculcation as a result of socialisation. They are artificial causes of belief[54] because they do not originate in our natural constitution but in 'inventions' that respond to our needs arising from our constitution and circumstances.[55] Even if artificial in this sense, they are still natural in the sense of being non-transcendent and part of a mundane network of causes and effects: they have a foundation in and influence on human psychology and sociability.

The psychological foundation of education is *sympathy*: an imaginative faculty responsible for the interpersonal transmission of sentiments and beliefs. Due to Hume's doxastic sentimentalism, sentiments and beliefs are closer relatives than they might seem to non-Humeans, because 'belief is more properly an act of the sensitive than of the cogitative part of our natures'.[56] Sympathy facilitates the adoption of beliefs that we receive by communication into our own system of beliefs, and human constitution is very susceptible of this kind of contagion, especially from those in our physical and social vicinity. This is true even if the transmitted beliefs are 'different from, or even contrary to our own':[57] even 'the bare opinion of another' can induce an idea, 'which wou'd otherwise have been entirely neglected', to have an effect on us.[58] This phenomenon is most 'conspicuous in children . . . who implicitly embrace every opinion propos'd to them'.[59]

The same holds for our inferential habits and practices. Although we can and do form them on the basis of individual experience and reasoning, education is still their dominant source: general rules so acquired 'over-ballance those, which are owing either to abstract reasoning or experience'.[60] General rules can be taught explicitly, but most of them are sympathetically transmitted and 'implicitly embrac'd':[61] they are read or distilled from beliefs and opinions acquired from others. The lack of explicit representation of general rules is no obstacle to their influence on behaviour whose causal intricacies are not transparent anyway – only careful experimental inquiry can reveal them. Their 'mighty influence' on action,[62] understanding and even on the senses creates 'a species of probability, which sometimes influences the judgment, and always the imagination',[63] and due to the widespread influence of the imagination on the senses and reason, they influence perception and our epistemic evaluations. Thus, in the context of inquiry, general rules influence what questions and solutions one can imagine in a particular field, the way problems can be structured and phenomena conceptualised, what moves can be perceived as right and wrong epistemically and what is perceived as an epistemic virtue. Facilitated by general rules, 'the imagination passes easily from the cause to the effect, without considering that there are still some circumstances wanting to render the cause a compleat one'.[64] Thus distributing significance among perceptions, general rules contribute to the process of presenting us with 'systems of reality' not less crucially than the principles of our natural cognitive endowment. And this also means that the natural and artificial causes of belief are in reality intertwined; they are only separated by Hume's analysis.[65]

The influence of socially transmitted beliefs and general rules explains why certain traditions of thought, ways of thinking, forms of discourse and ideologies can prevail for long, even when they are contrary to reason, experience or even to the interest of those concerned. However much we are 'governed by interest; yet even interest itself, and all human affairs, are entirely governed by *opinion*' – and opinion is predominantly transmitted by sympathy.[66] This transmission is the more efficacious the shorter the physical and social distance between the source and the recipient. In closely connected groups the consequences of sympathetic transmission extend even to 'men of the greatest judgment and understanding, who find it very difficult to follow their own reason or inclination, in opposition to that of their friends and daily companions'.[67] Sympathetic transmission introduces a certain inertia into commonly held systems of belief and prevents the adoption of alternatives: education 'is the cause why all systems are apt to be rejected at first as new and unusual'.[68] It sets imagination into 'a train of thinking', and thus it 'is apt to continue, even when its object fails it, and like a galley put in motion by the oars, carries on its course without any new impulse' – because 'men are mightily addicted to *general rules*'.[69] The origins of systems of philosophy can be explained by reference to the principles of human nature, their interaction and occasional conflict,[70] but their prolonged survival can be explained in terms of our social practices of epistemic approval.

Philosophers, natural and moral, ancient and modern, inherit concepts, standards of evaluation and methods of reasoning this way. This seems to apply, for example, to the first of Hume's own rules for judging causes and effects.[71] This rule requires that causes and effects be contiguous in space and hints at its foundation in human nature: we tend to associate the communication of motion with contact action because of the resemblance between cause and effect.[72] This general rule is consonant with the requirements of mechanical philosophy but not so much with the role that forces play in Newton's *Principia*. In fact, the mechanism by which gravity exerts its influence had been a crucial issue for Newton because, according to the prevailing standards of intelligibility, phenomena of motion could be adequately explained only in terms of contact action, and he could not provide this explanation for gravity. Newton made significant efforts to explicate his system according to these mechanical (Cartesian) rules and, when he failed, he would choose to revise the rules and make 'action at a distance' acceptable.[73] Eventually, Newton's rules have successfully replaced the rules of mechanical philosophy, and this success can be seen reflected in Hume's discussion of causation in his *Enquiry concerning Human Understanding* (1748), where Hume drops the criterion of spatial contiguity.

Hume's first rule might have a root in human nature, just like several other philosophical doctrines that Hume deems untenable. And the conceptual tools sketched above afford Humean explanations of how such rules get entrenched, maintained and eventually replaced. Notably, these explanations are irrespective of the truth or falsity of our beliefs; instead they invoke the same natural and artificial causes: the principles of human nature and the way they open the way for artificial (social) causes to operate on our cognitive and affective nature.[74] This is the core of Humean symmetry and impartiality: there are the same types of cause behind the credibility of beliefs and the conformity to general rules, and their explanation exploits the same causal resources – irrespective of their epistemic evaluation:[75] valid insights and philosophical maladies are both to be seen 'as arising from natural causes'.[76]

Reflective evaluation and revision of beliefs, belief-forming mechanisms and rules are still possible,[77] but our epistemic judgements remain within the psychosocial causal network; they cannot transcend it. Moral education is the most widely discussed process of sympathetic inculcation of general rules in Hume scholarship, but epistemic norms are also transmitted similarly: they are acquired as general rules to regulate one's thinking and doxastic feeling; and they are the products of individual and collective judgement on the reliability of sources of belief and forms of reasoning. So the general rules we deploy while evaluating belief-forming mechanisms are formed in the same way as the general rules we reflect on.

For Hume, just like for Bloor, the only way of epistemic justification (if it is worthy of its name at all) is thus question begging, because the rules to be evaluated are integral to our practices of evaluation.[78] As Hume puts it, we might correct our propensities by reflection, but "tis still certain, that custom takes the start, and gives a biass to the imagination'.[79] Given the way general rules get a grip on the understanding via custom and education, the 'following of general rules is a very unphilosophical species of probability; and yet 'tis only by following them that we can correct this, and all other unphilosophical probabilities'.[80] Consequently, our philosophical reflections cannot 'end in a state of epistemic grace':[81] epistemic evaluation cannot take us to a dignified epistemic realm above the world of causes and effects.[82] The realm of Cartesian reason of quasi-divine clear and distinct insight is an illusion. Reflection keeps us within the realm of Humean reason that is conditioned by the imagination, exposed to disturbing influences and prone to undermine itself, and requires combination with some other 'propensity' to be 'assented to'.[83]

All these lessons are valid for Hume's own convictions as well – this is the Humean equivalent of Bloor's reflexivity thesis. The products of philosophical reflection are also subject to doxastic sentimentalism and involuntarism, and they emerge from a network of causes:

> 'Tis not solely in poetry and music, we must follow our taste and sentiment, but likewise in philosophy. When I am convinc'd of any principle, 'tis only an idea, which strikes more strongly upon me. When I give the preference to one set of arguments above another, I do nothing but decide from my feeling concerning the superiority of their influence.[84]

This sentiment, just like any other, is not subject to the will even if it can be the subject of reflection and revision – and they also fit into the causal network of our cognitive and affective functioning. Epistemic reflection is part of our cognitive capacities and, just like them, it depends on the configuration of our overall intellectual system whose parts can be separated for the purposes of analysis but always function in mutual interdependence. The properties of this system do not allow the production of beliefs with an epistemic standing higher than that granted by collective reflected acceptance. Epistemic grace is an illusion.

Moral Causes in Knowledge Production

Perhaps the strongest candidate for a field of knowledge where the state of 'epistemic grace' seems attainable is mathematics. Mathematics for Hume is the exemplary field of demonstrative knowledge where certainty, infallibility and justification seem to be within reach – at least prima facie. But in Hume's hands, geometry turns out to be fallible because of the nature of the ideas it deals with: they are ideas of shapes and figures that are derived directly from sense experience; consequently, they are not exact. Our senses cannot convey ideas with the precision required for demonstratively certain conclusions. Arithmetic and algebra fare better because they are founded on the abstract and exact idea of a 'unit', but our cognitive capacities are constrained in this respect too. Even if the nature of our arithmetic ideas could afford demonstration, our reason is fallible. The sceptical conclusion is unavoidable: mathematical knowledge is inevitably fallible and lacks rational justification.[85] The only refuge we can take is in peer recognition: it is the dynamics of approval and disapproval within the epistemic community of mathematicians that provides the surrogate of rational justification.[86]

In the last several decades, mathematics has been one focus of Bloor's sociological investigations. The conceptual tools Hume provides make the results of these investigations translatable into a Humean proto-sociological idiom, and so they can be presented as a form of sociological Humeanism. Bloor's early explorative case study, offered as 'an example of a type of explanation',[87] takes us back to the German academic world in the first half of the nineteenth century and asks why it was there and then that the new mathematical method of 'proofs and refutations' took shape.

In Bloor's presentation, the university reforms of 1812 intended to reorganise the corporate universities inherited from the eighteenth century and to replace their guild-like scholarly functioning with an effective system to produce excellent teachers and bureaucrats. 'The aim was not to produce innovation but merely to achieve excellence', and the means of reaching this was to appoint scholars with high-quality output and reputation. These appointments were made as the result of bureaucratic procedures replacing the internal guild-like mechanisms of the universities. An unintended consequence of the need to show excellence was the emergence of an innovative scholarly culture: 'making discoveries became a necessity for those who aspired to chairs'.[88] This explains the change of methodology in mathematical inquiry: the introduction of the dialectical method of 'proofs and refutations', of invoking counter-examples to proofs then reconsidering and revising them in the new light. The new method would complement the classical method of analysis and synthesis that could help to prove true conjectures but could not help to improve false ones. The method of proofs and refutations was thus more fitting to produce mathematical innovations – and thus more fitting for the invention-oriented institutional environment that would emerge after the university reforms of 1812.

The general framework of unintended consequences meticulously studied by Hume and his fellow Scottish contemporaries is apparent in Bloor's reconstruction.[89] But more interestingly, the more refined tools of Bloor's analysis seem to have Humean counterparts, and they constitute a conceptual system that could deliver similar analytical insights. The idea that institutional change is a cause of change in customs, motives and sentiments is the core idea of Hume's essay 'On National Characters'. In Hume's language, 'institutional change' belongs to the class of 'moral causes': social circumstances 'fitted to work on the mind as motives or reasons, and which render a peculiar set of manners habitual to us'. The 'principle of moral causes fixes the character of different professions',[90] presumably by the different general rules inculcated through training and education, so changing the pertinent moral causes naturally leads to a change in the procedures that define the activity of mathematicians. These processes are akin to those large-scale social transformations induced by the different institutional structures characteristic to a republican and a monarchical government. Hume's discussion of these structures reveals how they foster values and patterns characteristic to feudal and capitalistic forms of social-economic activity.[91]

As we have seen in the previous section, Hume also provides socio-psychological mechanisms for the communication of social pressure and for the resulting transformation of beliefs and behaviour. From this angle, changes in the culture of mathematical inquiry can unfold either through changing beliefs about the circumstances under which actors must act, perceiving their own interests in the light of those newly acquired beliefs and adjusting their behaviour accordingly, or alternatively through the spontaneous emergence, transmission and wide-scale adoption of general rules by particular instances of problem solving that turn out to be advantageous under the changing circumstances. Bloor's case of Prussian university reforms of 1812 is closer to the latter schema. The pressure for innovative thought arising from institutional causes in German academia provides an evolutionary environment in which the emerging method of proofs and refutations is fitness-enhancing and so it can proliferate.

For the analysis of the so changing institutional structure Bloor deploys Mary Douglas's group-grid model. Douglas's model is an attempt at a systematic ordering and typology of social forms in general. This exercise has always been in the forefront of sociological interest, and Hume, as well as his enlightened Scottish contemporaries, made efforts along these lines.[92] In Douglas's account, 'group' features express how rigid and closed the boundaries of a group are; how easy it is to enter the group or interact with its members from the outside. The degree of 'grid' shows the refinement of hierarchy within the group, the complexity of its internal stratification.

One can find conceptual resources in Hume allowing for a similar analysis, too. 'Group' features can be explored in terms of Hume's 'circles of sympathy' that introduce the idea of sympathy fading away in direct proportion with the increase of social distance. Hume's language of one's 'narrow circle' of sympathy can be naturally deployed not only in affective but also in epistemic contexts.[93] As sympathy is a way of belief transmission, the 'group' features of a circle can be interpreted in terms of the frequency and efficiency of transmitting beliefs and evaluations, the exercise of epistemic authority and the sphere of epistemic acknowledgement and recognition.[94] Prussian university reforms so considered eroded a 'narrow circle' of epistemic sympathy: they broadened and blurred the boundaries of the collegiate circle by introducing bureaucratic standards that favoured scholarly reputation outside a candidate's narrow circle of sympathy.[95]

A similar Humean translation of 'grid' features is also made possible by exploiting Hume's framework for discussing social stratification centred on the concept of 'ranks'. Hume discusses ranks primarily in social and economic contexts and explores how different characteristic sentiments, rules of behaviour and evaluation relate to different ranks in society. These relations inculcate 'general rules' that facilitate inference from social position to economic status and expected social activity.[96] This framework of social analysis can be extended to the study of stratification in epistemic communities. Economic wealth (or 'riches') can be compared to epistemic capital, and the corresponding epistemic authority, accumulated through successful contributions to knowledge production (in Bloor's case to the exercise of proofs and refutations). Social ranks can be compared to institutional positions in terms of, for example, professorships and memberships in learned societies. The two can come apart just as in the case of economic wealth and social status, yet with institutional position we are inclined to infer the presence of adequate epistemic capital even when it is in fact lacking.

'Integrity' and 'reputation' are important features while evaluating knowledge claims, and so is expertise, just like 'unquestioned good sense, education, and learning' are while evaluating testimony.[97] These components of epistemic authority are independent of other social, personal or moral traits: having the moral standing of a prophet or an apostle or Cato contributes little to the sustainability of a knowledge claim if the person otherwise lacks epistemic capital. This epistemic capital is significant in mathematical communities: it specifies the degree one can contribute to the social production of mathematical certainty. It is peer approbation alone that can provide some remedy for Hume's sceptical worries arising from the fallibility of individual reason in mathematical problem solving. The epistemic significance of someone's approbation depends on the epistemic capital he accumulated through the approbation by others of his previous contributions to mathematical problem solving.[98]

Seen through the lenses of Hume's terminology, the new Prussian system of university appointments, with its increased emphasis on innovation, scholarly contribution and reputation, increased the significance of epistemic capital at the expense of institutional position in the former guild-like structure. In this environment, following the method of proofs and refutations would emerge as a more fitting way to accumulate the necessary epistemic capital than following the traditional method of analysis and synthesis only. As a consequence, the emerging 'competitive individualism' eroded the narrow circles of collegiate sympathy, and the increased significance of epistemic capital undermined the significance of ranks. This explains in Humean terms the low-grid low-group features of German academia emerging from the reforms.[99]

The Importance of General Rules

The Enigma of the Aerofoil offers Bloor's most elaborated case study on the influence of sociological (or, for Hume, moral) causes on knowledge production. Contrasting British and German programmes for aeroplane construction in the early decades of the twentieth century, Bloor explores the difference in their epistemic commitments, practices and evaluations arising from the different institutional environments in which they emerged and flourished. The German programme had developed in an institutional setting dominated by a culture of engineering that fostered a keen eye for practical necessities, applicability and efficient solutions of technical problems even at the expense of theoretical rigour. The British programme, however, had been dominated by an outlook trained in mathematical education: the solution of technical problems was to be derived only after a mathematically impeccable treatment of aerodynamic phenomena had been at hand.

Bloor's narrative is focused on the different understanding of what 'applied mathematics' meant in the two epistemic communities. In the German context mathematics was considered a *Hilfswissenschaft*: mathematical analysis was a tool for understanding interconnections among the facts of observation with an eye to developing applicable technology. Theoretical understanding had to operate under pressure from practical needs and necessities, and mathematics was a handmaiden in pursuing solutions to actual technical problems.[100] Consequently, those working in the German programme wanted manageable calculations, and not a mathematically impeccable theory, to make progress. They were willing to work with idealisations based on knowingly false presuppositions. So, without scruples, they relied on the 'circulatory theory' built upon the notion of non-viscous fluids without friction and turbulence to be able to deal with an 'otherwise intractable reality'.[101]

Those working in the British programme, by contrast, considered mathematics as a *Grundwissenschaft*: they wanted mathematical analysis based on the most realistic modelling. They insisted on the 'discontinuity theory' that seemed to them to be a better candidate for dealing with reality.[102] Instead of deploying mathematics to refine practical solutions, they took real problems and wanted to refine their mathematical analysis and instrumentalise the results only after they reached their rigorous theoretical understanding. And they would stick to this way of inquiry even though they were better equipped for experiments and technical refinements than their German counterparts.

Bloor himself points out that the core of his account 'can be understood in the humane, skeptical, and sophisticated terms' Hume offered.[103] And indeed, Hume's 'general rules' introduced above can serve as a connective between cognitive psychology and sociology of knowledge. General rules are inferential habits formed naturally as a result of repeated exposure to the same experience or education.[104] Once inculcated, they extend our expectations to situations similar to the ones that gave rise to the general rule. They are also 'able to impose on the very senses' and thus influence even our perceptual judgements: although 'the eye at all times sees an equal number of physical points', still by general rules distilled from experience we can infer the size of objects at different distances, and this judgement is so lively that we even confound it with sensation.[105] In their first appearance, general rules get entrenched due to the way we are constituted, and in that sense they are 'unphilosophical'. Reflection can reveal that some of these rules are mere prejudices and force their revision, but reflection can also vindicate them and turn them into epistemic norms or rules of inquiry – as is illustrated in Hume's rules for judging causes and effects.[106] Such revisions and vindications, even if they are conducted knowingly, are not guided by some ideal rationality but by reflective practices acquired in the context of psychological and social causes.

Although Hume discusses the connection between education and general rules mainly in the context of morality and property, with just a little adjustment these passages can be easily read as providing an account of cognitive socialisation. 'Education takes possession of the ductile minds' of children as it inculcates those rules considered 'worthy and honourable, and their violation as base and infamous'.[107] This is how general rules for the proper way of looking at theoretical problems 'take root in their tender minds, and acquire such firmness and solidity, that they may fall little short of those principles, which are the most essential to our natures, and the most deeply radicated in our internal constitution'.[108]

As students, we are repeatedly exposed to many cases of successful problem solving by adhering to specific rules. Education induces us to approach our problems in conformity to those rules that have a good track record in problem solving by presenting 'a great superiority of those instances, which are conformable to the rule, above the contrary'.[109] The habit so inculcated 'readily carries us beyond the just bounds' of its scope as it influences the imagination and the senses.[110] No wonder then that we are prone to

> carry our maxims beyond those reasons, which first induc'd us to establish them. Where cases are similar in many circumstances, we are apt

to put them on the same footing, without considering, that they differ in the most material circumstances, and that the resemblance is more apparent than real ... general rules commonly extend beyond the principles, on which they are founded; and that we seldom make any exception to them, unless that exception have the qualities of a general rule, and be founded on very numerous and common instances.[111]

The general rules we acquire through education establish specific ways of viewing and dealing with our problems. They constrain the prospects of adopting different perspectives because 'a constant perseverance in any course of life produces a strong inclination and tendency to continue for the future'.[112] Their revision requires the adoption of different general rules – that is, a different course of education presenting 'a great superiority' of different instances of successful problem solving.

This framework of general rules is indeed suitable for a Humean understanding of Bloor's narrative through the core difference between the German and the British programmes of aircraft design. The cultures of problem solving in *technische Hochschulen* and in mathematical physics rooted in the Cambridge mathematical tripos equipped students with different general rules for approaching and solving problems. And given the character of the problems they faced in the given case, the general rules of engineers fared better and illustrated Hume's wisdom: 'speculative reasonings, which cost so much pains to philosophers, are often form'd by the world naturally, and without reflection: As difficulties, which seem unsurmountable in theory, are easily got over in practice'.[113]

Conclusion

Although rudimentary, Hume's network of concepts offers a clear prospect of sociological analysis pertaining to the production of knowledge as collectively accepted system of beliefs. These interrelating concepts can be effortlessly extended to the study of dynamics in and around epistemic communities: due to these concepts, Hume's discussion of individual cognitive and affective functioning connects organically with his discussion of social interactions. Concepts like 'sympathy' and 'general rules' play equally central parts in the explanation of individual cognition and social organisation, revealing how those processes are inextricably interwoven and separable only for the purposes of analysis.

Not so much a representative of 'adventitious sociology', as Kenneth Macdonald likes to view the Scottish contribution to the history of sociology, Hume provides conceptual tools for a (proto-)sociology of knowledge: a sociological way of looking at epistemic phenomena, and conceptual resources that can be easily put into the service of sociological explanation. Hume is thus path-breaking in the direction not only of psychological naturalism but also of a sociological naturalism. Quine had already made Hume a hero of naturalised epistemology – and Hume's contribution is widely recognised in that context.[114] But Hume naturalises knowledge in the directions of both present-day cognitive psychology and sociology, and while Jerry Fodor aptly characterised the *Treatise* as the 'foundational document of cognitive science',[115] it can also be said to be the foundational document of the sociology of knowledge. The connection is the opposite of adventitious: the connection is fundamental to understanding Hume's enterprise. It is in no way accidental, indirect or irrelevant to his central purpose. Some sociologists have begun to recognise this, and perhaps philosophers and historians of philosophy could follow that path with advantage.

Notes

The chapter has benefited from helpful discussions with Gábor Bíró, David Bloor, Catherine Dromelet and Kenneth Macdonald. I am especially grateful to David Bloor for his extended comments on an earlier version of this essay.

1. The phrase has been coined by Dave F. Norton, 'From Moral Sense to Common Sense: An Essay on the Development of Scottish Common Sense Philosophy, 1700–1765' (PhD dissertation, University of California, San Diego, 1966). See also David Fate Norton, *David Hume: Common-Sense Moralist, Sceptical Metaphysician* (Princeton: Princeton University Press, 1982), p. 19.
2. David Fordyce, *The Elements of Moral Philosophy* (Indianapolis, IN: Liberty Fund, 2003), p. 6.
3. George Turnbull, *The Principles of Moral and Christian Philosophy*, vol. I (Indianapolis, IN: Liberty Fund, 2005), p. 10.
4. Francis Hutcheson, *Philosophiae Moralis Institutio Compendiaria with A Short Introduction to Moral Philosophy* (Indianapolis, IN: Liberty Fund, 2007), p. 23.

5. For a more detailed discussion see Tamás Demeter, 'Philosophical Methods' in Aaron Garrett and James Harris (eds), *Scottish Philosophy in the Eighteenth Century, Volume II: Method, Metaphysics, Mind, Language* (Oxford: Oxford University Press, 2023), pp. 53–107, pp. 71–3.
6. J. Y. T. Greig (ed.), *The Letters of David Hume* (Oxford: Clarendon Press, 1932), p. 33.
7. Gary Hatfield, *The Natural and the Normative* (Cambridge, MA: MIT Press, 1990), p. 27.
8. See Robert Pasnau, 'Epistemology Idealized', *Mind* 122 (2014), pp. 987–1021.
9. Hatfield, *The Natural and the Normative*, pp. 63 and 27.
10. Jerry Fodor, *Hume Variations* (Oxford: Clarendon, 2003), p. 4. There is an important contribution to the Hume literature whose representatives clearly see otherwise. See for example Louis E. Loeb, *Stability and Justification in Hume's* Treatise (New York: Oxford University Press, 2002).
11. While I sympathise with Fodor's claim, I also agree with Hsueh M. Qu's suggestion, in *Hume's Epistemological Evolution* (New York: Oxford University Press, 2020), that Hume's *Enquiry concerning Human Understanding* (Oxford: Clarendon Press, 2000) (hereafter EHU) represents a turn to normative epistemology.
12. Howard Stein, 'Newton's Metaphysics' in I. B. Cohen and George E. Smith (eds), *The Cambridge Companion to Newton* (Cambridge: Cambridge University Press 2002), pp. 261 f., 269 f., 277.
13. David Hume, *A Treatise of Human Nature* (Oxford: Clarendon Press, 2007) (hereafter T), 3.1.1.27.
14. Several of these ways have been explored in the literature. It has been suggested that exploring the normal functioning, or 'the nature' of our faculties and contrasting it with its pathologies can lead to normative conclusions. See Tamás Demeter, *David Hume and the Culture of Scottish Newtonianism* (Leiden: Brill, 2016), ch. 10. Normative considerations can also be conceived as arising from a reflection on, refinement and correction of our natural cognitive mechanisms as in Hsueh Qu, 'Prescription, Description, and Hume's Experimental Method', *British Journal for the History of Philosophy* 24 (2016), pp. 279–301. And Hume can also be plausibly represented as giving up the quest of rational justification for the sake of practical justification, as for example in Michael Ridge, 'Epistemology Moralized: David Hume's Practical Epistemology', *Hume Studies* 29 (2003), pp. 165–204.

15. EHU 12.25.
16. Martin Kusch, 'Philosophy and the Sociology of Knowledge', *Studies in History and Philosophy of Science, Part A* 30 (1999), pp. 651–85, explores the roots of aversion towards a sociological naturalisation of epistemology, as opposed to its more popular psychological naturalisation. Commentators emphasising Hume's naturalism, in consonance with Kusch's diagnosis, also tend to focus on the psychological side of Hume's naturalism at the expense of its sociological import.
17. T Abstract.3 and Introduction.8
18. T Introduction.4 and 8.
19. See Kenneth Macdonald, 'Did British Sociology Begin with the Scottish Enlightenment?' in Plamena Panayotova (ed.), *The History of Sociology in Britain* (Cham: Palgrave Macmillan, 2019), pp. 37–69. See also his chapter on 'Adventitious Sociology' in the present volume.
20. Bernard Williams, *Truth and Truthfulness* (Princeton: Princeton University Press, 2002), p. 21.
21. On Hume's genealogical strategies see Peter Kail, 'Hume and Nietzsche' in Paul Russell (ed.), *The Oxford Handbook of Hume* (Oxford: Oxford University Press, 2016), pp. 755–76. For a different take see Matthieu Queloz, *The Practical Origins of Ideas* (Oxford: Oxford University Press, 2021), pp. 71–99.
22. Miranda Fricker, 'Skepticism and the Genealogy of Knowledge: Situating Epistemology in Time', *Philosophical Papers* 37 (2008), pp. 27–50. I offer a case study in Tamás Demeter, 'Hume on the Social Construction of Mathematical Knowledge', *Synthese* 196 (2019), pp. 3615–31.
23. David Bloor, 'Relativism and Antinomianism' in Martin Kusch (ed.), *Routledge Handbook of the Philosophy of Relativism* (London: Routledge, 2020), p. 392.
24. David Bloor, *The Enigma of the Aerofoil* (Chicago: University of Chicago Press, 2010), p. 3.
25. Bloor, 'Relativism and Antinomianism', p. 394.
26. David Bloor, 'Epistemic Grace', *Common Knowledge* 13 (2007), pp. 250–80, p. 268.
27. See for example David Bloor, *Wittgenstein, Rules and Institutions* (London: Routledge, 1999); Bloor, 'Epistemic Grace'; Bloor, 'Relativism and Antinomianism'.
28. David Bloor, *Knowledge and Social Imagery*, 2nd ed. (Chicago: University of Chicago Press, 1991), p. 2, and Barry Barnes and David Bloor, 'Relativism, Rationalism and the Sociology of Knowledge' in

Martin Hollis and Steven Lukes (eds), *Rationality and Relativism* (Cambridge, MA: MIT Press, 1982), pp. 21–47, p. 22n5.
29. Bloor, 'Relativism and Antinomianism', p. 393.
30. Bloor, *Enigma of the Aerofoil*, p. 430; 'Epistemic Grace', p. 268; 'Relativism and Antinomianism', p. 391.
31. Fricker, 'Skepticism and the Genealogy of Knowledge', p. 29.
32. Bloor quotes G. H. Bryan; *Enigma of the Aerofoil*, p. 9.
33. The problem was that they could not solve the Stokes equations of viscous flow. See Bloor, *Enigma of the Aerofoil*, e.g. pp. 394–6.
34. See Jacqueline Taylor, *Reflecting Subjects: Passion, Sympathy, and Society in Hume's Philosophy* (Oxford: Oxford University Press, 2015), ch. 2. Taylor provides a clear and inspiring reconstruction of Hume's views primarily, but not exclusively, in the context of socialisation.
35. T 2.1.6.8.
36. T 1.3.9.19.
37. For a summary of Bloor's methodological theses see Bloor, *Knowledge and Social Imagery*, ch. 1.
38. For Bloor, 'objective' means something like impersonal and collective, so it has a social character. With respect to 'universal', Bloor acknowledges contingent cultural universals but denies universals allegedly sanctioned by absolute values. See David Bloor, 'Relativism and the Sociology of Knowledge' in Steven D. Hales (ed.), *A Companion to Relativism* (Oxford: Blackwell, 2011), pp. 433–55.
39. See Michael Williams, 'Hume's Skepticism' in John Greco (ed.), *The Oxford Handbook of Scepticism* (Oxford: Oxford University Press, 2008), pp. 80–107, p. 94.
40. Bloor, *Enigma of the Aerofoil*, p. 444.
41. On Hume's 'consequent scepticism' resulting from an enquiry into our epistemic prospects see Qu, *Hume's Epistemological Evolution*, pp. 179–86.
42. See T 1.4.1.1. and I.5 and A.3. On Hume's psychologism about necessity see Tom Holden, 'Hume's Absolute Necessity', *Mind* 123 (2014), pp. 377–413.
43. Bloor, *Enigma of the Aerofoil*, p. 444.
44. T 1.4.1.1. As Peter Kail aptly points out (Kail, 'Hume and Nietzsche', p. 759): 'Hume's investigation into our inferential faculties reveals that a non-naturalistic account of such inferences is incorrect.'
45. T Appendix.2.
46. T Introduction.5, Abstract.3.
47. Hume's famous 'title principle' is consonant with this stance: 'Where reason is lively, and mixes itself with some propensity, it

ought to be assented to. Where it does not, it never can have any title to operate upon us' (T 1.4.7.11). For the classic discussion see Don Garrett, *Cognition and Commitment in Hume* (New York: Oxford University Press, 1997), pp. 234–7.
48. See Louis E. Loeb, *Reflection and the Stability of Belief* (New York: Oxford University Press, 2010), pp. 143–164, although Loeb thinks that these causal mechanisms are also sources of epistemic justification.
49. T 1.3.7.7.
50. T 1.4.4.1.
51. For the influence of the understanding on the senses see T 1.3.9.11, 1.3.10.12, 2.2.8.6; for that of the imagination (natural relations) on reason (philosophical relations) see 1.3.6.16, 1.3.14.31.
52. T 1.3.9.3; see also 1.3.9.5.
53. T 1.4.4.2.
54. T 1.3.9.19.
55. T 3.2.1.19, 3.2.6.1, 3.3.1.9.
56. T 1.4.1.8.
57. T 2.1.11.2.
58. T 2.3.6.8.
59. T 2.1.11.2.
60. T 1.3.9.19.
61. T 1.3.9.19.
62. T 2.2.8.5.
63. T 3.3.1.19–20.
64. T 3.3.1.20.
65. Hume is congruent in this respect with the Edinburgh-style Sociology of Scientific Knowledge (SSK). While arguing that knowledge is constitutively social, the representatives of SSK raised fundamental questions about taken-for-granted divisions between social versus cognitive, or natural, factors. See for example Steven Shapin, 'Here and Everywhere – Sociology of Scientific Knowledge', *Annual Review of Sociology* 21 (1995), pp. 289–321. This division does not exist for Hume.
66. David Hume, 'Whether the British Government Inclines More to Absolute Monarchy or to a Republic' in *David Hume: Essays. Moral, Political and Literary*, ed. Eugene F. Miller (Indianapolis, IN: Liberty Fund, 1987) (hereafter EMPL), pp. 47–53, p. 51.
67. T 2.1.11.2.
68. T 1.3.10.1.
69. T 1.4.2.22 and 3.2.9.3.
70. Hume does that, for example, in T 1.4.4.

71. T 1.3.15.3.
72. T 1.3.9.10.
73. These changes are introduced in the second (1713) and third (1726) editions of the *Principia*. For a useful discussion see Imre Lakatos, 'Newton's Effect on Scientific Standards' in John Worall and Gregory Currie (eds), *The Methodology of Scientific Research Programmes* (Cambridge: Cambridge University Press, 1978), pp. 193–222, pp. 202–8. On the changing standards of intelligibility see Peter Dear, *Intelligibility of Nature* (Chicago: University of Chicago Press, 2006), p. 26.
74. For a discussion of moral causes in the Scottish Enlightenment see Christopher Berry, *Social Theory of the Scottish Enlightenment* (Edinburgh: Edinburgh University Press, 1997), pp. 77–88, and his 'Hume and the Customary Causes of Industry, Knowledge and Commerce', *History of Political Economy* 38 (2006), pp. 291–317.
75. This can be taken to be the methodological hard core of Edinburgh-style Sociology of Scientific Knowledge: 'regardless of whether the sociologist evaluates a belief as true or rational, or as false and irrational, he must search for the causes of its credibility. In all cases he will ask, for instance, if a belief is part of the routine cognitive and technical competences handed down from generation to generation. Is it enjoined by the authorities of the society? Is it transmitted by established institutions of socialization or supported by accepted agencies of social control? Is it bound up with patterns of vested interest? . . . All of these questions can, and should, be answered without regard to the status of the belief as it is judged and evaluated by the sociologist's own standards.' Barnes and Bloor, 'Relativism, Rationalism and the Sociology of Knowledge', p. 23.
76. T 1.4.4.1.
77. See for example Hsueh Qu, 'Hume's Doxastic Involuntarism', *Mind* 126 (2017), pp. 53–92.
78. Bloor, *Enigma of the Aerofoil*, p. 444.
79. T 1.3.13.9.
80. T 1.3.13.12.
81. Bloor, 'Epistemic Grace', p. 267.
82. In some reconstructions, Hume describes reflective mechanisms from which epistemic justification and moral evaluation arise. Yet, there seems to be no Humean way to take reason or moral sense outside of the causal influence of custom, sympathy and general rules. Albeit the product of these reflective mechanisms are second-order, reflective evaluations, they cannot end in moral or epistemic grace. See for

example Loeb, *Reflection and the Stability of Belief*; Karl Schafer, 'Curious Virtues in Hume's Epistemology', *Philosophers' Imprint* 14 (2014), pp. 1–20.
83. As the 'title principle' (T 1.4.7.11) proclaims, one central conclusion of Hume's sceptical arguments concerning reason. For an introductory discussion of the 'title principle' see Don Garrett, 'Reason, Normativity, and Hume's "Title Principle"' in Paul Russell (ed.), *The Oxford Handbook of Hume* (Oxford: Oxford University Press, 2016), pp. 32–53.
84. T 1.3.8.12.
85. That is of course Hume's conclusion also with respect to empirical knowledge based on induction and causal inference, succinctly summarized in sections 4, 5 and 7 of EHU.
86. A detailed discussion is offered in Demeter, 'Hume on the Social Construction of Mathematical Knowledge'.
87. David Bloor, 'Polyhedra and the Abominations of Leviticus', *British Journal for the History of Science* 11 (1978), pp. 245–72, p. 265.
88. Ibid. p. 264.
89. See for example Berry, *Social Theory*, pp. 39–47.
90. David Hume, 'Of National Characters' in EMPL pp. 197–215, p. 198.
91. For more details see Tamás Demeter, 'Sympathies for Common Ends: The Principles of Organization in Hume's Psychology and Political Economy' in Gábor Bíró (ed.), *Humanity and Nature in Economic Thought* (London: Routledge, 2022), pp. 3–23.
92. The most well-known attempt being the stadial histories of society developed widely among Scottish Enlightenment thinkers. In the present volume the chapters by R. J. W. Mills, Spyridon Tegos and Nicholas Miller discuss them in more detail.
93. For proposals of such extension see for example Schafer, 'Curious Virtues'; Taylor, *Reflecting Subjects*.
94. T 3.3.3.2. Circles of sympathy also figure in T 3.2.1.12 where Hume mentions that an Englishman in Italy, or a European in China, or any man on the moon will evoke the feeling of a close bond.
95. Bloor, 'Polyhedra', p. 264.
96. See e.g. T 2.1.6.8, 2.3.1.8, 3.3.2.11. For discussion see Taylor, *Reflecting Subjects*, ch. 3.
97. EHU 10.15.
98. See especially T 2.1.1.9–13. For a detailed discussion see Demeter, 'Hume on the Social Construction of Mathematical Knowledge'.
99. See Bloor, 'Polyhedra', p. 265 for a diagram.

100. The quotations Bloor (*Enigma of the Aerofoil*, pp. 188–92) takes from August Föppl amply illustrate this stance of taking mathematics as a *Hilfswissenschaft*. Curiously, this view is also congruent with the role Hume assigns to mathematics in empirical matters; see for example T 2.3.3.2.
101. Bloor, *Enigma of the Aerofoil*, p. 445. According to the circulatory theory, movement generates steady wind, and the wing generates vortices bound to the position of the wing. This is responsible for lift and drag.
102. According to the discontinuity theory, the flow breaks away from the edges and creates a wake behind, so the pressure on the front is greater than behind. This generates lift and drag.
103. Bloor, *Enigma of the Aerofoil*, p. 446.
104. T 1.3.13.8–9.
105. T 2.2.8.5, 1.3.9.11., 1.3.10.12, 2.2.8.6.
106. T 1.3.13.7, 1.3.15.
107. T 3.2.12.7; see also 3.2.2.4
108. T 3.2.3.26.
109. T 2.2.5.13.
110. T 2.1.6.8.
111. T 3.2.9.3
112. T 1.3.12.6.
113. T 3.2.12.7.
114. W. V. O. Quine, 'Epistemology Naturalized' in *Ontological Relativity and Other Essays* (New York: Columbia University Press, 1969), pp. 69–90.
115. Fodor, *Hume Variations*, p. 134.

Notes on Contributors

Christopher J. Berry is Professor (Emeritus) of Political Theory and Honorary Professorial Research Fellow at the University of Glasgow. He has written extensively on the Scottish Enlightenment. His most recent publications are *Essays on Hume, Smith and the Scottish Enlightenment* (Edinburgh University Press, 2018), a selection from his past work with new pieces, and the *Very Short Introduction to Adam Smith* (2018). He has given invited series of lectures in Japan, China and Chile on several occasions as well as in Brazil, Europe and the US. He is an elected Fellow of the Royal Society of Edinburgh of which Adam Smith was a founder member.

Angela M. Coventry is Professor of Philosophy at Portland State University. She is the author of two books: *Hume's Theory of Causation: A Quasi-Realist Interpretation* (2006) and *Hume: A Guide for the Perplexed* (2007). She has co-edited *David Hume: Morals, Politics and Society*, with Andrew Valls (2018), *The Humean Mind*, with Alex Sager (2019) and co-wrote *The Historical Dictionary of Hume's Philosophy*, with Kenneth Merrill (2018). Most recently, Angela published an edition of Hume's *A Treatise of Human Nature* for Broadview Press in 2023. In addition, she has published several book chapters in edited collections as well as articles and book reviews in journals.

Tamás Demeter is Professor of Philosophy at Corvinus University of Budapest and Senior Research Fellow at the HUN-REN Research Centre for the Humanities, Budapest. He has published widely on the connections between moral and natural philosophy in the Scottish Enlightenment with a focus on David Hume. He is the author of *David Hume and the Culture of Scottish Newtonianism*

(2016) and co-editor of *Recasting Hume's Treatise*, with Peter Millican (forthcoming).

Catherine Dromelet holds a PhD in philosophy from the University of Roma II. She has published in several languages on Scottish, English and French Enlightenment philosophers and on nineteenth-century French philosophy, focusing on the concepts of custom, habit and moral duty. She has been an FWO postdoctoral fellow at the University of Antwerp and has had visiting fellowships at the University of Edinburgh, Boston University and the Hungarian Academy of Sciences in Budapest. Her recent publications include papers in the *Journal of Scottish Philosophy* and *Archives de Philosophie*, a paper on David Hartley in *Habit and the History of Philosophy* (ed. J. Dunham and K. Romdenh-Romluc, 2022) and co-authored entries for the Springer *Encyclopedia of Early Modern Philosophy and the Sciences*.

John A. Hall is the James McGill Professor of Comparative Historical Sociology Emeritus at McGill University. He is the author of several books, including a biography of Ernest Gellner and, most recently, *Nations, States and Empires* (2024).

Kenneth Macdonald is an Emeritus Fellow of Nuffield College, University of Oxford. His research interests have been in social theory and in the development and interpretation of quantitative techniques within sociology (with particular reference to social mobility). In recent years he has published on Adam Smith (arguing, contrary to current academic orthodoxy, that Smith did not regard poverty as deeply problematic and in need of remediation). He has also queried the traditional invocation of grand theory to substantiate the role of the Scottish Enlightenment in the historical development of sociology.

Aldo Mascareño holds a PhD in sociology from the University of Bielefeld, Germany. Currently, he is Senior Researcher at Centro de Estudios Públicos, Chile, Editor-in-Chief of the journal *Estudios Públicos* and Professor of Sociology at Universidad Adolfo Ibáñez, Chile. His publications include *Diferenciación y contingencia en América Latina* (2010), *Die Moderne Lateinamerikas* (2012), *Durch Luhmanns Brille*, co-edited with P. Birle and M. Dewey (2012), *Legitimization in World Society*, co-edited with

K. Araujo (2016), and more than one hundred articles and book chapters in the areas of sociological theory, sociology of law and complexity theories.

Nicholas B. Miller is Associate Professor of History at Flagler College. He is a social and intellectual historian whose research spans early modern and modern history, including the Enlightenment, cross-cultural encounters, international migration and comparative studies of plantations. His books include *John Millar and the Scottish Enlightenment: Family Life and World History* (2017); with Ere Nokkala, *Cameralism and the Enlightenment: Happiness, Governance and Reform in Transnational Perspective* (2020); and with Ulrike Lindner, *Plantation Knowledge: Agricultural Colonization, Exploitation and Exchange since 1500* (forthcoming).

R. J. W. Mills is an Honorary Fellow at the Institute of Intellectual History, University of St Andrews and the author of *The Religious Innatism Debate in Early Modern Britain* (2021) and *Religion and the Science of Human Nature in the Scottish Enlightenment* (2024).

Leonidas Montes is Director of Centro de Estudios Publicis (www.cepchile.cl) and Adam Smith Professor at Universidad Adolfo Ibáñez (www.uai.cl) in Chile. He is the author of *Adam Smith in Context* (2004) and co-editor of *New Voices on Adam Smith* with Eric Schliesser (2006) and has published papers on Adam Smith, Friedrich Hayek and his visits to Chile (with Bruce Caldwell) and on Milton Friedman and his visits to Chile (with Sebastian Edwards).

Otto Pipatti is a researcher in sociology and social anthropology. His first book is *Morality Made Visible: Edward Westermarck's Moral and Social Theory* (2019). His second book, *The Origins of Human Social Nature – Westermarckian Sociology and Social Anthropology*, deals with Westermarck's disciples in Finland and Britain (to be published in 2024). In 2023 Pipatti spent a year as a visiting researcher at the Royal Anthropological Institute in London.

Dirk Schuck holds an MA in philosophy from the University of Frankfurt am Main and a doctorate in political science from the University of Leipzig. He has taught political theory at the University of Leipzig and at the Alberts-Ludwigs-University Freiburg im Breisgau. Currently, he is a postdoctoral researcher at the Collaborative Research Centre 'Structural Change of Property' at the University of Erfurt, and his work is funded by the Deutsche Forschungsgemeinschaft (SFB TRR 294/1-424638267). So far, his research has mainly dealt with the intellectual, social and economic history of early modern Europe, as well as with comparing Eastern and Western ethics. His current research focuses on an ecological approach to the history of ideas, on the cultural history of luxury and on anthropological theories of consumption.

Craig Smith is Professor of the History of Political Thought in the School of Social and Political Sciences at the University of Glasgow. His research focuses on the moral and political theory of the Scottish Enlightenment. He is the author of *Adam Smith's Political Philosophy: The Invisible Hand and Spontaneous Order* (2006), *Adam Ferguson and the Idea of Civil Society: Moral Science in the Scottish Enlightenment* (Edinburgh University Press, 2019) and *Adam Smith* (2020).

Spyridon Tegos is an assistant professor of early modern philosophy at the University of Crete, Greece. In his research, he concentrates on the history of moral and political philosophy (Scottish and French Enlightenment). He is currently preparing a book on the classical French sources (early modern theatre and belles-lettres) that inspired early Scottish liberalism (David Hume, Adam Smith) and, in its aftermath, French liberalism (Germaine de Staël, Alexis de Tocqueville). He is also working on a project regarding the legacy of Hellenistic ethics and philosophical anthropology in early modern moral and political thought. He holds a PhD from the University of Paris X-Nanterre with a thesis on the concept of social sentiments (friendship, sympathy, compassion) in early modern philosophy. His recent publications include 'The Joke Is Not Funny Anymore: Irony, Laughter and Ridicule in Adam Smith' in *Adam Smith and Modernity* (ed. Alberto Burgio, 2023).

Index of Names

Adelung, Johann, 342
Alexander, Jeffrey, 292
Alexander, William, 336
Allan, David, 92, 96
Aristotle, 9, 382
Aron, Raymond, 3–4, 220, 292, 316

Bachofen, Johann Jakob, 333, 336
Barnave, Antoine, 342–3, 345
Berger, Peter, 229
Bergson, Henri, 247
Berkeley, George, 247
Berry, Christopher J., 6–8, 49, 60, 90, 112
Bloor, David, 14, 385–8, 393–401
Bourdieu, Pierre, 229, 313
Brewer, John, 46
Bryson, Gladys, 219

Cahen, Léon, 342
Cassirer, Ernst, 348
Clarke, Samuel, 124
Collier, James, 337
Comte, August, 11, 220–1, 248–9, 256
Condillac, Étienne Bonnot de, 143, 247
Cooley, Charles, 229
Cooper, Anna J., 221–2
Cousin, Victor, 248
Cunow, Heinrich, 343

Dalrymple, Sir John, 106
Descartes, René, 247
Douglas, Mary, 397
Dunbar, James, 25–6
Durkheim, Émile, 11–12, 228–30, 245–62

Engels, Fredrich, 213, 230, 331, 342
Eriksson, Björn, 106, 220
Espinas, Alfred, 256
Evans-Pritchard, E. E., 103–4

Ferguson, Adam, 7–8, 21, 30, 47, 88–97, 209
Feuerbach, Ludwig, 345
Fleischacker, Samuel, 54
Fodor, Jerry, 14, 383, 402
Forbes, Duncan, 85–6
Fordyce, David, 381
Frazer, James, 250
Freud, Sigmund, 300
Freyer, Hans, 347
Friedman, Milton, 120
Fustel de Coulanges, Numa Denis, 249

Gellner, Ernest, 230, 250
Giddens, Anthony, 292
Goffman, Erwing, 233–4, 299
Graeber, David, 350

Index of Names

Hamilton, Alexander, 319
Hazard, Paul, 348
Hegel, Georg Wilhelm Friedrich, 10, 199–200, 207, 210
Heinzen, Karl, 336
Hill, Lisa, 92
Himmelfarb, Gertrude, 53, 57
Hirschman, Albert 307
Hobbes, Thomas, 104, 333
Hume, David, 14, 219, 224–31, 273, 300, 385, 389, 402
Hutcheson, Francis, 69, 101, 141, 219, 340, 359, 381, 382

Ignatieff, Michael, 333, 348

Janet, Paul, 244
Johnson, Samuel, 307

Kames, Lord (Henry Home), 8, 25, 35, 103–26
Kant, Immanuel, 109, 246, 257
Keynes, John Maynard, 48, 312, 320
Kuhn, Thomas, 2, 51

Landtman, Gunnar, 284, 341–2
Lang, Andrew, 333, 339
Lehmann, William C., 330, 331
Linguet, Simon-Nicholas Henri, 343
List, Friedrich, 319, 358
Locke, John, 104, 150, 202, 207, 214, 247, 253, 296
Lueder, August Ferdinand, 342
Luhmann, Niklas, 14, 365–75
Lukács, Georg, 202, 215
Lukes, Steven, 11, 246, 250, 266

McLennan, James, 337
Maine de Biran, 247–8
Mandeville, Bernard, 112

Mannheim, Karl, 3
Marx, Karl, 3, 335–6
Mauss, Marcel, 259
Mead, George Herbert, 232–3
Meiners, Christoph, 334
Meyer, Annette, 88
Mill, James, 224, 335
Mill, John Stuart, 335, 349
Millar, John, 13, 155, 330–50
Montaigne, Michel de, 249
Montesquieu, 7, 104, 208, 296
Müller, Max, 339

Newton, Isaac, 392–3
Nietzsche, Friedrich, 292, 300
Nussbaum, Martha, 55

Parsons, Talcott, 292
Pascal, Roy, 347
Philippon, Thomas, 314
Pocock, J. G. A., 348
Pollock, Friedrich, 346
Pope, Alexander, 168–9

Quine, W. V. O., 402

Raphael, D. D., 359
Reddie, James, 335
Reid, Thomas, 39, 246–8, 327, 385
Renouvier, Charles, 249
Riazanov, David, 346
Riesman, David, 299
Robertson, John Mackinson, 337, 340
Rousseau, Jean-Jacques, 85, 88, 104, 117, 247, 296, 298, 301, 315–16, 341, 342
Royer-Collard, Pierre Paul, 248

Saint-Simon, Henri de, 256
Schliesser, Eric, 53, 365

Schmaus, Warren, 11, 246
Sen, Amartya, 7, 48, 53
Simmel, Georg, 109, 271
Sinclair, Sir John, 153–4
Skinner, Quentin, 74
Smith, Adam, 7, 9, 12–13, 52–6, 134–41, 143, 147, 274, 293–319, 361–3
Smith, Craig, 70
Sombart, Werner, 330–4, 344–9
Sorokin, Pitirim A., 346
Spencer, Herbert, 337
Steuart, James, 7, 50–2, 64–74, 156
Stewart, Dugald, 155, 344
Stocking, George W., 122
Stuart-Glennie, John, 337–40
Sulzbach, Walter, 342–5
Swift, Jonathan, 185
Swingewood, Alan, 126, 219, 348

Tocqueville, Alexis de, 318
Tönnies, Ferdinand, 11, 226
Turgot, Anne Robert Jacques, 338

Vico, Giambattista, 342
Vygotsky, Lev, 233

Weber, Max, 3, 5, 6, 13, 134–7, 145–7, 222, 225–6, 228, 230, 271, 292, 293, 312, 317–18, 331
Wengrow, David, 350
Westermarck, Edward, 12, 231, 269–84

Young, Arthur, 57

Index of Subjects

abolitionism, 340
accidents, 159, 349
Adam Smith Problem, 355
agitation, 111–12
agriculture, 107–8, 113–23, 306
alienation, 88
anomie, 293
anthropology, 47, 103, 110, 135, 235, 250, 271–2, 284, 337, 339, 341
antiquity, 209, 340, 341
authority, 23, 28, 73, 134–5, 137, 141, 144–7, 166, 202–3, 225, 250–3, 258, 260–2, 313, 337, 341, 344, 346
  epistemic, 397–8
  moral, 258
  natural, 202, 215
  political, 116–18
autonomy, 317, 320, 357, 365–9, 372
autopoiesis, 356

Britain, 72, 115, 132, 180, 269, 284, 308–10, 327, 335, 358, 386

Cambridge school, 331
census, 154
character, 166, 210, 258–9
citizenship, 208–9, 230, 309, 315, 340
civic humanism, 96, 348

civil society, 87–91, 93–7, 111, 113, 116, 122, 209, 334
civilisation, 113, 316, 333
class, 3, 62–70, 316–17, 342–6
  and demography, 62
  and mortality, 71
colonialism, 308, 339
commerce, 61, 107–8, 114–16, 130, 131, 201, 205, 208–10, 212, 294–8, 307, 343, 345
commercial society, 3–4, 26–6, 126, 296–317, 326, 349, 356, 362
communication, 232, 360, 366, 371, 372, 396
Communism, 345–6
comparative advantage, 303, 310
comparison, 3, 23, 65–6, 71–2, 87, 89, 123, 147, 157, 159, 168, 210, 249–51, 255–6, 270–1, 284, 315, 341, 362–3
complexity, 29, 32, 332, 356–8, 363, 365–7, 369, 372
contingency, 65, 199, 203, 207, 210, 213, 217, 367, 371
convention, 89, 126, 220, 222, 225–7, 231, 266, 295, 286
cooperation, cooperatives, 94, 107–8, 177, 280
corruption, 90–1, 122, 126, 131
curling, 9, 178, 194–5
  as indicator of mental health, 178, 184
  social interpretation of, 9, 183–4

417

custom, 24–5, 29, 36, 79, 88, 207, 227–8, 245, 246, 249–55, 260 144–6, 411, 279–81, 303, 341, 387–8, 393–4, 396

demand, 58, 76, 166, 172, 372
democracy, 208, 313, 345
depopulation, 178, 184
depression, 178
differentiation, 26, 32, 341, 370
divine origins of kings, 337
Dogmengeschichte, 342
duty, 64, 69, 174, 381
   moral, 41, 96–7, 183, 250–1, 257–8

economy, 112, 223, 307–8, 314–20
   service economy, 67
education, 33, 36, 56–7, 153, 161, 169, 191, 192, 220, 221, 248–9, 252, 303, 307–8, 311, 386–8, 390–401
   moral, 91, 97, 253, 393
empire, 30, 191, 308–9
Enlightenment, 3, 57, 69, 104–5, 348
epistemology, 199–200, 202–6, 260, 383, 382–5
ethics, 231, 261, 273–4, 357, 360, 363
   indirect, 54–5
ethnocentrism, 87, 96, 121
evidence, 54–9, 88–9, 92–3, 97, 120–6
evolution, 26, 121, 138, 200, 203, 220, 231, 270, 272, 274, 280, 284, 338, 340, 363, 368–70, 372–3, 378–9
exchange, 27, 34–5, 42, 77, 215, 222, 224, 303, 306, 309, 369, 372

expectations, 28–9, 181, 233, 356–8, 365–75
   cognitive and normative, 356, 367
   disappointment, 367
   of expectations, 367
   reciprocal, 356, 372
   social, 375
experiments, 143, 159–60, 173, 379, 383, 391

feudalism, 27, 203–7, 210, 305–7, 343, 345
folklore, 337
French Revolution, 159, 331
functional explanation, 87–9

gender, 47, 293, 318, 330, 332, 335–7, 340, 343
German Historical School, 335, 357–8
government, 22–8, 47, 56, 60, 62, 64, 78, 79, 107–8, 116–19, 123, 137, 144, 149, 158, 166, 180, 227–8, 250–1, 257, 304–5, 307, 334–5, 344, 396
grand theory, 7, 46, 51, 70, 74
groups, 89, 94, 107, 119, 124, 144, 259, 276, 279, 337, 339, 356, 392
   occupational, 65

habit, 25, 27, 89, 118, 190, 227–9, 252, 281, 295, 360, 400
historical materialism, 120, 342–3
historicism, historicist, 104, 110, 350
history
   conjectural, 48, 87–8, 106, 123–4, 185, 201–16, 211–12, 297, 334

Index of Subjects 419

disciplinary, 3, 97, 164, 331, 340, 342, 347–8
intellectual, 74, 330, 347–8
natural, 23, 29, 35, 135, 141, 201–3, 229–30, 330
of law, 123
of man/mankind, 21, 29, 110–11, 124, 150, 341, 125
of marriage, 334
of political thought, 413
household, 61, 168, 330, 334, 341
housing, 34, 57, 72, 183
humanity, 34, 60–2, 87, 89, 95, 109, 111, 113, 118–19, 142, 177, 180, 222, 252–5, 258–9, 261–2
Humean, 32, 137, 210, 245, 250, 256, 270, 388, 395

ideology, 101–2, 202, 212, 214, 215, 392
imagination, 135, 139–41, 200, 210–11, 296, 298, 383, 389–92, 394
India, 335
industry, 4, 34, 70, 73, 79, 107, 115, 120, 130, 157, 168, 170, 226, 307, 310, 314, 345, 358, 36–5, 373
inequality, 26, 55, 209, 305, 313, 326, 330, 332–3, 341–2, 346
inheritance, 280, 308
inoculation, 178–81
interaction, 89, 107–10, 120, 232, 257, 355–6, 360–1, 366–70
interdependence, 357, 366, 272
institutions, 21–36, 55, 60, 70, 90, 104–6, 112, 121, 123–4, 126, 146–7, 202–4, 226–7, 253–4, 257, 259, 345–6, 396–9
insurance, 176, 181

justice, 34, 61, 117, 225–7, 231, 250–3, 309, 311, 370
justification, 73, 155, 260, 386, 389

Kantian, 12, 216, 244
kirk, 173, 175, 177, 178, 192

labour 25, 29, 31, 56–62, 87–8, 108, 120, 174, 176, 182, 184, 223–4, 301–3, 344
child, 184
division of, 36, 44, 90, 95, 97, 110, 167, 209, 228, 282, 297, 316–17, 362, 369, 373–4
household, 168
pool for national service, 67–8
unproductive, 155, 187
women's, 48, 72–3, 167–8
landlords, 167, 177, 303–4, 306
laws
rule of, 28–9, 34, 305–6
sumptuary, 58–9
legislators, 88, 146, 307
liberty, 120
natural, 302–4
political, 208, 226, 318
Lockean, 150, 202, 207, 214
luxury, 58–9, 114–15, 122, 209–10, 343

machinery, 171
manners, 22, 27, 29, 31, 48, 69, 71, 117–18, 165, 168, 170, 396
market 4, 28–9, 172, 176, 227, 302–4, 310–11, 369–70
marriage, 184
marriage, 272, 331, 338
matriarchy, 334, 336–7
matrilineality, 340
measurement, 159

merchants, 303–4
methodology, 64–5, 86–7, 92, 123, 160, 349
moral
  obligation, 250–3, 257–9
  philosophy, 53, 91–7, 124, 274, 282
  science, 86, 91–7
morality, 92–3, 121, 221, 231, 250–4, 260–2, 270, 272–6, 282–3, 316
  aesthetic, 142
mortality, 62
myth, 87–8, 90, 96, 138

necessity
  retroactive, 199
nomadism, 345
norms, 66, 142, 280–1, 356–7, 382–3

occupation, 65–7, 155–6, 166

papistry, 165
passion, passions, 30–1, 35, 108–13, 116–19, 125, 135–8, 163–4, 251–3, 360–1, 371–2
pastoralism, 27, 202
patriotism, 116, 119
political economy, 52, 63, 156, 170, 187, 223–4, 193–4, 297, 304, 311, 362
population, 59–65, 153–4
positivism, 220–2, 245–6, 248–50
poverty, the poor, 27, 29, 48, 52–62, 298–9, 301, 308, 363
  child, 59
  provision for, 173–82
predestination, 178–9, 213
primitive, 31, 139–41, 230, 338–41

production, 62–3, 68, 108, 157, 171–2
  of knowledge, 383, 385, 387
progress, 24–5, 104–6, 113–14, 120–5, 171, 201, 362
promise, 108, 110, 225, 250–1, 256
property, 26–7, 41, 105–10, 184, 202–6, 210
prudence, 363–5

race, 222, 334
rank, 57–62, 70, 166, 169, 175, 299–300, 326, 334, 341, 343–4, 363–4, 397–8
reception
  Marxist, 90, 120, 212–13, 331, 342–7
relativism, 69, 260, 386, 388
religion, 30–4, 160, 163, 165–6, 220–22, 229–30, 250–1, 259–62
resentment, 274–5, 281
roles
  gender, 329
  intersecting, 69
  social, 28, 90, 182
Rome, 47, 306
rule of law, 28–9, 305–6
rules, 92, 225, 233, 251–2, 272–3, 279, 281, 370
  general, 249, 387–9, 391–4, 398–401
Russian Revolution, 331, 346

sacred, sacredness, 254
savage, 30–1, 35–6, 113–14, 121–2, 340, 341, 362
scepticism, 206, 248, 296, 389
sects, 166, 307
secular religion, 250, 262
security/stability, 28, 32, 107, 111, 113, 121, 140–1, 364

Index of Subjects 421

sedition trials, 159
self, 166, 201, 229, 232–5, 248, 256, 296, 373
self-interest, 356, 365, 373
selfishness, 35
sentiments, 34, 134, 253, 273
service economy, 67
shame, 56
shorter Catechism, 157
signalling theory, 7, 51, 73–4
slavery, 297
social
  arithmetic, 154
  change, 27, 47, 124, 304, 318
  determinism, 120
  epistemology, 202, 387
  evolutionism, 121
  mobility, 51, 65–6, 169–70
  policy, 60, 63, 176
  theory, 87, 104, 116, 275, 315
sociality, sociability
  commercial, 13, 292, 297, 300
  natural, 344
socialisation, 109–10, 244–5, 252
socialism, 331
society
  commercial, 34, 122, 126, 215, 296–8, 316, 349
  emergence, 297, 334, 356
  modern, 91, 262, 272, 356
  natural history of, 330
sociology
  adventitious, 3, 7, 46–9, 402
  conflict, 96
  Marxist, 342
  of Cambuslang conversions, 163
  of ideas, 182
  of inoculation, 180
  of knowledge, 14, 381, 402
  of marketing, 172
  of morality, 272–4, 283
  of political unrest, 161
  of religion, 139, 230, 318
  seminars, 51

Soviet Union, 345
spirit, 9, 143, 145, 207–8, 217, 248
stadial theory, 32, 87, 90, 317, 342
statistics, statistical, 153, 155
superstructure, 90, 345
symbolic interactionism, 12, 321
sympathy, 163–4, 231–3, 245, 250, 252–3, 256–62, 278–81, 298–300, 355–75, 387–8, 391–2, 397–8
  deliberation, 361
  for labour, 302–3
system
  environment, 366
  psychic, 366, 375
  social, 14, 109, 356, 366

tax, taxation 58–9, 176
  on land, 55
technology, 160, 166, 171, 301, 314
toleration, 166
tourism, 70–1

Umschwungstheorie, 358
unintended consequences, 35, 70–1, 87, 89, 96, 307, 356, 362, 395–6
unrest, 160–1
utility, 56, 73, 142–3, 166, 176, 225–6, 252–3, 257, 363–5
  of population, 62

values, 36, 97, 222, 224, 299, 313, 386–7, 396
  epistemic, 53
  political, 304

welfare, 297, 319, 373
witchcraft, 182–3
women, 47–8, 271, 333, 346
work, 228, 251, 283, 294

EU Authorised Representative:
Easy Access System Europe Mustamäe tee 50, 10621 Tallinn, Estonia
gpsr.requests@easproject.com

Printed and bound by CPI Group (UK) Ltd, Croydon, CR0 4YY

02/03/2026

02063692-0020